EARLY
CHILDHOOD PROGRAMS
HUMAN RELATIONSHIPS AND LEARNING

EARLY CHILDHOOD PROGRAMS

HUMAN RELATIONSHIPS AND LEARNING

NINTH EDITION

Katherine Read
Professor Emeritus
School of Home Economics
Oregon State University

Pat Gardner
Child Development Program
Santa Monica College

Barbara Child Mahler
Child Development Program
California State University, Chico

Harcourt Brace College Publishers
Fort Worth   Philadelphia   San Diego   New York   Orlando   Austin   San Antonio
Toronto   Montreal   London   Sydney   Tokyo

Publisher	Ted Buchholz
Acquisitions Editor	Jo-Anne Weaver
Developmental Editor	Laurie Runion
Project Editor	Mike Hinshaw
Production Manager	Kathleen Ferguson
Book Designer	Pat Bracken

Cover photography and color separations by Phase One Graphics, Sunbury, PA. Photo courtesy of Playworld Systems, Inc.

Address for Editorial Correspondence:
Harcourt Brace College Publishers, 301 Commerce Street, Suite 3700, Fort Worth, TX 76102.

Address for Orders:
Harcourt Brace & Company, 6277 Sea Harbor Drive, Orlando, Florida 32887.
1-800-782-4479, or 1-800-433-0001 (in Florida).

ISBN: 0-03-074166-1

Library of Congress Catalog Card Number: 92–82727

Printed in the United States of America

3 4 5 6 7 8 9 0 1 039 0 9 8 7 6 5 4 3

Katherine Read
1904–1991

This book is dedicated to Katherine,
who deeply touched the personal and professional lives of countless people.
In the same spirit the book is dedicated
to the young children
who will benefit in the future
from your learning, and teaching to others,
Katherine's tenets and philosophy.

Preface

The ninth edition of *Early Childhood Programs: Human Relationships and Learning* prepares adults to work with young children in group settings. Changes to this edition show what is happening in the rapidly changing field of early childhood education. The following topics have been added: accreditation of programs, diversity curriculum, appropriate curriculum and assessment in programs, developmental screening, code of ethics, emergent literacy, and educational technology. The point of view expressed continues to emphasize the feelings and attitudes of children involved in the learning process. Because physical, social-emotional, and intellectual development are viewed as interrelated, all must be considered if children are to grow and fully develop their capacities. We believe that children learn more readily when teachers understand them and give them opportunities to grow as individuals. The central focus of this book is learning for children, teachers, and parents through exploring and discovery in early childhood programs. This textbook is appropriate reading for adults preparing to teach, for parents wanting information about children's social and educational needs, and for anyone else with interest in the ever-expanding field of early childhood education.

We have organized the chapters according to crucial introductory ideas, and we have provided a chapter overview, projects for the student, an annotated bibliography, and a list of resources in the Appendix. Illustrations have been selected to highlight or explain textual information, and case studies and anecdotal observations have been provided to clarify or expand subject matter.

This edition contains six main parts: The Setting; Basic Teaching Skills; Guidance in Experiences Common to Everyone; Understanding Behavior; The Program Evolves From Experiences; and Concerns of Parents and Teachers. We have presented the material as simply and directly as possible so that it may be easily understood by anyone interested in young children. We start with essential points, things most necessary to know in dealing with young children. We then return to these points, amplifying them in later sections, and adding information that can lead to more advanced or profound thoughts.

Although the material in *Early Childhood Programs* is based on research findings, we have not stressed the academic approach. The emphasis remains the understanding of human behavior, the child's as well as our own, and the process of learning. Anyone working with young children needs to understand the significance of behavior and the needs of individuals in order to guide children wisely and help them learn.

We express our thanks to Millie Almy for her suggestion of the title and its definition. We continue to be indebted to Betty Lark-Horovitz for her gift of children's drawings to be used as headings in the chapters of the book. We are also indebted to the professional organization, The National Association for the Education of Young Children, for many quotations from their recent publications and for their emphasis on quality education for young children. We are equally grateful to The Children's Defense Fund for providing current information about changes taking place in program funding. We are also grateful to the many colleagues who have helped us in writing this book. A special thanks to Alise Shafer and her assistance with the emergent literacy material and to Gwen Dophna for the ecology information. We further wish to thank those whose thoughtful reading and comments have helped to shape this edition: Diane Cromwell, American River College; Kathy Fite, Southwest Texas State University; Karen S. Gaston, Georgia Southern University; Lynn Hartle, University of Florida; Sally Jennings, St. Louis Community College; Cecilia Kuster, Santa Barbara City College; Ann Marie Leonard, James Madison University; Ronald Linder, University of South Florida.

We appreciate the valuable contribution Jean Berlfein has made by the photographs she has provided for this edition. Our thanks are also extended to Laurie Schneider for her skill in capturing children in action at John Adams Children's Center and Hill 'n Dale Family Learning Center. Other excellent photographs were contributed by Deborah Hansen and Denise Maldonada, teachers at First Step School in Santa Monica. Louise Dean and Marc Pettigrew were generous in providing fine pictures of the outdoor setting and children at Los Angeles Valley College Campus Child Development Center. Vida Krakovska, a student at Santa Monica College provided pictures of the College Child Development Center. Barbara Mahler provided pictures from the California State University, Chico, Child Development

Program and from the Migrant Headstart Program, also of Chico, California.

We acknowledge the contribution our husbands have made by their support and patience. We especially want to thank Chuck Gardner for his hard work and effort in the preparation of this ninth edition manuscript.

We also express our thanks to Jo-Anne Weaver, our Acquisitions Editor; Tracy Napper, Editorial Assistant; Laurie Runion, our Developmental Editor; Mike Hinshaw, our Project Editor; and to the other staff members of Harcourt Brace Jovanovich who worked with us on this edition.

We have pooled our knowledge and our different experiences in the production of this edition. Communicating from a distance has often been difficult but we have found the process stimulating. We have enjoyed our contacts and hope that we have produced a more useful book than any one of us might have achieved alone.

K.R.
P.G.
B.C.M.

Contents

Part Five: The Program Evolves from Experiences   277

16 The Process of Learning in Early Childhood   278

17 Areas of Learning in the Program: Motor and Sensory Development   295

18 Areas of Learning in the Program: Language and Literature   308

EARLY
CHILDHOOD PROGRAMS
HUMAN RELATIONSHIPS AND LEARNING

PART ONE

The Setting

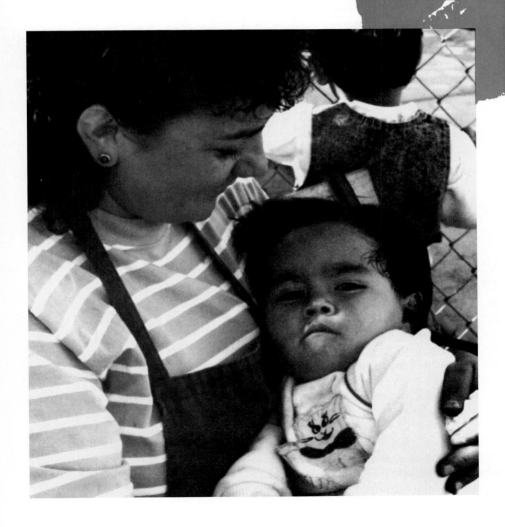

CHAPTER 1

Introduction to the Human Relations Laboratory

Taylor and her sister (*girl, 3 years, 6 months*)

This chapter introduces you to:

▶ The main ideas and underlying beliefs of this book
▶ Children like some of those you will encounter in centers
▶ Parents, very important people
▶ Adults in the center, who begin their work with many feelings
▶ Some self-understandings you will want to explore
▶ The center as a human relations laboratory.

This book is about the care and well-being of young children and the people who work with them. "The single most important thing in human cultural behavior is literally and specifically the way we bring up our children." (LaBarre, 1949) This statement by an anthropologist points to the significance of the task of those responsible for bringing up children, whether they are parents, or teachers, or members of any other group relating to young children.

The material presented here is addressed specifically to those who are beginning to teach in centers, but it can serve those who care for young children anywhere. Anyone with young children, even the most experienced person, needs to learn as well as to teach. The two processes are inseparable.

For many years people have been concerned about meeting the needs of children. Today this concern is supported by more knowledge than in the past. However, with more knowledge comes increased responsibility for providing children with what they need for sound growth. Research findings have emphasized the importance of the early years and the necessity of meeting the physical, emotional, social, and intellectual needs of the young child.

The educational programs we describe not only support, complement, and supplement parental care but also enhance the child's development. They are programs in which children learn as they play and share their day-to-day experiences with other children, guided by adults who have an understanding of child growth and development and of the learning process. These are also programs in which adults learn more about human behavior and relationships as they observe and participate.

The authors recognize the difficulty of using acceptable terms to describe race, gender, ethnicity, and persons who are disabled. An example of the problems facing writers, editors, and educators is the term *handicapped*. Jack Smith of the *Los Angeles Times* recently wrote a telling essay about the problems of euphemisms invented to shield various minorities from insensitive labels. He writes, "Handicapped is now in disfavor with some of those who work with the handicapped, though I have never heard a complaint from a handicapped person." John Leo of *US News and World Report* writes, "'Colored people', as in NAACP, is racist, but the backward construction 'people of color', is progressive." (*Los Angeles Times*, August 22, 1991) The Children's Defense Fund provides a disclaimer in their publications concerning the terms black and Latino, recognizing that African American and Hispanic are terms preferred by many. (CDF 1991 *State of America's Children*, page iv) The language struggles to keep pace as society reshapes itself in the attempt to become more egalitarian.

A long-standing problem has been the use of the universal "he" to stand for women or men, boys or girls, and the stereotyping of teachers as women. To avoid these problems, we have varied the anecdotes of children from passage to passage throughout the book; here, the child is female, there male. "The teacher" has been treated more as a role, with the focus more on duties and characteristics of the job at hand, rather than on any gender-specific traits. Donaldson (1978) stated, "While the word 'child' does not convey any information as to sex, there is no similarly neutral personal pronoun in English . . . The ideas in this book apply equally to boys and to girls." As Smith added, "We wish to acknowledge the known fact that teachers and students are both male and female. Their excellence

Each child needs a rich variety of experiences as he tries to make sense out of the world.
John Adams Children's Center, Santa Monica, California

in either of these positions is not determined by their sex." (A. Smith. 1985. From a personal paper, "Mistakes, a tool for learning.")

Let us now turn to the issues confronting educators. What promotes optimum overall development in young children? What do teachers need to know about development and learning? What skills do they need in guiding young children? We shall be looking for answers to these and other questions—even though the answers may often be incomplete.

There is a tendency today to try to hasten a child's intellectual development by teaching to much younger children what may be more appropriate for first-graders. Pushing children in their development may shortchange them, depriving them of firsthand experiences on which later learning depends. The best preparation lies in children's completing each stage, having as full and as rich a variety of experiences as possible, consistent with each child's own style and pace of learning. Each child should feel more self-confidence because of successful learning.

Children's needs are the same, whether at home or in a center. Young children are in a crucial period of development, physically, socially, emotionally, and intellectually. Each child is an individual, different from any other. Each child needs understanding guidance that respects individual rates and styles of growing and learning. Each child needs a rich variety of experiences in exploring and discovering while trying to make sense out of the world.

The emphases in this book are on human relationships and learning and on teaching as a creative process. The order or presentation of the material does not indicate the degree of its importance. We must begin somewhere and spiral our way upward, going over subjects at new levels. Some matters of immediate importance are presented simply and later developed in more depth. Although we may wish we could start out with a complete background of knowledge, we must be content to learn each step of the way. The more knowledge we have, the more we need to know. The journey demands our best efforts. It is never dull. It remains challenging. It is always rewarding.

The Children

A center for young children is a place where people are important. We start by introducing the people one finds there, beginning with the children.

The children are the most important people we will meet in the center. They are the people from whom we will learn the most, not just because they are the most active and the noisiest but also because they show us more clearly how they feel. Their responses are relatively simple and direct, and they act as they feel. An angry child may cry, or kick, or throw something, or yell at his mother or his teacher, "Go away. I don't like you." With neither an adult's capacity nor inclination to modify their responses, children's patterns of behavior are less likely than an adult's to be influenced by a fear of consequences.

We learn from children for another reason. Their behavior changes rapidly. In different environments or under different circumstances they blossom forth with quite different behavior. We can see the effects of our guidance when we observe a child's response.

By watching children, we see too that each is surprisingly different. Each has a unique way of meeting situations. Let us introduce some children, so that we may feel acquainted and thus be better able to understand what may lie behind the behavior of other children with other names.

 Kevin, Who Often Surprises Children and Teachers   Kevin, a sturdy 3 1/2-year-old, always on the move, comes running into the school each morning, greeting the teachers and the children with enthusiasm and plunging into activity. Everything captures his attention: a new book on the table, a bird's nest brought in by one of the children, the pin on the teacher's dress, the garage of blocks that some children are building. Observed over one 50-minute period, he engaged in or paused at more than thirty activities with apparent, if brief, interest.

Kevin is eager to join other children in whatever they are doing and makes many attempts to get others to join him. He tries to direct any play in which he is engaged with a flow of excellent language and a vigor and enthusiasm that overwhelms the opposition. But other children drift away from him or reject his advances, perhaps because he cannot accept their ideas for play. He hits or bites

The children are the most important people we will meet in the center.
Santa Monica College, Child Development Center, Santa Monica, California

when blocked, or sometimes for no apparent provocation. He is impulsive and quick, and therefore it is difficult for the teachers to keep him from attacking others. He is constantly taking things from other children. If he sees someone using equipment or a toy, he immediately wants it.

He has picked up many adult verbalizations that he only partially understands. He knows that words are often used to justify acts. "I *need* to swing," he says emphatically when he sees Jill on the swing. "Why?" asks Jill reflectively. "Because I have to learn how," he answers. He quickly gets on the tricycle that Bruce has left for a moment to pick up his hat. When Bruce cries, "I want it," Kevin's answer is, "When people get off trikes, I have to get on and ride around." Usually he does not wait until people get off. When he is absent with one of his rare colds, LaBrita's comment is, "I'm glad. Now he won't bite me today."

His behavior often surprises teachers as well as children. One morning as he started to pour a drink, he said to the teacher cheerfully, "Do you know what I'm going to do?" To her negative reply, he answered, "I'm going to pour this water on the floor." He did just that before her startled eyes. Then he mopped it up willingly and became absorbed in watching the way it ran down the corridor, exclaiming, "The water doesn't wait for me."

Kevin's observations and his approach to problems reveal an attention to detail. He enjoys stories and listens with attention as an adult reads, though he may not remain for the story's end. He looks thoughtful when adults give explanations and nods as if he understands the reasons for requests. One gets the impression that he can see the value of constructive ways of interacting with people but that his own feelings get in his way and are often more than he can manage. He is eager for social contacts but gets carried away by his impulses, and he appears genuinely sorry when he hurts another child.

Typical of Kevin's behavior is the following incident. As he entered the playground one morning he saw Roberto on a tricycle. He ran to him, grasping the handlebars firmly and saying in a persuasive voice, "Give me your trike, 'Berto. I want to pull you." Roberto made no move to give up the tricycle, and Kevin repeated the request several times in the same persuasive tone. Then, still talking, he pushed Roberto off and rode away, calling back, "I'll be right back. I'm only going to take a little ride." Roberto ran after him and grabbed for the tricycle. Kevin hit him, and the teacher had to intervene and help Roberto recover his tricycle. Deprived of the tricycle, Kevin threw himself on the ground, crying loudly. Suddenly he jumped up and ran to the trike shed, calling, "Wait for me." He came out with another tricycle and rode after Roberto, trying in vain to get him to play.

The demands for adjustment at home have been heavy for Kevin. The family has moved many times. Kevin's parents think he is a difficult child to manage. They seem to expect adult behavior from their son. He has been spanked, threatened, made to sit on a chair, reasoned with, and given rewards. They appear to have little understanding about what a load their expectations have been for him or how often he has been confused about what is expected. A new baby at home has complicated the situation further. His parents have not recognized what the addition of the baby to the family may have meant to Kevin. They have succeeded in making him hide his feelings to such an extent that they report that "he adores his baby sister and is very sweet to her." His biting at school may be related to these pressures at home.

Contradictory about adult standards, eager for friendships with children, having impulsive actions and confused feelings, Kevin is very much in need of guidance. He needs to be with people who will reduce the difficulties he has to face, who will give him suggestions for solving his problems, and who will interpret the needs of others to him. Because of his intellectual capacity, his strong drives, and his physical vigor, he can be either a damaging influence or an inspiring one in the group, depending on the guidance he receives. With the potential leadership qualities he possesses, he may go in either direction.

Alicia, Who Has Lived Under Favorable Conditions   Alicia, who has just turned 3, is a small, sturdy child. Although one of the youngest children in the group, she is independent and resourceful, but she plays with all the children. She entered the group several months after school had begun, but she was soon acquainted with everyone and everything. Being the youngest in a family of four children may have helped her to adapt easily.

Alicia appears to like people and to trust them. She approaches other children easily and is not defensive in her responses to them. If they reject her, she turns to something else. She is seldom rejected, however, for when she joins a group it is with a purpose. She brings an idea or some new material. She is primarily interested in activity and joins groups of active children who are carrying on projects.

Alicia loves music and, although a vigorous, active child, will occasionally spend as much as half an hour listening to music. She paints, uses clay, builds with big blocks, and is often busy in the housekeeping corner. She stands up for herself and will hit another child who tries to take something from her. Her social skills are excellent and seem to reflect a realistic appraisal of what other children are like. She solves her problems well, both with materials and people. She is sure of herself and impartial in playing with other children. Her sympathy is apparent and intelligently given. One day, for example, she took a child with a scratch to the first-aid cabinet to get a bandage.

An example of how she copes with experience occurred on the second day she stayed at the center for lunch. She followed the teacher's directions carefully and seemed to enjoy the experience very much, taking additional servings of everything, including dessert. The dessert consisted of fruit and cookies that the children had helped make earlier in the morning. When Alicia asked for another cookie, the teacher told her to go to the kitchen and ask the cook for one, because there were no more on the table. This teacher was not aware that plans had been made to let each child take a cookie home after lunch. Alicia trotted off toward the kitchen. When the teacher glanced up two or three minutes later, she saw Alicia again heading for the kitchen, but this time she had her coat on. For a moment the teacher was puzzled, and then she realized what must have happened. The cook, when asked for a cookie, had told Alicia, "You may have one when you have your coat on ready to go home." So Alicia went to the coat room and put on her coat. She must have thought that adults make strange requests! With her second cookie in hand she went back to the coat room, removed her coat, and happily returned to the table.

Alicia had kept her purpose in mind and carried out the confusing directions. She accepts things as they are.

Alicia's confidence spills over to others. She takes care of herself, faces problems, and feels comfortable. Others are more comfortable and confident and purposeful because of her presence. Without actively leading, Alicia is a strong force in the group.

 Juan, Who Watches Others   Juan is a serious Hispanic 4-year-old who shyly watches what goes on around him. Occasionally his mother has had relatives nearby to "watch him," but they have moved on to work in the fields or have returned home. Much of the time she took him with her when she worked. He had been a good baby and fussed very little, but it had not been easy for her, a single parent, to manage. As Juan grew older, he played quietly or watched her as she worked. He understood that he was not to touch the things around him or to disturb other people.

Each child has his own way of meeting situations in the center. Migrant Head Start, Chico, California

His mother wanted Juan to learn English before beginning kindergarten. She wanted him to be with other children and to start learning what he would need to be successful in school. She spoke only Spanish with Juan. She had already tried to teach him his letters, without much success. She was relieved when she found that the center would accept him.

When Juan entered the center he was able to let his mother leave after the first day. He made no protest, but after several weeks in the center he was still a "watcher." He seemed interested in what the other children did. He watched them, but he left an activity when another child approached. He preferred to play alone. Teachers have not heard Juan speak in Spanish or English.

When he does enter into play, Juan cautiously uses large-muscle materials, like riding tricycles or building with large hollow blocks. He does not often approach small-muscle play like pegboards, puzzles, or other manipulative toys. He follows the teachers' directions, given in English or the minimal Spanish spoken by two of the staff. He fits into the routines of the school and watches other children to gain cues for expected behavior. He sits quietly at the table at lunch time, though not eating much, and rests when told to do so. He remains passive and compliant, doing what is suggested but initiating little.

What is Juan really like? The teachers do not know. Is he responding to his early experiences in which he needed to be "good" at his mother's workplace? Is he a child who, by temperament, simply needs more time to move into new situations? How can he be helped to do more exploring, discovering, and creating on his own?

His teachers realize that they need to learn more about his cultural patterns in order to see him as the individual that he is. How can he be helped to communicate in Spanish and English? If they could see him with other children who speak his language, they could observe his social skills and perhaps facilitate his play with other children.

The teachers are slowly finding ways to win Juan's trust. They hope to help him change his passivity into a confident zest for experience. They hope to help him find friends. They hope to help him discover his own patterns of learning as he grows in the center.

Atousa, Who Finds It Hard to Trust the World and the People In It

Atousa, nearly 5, was born with a deformity requiring surgery. She was in the hospital several times as an infant and young child. Her mother was not able to stay with her and could only see her during visiting hours.

Atousa is physically normal now, but she bears both the scars of her operations and the psychological scars left by her hospital experiences. Her hospitalizations and surgery came at a critical time in her development, when she should have been learning to trust herself in the world. Instead, she learned to be suspicious and unsure of herself. She is very jealous of a younger brother born shortly after her last hospital stay.

Atousa's parents were eager for her to enter the center. She and her parents are close, but the parents believed she would gain a great deal from being with others. They were delighted when she was enrolled.

At first, Atousa moved rather clumsily and often pouted. She was a heavyset girl with thick dark hair. Her motor coordination was poor for a child of her age, and she avoided active play. She did not join the children on the jungle gym or the ladder bars. She seemed aware of her lack of skill and defensive about it.

Atousa needed her mother when she first entered. She did not remain near her mother, but she would protest vigorously if her mother indicated that she was going to leave. She seemed to want to be sure that she could control the matter of her mother's leaving. Both the staff and the mother believed it was important for Atousa to feel that she could keep her mother there. They knew she would feel sure of herself in time. Meanwhile, the teacher tried to build a good relationship with Atousa. Atousa had accepted help from her teacher from the beginning but kept the interaction on an impersonal level. She was suspicious of people.

For many weeks, her teacher continued trying to maintain a warm, friendly relationship, giving Atousa extra encouragement when she tried something new or was successful in any motor skill. She also let Atousa decide as many things as possible. When she had to refuse to comply with one of Atousa's requests, she did so in a firm, matter-of-fact manner, explaining the reason and adding, "I would like to let you do it, but I can't because . . ."

The teacher made a point of including many items for dramatic play of the doctor-nurse-hospital variety. She read stories about children and hospital experiences. It took a long time before Atousa became interested in these books after she had enjoyed a lot of messy play—getting her hands into sticky clay and playing with water. By this time, she viewed her teacher as her special friend, which seemed to make her feel more secure, and she began using the dramatic play materials.

The change in Atousa by the end of the year was rewarding to everyone. She was enjoying active play, using her body freely, and keeping up with the other children in climbing, riding a tricycle, and engaging in other large-muscle activities.

She sometimes talked with her teacher about what had happened to her in the hospital as though what she experienced there really was a thing of the past. She was steadily making progress in learning about the world and the people in it and in finding it rewarding to achieve, to build skills, and to cope with stress. The center had been successful in providing Atousa with some of the support she needed.

The Parents

Parents Are Important People

Parents are the child's first teachers. They give children their first experiences with loving relationships and serve as their first models. Parents direct the child's first learning opportunities.

Parents also are important because they are people with feelings and needs. They must cope with difficulties and seek personal satisfactions. Their relationships with the child are loaded with some of the deepest human feelings. We need to know something about parents and to respect the part they play in bringing up the children we meet.

Parents are all different. What are they like? What does the center offer them?

Kevin's parents are glad to have him attend the center. They are both busy people. While they are proud of this active little boy and love him very much, they often find him difficult and trying. He does not fit easily into the dream they have of a well-behaved child who does them credit. They look forward to the time when it will be easier for him to understand what they want. They are glad to shift the burden of caring for Kevin to the center for a time. Kevin's father has never come to the center, and his mother seldom has time to visit. She has to get home to the baby or on to some engagement.

Alicia's parents lead a full life, too. At the moment it is full because of their four active children. They enjoy them all, but Alicia has a special place because she is the baby. Alicia is well able to hold her own with the others. The mother really intended to keep her at home, but she knows Alicia wants to play with children and is eager to go to school. The mother often drops by for a visit and has stepped in quietly to help on occasions. She thinks teaching in a center would be a delightful experience and wonders if it might be possible for her to do so when her children are older.

Juan's mother is relieved that the center has a place for Juan. Having her son in the center makes it much easier for her to manage her work. She feels glad that Juan is with other children, learning English and learning what he needs to be ready for school. The mother is hesitant to talk to teachers, but she did shyly say that she hopes the center will observe some Hispanic customs with holidays and foods. She believes education is important and knows she herself was denied many opportunities. As they leave each day, she asks Juan in Spanish, "What did you learn from your teacher today?" She is not sure just what the center does to teach the children, but she is happy that Juan enjoys going there.

Atousa's parents are grateful to have Atousa in the center. They believe she is thriving in this situation, so different from her separation experiences when she was hospitalized.

Atousa's mother was glad to stay with Atousa as long as the teacher felt it helped her. Atousa's father willingly carried the extra work at home. The mother observed with interest what the teachers did and how they guided the children. She says she learned many things that have helped her understand better what Atousa needs and how she and her husband can encourage Atousa's development at home. Both parents think the teachers care about Atousa and are watching her development with pleasure. The burden of concern they had known earlier has been lifted. They welcome conferences with the teacher and appreciate the help they have received.

As we can see, all of these parents have different needs. They look at the center and the teachers in different ways. For all of them the school and the teachers play an important role in their lives.

Kevin, Alicia, Juan, and Atousa are like some of the children we will meet in the center. Their parents are like some of the parents there. What are the other adults in the center like?

The Adults in the Center

Adults Are People with Feelings that Need to Be Understood

Adults are people with the same kinds of feelings as children, but they are likely to express their feelings less directly and openly. Their responses have been modified by experiences that have taught them to control and often to conceal their feelings even from themselves. An adult who is angry seldom hits or throws but may demonstrate anger by performing a task poorly or criticizing for no apparent reason. Many times the adult's responses are as inappropriate or unacceptable as the child's, but they are harder for us to relate to the cause. The responses of an adult do not change as quickly as a child's, perhaps because these responses are behavior patterns that have been in place a long time.

But an important difference between the child and the adult gives the adult an advantage. The adult has a greater capacity to be reflective, to examine personal feelings and behavior. Because of this capacity, the adults can modify responses and make them more appropriate as understanding grows. Understanding ourselves—what we feel and why we respond as we do—is very important. We need to understand ourselves, for our feelings will influence the relationships we build and maintain with other people.

Self-understanding is especially important for teachers so we can be honest and realistic and respond in appropriate and constructive ways to people and to situations. We are in a better position to help children understand themselves when we understand ourselves.

Parents are the child's first teachers about loving relationships. Santa Monica College, Santa Monica, California

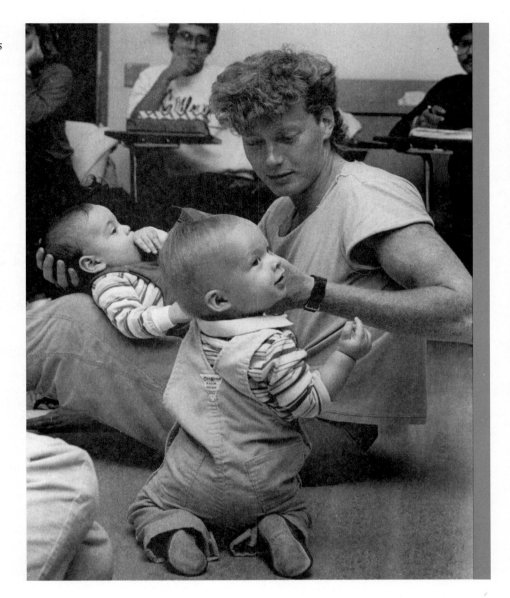

We Are Likely to Feel Inadequate in a New Situation

Most people who begin working with children in centers are entering a situation that is new to them. They may not be sure of what to do. They do not know the children or the teachers, and they are unfamiliar with school procedures. They may not know simple things such as where the paints or the mops are kept. Even though they have been given directions and have been shown through the school, they are sure to find that they have forgotten or were not told many of the things they need to know. Unexpected things keep happening, things for which they are not prepared.

In these situations a new teacher may try something that does not work. Cheerfully greeting a child may draw the response, "I don't like you." Following the example of a more experienced teacher in approaching a group with the words, "It's time to put things away now," may get a different response from the children, such as, "We're not going to."

The new teacher has many questions. What is the proper response when one child hits another? To just watch? To ask an experienced teacher for help?

It is not comfortable to feel unsure and inadequate. It is easy to blame someone or something as a defense against this feeling. A student teacher may become critical, disapproving of the teachers and the program and what the children are allowed to do. Or she may turn away from the unfamiliar or difficult situations. Others may busy themselves with familiar things or spend time with the passive, "easy" children. A new teacher may even take personal blame for not knowing what to do. Any of these responses may make it harder to feel comfortable and effective with young children.

We Need to Feel Comfortable about Being Inadequate in the Beginning

All of these responses are natural. In a new situation everyone has feelings of inadequacy, and these feelings are not easy to face. The important thing is to realize the feelings and to understand something about why they are there.

Most adults and all students can expect to feel inadequate when they begin participating in the center and probably for some time after that. They cannot possibly be prepared for all that may happen. No one can give instructions that will cover everything, certainly not in the sometimes limited time available for preparation. Of course, students will not feel sure of what is expected of them or of what they are supposed to do. The teacher who is guiding them may not even be sure of these things.

What student teachers can do about the feeling of inadequacy at this point is to feel comfortable about having it. It is all right to be inadequate when one begins a learning experience. No one should expect to know in the beginning what will be learned in time. There is a lot to learn at first. Student teachers might as well try to live as comfortably as they can with this feeling and enjoy their successes as they come.

We Have Other Feelings, Too

The feelings we must face and deal with first are usually feelings of inadequacy. But other feelings encourage us. A boy's face lights up when he sees us come into the room, and we know that our relationship with him is a source of strength. He sees us as someone who cares, who can be depended on, someone who has something significant to give. It makes us feel good inside to be this kind of person for a child. It gives us confidence.

Or a girl may bring us a drawing she has made, saying softly, "It's for you." It is the kind of gift that warms the heart. We are rewarded, also, when we watch her struggle and then succeed in actually cutting through the piece of wood with the saw or spooning pancake batter into a pan, all on her own. The glow of satisfaction on her face or expressed through her body makes all of our planning and teaching efforts seem worthwhile. We share in her accomplishment. We can truly feel that we are engaged in "the most important thing in human cultural behavior," as we succeed in helping a child to act and to learn with confidence.

What Do We Need to Understand About Ourselves?

We Were All Children Once

It is important for us to understand ourselves if we are to understand others. We are all alike in many respects, and we all have common experiences that may influence our responses. In the first place, all of us were children once. We can never escape that fact. What happened to us then influences what we are like now. Some of us may wish that our childhood experiences had been different. Others may feel grateful for the events of their childhood. Whatever the case, we can understand ourselves better by trying to understand what children are like and by observing how things affect them.

The way our needs were met during the period of dependency, when we were tiny and helpless and dependent on the adults around us, still affects what we do. If we lived with people who met our needs with warmth and love, if we were fed when we felt hungry and played with and cuddled when we wanted attention, then we were satisfied during this period of dependency. If the adults around us were themselves satisfied people who did not try to prolong needlessly our dependence, then we were free to become independent when we were ready. If we grew up under conditions like these, we are now neither fighting against being dependent nor seeking reassurance by constantly demanding more protection than we need.

Others of us may have lived with people who did not provide pleasant experiences during our period of dependency. We were not fed when we felt hungry. We were left to "cry it out" when we felt helpless and alone. There may have been reasons for such handling by our parents, such as lack of knowledge of the real needs of infants, poor health, too many responsibilities, or the influences of their own childhood experiences. Under these circumstances, we may have fought against being dependent, finding it hard later to accept the necessity of being dependent in any situation. Or we may have continued seeking to have our "dependency needs" met by trying to be more dependent than we need to be, as though to make up for what we did not have earlier.

We were all children once and can remember events that delighted us. Valley College, Campus Child Development Center, Los Angeles

We Were All Members of Families

Another factor influencing our behavior is the position each of us held in our families. Some of us were only children; others were oldest, youngest, or any number of middle positions. The position means different things in different families. Families are likely to be competitive. Children want attention and compete for their parents' or each other's attention. Some are more successful than others in getting it.

In the center, for example, a teacher who happens to be the youngest in her family may identify with the youngest child and resent seeing him teased. She may want to see the aggressor punished, just as she wanted to see punishment for those who teased her when she was a child. Under the guise of wanting to be "fair" she may try to impose a "justice" that really belongs to a situation from her own past, from which she has not yet succeeded in untangling herself. When we recognize that patterns of past feelings still exist, we have a better chance of handling situations in the present with understanding.

We All Met Frustrations in the Growing-Up Process

As a result of the frustrations that are an inevitable part of growing up, we all have feelings of resentment and hostility; we handle them better if we can recognize them. It is needless, and may be damaging, to try to deny these feelings. We have them because as babies we were subjected to limitations. The baby girl can't reach the toy she dropped. Or a boy trips and falls when he tries to walk. He isn't allowed to touch interesting objects. Frustration rouses resentful and sometimes hostile feelings.

How much hostility a child feels depends somewhat on whether the adults in his world help to minimize the inevitable frustrations or whether they increase frustration by a mistaken idea of "teaching" the child. If the necessary limitations are imposed firmly but with gentleness by a comfortable, confident, loving person, they will not rouse much resentment. If limitations are imposed by a teacher who is cross, confused, and struggling with personal feelings of hostility, such behavior will rouse a great deal of negative feeling in the child. The child will want to fight and hurt in return, and these feelings will spill out in many situations against anyone who interferes with the child.

Few of us are fortunate enough to have been handled all the time by people who tried to decrease the feelings of hostility and resentment that are part of growing up. Most of us feel more resentment than we can manage comfortably on all occasions, and these feelings spill out in inappropriate ways. When these negative feelings overflow, they may make us feel guilty and afraid without knowing what is wrong. They may keep us from learning things that we may really want to learn.

We Need to Identify Our Negative Feelings

All of us have a store of negative feelings. So that we may be productive, these feelings need to be released in vigorous activity, artistic or musical expression, talking to a friend, in doing anything that makes us feel more adequate. When we have such outlets, we keep our negative feelings down to manageable proportions.

Negative feelings that are not released productively may come out later in ways that are difficult to identify. Feeling very strongly about a thing, for example, is an indication that it is serving as an outlet for extra emotion, especially if most people do not seem to feel as strongly as we do about the same thing. It may be good to stop and ask, "Why do I feel so strongly about this?" We can direct strong feeling more safely when we understand why we feel as we do. The likelihood of our meeting a child's needs is increased if we understand our own needs and feelings.

Consider, for example, a teacher who is feeling very indignant that a child is allowed to play with food at the table and even to leave some of it uneaten. These feelings may be the result of not being allowed to play with food as a child. Now, having accepted adult patterns and identifying with the adults in this situation, all the resentment that the teacher felt at being denied the delightful experience of playing with food, as well as tasting it, is turned into resentment about seeing a child permitted to do what the adult was denied and was forced to consider "bad." It is not easy to take on values, and we often pay a heavy emotional price when they are forced on us too early. We cannot bear to see others getting by cheaply.

The point here is not whether a child should be allowed to play with food—what is important is to be able to identify the emotional forces that lie behind our reasoning.

All of Us Tend to Resist Change

In spite of ourselves we find all kinds of reasons for avoiding real change in our thinking and behavior. New ways of behaving, regardless of their merit, are rejected until we manage to handle our resistances. Most resistances result from childhood experiences. Recognizing this, a teacher can handle resistance more appropriately, reasoning, "I don't have to feel and behave as I did when my mother (or my big sister or my father) was bossing me. I'm no longer a child. I'm grown and I'm free to use a suggestion, if I think it is a good one, or to reject it, if I think it is a poor one." The adult can be free from the control that childhood patterns may still be exerting.

The more insecure we are, the less likely we are to feel that we can afford to change, for change involves uncertainties. Even a too-ready acceptance of a new viewpoint may result in only a superficial acceptance, in itself a defense against any real change. It is important for us to be aware of this universal tendency to resist the new, the different, so that it will not block us when we try to profit from others' thinking. We must assert our right to use opportunities—whether it is a morning in the school, a discussion period, or the reading of a book—to reach our own conclusions.

We Need to Accept All the Feelings We Have

It is essential not to feel ashamed or guilty about our feelings. We have been taught so often that we must be "good" that we may be afraid to face our negative feelings. They go unrecognized and thus interfere with our thinking more than they would if we had accepted them.

As adults we can afford to look at our feelings. As children, our strong feelings often overwhelmed us. Perhaps anger turned into a temper tantrum. We may have felt guilty and afraid, and we may not have had much help from the adults around us. Now that we are grown, we have less need to feel afraid. We are not as helpless as when we were children. We have more ability to handle feelings when we know that they exist. We realize that everyone has negative feelings at times.

We Need to Recognize the Ambivalence of Our Feelings

Feelings are usually mixed. Feeling comfortable or uncomfortable, enjoying and not enjoying, loving and hating, are all mixed together, although we may be aware of only the feeling that is strongest at the moment. We may be surprised at sudden changes in feeling. We may want to learn more about people and yet resist learning. We may like and dislike the same person, who, in turn, may have some of both kinds of feelings about us. We seldom feel all one way or the other about a person or an experience.

We Need to Try to Understand Rather than Judge Ourselves and Others

We all have many kinds of feelings, pleasant and unpleasant, and most of us want to make changes in some of our feelings and ways of behaving. Real change is not likely to take place as a result of disapproval or blaming ourselves or anyone else. Change more often occurs as a result of being able to consider feelings and circumstances and to make an effort to understand them.

It does not help to blame ourselves and feel discouraged, for example, when we are unsuccessful in dealing with a child's behavior. It does help if we think about how we felt at the time, what we did, what we might have done instead, and what the situation may have meant to the child. By reflecting in this way we gain new insights into the situation. It is tremendously profitable to recognize that we can do something to change our ways of feeling and acting if we are willing to try. We can grow in understanding ourselves and others.

The things we may discover about ourselves and others may be confusing or disturbing. Understanding is not a simple task, for human behavior is complex. Needs differ as people grow. It may be important to talk problems over with someone. Certain questions may be brought up for discussion. Some less clear or more personal matters may be talked over with a teacher whose longer experience has yielded a wider understanding of behavior.

The Center Is A Human Relations Laboratory

The entire center is thus full of human beings who must understand and accept their feelings and those of others. Each adult shares some common problems.

Student teachers, as they start teaching, have the problem of facing and accepting the almost inevitable feelings of inadequacy that a new situation brings.

Parents with children in the center face the problem of being able to leave the child free to take a step toward greater independence.

Teachers must continue their professional growth and deepen their understanding of the ways to meet the needs of children and parents.

The director and family services coordinator build staff relationships that support the educational program.
Migrant Head Start, Chico, California

The *cook* must share in the center's goals, too, finding satisfaction in the job and interaction with the children, as the food is prepared and served.

The *custodian* must be able to understand and accept the needs of children. This includes regarding the job as one of making a satisfying place for children instead of merely a good place for a custodian.

The *director* must continue professional growth and deepen understanding of ways to support children's and teachers' learning. The director must be able to help build staff relationships that facilitate human relations and support the educational problem.

For everyone the center can be a human relations laboratory. It can be a place where we learn more about ourselves and others, as we gain skill in guiding children's development.

Chapter Overview

This chapter has focused on the issues confronting educators. What promotes optimal development, the concerns of hastening intellectual development, and the concept that children's needs are the same, whether at home or in the center, are addressed. Children, parents, and adults in the center have been introduced with the emphasis that the center is a human relationships laboratory. It can be a place where we learn more about ourselves and others, as we gain skill in guiding children's development.

Projects

1. What were your favorite toys and play activities when you were young?
2. List some of the things children do that annoy you. List some of the things children do that you enjoy watching. Check these lists later to see whether your feelings have changed. If they have, how would you explain the changes?

For Your Further Reading

Beardsley, L. (1990). *Good day/bad day: The child's experience of child care.* New York: Teachers College Press. Describes from the viewpoint of preschool children their experiences in child care, with annotated discussions linking research on child care quality to actual day-to-day practice in poor and high-quality child care settings.

Bredekamp, S. (Ed.). (1987). *Developmentally appropriate practice in early childhood programs serving children from birth through age 8.* (Exp. ed.). Washington, DC: National Association for the Education of Young Children. The best-selling book that defines the fundamentals of both appropriate and inappropriate practices for teachers of children from birth through 8. Each age group has separate sections. This book should be in every early childhood center, and every teacher will want to be familiar with it.

Greenberg, P., (Ed.) (1991). *Beginner's bibliography—1991.* Washington, DC: National Association for the Education of Young Children. Excellent brief listing of recent books, periodicals, and leaflets on how young children grow and learn, intended for parents as well as teachers. Updated periodically.

Hendrick, J. (1987). *Why teach?* Washington, DC: National Association for the Education of Young Children. A look at careers in early childhood education and care, especially helpful to college students and even high school students and other adults who are exploring why and where they can teach in infant, toddler, preschool, and school-age programs.

Martyna, W. (1983). Beyond the he/man approach: The case for non-sexist language. In B. Thorne, C. Kramarae, and N. Henley (Eds.). *Language, gender, and society* (pp. 25–37). Rowley, MA: Newbury House. Challenging reading for those who are further interested in problems associated with unbiased gender language.

National Association for the Education of Young Children (1986). *What are the benefits of quality child care for preschool children?* Brochure #540; single copies $0.50. Washington, DC: Author. Briefly lists research findings which confirm that high-quality programs are cost-effective, save money and provide lasting benefits for children and their families and for society.

Sheldon, A. (1990). "Kings are royaler than queens": Language and socialization. *Young Children, 45*(2), 4–9. How to take an active role in promoting language that promotes female visibility. Includes "Checklist for a non-sexist classroom," from B. Sprung, *Non-sexist education for young children: A practical guide.* (1975). New York: Women's Action Alliance.

Stone, J. G. (1990). *Teaching preschoolers: It looks like this . . . in pictures.* Washington, DC: National Association for the Education of Young Children. In vivid pictorial form this book illustrates developmentally appropriate practice in preschools.

The Center

Going to school (*girl*, 4 *years*)

This chapter addresses these topics:

▶ What is a *center*?
▶ Why is child care needed?
▶ What characteristics are seen in quality early childhood centers?
▶ What kinds of centers exist and how are they funded?
▶ What are licensing and accreditation?
▶ How does one choose a center?

The word *center* as used in this book refers to programs in places where young children are cared for in groups outside their homes with a qualified teacher and assistants. The centers provide adequate care and learning opportunities appropriate to each child's age and interests. The centers may be in session for a half-day, or they may provide longer care to meet the needs of parents who work. What we will discuss can be applied to children who are cared for in family day-care settings, nonprofit and for-profit child-care centers, and public or private prekindergarten programs.

The Need For Child Care

The need for centers that care for young children has grown rapidly during the past few decades. Many more women today are employed than in the past; some work for economic reasons, others for the job opportunities now open to women. "Researchers estimate that by 1995 two-thirds of all preschool children and three-fourths of school-age children will have mothers in the work force." (Children's Defense Fund, 1991, p. 38) As our knowledge about child growth and development increases, we are more aware of the extent of learning that takes place in the early months and years of life. Children need a variety of firsthand experiences if they are to thrive.

A center caring for young children can be of value because it offers parents and children an opportunity to spend some time apart. When families live in small homes or apartments under crowded conditions with little or no space for play, children can profit from spending time in an environment that provides space, adults, peers, and rich learning activities. Some centers give priority to children who have been abused because parents under stress need a respite from constant interaction with their children, and the children need experiences with other adults.

Children need quality programs in the centers they attend, but programs differ. All programs should meet certain standards. They should provide an environment that is safe, that promotes health, and that offers learning opportunities adapted to what is known about developmental needs of young children. The adults in a center share with parents the re-

*Teachers are important in providing appropriate care and learning opportunities for each child.
Migrant Head Start, Chico, California*

sponsibility for promoting sound growth in this period when growth and learning are most significant. The needs of the children should be the main concern of the adults in any center. Respect for the individual child is the basis for a quality program.

Characteristics Of Quality Programs For Young Children

The center can be thought of as a laboratory for developing human relationships and learning. Although centers differ in appearance and program offerings, universal themes are apparent in all quality settings, including opportunities to:

▶ play with other children
▶ manipulate objects and materials
▶ discover what works
▶ make mistakes
▶ imagine and create.

Programs should be planned with these ideas in mind. In this type of program children are seldom all doing the same thing at the same time. An observer may see one group of children engaged in dramatic play in the homemaking corner; another group building with blocks; a child or two working in the woodworking corner; another child painting at an easel; another small group making play dough; and a child watching others play.

Play is an important avenue for learning, so ample opportunity must be provided for a variety of play experiences. Young children need many

Preschoolers can be independent when the environment is planned to support developmental needs. Migrant Head Start, Chico, California

opportunities for looking, touching, listening, tasting, smelling, and moving. They also use play as a way to discover more about themselves and their world. In play they re-create what they have observed, rehearsing roles and making representations of objects. We see children using blocks to build roads or towers representing what they have seen. We also see them in the housekeeping corner imitating adult roles they have observed by caring for the dolls and setting the table. Discovery of how things work, of how to manage feelings and relationships, and developing concepts about the world around them, all are a part of the active process of learning.

In a quality program the environment is planned to support the developmental needs of the children through the equipment and materials supplied and the planning of space and time. (This is discussed in more detail in Chapter 4.) The teachers encourage and guide children in their use of the environment. They observe carefully and plan to meet the changing needs of the group and of individuals. The teachers are careful observers. (The teacher's role is discussed more in Chapter 12.)

Types of Centers and Their Funding

Many different types of centers care for young children from infancy to school age, and funding for these centers comes from a variety of sources. Usually nursery schools are half-day programs, and day-care centers are full-day programs. Infants and toddlers can be found in either setting. School-age child care occurs before and after the regular school day and provides care for children ages 5 to 12. Within these general classifications are a variety of arrangements and complex funding patterns depending on families' needs and socioeconomic status.

Some centers are in churches or temples because space is available on weekdays. Some of these centers are supported by a religious group, while others are sponsored by agencies or private groups. In most instances parents pay a fee for their child's care. These centers serve the needs of working parents as well as of parents who want their child to have a group experience. Generally they are nonprofit.

Private early childhood programs take many forms. Parent fees usually are the main source of funding. Often proprietary centers are run by individuals interested and educated in early childhood education. Many private schools serve the needs of working parents by providing full-day programs. Some private schools, such as Montessori, have their own methods, materials, and specially trained teachers. Others, such as High/Scope, have a specified curriculum and environment with teachers trained in using High/Scope methods. The High/Scope Curriculum can be found in both private centers as well as publicly funded programs. Still others follow guidelines established by the National Association for the Education of Young Children (NAEYC) for Developmentally Appropriate Curriculum. (Bredekamp, 1987)

Many young children are in some kind of home care. While the parent is at work, a child may be left with a neighbor, or several children may go to the licensed home of someone who cares for a group of children. Many reasons exist for these arrangements, including parents' preference for a home setting, economic conditions, and a shortage of centers. Quality standards for the number of children in the care of one caretaker depend on the ages of the children. (See Table 2–1, p. 33 for the preferred group size and staff-child ratio.)

Availability of care for infants and toddlers is one of the fastest growing needs in the field. Children in this age group need a great deal of individual attention. The standards for quality group care of infants and

The ratio of one adult to three older infants or young toddlers provides for individual attention.
Migrant Head Start, Chico, California

toddlers recommend that one adult should care for not more than four infants at a time. Whenever possible, no infant should have more than two caregivers during a day. Most children under 3 have not developed a large enough measure of trust to feel secure when the caregivers change frequently. Even 3-year-olds entering a center usually need to depend on the same teacher for a time before they adjust to life in the group. Infant and toddler care is a costly arrangement because of the need for small groups and low adult-child ratios.

At parent cooperative nursery schools, interested parents form a group and arrange to open a school for their own children, then hire a trained teacher and act as the teacher's assistants. Generally, parent cooperatives have lower fees due to the parents' participation. These usually are half-day programs. Parent cooperative nursery schools became popular after World War II. Today their numbers are diminishing, perhaps due to social change, such as the increase in two-income families.

Some day-care centers receive federal and state support under Social Services Block Grants (SSBG), also known as Title XX. According to the Children's Defense Fund, Title XX is the largest program providing federal support directly for child care. Most of the families using Title XX programs are headed by single women who work due to economic necessity. Title XX provides a variety of assistance, one type being subsidized care in licensed child-care centers and in family day-care homes. The federal programs Congress approved and funded for 1991—The Child Care and Development Block Grant and the "At Risk" Child Care Program—will give the states new money to subsidize child care for low-income families. (Children's Defense Fund, 1991, p. 44)

"As of 1990, 30 states had developed preschool programs, although most states only provide part-day services." (CDF, 1991, p. 45) A few state governments fund centers as part of school programs. An example is the state-funded Children's Center Program in California. These centers are usually found in or near a public school.

Head Start is a federally funded program that began in the summer of 1965. Head Start provides comprehensive services including health, education, social services, and parent involvement to children from low-income families usually in the year before they enter kindergarten. In 1990 Congress recognized the program's unique effectiveness by authorizing for the first time a series of funding increases which, if appropriated, would allow all eligible 3- and 4-year-olds and 30 percent of eligible 5-year-olds to participate by 1994. (CDF, 1991, p. 45) At present these programs are part-day and are closed in the summer. The community is required to make a contribution in the running of the center, usually by providing the site and some services. Funding is provided under Title XX.

Many colleges and universities have established child development centers for students in classes or as laboratories for research. These usually are half-day programs, and the waiting lists are long. In addition, many colleges and universities have campus child-care programs for the children of students and staff members. Some have full-day programs operating on the campus as well as laboratory nursery schools.

A relatively new trend in child care comes from private business that supports different options as part of employee benefits. This may include a center at the workplace, vouchers to help parents pay for child care at already existing centers, or direct contributions to centers where employees' children are enrolled. An employer or group of businesses may employ a child-care referral person to consult with parents about their needs. Hospitals have been leaders in providing on-site centers, finding them to be cost effective in attracting employees and reducing staff turnover. The largest and most comprehensive employer-supported child day-care program in the United States is that operated by the Department of Defense. (Cook, 1985) At military installations across the country, programs provide a variety of services for children and families.

Kindergarten is available in public school systems in most states, and many private early childhood centers offer kindergarten programs. Kindergartens were to be a bridge between home and school, and it was felt a shorter day would be more developmentally appropriate. Times have changed and preschools now serve as this bridge. Kindergartens traditionally are half-day programs, with many schools now providing extended care to accommodate working families. Some children attend public school kindergarten and a day-care program before or after the school day. Interest nationwide is causing a societal push for full-day kindergartens, both to meet the need of working parents and to ensure greater academic accomplishments from young children.

Still another trend involves franchised child-care programs. These are chains of day-care centers found mainly in suburban areas and operated as large-scale businesses. In general, franchised child care provides fewer social services and other supportive elements for families than more traditional early childhood programs. (Cook, 1985)

A growing concern is that of so-called "latchkey" children, school-age children who let themselves into an empty house or apartment after their school day is over. "A poll in Washington, D.C., for example, showed that one in every seven children between the ages of eight and thirteen generally was left to care for himself or herself after school for at least part of the day, and that some children as young as six and seven were left on their own regularly." (CDF, 1991, p. 46) Many school districts are responding to the concern for these children by providing space and materials for before- and after-school programs. Local agencies, such as Boys Clubs and Girls Clubs, city recreation programs, and the YWCA and YMCA, also provide programs for this age group. School-age child care often overlaps center-based care and family day-care.

Although many kinds of centers exist, the number of quality day-care programs falls far short of meeting the demand. One of the barriers to expanding the availability of child care is the start-up cost, which can discourage many religious organizations, businesses, community groups, and individual family day-care providers from establishing programs. (CDF, 1991, p. 46) The cost of good day-care is high, especially for any center that cares for children under 2 years of age. Budgets in most centers are inadequate. Infant and toddler care costs more than care for preschoolers, and center-based care often costs more than family day-care. Rates also vary widely around the country. In 1990, a survey of selected cities revealed that the average annual cost for an infant in a licensed center ranged from almost $4,000 in Dallas to almost $11,000 in Boston. In Dallas, a single mother who works full time at the minimum wage would have to spend almost half her income to pay for infant child care. (CDF, 1991, p. 42)

> The availability of child care lags so far behind the demand for it that approximately 7 million children 13 years old and under, or more than one in six, may be going without adult supervision for part of each day. The need for infant care is climbing as is the demand for after-school programs. As more parents of young children work, child care needs will become an even greater problem. (CDF, 1991, p. 46)

Standards, Licensing, and Accreditation

Most states set legal minimum standards for the care of young children outside the home. The NAEYC affirms the importance of child-care licensing as a means of controlling the quality of care for young children in settings outside the home. The NAEYC advocates licensing procedures that take into account the nature of the child-care setting and the number of children to be served; set standards for centers, group homes, and family homes; include care of children from infancy through school age; and cover full-time, part-time, and drop-in arrangements. Research demonstrates the relationship between the quality of care provided and such factors as group size, staff-child ratio, and staff education and experience. The NAEYC believes that standards should be clearly written and vigorously enforced. The standards should deal with patterns of safety and health, including nutrition, staff-child ratio, and numbers in a group. Licensing should be administered by agencies that are known and accessible to parents and to the individuals providing care. The standards should include written policies and should describe processes for initial licensing, renewal of license, inspections, revocation of a license, and appeals. (NAEYC, 1987d)

Because licensing requirements stipulate the basic necessary conditions for protecting children's well-being, the NAEYC firmly believes that all forms of supplementary care of young children should be licensed and that exceptions from licensing standards should not be permitted. Giving a single program or group of programs exemption or special treatment weakens the entire fabric of licensing.

Because licensing is not mandatory in many states, and because licensing represents minimum requirements, there has been a movement toward higher standards through accreditation. The "only professionally sponsored, national voluntary accreditation system for preschools, child-care centers, and school-age child-care programs" (National Academy of Early Childhood Programs, *Academy Update*, 1986) is the program of the National Academy of Early Childhood Programs, a division of the NAEYC. The system has been in full operation since 1986 and as of fall 1991 had accredited 1800 programs nationwide. Another organization, the National Family Day Care Association, has recently instituted a voluntary accreditation system for family day-care homes and had accredited about 300 pro-

In selecting a center a parent will visit with her child. Valley College, Campus Child Development Center, Los Angeles

grams in 32 states and the District of Columbia by fall 1991. (National Academy of Early Childhood Programs, personal communication; National Association for Family Day Care, personal communication, 1991)

The public has a responsibility to ensure that child-care programs promote optimal development in a safe, healthy setting. All parents who need child care have the right to choose from settings that will protect and educate their children in a nurturing environment. (NAEYC, 1987d)

Selecting a Center

Most children under 3 or even 4 need the support of a parent before they are comfortable enough to enjoy going into a group alone. It takes longer for some children than for others, depending in part on earlier experiences and temperament. Pushing a child's entry only makes it harder for the child.

Many parents benefit from watching the teacher encourage the child to play with the materials and other children. The parent may also gain insights about the kind of play suitable for young children and its value. They may learn about the needs of children this age as they watch the teacher encouraging the children to play and manage the situations that arise.

What Information Does a Parent Want About a Center?

In selecting a center parents will need to visit one or more centers before deciding to enter their child. Talking with someone who has had a child in those centers is helpful in making decisions about placement. The adults in the center play the major role in caring for young children. Parents should observe the quality of adult-child interactions as they visit centers. The teachers' education and experience, the size of the group, and the staff-child ratio play important roles in determining the quality of the experience for children.

The head teacher is a very important person. Typical questions parents should ask the head teacher include: What education and experience have you had? Do you enjoy children? What is your philosophy about learning? What are your expectations for the children and their behavior? Do you respect individual differences among children? Also, parents will want to look for cultural diversity among the teachers. Are multicultural materials present? Parents will want to ask these questions about the other teachers in the center, also.

The size of the group and the staff-child ratio are also important points. Young children profit most when the group is small so that teachers can help individuals. We suggest these guidelines in Table 2–1 for optimal group size and minimum staff-child ratio for centers. (NAEYC, 1991a, p. 41)

TABLE 2–1	Recommended Staff-Child Ratios Within Group Size

Age of Children*	Group Size									
	6	8	10	12	14	16	18	20	22	24
Infants (birth–12 mo)	1:3	1:4								
Toddlers (12–24 mo)	1:3	1:4	1:5	1:4						
2-year-olds (24–36 mo)		1:4	1:5	1:6*						
2- and 3-year-olds			1:5	1:6	1:7*					
3-year-olds					1:7	1:8	1:9	1:10*		
4- and 5-year-olds						1:8	1:9	1:10*		
5-year-olds						1:8	1:9	1:10		
6- to 8-year-olds								1:10	1:11	1:12

*Small group sizes and lower staff-child ratios have been found to be strong predictors of compliance with indicators of quality such as positive interactions among staff and children and developmentally appropriate curriculum.
Multi-age grouping is both permissible and desirable. When no infants are included, the staff-child ratio and group size requirements shall be based on the age of the majority of the children in the group. When infants are included, ratios and group size for infants must be maintained. (p. 40)

Is there adequate space indoors and outdoors? A minimum of 35 square feet of usable playroom floor space indoors per child and a minimum of 75 square feet of play space outdoors per child are suggested by the NAEYC. (NAEYC, 1991a, p. 43) Is it a safe place? The space should

In selecting a center a parent looks for adequate space outdoors and a variety of equipment for active play.
Valley College, Campus Child Development Center, Los Angeles

be free of hazards such as broken equipment, sharp corners, and steep stairs without hand rails. There should be latches, a childproof fence around the outside play area, no fire hazards, and fire extinguishers well-placed.

Is there visible concern for health? Are the kitchen and bathroom clean? Are toilets and facilities for washing and drying hands and face near the play area and easily supervised? Are the snacks and meals planned with nutrition in mind? What are the procedures if a child becomes ill?

Is there a wide variety of equipment available for active and for quiet play? Is the equipment well arranged, with space for block play, props for dramatic play, provisions for children's books, music, and a variety of art activities?

The program evolves through teacher-child relationships. Do teachers value play? Do teachers value books and read often to small groups? Do teachers encourage talking with children rather than at them? Is a limited time spent in whole group activities with most of the time spent in small groups with self-initiated activities including projects? How do teachers deal with children's conflicts or a very quiet child?

The setting should support emotional well-being. What is the atmosphere in the school? Is it relaxed but alert? Are children happy and busy with activities in an independent way?

Parent–teacher relations are an integral part of a young child's experience in a center. Are parents or other caregivers welcome to visit at any time? Are opportunities planned for conferences with the teachers? Are parent meetings scheduled?

These guidelines for selecting a center are elaborated in other parts of this book and are provided here as a beginning guide. The NAEYC has published a useful guide called "How to Choose a Good Early Childhood Program." (NAEYC, 1990b) The parent will need to take some time observing to find answers to these points and may want to talk with the teacher again later. Unfortunately, a parent may not have much latitude in the selection of a center for the child, and decisions may be made out of necessity rather than choice.

The Program as it Functions for a Child

Many similarities exist between half-day programs and full-day programs, but some differences are notable. Children in full-day programs have needs that differ from children who spend a morning away from their homes. In full-day programs the homelike atmosphere becomes more important, as does the provision for rest. The need for softness, privacy, and perhaps a slower pace should be carefully considered by both the staff and the parents. The child's participation in keeping the room clean and tidy takes on another dimension beyond learning how to put things away. Parent–staff relations become more important due to the longer period of time the child spends away from home.

Chapter Overview

The care of young children is provided in a variety of settings reflecting the diverse needs of today's families. Types of programs range from private and for-profit to public or federally funded programs. Along with the selection of an appropriate program for a child, considerations such as philosophy of the school, standards and licensing, school policies, staff-child ratios, and space requirements are important. Selecting the right program is a complicated process. Parents should consider carefully the choices available if they are to find the one that matches their needs and philosophy of early childhood education. They should consider a center that suits their child's temperament and needs.

Projects

1. Survey your community and report on the number and types of early childhood programs available. What are the most common kinds? (The local NAEYC affiliate and the day-care licensing department are good resources.)
2. Interview the personnel officer of a large company in your area and learn what provisions are made for child care for employees. If child care is not offered, discuss the possibilities and what other companies are doing. Check your library for information about employer-sponsored child care.
3. Visit a college campus child-care center. What are the arrangements for students attending school who need child care? What are the goals of the program? How well are these goals met?

For Your Further Reading

Clarke-Stewart, S. (1982). *Daycare*. The developing child series. Cambridge, MA: Harvard University press. A sound and very readable book about day-care that includes discussion of why American society seems biased against day-care.

Day, M. C., & Parker, R. K. (Eds.). (1977). *The preschool in action* (2nd ed.) Boston: Allyn & Bacon. An often-cited book giving a thorough overview of fourteen kinds of programs ranging from infant and home-based to center-based preschools; excellent comparative analyses.

Dittman, L. L. (1985). *Finding the best care for your infant or toddler*. Brochure #518; single copies $0.50. Washington, DC: National Association for the Education of Young Children. Discusses options to consider in seeking infant and toddler care. Companion brochure to Dittmann, L. L., *The infants we care for*.

Hohmann, M., Banet, B. & Weikart, D. P.

(1979). *Young children in action: A manual for preschool educators*. Ypsilanti MI: High/Scope Press.

Hohmann, M. (1983). *Study guide to "Young children in action."* Ypsilanti MI: High/Scope Press. Two books on the High/Scope model, which is seen in many centers where teachers have been trained in this approach, based on Piagetian principles.

Keyes, C. R., & Schwartz, S. L. (1991). Special issue: Campus Children's Centers: Coming of age. *Early Childhood Research Quarterly, 6*(1). Twelve articles reviewing two decades of campus child care, challenges and problems for these programs, and issues of professional identity and development.

Montessori, M. (1964). *The Montessori method*. Cambridge, MA: Robert Bentley.

Montessori, M. (1967). *The absorbent mind*. New York: Dell Publishing. Teachers of young children need to be aware of the great debt owed to Dr. Maria Montessori by all in the early childhood field. These books are worth searching for in the library.

National Association for the Education of Young Children (1990) *How to choose a good early childhood program*. Brochure #525. Also available as *Como escoger un buen programa de educación pre-escolar*. Brochure #510. Single copies $0.50. Washington, DC: Author. A brief, convenient guide to evaluating and selecting programs; good for parents and teachers. Discusses thirteen criteria.

National Association for the Education of Young Children (1987). *NAEYC position statement on licensing and regulation of early childhood programs in centers and family day care*. Brochure #535; single copies $0.50. Washington, DC: Author. Includes health, safety, zoning, and building codes, which can be confusing because the fifty states differ in regulations.

National Association for the Education of Young Children (1991). *Accreditation criteria and procedures of the National Academy of Early Childhood Programs*. (rev. ed.) Washington, DC: Author. A detailed guide for programs considering national accreditation, it also is useful in its descriptions of ten areas of characteristics of quality early childhood centers. Every center will find it useful.

The People in the Center

Lady and dog (*girl, 3 years*)

This chapter acquaints you with:

▶ The children in the center, the size of the groups, and the children's ages
▶ The length of the center's day
▶ The adult staff and their numbers in relation to children's needs
▶ Teachers' qualifications and paths for professional development
▶ Volunteers
▶ Growth experiences for staff within the center
▶ Improving staff insights through observation
▶ Maintaining positive staff relationships.

GOAL for Interactions among Staff and Children: Interactions between children and staff provide opportunities for children to develop an understanding of self and others and are characterized by warmth, personal respect, individuality, positive support, and responsiveness. Staff facilitate interactions among children to provide opportunities for development of self-esteem, social competence, and intellectual growth. (NAEYC, 1991a, *Accreditation Criteria . . .*, p. 15)

The center as we have defined it serves the needs of children by offering them experiences appropriate to what is now known about growth needs at these age levels. It shares with parents the responsibility for promoting sound growth and learning in a period when growth is rapid and significant. Respect for the individual child is the basis for a good program.

In a good center the groups are small. Children are seldom all together, doing the same things at the same time. They work or play in groups of two, or three, or four. A great deal of talking takes place, for language skills are valued. Children are active. They make choices among many meaningful activities.

The Children

Children attend an early childhood program because it meets their needs or the needs of their parents. Some centers *mainstream* children with physical or mental disabilities into groups of nondisabled children. Many parents, of course, seek care for their children because of their work. Others look for part-day programs for their children's learning and social experience. All quality centers, whatever the parents' needs, are interested in the healthy development of young children.

Centers are fortunate when they enroll children from diverse cultural backgrounds. Under the guidance of understanding teachers, such diversity brings significant enrichment in the opportunities for all children. Children can develop positive attitudes about people who differ from themselves. In doing this, children broaden their understanding of the world around them. Positive attitudes about race and culture can develop early in life.

Number of Children in a Group

The size of groups in centers for young children is now considered as important as adult–child ratio. Both factors must be taken into account. To meet the individual needs of children the group size should be small.

As discussed in Chapter 2, the children's ages, the range in age in the group, and the teacher–child ratio should determine the number of children in a group. For infants and toddlers the size of the group should be very small. In groups set up to include children with special needs the number should be reduced to allow more individual attention. The numbers of children in full-day groups should also be determined by children's ages.

Full day-care programs make heavy demands on the staff as well as the child. Limits in the size of the group are too often disregarded for economic reasons. State and federal guidelines have been established to ensure that the number of children cared for in groups is based upon sound early childhood practices, but some state licensing standards may allow larger than optimum group size. Accreditation standards for group size and staff–child ratio promote positive interactions between adults and children. (NAEYC, 1991a, p. 41).

Ages of Children

Most centers are flexible in the range of ages, the age span depending on the goals of the program, the needs of the community, and the children served. Some evidence shows that a narrow age range in a group may increase competitiveness among children and offer less chance for the learnings that come from being with children who are both younger and older. Teachers may find it easier to provide opportunities adapted to each child's needs when the age range is within a year. Chronological age is not, however, the only measure of maturity. The range in levels of development is large in any group, whatever the age range.

In a "family type" or "mixed age" group the younger children have the opportunity to learn through watching and playing with older children. The older children, in turn, may gain from helping and playing with the younger ones. Cooperative play seems to occur more easily. The mixed age group takes skillful teacher guidance at times to prevent the younger children from continually taking passive roles and to prevent the older children from interfering in the play of younger children. Patterns of relating to siblings at home may be repeated at the center. These patterns of behavior may then be worked through in the center.

We can conclude on the evidence we have at present that the ages served and optimum range in age may depend on space arrangements, funding constraints, staffing patterns, preferences of the teachers, and needs of parents.

Length of the Day

Young children gain from attendance that supplements their home experience. In day care, where the needs of the family make a longer day necessary, the program will adapt its pace to meet the demands that a longer day makes on the child. Two-and-a-half hours a day spent away from home with other children meets the needs of most children when parents are looking for a group experience for their child. Other children may need to stay longer because parents are employed. Strains in the family situation, such as poor housing, ill health of parent or sibling or stress that might lead to child abuse, also necessitate children having longer days in centers. Children spending the major part of the day in a center have different needs than those in half-day programs. Group life at this early age is difficult for some children. Adults are needed who understand that children need plenty of loving care on an individual basis.

The Staff
Number of Staff

The number and type of staff members in a center depend on its size and purposes. A large program will employ a variety of staff members—a

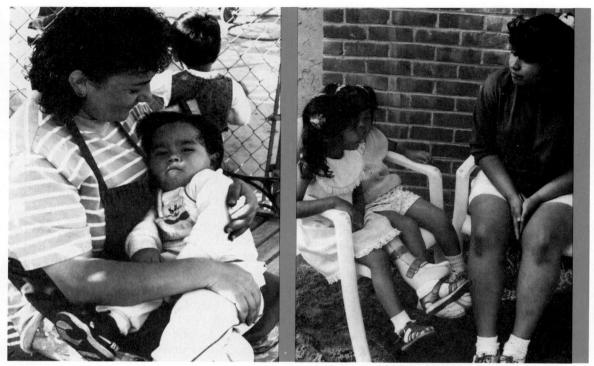

Caregivers for infants must be consistent in order for a
trusting relationship to develop.
Migrant Head Start, Chico, California

When children with physical disabilities are enrolled,
the center may need additional staff.
Migrant Head Start, Chico, California

director, teachers, assistant teachers, aides, perhaps students in training,
and volunteers who may or may not be parents. There also may be a secre-
tary, a cook, and a person responsible for building maintenance. There
may be people from other professions, such as a social worker, speech therapist, nurse, or perhaps a doctor, psychologist, or psychiatrist who act as
consultants. In a program planned to meet the needs of young children
there will always be more than one adult with each group of children, regardless of the size of the group.

Infants require a very different kind of care than toddlers and older
children. They are working at establishing trust in their environment and
the people around them. Caregivers must be consistent and reliable for
this trusting relationship to occur. Infants need an environment that supports sensorimotor development with just the right amount of space to enhance their development. Infants are acquiring language in these
beginning months, and a setting where adults talk to them is a necessity.
A small group is best, with one adult to three infants.

Toddlers need attention and individual care from a teacher, such as help in dressing, in using the toilet, and in eating. Two-year-olds also need someone to turn to for encouragement or comfort. They are just beginning to master the strong urges for being independent. The teacher must be there when needed and must be a person who enjoys, but does not foster, the dependency of young children.

Children with special needs require additional staff. A child who is blind or partially sighted, hearing impaired, emotionally disabled, or developmentally delayed demands more help from teachers than do other children. All these children may gain from being "mainstreamed" in a group of children. They may contribute to the experiences of the other children when the situation is well planned and well staffed. A balance must be maintained between meeting the needs of special children and the needs of the rest of the group. For the good of all, the group should not be overly weighted with children with special needs; otherwise the gains will be less for everyone.

The physical environment influences the number of staff needed. Teachers can direct all their energy to meeting the needs of children if the toilets and the playground are right next to the classroom, if ample storage space is adjacent to where materials will be used, if children can move freely from one area or room to another without needing adult help, and if rooms or yard contain no "blind spots."

Qualifications of Teachers

PERSONAL CHARACTERISTICS Evidence abounds that the teacher is the most important single factor in determining what a school experience will be like for children. It is not only the teacher's skill but also attitudes and feelings that will influence what that teacher does for, and with, the children. A teacher of young children must enjoy being with them.

To meet the daily demands of a group of active young children, a teacher needs to be in good physical health and emotionally stable. Moods cannot interfere with responses in the teaching situation. The teacher needs to have confidence in herself and in others, a capacity for warm personal relationships, and a zest for living and learning. A sense of humor and a "light touch" are essential.

A good teacher is flexible, resourceful, realistic, independent-thinking, capable of sustained effort. Sensitive and responsive, but able to use authority in constructive ways, the innovative teacher is willing to experiment and to act with spontaneity. With a sense of order, an appreciation for beauty and the wonders of life, this teacher is sustained by the belief that each child can learn.

It takes time for a teacher to grow in understanding and skill, just as it takes time for a child to grow. Becoming a competent teacher is a process that continues throughout one's career. Any group contains teachers in

A *good teacher has a zest for learning. She uses the marble game to encourage language and math concepts.*
Migrant Head Start, Chico, California

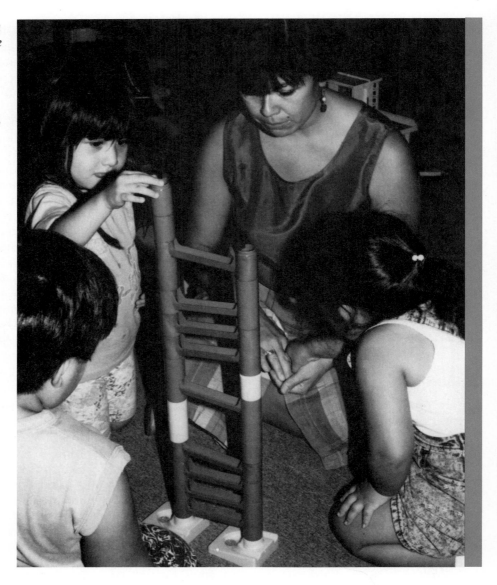

different stages of "becoming." A teacher must develop an awareness of what is significant. One cannot skip any stages in growth. The attempt to take shortcuts may preclude the possibilities for later growth.

PROFESSIONAL QUALIFICATIONS Becoming a professional teacher of young children is a developmental process. Early childhood education courses with emphasis on child development, principles and practices of working with young children, supervised field work experience, curriculum courses in art, music, science, language and literature, and health and safety provide the professional foundation. Courses in science, social studies, and the humanities provide the breadth necessary to enrich the teacher's own life as well as the lives around her. "Research demonstrates that a major factor in the quality and effectiveness of programs for young children is the specialized education of the staff." (NAEYC, 1984)

The assistant teacher also should have had courses, or be taking courses, in child development and in methods of working with young children. An assistant should have an understanding of personality development and the learning process of young children. Part of the assistant's education should include having worked with a group of young children under the supervision of a head teacher.

In nursery schools or day-care centers, associate teachers may be persons trained as Child Development Associates (CDAs) under a program funded by the federal government in which academic work is coordinated with field experience. Credit is given for previous practical experience. The Child Development Associate (CDA) program is a competency-based assessment system. On October 4, 1985, the Head Start Bureau; the Administration for Children, Youth and Families; the Office of Human Development Services; the Department of Health and Human Services; and the Employment and Training Administration of the Department of Labor signed an interagency agreement. The intent of the agreement was to enable more adults who were employed in programs such as Head Start or military child care to receive CDA training and assessment leading to the CDA credential. An important feature of the agreement was its emphasis on serving individuals who are economically disadvantaged. The CDA credential is now awarded by the Council for Early Childhood Professional Recognition.

Volunteers

Volunteers may be regularly scheduled, carrying out duties similar to those of an assistant teacher, or they may come for special purposes. They may be parents or grandparents (real or surrogate); they may be high school or college students; they may be people from the community or older children from an elementary school. One may come to play a musical instrument, such as a violin, flute, or horn. A volunteer might be one who loves animals and brings a pet to school or invites the children to visit and get acquainted with the animal at home. Someone who has a special collection may be willing to exhibit parts of it, to share with the children.

Volunteers can contribute needed services, too, helping with transportation on excursions or coming into the center to prepare snacks or to work with children on special days. Parents may be encouraged to share cultural aspects of their family life such as food, music, dance, stories,

The CDA program provides a career development ladder for teachers, based on competence.
Santa Monica College, Child Development Center
Santa Monica, California

clothes, and toys and games. They gain from taking part in the program, and the center is enriched by their participation.

Whatever their age, when volunteers offer a warm, loving, caring relationship to children, they bring something of great importance. If volunteers are to be successful, there must be someone responsible for giving them adequate directions and a background for understanding individual children, as well as some knowledge about how children can learn and what children need to learn. This guidance should be given without diminishing their spontaneity or interfering with their own "style" of relating to children. Success with even one child opens up the possibilities for success with other children.

Professional Growth Experiences for Staff Members

All teachers need continuing opportunities for learning. Some of these opportunities will occur within the center itself. Regular staff meetings provide time to discuss questions that arise about the program, about individual children, about the philosophy of the center, and about curriculum. Regular staff discussions are an important part of every program. Brief discussions can be held at the end of half-day programs or during rest time in full-day programs. Longer discussions may be held in a monthly evening meeting or a weekly potluck supper. Retreats, where teachers spend a weekend together in a setting other than school, are an ideal way to provide for cohesiveness and staff development. Staff meetings serve the important function of restoring teachers' energy and interest.

In group discussions, staff members may spend time planning for activities such as cooking with the children, deciding what supplies are needed, how they will share the responsibilities, what the goals may be, and how teaching and learning will be evaluated. They may discuss how the budget will be allocated. If a trip is planned, arrangements will have to be made. What and how will these be done? They may evaluate the day's learning opportunities and decide on a change in the arrangement of the housekeeping corner or the placement of the easels. More discussion about professional growth occurs in Chapter 23.

Improving Staff Insights Based on Observations

Teachers' discussions of their observations lead them to greater insight into the needs of individual children. A teacher may ask, "I wonder what happened today when Felicia and Michael were fighting over the blocks?" In describing the incident, another teacher may suddenly realize more clearly just what did happen and her part in it. Insights into situations and into the needs of individual children grow as a result of such thoughtful consideration.

Staff discussions may center around observing, evaluating, and planning.
Child Development Laboratory, California State University, Chico

As they recall a number of incidents about a particular child, staff members may begin to understand more clearly the meaning of that child's behavior. They may develop a more consistent and constructive plan for helping the child learn, or they may realize that they need to understand much more about the child. They may decide to observe and make notes about this child and to discuss the behavior again at the next staff meeting.

Another staff member may comment, "I realized today that I have never given much attention to Shawna. She doesn't seem to need it. Now I'm beginning to wonder if she is missing out somehow. She hasn't changed much since she entered school." The staff can then pool their feelings and observations of Shawna, trying to assess her behavior to see whether her patterns are those of independent competence or of passive avoidance of difficulty.

Then someone may say, "I really felt angry when Monty kicked me today and told me to go away when I was trying to help him." Others agree that Monty has made them angry, too, and they have felt frustrated and uneasy about their responses to him. In talking about the situation, they feel some relief and can begin to smile at themselves. Monty is such a little boy, rejecting these big grown-ups. They begin to wonder what the world must be like for Monty, if he sees everybody in it as an enemy. Why does he feel and act this way? What can they do to help him change his perceptions of people and of himself? How is one friendly and firm with such a child?

Maintaining Positive Staff Relations

Staff members become better teachers through such discussions, but discussions like this depend on good staff relationships. The development of good relations may be helped by drawing up some ground rules for conducting a discussion such as the following.

It is understood that all members agree to:

1. Respect individual differences in feeling and in "styles" of working and accept the fact that there are many possible ways of reaching a goal.
2. Refrain from passing judgment on what another person does. Instead they join in looking at questions and in thinking about them, rather than considering or criticizing. One may ask, "I wonder why you did that?" in attempting to understand; or, "I wonder what else could have been done" in attempting to seek alternative solutions.
3. Respect, as a matter of "professional ethics," the confidentiality of personal things that are discussed in the staff meeting and not to repeat these outside the professional setting.

In the climate of acceptance set up by such an agreement, staff members are better able to be honest and objective in looking at their own as well as at children's behavior. They are better able to function with competence, channeling their energies into common goals, less entangled by the universal problems of jealousy and rivalry. They are better able to work out ways of facing the problems of authority everyone must face. They are freer to grow in their insights into human relationships, just as they hope to help the children grow in understanding their relationships with others. These issues are discussed further in Chapter 23.

Chapter Overview

This chapter provides guidelines for number of children in a group and age grouping choices. Staff–child ratios and staff qualifications are discussed as well as professional qualifications. A reminder that all teachers need continuing opportunities for learning has been addressed. Finally, suggestions for improving and maintaining staff relations have been outlined.

Projects

1. In the school where you are observing or participating, check these points:

   a. The number of children in each group.
   b. The ratio of boys and girls in each group.
   c. The ratio of children and adults in each group.
   d. The education and the experience of the staff members.
   e. The scheduling of staff meetings and parent conferences.

2. Arrange to observe in a "family type" group where ages are mixed; also observe in a group where the ages of the children are within about a year. What differences are there between the two groups? What differences might be due to the difference in age range? What are the advantages and disadvantages? Compare the number of children in each group and the ratio of children and adults in each group.

3. Arrange to have an interview with a CDA candidate or someone who has received a CDA certificate. Report on cost of certificate, educational requirements, length of time involved in getting the certificate, and evaluation procedures.

For Your Further Reading

Dittmann, L. L. (Ed.). (1984). *The infants we care for.* Washington, DC: National Association for the Education of Young Children. Offers useful ideas for operating home- or center-based infant programs, including staff selection and training, budgeting, facilities, equipment, and program planning. T. B. Brazelton and B. L. White contributed.

Gonzalez-Mena, J. (1989). *Infants, toddlers, and caregivers.* (2nd ed.). Mountain View, CA: Mayfield Publishing Co. Revised and updated to include toddlers. Issues discussed in care situations, such as parent-caregiver relationships, separation problems, and cultural diversity, with helpful solutions.

Greenberg, P. (1989). Parents as partners in young children's development and education: A new American fad? Why does it matter? *Young Children 44*(4), 61–75. Parents are very often among the people in the early-childhood classroom. This article examines the historical and political roots of parent involvement in schools and challenges teachers to look at their own gender bias, racism, and classism in building parent partnerships.

Katz, L. G., Evangelou, D., & Hartman, J. A. (1990). *The case for mixed-age grouping in early childhood education.* Washington, DC: National Association for the Education of Young Children. Examines research, discusses benefits to children, and provides practical ideas for implementing mixed-age settings.

Phillips, C. B. (1990). The Child Development Associate Program: Entering a new era. *Young Children 45*(3), 24–27. Reviews the history of the CDA national credentialing program since 1971; now administered by the Council for Early Childhood Professional Recognition. Explains the new professional preparation program and revised procedures for assessment of individual applicants through fieldwork, course work, and evaluation.

Souweine, J., Crimmins, S., & Mazel, C. (1981). *Mainstreaming: Ideas for teaching young children.* Washington, DC: National Association for the Education of Young Children. Useful suggestions for integrating children with special needs into the classroom with other children, including possible difficulties to be solved.

The Physical Environment of the Center

My play yard (*girl, 3 years, 4 months*)

This chapter explores many aspects of the physical setting in good centers for young children such as:

▶ Buildings
▶ Health and safety considerations
▶ Play equipment of many kinds
▶ Materials to be selected
▶ The use of space
▶ The use of time.

GOAL for the physical environment: The indoor and outdoor physical environment fosters optimal growth and development through opportunities for exploration and learning.

RATIONALE: The physical environment affects the behavior and development of the people, both children and adults, who live and work in it. The quality of the physical space and materials provided affects the level of involvement of children and the quality of interaction between adults and children. . . (NAEYC, 1991a, *Accreditation Criteria . . .* , p. 43)

The Building

Children are active doers who learn best through firsthand experiences. This point of view serves as a guide in planning an indoor and outdoor environment that will enhance young children's development. A good deal of thought should go into planning the environment, for it extends or limits the experiences of children.

AMOUNT OF SPACE   The NAEYC recommends at least 35 square-feet of play space per child indoors and 75 square-feet of space outdoors. The association also suggests that centers located in warm climates can use ample outdoor space for activities often conducted indoors. Centers with limited outdoor areas may take advantage of indoor space such as a gym to provide equivalent activities.

EXPOSURE   A southern exposure is desirable for the playrooms so that they may be sunny and bright, with plenty of light coming in through low windows. Children want to be able to look out and see what is happening outside. One school surrounded by a block wall fence was able to have the fence on the street side of the yard replaced by a steel mesh fence so the children could see the rolling hills across the street from their school. This change was especially beneficial because sheep occasionally were unloaded at this point for grazing.

PARKING SPACE   Parking space near the entrance is not only convenient for parents but also reduces the hazards of traffic for children. By providing easy parking arrangements the center encourages parents to have more contact with the staff at arrival and departure times.

RELATION OF ROOMS   The entrance should be spacious enough to accommodate parents and children as they come and go. It should look attractive, and it should lead directly into the play areas. At one school a large doll house was located at child's eye level near the entrance. This served as a way of helping new children enter the area. They would arrange the furniture or put the dolls to bed as they gradually gained confidence in the new setting.

Doors leading outside must have childproof latches. Personal storage spaces for the children should be near the entrance. Bathrooms should open off the playroom. The outdoor play area should open directly off the inside play space if possible. This arrangement permits a more flexible program and easier group supervision.

ACTIVITY AREAS   The physical arrangement of space and its boundaries are important considerations in planning a program for young children. No single best way to arrange a classroom exists, although certain criteria should be considered such as locating books in a well-lit area and placing blocks out of the line of traffic. Space allows children to move freely and make choices about activities.

Activity areas should be bounded by low room dividers that can be used for storage and for protecting the play from interference. Low dividers also enable the teacher to see what is happening, in order to supervise from strategic points. The room and the yard should include places for privacy as well as for social interaction. Materials and equipment should be appropriate for the age level of the children and encourage independence.

STORAGE As every teacher knows, adequate storage space is essential. Individual spaces for children to hang their clothing and store their personal belongings are necessary. Space where supplies and equipment can be conveniently stored is needed both inside and outside. Some storage

Small manipulative toys need a good storage arrangement. Valley College, Campus Child Development Center, Los Angeles

space should be at the child's level for encouraging independent behavior. Paint supplies on low shelves near the easel, plus collage materials, paper, and glue located near low tables, encourages independence and free choice. Provision should be made for drying wet clothing.

Conveniently arranged storage space includes space for collections, space for "junk" of all kinds that may be used later, space for things that can be taken apart and examined, and space for raw materials from which things can be constructed. A work space for making and repairing equipment is needed. Teachers will appreciate space for their own belongings and materials, as well.

OUTDOOR ACTIVITY   The outdoor activity area should consist of sunny areas and shady areas and should have a variety of surfaces: grass, dirt, and hard-surfaced areas for wheel toys and for play when the ground is wet. A covered outdoor shelter is desirable adjacent to the building so that children can play outdoors even on snowy, rainy, or cold days. There should be a childproof fence around the playground with childproof fastenings on all gates. Good landscaping adds interest and variety to the children's experiences. Different kinds of areas, such as a slope, a digging area, and garden space, make different types of play possible.

ANTI-BIAS ENVIRONMENT   The center must provide opportunities for exploring gender, race, ethnicity, age, and disabilities. Materials that reflect the diverse backgrounds of the children and staff should be attractively displayed. Images that show people of various backgrounds working and playing together as well as diversity in family styles are needed.

BEAUTY   In addition to being safe and functional, a center should be an attractive place where attention is given to color and pleasing lines and shapes, such as a graceful arrangement of flowers in a bowl, a picture on the wall, an interesting mobile. Children respond to beauty in their surroundings.

Many centers are in buildings that do not have all of these features. Space may have to be adapted in churches, community centers, or schools that are far from ideal. Much can be done in remodeling and in the organization of available space, however, to make the facilities serve adequately the needs of children.

HEALTH AND SAFETY   Shades or blinds may be needed as a protection against glare. The center should be cleaned daily, bathroom fixtures and tables disinfected, and trash removed. Toys that children touch with their mouths should be washed daily. Both cleaning and sanitizing are necessary.

Toilets, drinking water, and hand-washing facilities must be easily accessible. Liquid soap and disposable towels are necessary, since cakes of soap and cloth towels spread germs. Electrical outlets need to be covered

When clean-up is convenient, accessible, and expected, children are enthusiastic participants.
Migrant Head Start, Chico, California

with protective caps at all times. Cushioning materials, such as mats, wood chips, or sand, are required under climbers, slides, and swings. Climbing equipment, swings, and large pieces of furniture should be securely anchored. Canvas seats are needed on swings rather than wooden seats.

The building and all equipment should be maintained in safe, clean condition and in good repair. Fire hazards should be eliminated and fire extinguishers, fire drills, and escapes provided as recommended by the fire authorities. Many states require smoke detectors in centers.

The health and safety of the children are a first responsibility for the center. Although every precaution should be taken, every center must carry accident and liability insurance to cover children and staff.

Equipment

Developmentally appropriate equipment and materials are important ingredients in a quality environment for young children. Play equipment must be durable for active use and sufficient in quantity to encourage social play. Storage of materials on open shelves at children's level makes them accessible for use and facilitates clean-up. Children's cooperative, creative and constructive play is facilitated when equipment is "accessible to them, organized to promote independent use, and periodically changed to provide variety." (NAEYC, 1991a. *Accreditation Criteria,* p. 45)

Equipment should be sturdy, safe, and capable of serving a variety of purposes. Sometimes equipment, such as real tools and outdoor climbing apparatus, seems dangerous at first glance. It must be remembered that children want to gain mastery, and they need a sense of adventure in play. Every child should have the pleasure of using a real workbench and hammer or digging with a small, real spade. All children should have the opportunity to experience the thrill of climbing up high and sliding down a slide or a pole. A child learns to use equipment by using it again and again. Our concern is with the safe use of equipment. Giving a child too much help may result in his doing something that is beyond his ability or skill level. It is at such times that he is likely to have an accident. Safe use means maintaining certain rules about the use of equipment, such as permitting only one child at a time on a ladder. Safe use means showing a child how to use equipment safely, such as placing a ladder in a secure way or carrying a sharp implement with the point downward. We help children learn to use equipment safely in order to allow them to become competent and to move freely. Learning about safety is an important aspect of learning to use equipment.

No one equipment list is ever complete, nor should it be, because the inventiveness of parents, teachers, and children can make a center's equipment unique. Yet there will be some equipment common to all quality centers.

 BLOCKS   Every center should have a variety of blocks of different sizes and shapes. Large blocks promote motor development and encourage cooperative and dramatic play. Small blocks offer many opportunities for children of all ages to construct and learn in areas such as mathematics, science, and art. Unit blocks include units, half units, and double and quadruple units as well as a variety of basic shapes and sizes. Large hollow blocks that are multiples of each other should be available, too. Blocks are useful in different ways to children at different stages of development. Shelves for the storage of the blocks are needed so that they can be organized and stored by shape and size. Learning is aided when outlines of each size and shape are provided on block shelves.

Block storage should be organized by shape and size to promote learning during clean-up time. Valley College, Campus Child Development Center, Los Angeles

DRAMATIC PLAY The dramatic play corner should include a stove, sink, cupboard, small table and chairs, doll bed and chests, and other furniture that allows children to create the world that they know. Racks for hanging clothes, shoe shelves, pegs on the wall for hats, mirrors, and doll buggies or strollers allow children to re-create life around them. The equipment, objects, and spatial organization of the dramatic play area should include and encourage diversity of gender play by including space other than the kitchen for playing out roles that children experience. A garage repair shop with real tools, a place to take the order, and a mock setup of a car made from blocks and an old car seat provided hours of pleasure in one center. Cultural diversity can be reflected in the center by having cooking and eating utensils and objects such as toys, dolls, or games that reflect different cultures. Personal objects such as different kinds of combs and brushes and items used for holiday celebrations help children understand that there are many ways of being in the world. The dramatic play area in one center gathered a variety of beds to help children realize that there are many ways of sleeping other than in a regular bed.

ART The art center provides materials for creative expression as well as art appreciation. It needs easels with space for two or more children, primary color paints along with tan, brown, and black paint, and a water supply. Crayons and marker pens in skin tones and other colors should be available. Racks or rope with clip clothes pins are needed for hanging paintings to dry. Low tables and chairs for collage, clay, and other activities should be provided. Art work representing various cultures should be displayed at child's eye level. Clay may be stored in a large crock or small trash container with a tight fitting lid.

BOOKS   The library center should look cozy, soft, and inviting. Cool colors—blue, green, lavender—help provide a quiet setting. Large cushions, book racks with book covers facing forward, and good lighting allow children to explore books comfortably. Books are selected that reflect diversity of gender roles, racial and cultural backgrounds, special needs and abilities, and a range of occupations. One center had a variety of books showing different languages. There was an alphabet book in Farsi, a story book in Braille, a sign language book, and several books in different languages.

SCIENCE   The center for exploration and experimentation may include magnets, magnifying glasses, balance scales, cages for insects and pets, shelves with egg timer, hourglass, abacus, measuring cups in sets, measuring spoons, steel tape, a ruler, a compass. Smell bottles, sound boxes, attribute blocks, and other items provide a setting for experimentation and discovery. The center should include both natural and physical science materials, and displays should be changed periodically as interests change.

PUZZLES AND QUIET PLAY   A center for quiet play consisting of low tables and chairs near shelves with manipulative toys, puzzles, and games will provide children with much pleasure. Felt pens or marking pencils, crayons, sheets of plain paper and colored paper, paste, and blunt scissors can be available in this area.

MUSIC   The music center might have an autoharp, a piano, a record player, tape recorder, or perhaps an electronic keyboard. Regularly heard music should reflect the various cultural styles of the children and staff. Instruments such as a large drum, smaller drums, bells, large gong, small wrist bells, xylophone, triangle, tone bars, sand blocks, maracas, castanets, and other sound-making items can be included. Scarves or colored squares of gauze for use in dancing and movement add to the experience.

"MESSY" PLAY   "Messy" play centers are important! Tables with washable surfaces are used for finger painting or wet clay, with a heavy piece of plastic used under the table if the floor needs protection. A tray for finger paint with a roll of butcher paper and cutter on the shelf or wall nearby provide the ingredients for rich experiences. Sand-and-water tables provide space for many sensory activities.

SAND A sand area is an indispensable place in which to dig roads and waterways, to make mountains and tunnels, with water available to fill pails and plastic jars, to discover the properties of sand and water, for dramatic play and for making pies, cakes, and cookies.

CLIMBING Climbing equipment of all kinds should be provided, such as a jungle gym, ladders, large crates, rope ladders, sewer pipes, planks, ladder boxes, and tree trunks. Stable bases of support provide challenging learning opportunities. It is desirable to include movable pieces and accessories to provide variety in climbing opportunities.

CONSTRUCTION Building equipment such as large hollow blocks, boards of different lengths, sawhorses, packing boxes, used tires, and canvas or nylon sail fabric to use as a tent or a roof allow children to construct their own play space.

WOODWORKING A heavy workbench, several sawhorses, and tools such as a vise, hammers, clamps, and saws are also important pieces of equipment. The tools should be real, functional, and carefully supervised.

GARDENING Gardening and dirt-digging areas offer opportunities to explore the properties of dirt and water, to plant a garden, and to find earthworms and insects. Small shovels, trowels, and rakes are useful additions here.

Materials

Materials should be selected that directly relate to the program's objectives and to the particular children in the program. The following outline provides some suggestions for basic materials. Some items could appear in more than one list.

BUILDING MATERIALS boxes, large and small, carpet pieces, boards, old sheets, blankets, plexiglass pieces, styrofoam packing pieces, string, rope and pulleys, scrap lumber, cardboard.

MATERIALS TO TAKE APART AND PUT TOGETHER dump trucks, pickup trucks, barn with animals and people, dollhouse, dollhouse furniture, baskets, cans, buckets, crates, spools, small blocks, stones, small cars, shells, pegs and pegboards, Tinkertoys, Lego blocks, nuts, bolts, screws, puzzles.

MATERIALS FOR PRETENDING play stove, sink, refrigerator, tables, chairs, dishes, pots, pans, dolls of various ethnic and special backgrounds (including those with disabilities), doll beds, broom, dustpan, telephones, cash register, dress-up clothes (hats and shoes for boys and girls, purses, dresses, scarves, jewelry, neckties, vests, boots), watches, wallets, brief-cases, lunch box, picnic basket, play money, canceled stamps, prop boxes.

OTHER MATERIALS: hot plate, toaster oven, electric frying pan, popcorn popper with see-through lid, blender, meat grinder, food mill.

The chapters on curriculum areas will give further examples of materials related to objectives and to planned learning opportunities.

Housekeeping

Just as a parent at home knows that order reduces needless frustration, the teacher in the center knows that having a place for materials and equipment and keeping things in their place make for a smoother program. Students, assistants, or volunteer workers find it easier when they know where materials are kept. A neat label on a shelf indicating what is stored there helps those working in a center to be clear about what to replace there. Children, too, gain from knowing that things have a place. They can expect to find them in this place and to take responsibility for putting them back in the place where they can find them again. The High/Scope program promotes labeling of all objects in the classroom, not only for housekeeping purposes but also to provide matching experiences for children as they return items to their proper places.

When teachers find material scattered during the day, they will take time to restore order, not in such a way that it interferes with children's activity, but in a way that it adds to the activity. Carmen, a student teacher, started picking up some of the blocks that appeared to be interfering with the construction of a tower that two children were building. One of the children smiled and said, "Now we can build a road to the tower!" Carmen enhanced this block building by helping the children clear the way for further building.

Staff must also be alert to wiping up spilled water or paint or washing a table that may need to be cleaned. Keeping the sand swept off the sidewalk is a safety factor as well as a housekeeping one. It is important to have mop, cleaning cloths, broom, and dustpan conveniently near for both children and adults to use. Good housekeeping is part of good teaching.

The center should look comfortably lived in, but it should also look attractive. Fresh flowers in a vase, artistically arranged, bright-colored autumn foliage, perhaps a plant, the children's pictures mounted and carefully hung at their eye level or fastened to a display board, an interesting mobile, perhaps a piece of fabric with vivid colors, pattern, or texture as a wall hanging, an arrangement of forms and shapes that is pleasing—all of these add to the charm of a room that should be full of life and color. One teacher brought in a homemade quilt with a bold repeat design to introduce the children to patterns that are repeated. This led to looking at rug patterns in a local shop, sweater designs, and a new experience of looking at the world for these children. Children are sensitive to beauty. It becomes part of them. Their attention is caught by the introduction of something lovely. They are aware of these things even though they make no comment. The center may often be in disorder while it is in use; but if there is an underlying sense of orderliness and of attention to beauty, it can be felt. All of us are influenced by the atmosphere of a room.

Another important aspect of housekeeping in which even the beginning teacher in the center can assist is ensuring that materials are available and equipment is in working order. When the easel is set up, it needs to be checked to be sure that the paint jars still have plenty of paint in them. When the woodworking table is set up, nails and soft wood pieces are provided that are usable and inviting.

A piece of broken equipment should always be removed or repaired. A child gets discouraged struggling with a toy that is supposed to stand upright but does not because a part is missing. He may feel that something is wrong with him. As a result, he may carry this frustration into his next encounter with things or people where it may again interfere with his learning. Difficulties may be avoided by keeping materials in good condition. Keeping equipment in good condition also means keeping surfaces smooth to prevent splinters or renewing the paint on painted surfaces as it wears off. Equipment kept in order, freshly painted, and stored in a proper place is more likely to be treated with care. We encourage the child to treat equipment with care when we keep it in good order and respect its upkeep ourselves. We are setting a pattern for the child to follow.

The Use of Space

ARRANGEMENT OF EQUIPMENT   The way equipment is placed in the space available for it influences the use that children will make of the equipment. A housekeeping center with plenty of room encourages more children to play there and reduces the amount of conflict. Two or more items of a kind, like two doll buggies or several large trucks, encourage social play. Easels placed side by side give children a social experience as well as an art experience. Even the use made of wheel toys will depend in part on the amount and arrangement of the hard-surface space available. A broad walk that circles the playground will handle traffic in a way that an unbroken block of hard surfacing in one part of the playground cannot.

Storage space where the children can reach the equipment and put it away easily offers opportunity for them to be independent and self-sufficient. Areas labeled for storage of items such as blocks allow matching opportunities for the children.

THE NEED FOR SPACE   Young children need ample space. They need space for vigorous active play, space for social play, space for "messy" play, space to play alone and undisturbed. In centers where children stay all

*Private places are important both outdoors and indoors. They can be shared with a friend.
Valley College, Campus Child Development Center, Los Angeles*

day it is especially important to provide private or protected areas both indoors and outdoors. Just as adults need a place to be alone and undisturbed, so do young children. A card table or wooden crate covered with a blanket, a closet with the door removed, or some soft cushions on the floor can achieve this.

THE CONTENTS AND ORGANIZATION OF SPACE   Our concern is with the quality of space as well as the quantity of space. In research analyzing use of space, Kritchevsky, Prescott, and Walling (1977) studied children's uses of play space and presented a useful analysis, based on a three-year study in day-care centers. According to their analysis, quality depends on the content and organization of the space. They classify contents into *simple* *units,* such as a swing or a wagon; *complex units,* such as a sand table with digging equipment; and *super units* consisting of three or more play materials combined, such as a sandbox with play materials and water. Complex and super units allow for more types of activities and for use by more children at one time.

Using such a classification the teacher can check play areas to see whether there is a sufficiently wide choice of activities and enough activity for each child. Is a sufficiently wide choice of things in the units available, or are there a lot of tricycles and no wheelbarrows or wagons? Are the number of play spaces sufficient to provide a place for every child to be doing something and also to permit a change of activity? For example, a housekeeping center equipped with a table and dishes, a stove and cooking utensils, dolls and doll bed, doll clothes and an iron and ironing board may accommodate four children at one time. If three children are using this "super unit," they can shift activities or make room for another child to enter.

The study also lists these characteristics of well-organized space:

1. sufficient empty space
2. a broad, easily visible path through it
3. ease of supervision
4. efficient placement of storage units.

Based on their observations, the authors of this study conclude that not less than one-third and not more than one-half of the play space should be empty. The empty space should be capable of being used in different ways, such as for setting up a store or for building with blocks. It should be easy for a child to see how to get from one place to another without interfering with any activities. It should also be easy for the teacher to see what is going on without having to walk through the room. Low room dividers that separate play centers make this possible.

The authors point out that the advantage of well-organized space is that the teacher has more *discretionary time.* "She can act out of her own choices made in terms of her knowledge, experience, and sensitivities, just as the children are acting out of their own choices." (Kritchevsky et al, 1977, p. 25)

By proper organization of space, the teacher can make the available space serve the needs of the group most effectively, eliminating points where activity is likely to be unproductive or full of conflict. Doing so also allows more time to observe and to work with individuals or small groups. Using space well is an important aspect of good teaching.

The Use Of Time

Decisions about the length of the day or year are usually made on the basis of money, facilities, precedent, and the purposes of the center. A child-care center that serves the needs of children of working parents may be open from early in the morning until evening each working day. A college or university laboratory preschool may follow the institution's calendar and have morning sessions only. Head Start programs typically operate four hours a day, but schedules vary throughout the country. Most nursery and kindergarten children attend school two-and-a-half to three hours a day, but there is some interest nationwide in all-day kindergarten.

Within the given time of each day, teachers will work out a schedule that meets the needs of the particular children in a particular group. Schedules will consider the children's interests and involvement and will revolve around such activities as arrival, snack, and departure in a part-day program and snack, lunch, sleep or rest, and departure in a full-day program. The availability of special staff such as volunteers or specialists like a speech therapist or access to space or facilities like a gym may also

A child enjoys his turn in setting the table for lunch, a significant event of the day.
Migrant Head Start, Chico, California

determine a daily schedule. Large blocks of time should be planned so that children have freedom and learn to use it to make choices within the structure.

Generalizations can be made about a schedule, because all children have some needs in common. Any program for young children should provide for the following:

1. Active involvement in work and play outdoors.
2. Quiet involvement in work and play indoors.
3. Opportunities for not being involved and for rest and relaxation.
4. Toileting, washing, dressing, and other routines.
5. Nourishment of some kind.

Children also need an order in the events of the day. Children who have known little order in their lives at home may especially need order in their school day. A fixed sequence to parts of the program gives a child confidence in himself, because he knows what to expect. He can predict the order of the day. The order should be flexible, and it should be modified, from time to time, for a trip or a special event. Flexibility can be predictable, too. Children should be a part of this planning for flexibility.

A Schedule

A schedule will include:

ARRIVAL   Children like to know what to expect when they arrive at the center. They like to know that the teacher will be there to greet them, that she is waiting for them to come, and that she expects them to greet her, too. Then they go on to hang up their coats in their lockers to begin indoor activities or they will proceed outdoors.

SNACK TIME   A midmorning snack and a snack after naps in an all-day group.

MEALTIME   A fixed point of time when meals are served, preceded by toileting and washing and followed by tooth brushing after meals. Some centers serve breakfast as well as lunch.

REST OR NAP   A period of quiet activity before lunch, a rest period on cots or mats after lunch in the all-day program (not exceeding an hour if the child does not sleep).

GROUP TIME   This may be a period before the end of the morning or before lunch and after rest in a full-day program. Teachers may read to small groups, or they may have something to show to the group such as an interesting plant or a special picture or game. It may be discussion, making plans or talking over what has happened or reporting on experiences. It will be a period for thinking, talking, learning.

PICK-UP TIME   A time for putting away materials at the end of the morning and at the end of the afternoon in the all-day program.

DEPARTURE   After preparations for ending the day are completed, the time comes to say "good-bye" to the teacher, something to give a sense of an ending before welcoming the arrival of the parent. In the all-day program children usually depart gradually during the last hour or two.

Children should have large blocks of uninterrupted time for play between these regularly occurring points in the program. Someone has said, "No child has enough time for play." The center should make sure that children have plenty of time for play, especially for dramatic play. The teacher will make some of her most significant contributions to children's development by extending and enriching their play, skillfully and unobtrusively, and by observing them at play so she may understand them better.

Over a period of days teachers will plan for and children should have the opportunity to participate according to their individual interests in:

MUSIC AND MOVEMENT   Teachers should be ready to sing with children frequently, to make music together using simple instruments, or have music and movement experiences.

ART   A variety of art materials should be available for use every day.

BOOKS AND STORIES   Teachers should be ready to read to a child or to small groups. Children should have available plenty of books, displayed in an attractive manner, and soft cushions to sit on while using the books.

LANGUAGE   Teachers should be ready to talk with children, answer questions, listen, and encourage children to create with words.

EXPLORING AND DISCOVERY   Teachers should plan to introduce new materials and experiences for discovery in the school as well as plan walks and excursions to broaden the children's experiences outside the school.

A flexible schedule for activities encourages initiative on the part of children and teachers and sustains interest. It allows for planning individual and group experiences and includes time for review of what has happened during the day. It permits the group to develop projects. A schedule exists as a framework only. It gives a sense of sureness and order to the day.

The daily schedule, which includes toothbrushing, gives children a framework and sense of order. Migrant Head Start, Chico, California

Chapter Overview

The physical environment of the center sets the stage for children growing and learning together. The building plays an important role in creating the kind of atmosphere that promotes quality experiences. Health and safety factors must be considered when selecting the appropriate equipment and materials to be used. Teachers are responsible for housekeeping in the center, remembering that good organization will make this task easier. Finally, the use of space and the use of time in that space are explored in this chapter. Children need space that is well-arranged along with large blocks of time to actively work and play. Consideration of these factors is necessary to preparing a program for meeting the needs of young children.

Projects

1. Draw a diagram of the indoor space and a diagram of the outdoor space in your center. Indicate where a teacher is needed if the areas are to be adequately supervised. List five things you see children playing with in the various areas of the setting. Show on your diagram where those things are located. Considering the units of equipment as simple, complex, and super, check to see if the number of play units or "spaces" is adequate for the number of children who may be using them.

2. Analyze the organization of the play space. Are the pathways clearly visible? Does supervision appear to be easily given? Is there enough but not too much empty space?

3. Consider one learning center of the classroom (art, science, dramatic play, books, etc.) and list all of the equipment and materials located there to enhance young children's development.

For Your Further Reading

Esbensen, S. (1987). *The early childhood playground: An outdoor classroom.* Ypsilanti, MI: High/Scope Press. Helpful in selecting equipment and materials that are developmentally appropriate with tips on playground safety.

Greenman, J. (1988). *Caring spaces, learning spaces: Children's environments that work.* Redmond, WA: Exchange Press, Inc. A comprehensive look at indoor and outdoor environments. First examines needs of staff, parents, and children from infancy through preschool, including school-age and special needs children; then designs environments from those needs.

Harms, T., & Clifford, R. (1980). *Early childhood environment rating scale.* New York: Teachers College Press. A classroom evaluation instrument with seven easy-to-rate areas: routines, furnishings, reasoning and language experiences, large and small motor activities, creative activities, social development, and staff needs.

Harms, T., & Clifford, R. M. (1989). *Family day care rating scale.* New York: Teachers College Press. A similarly valuable guide for evaluating a family day-care center in six dimensions.

Harms, T., Cryer, D., & Clifford, R. M. (1990). *Infant/toddler environment rating scale.* New York: Teachers College Press. Group care settings for children up to 30 months of age can be evaluated using this assessment guide; looks at seven categories.

Kendrick, A. S., Kaufmann, R., & Messenger, K. P. (Eds.). (1991). *Healthy young children: A manual for programs.* (rev. ed.) Washington, DC: National Association for the Education of Young Children. An eye-opening guide for teachers wanting to provide a healthy environment. Includes principles of disease control, cleaning, sanitizing, and hand-washing, as well as specific information about common infections in group settings. A helpful feature is sample letters to parents about a number of diseases.

Kendrick, A. S., Kaufmann, R., & Messenger, K. P. (1988). *Keeping healthy: Parents, teachers, and children.* Brochure #577; single copy $0.50. Washington, DC: National Association for the Education of Young Children. A companion poster, #777, is available along with the brochure; it illustrates good handwashing and proper preparation of sanitizing solution.

Moore, R. C., Goltsman, S., & Iacafano, D. C. (Eds.) (1987). *Play for all guidelines: Planning, design, and management of outdoor play settings for all children.* Berkeley, CA: MIG Communications. A comprehensive planning guide with diverse contributions. Unusual in that it includes planning for children with special needs, along with safety and how children learn through outdoor play.

Moukaddem, V. (1990). Preventing infectious diseases in your child-care setting. *Young Children* 45(2), 28–29. Useful two-page chart that could serve well for beginning teachers, in-service staff training, and parent education. Every teacher needs this information defining infectious diseases, vaccinations, medical care, and sanitation.

Moyer, J. (Ed.). (1986). *Selecting educational equipment and materials: For school and home.* Wheaton, MD: Association for Childhood Education International. As well as chapters for infant, toddler, preschool, and kindergarten equipment, this valuable book rank-orders needed purchases by first, second, and third year and "luxury" items.

National Association for the Education of Young Children. (1991). *Accreditation criteria and procedures of the National Academy of Early Childhood Programs.* (rev. ed.) Washington, DC: Author. Pp. 43–46, "The physical environment," gives detailed description of components to be included in the physical environment of a quality center. Includes much more than the usual square footage requirements: space arrangement, age difference needs, private areas, soft elements, variety of surfaces, and sound absorbency.

Vergeront, J. (1987). *Places and spaces for preschool and primary (INDOORS).* Washington, DC: National Association for the Education of Young Children.

Vergeront, J. (1988). *Places and spaces for preschool and primary (OUTDOORS).* Washington, DC: National Association for the Education of Young Children. These two little books emphasize "do it yourself" ideas with sketches for indoor activity areas, "soft" places, and play structures.

PART TWO

Basic Teaching Skills

CHAPTER 5

Observing and Assessing Children

Cobweb (*boy, 4 years*)

This chapter explains two of the most important skills teachers can develop:

▶ Observing and Recording
   Types of observation records
   Contrast in observations
▶ Assessment and Evaluation
   Types of assessment
   Questions to ask about assessment procedures.

GOAL FOR EVALUATION: Systematic assessment of the effectiveness of the program in meeting its goals for children, parents, and staff is conducted to ensure that good quality care and education are provided and maintained.

CRITERION FOR OBSERVING: Individual descriptions of children's development and learning are written and compiled as a basis for planning appropriate learning activities, as a means of facilitating optimal development of each child, and as records for use in communications with parents. (NAEYC, 1991a, *Accreditation Criteria . . .* , p. 59).

"If understanding a child is like unraveling a mystery, then taking records is the gathering of clues. Like experienced detectives we must recognize the significant clues, we must develop special skills." (Cohen & Stern, 1983).

All teachers need to develop skills as observers of children. They learn most about children by studying their behavior directly. By learning to observe with objectivity, making careful notes, and going over them thoughtfully, a teacher increases her understanding of the meaning behind a child's behavior. Accurate observation records make valuable contributions toward planning for one child's learning or improving curriculum for the entire group. Teachers may find it easier to see the importance of observing and recording children's behavior than to learn how to do it.

As part of education for teaching, beginning teachers need to spend time observing and recording their observations of young children. In order to see the significance of the child's behavior, a teacher becomes an involved observer.

Teachers also need to develop skills in assessing and evaluating children. Centers that receive state or federal money require assessment of children's progress for continued funding; but teachers in all programs, regardless of the funding sources, want to know how children in their care are learning and growing.

It is not easy to decide on assessment methods that can be useful with the children in our care. Controversy continues about standardized testing for young children, "accountability," and misuse of methods of assessment. Such controversy has raged since the early days of Head Start, when poorly designed evaluation procedures seemed to indicate that the program had only transient effects, which nearly resulted in the dismantling of Head Start. Teachers need to see how children are benefited, as well as how their own jobs are made more rewarding, by assessment and evaluation.

Let us consider some purposes of observing and recording behavior as well as methods. Then we will look at how assessment evolves from observation and some ways to evaluate a center's assessment procedures.

Observing and Recording

PURPOSES   As teachers make written observations, they learn about each child as an individual as well as learning more about the group—its energy level, its interests, its timing. Notes become part of a record about each child. These observations also are valuable in assessing the center's program.

SUGGESTIONS FOR OBSERVATIONS   Acquiring the skill of behavioral description is not easy. To achieve even a measure of objectivity takes practice and self-discipline. Objectivity means seeing what is actually

The observer looks for details of behavior to gain insights. Migrant Head Start, Chico, California

The observer looks for details of behavior to gain insights. Migrant Head Start, Chico, California

taking place, not what "should" happen or what a child's motive might have been. It means observing without being influenced by value judgments like "bad," "good," "right," or "wrong." It means trying to reduce the distortions that result from one's own biases, defenses, or preconceptions. In other words, we can observe and we can interpret, but we must be very careful not to judge.

Teachers need to make written observations as a part of their daily teaching. They can carry a pad and pen in a pocket to make notes describing behavior as it occurs. They should quote the words said by the child, for exact words are hard to recall later. Words describing how a child acts, speaks, moves, or looks add to the unique picture. The date should always be included, as well as a word or two about the setting or circumstances. Sometimes fragments of notes need to be rewritten later in the day if they have been jotted down in a hurry.

Teachers should also try to manage time during each week when they can step aside and do more sustained, planned observing. They may have a special purpose in mind, such as trying to discover how a certain child approaches other children, or why there is trouble so frequently in the block-building corner, or how the setup for finger painting might be improved. If staff members believe a particular child is having difficulty or is not being observed as much as others, they may all observe him throughout a week. One teacher may take time to do a longer observation in order to add still more information. Pooling these records, the staff can discuss a child's behavior in a meeting. They will have more accurate information about a child's strengths and vulnerabilities and be better able to plan for the child's success. They will be better able to plan activities for an individual child based on individual assessment of his needs and interests. (NAEYC, 1991a. *Accreditation Criteria . . .* p. 20)

Such notes are invaluable raw material from which understanding grows. When written up more completely later and filed, notes become part of a record about a child. This record should be reviewed and summarized at intervals.

Types of Observation Records

There are many types of observational records. The *informal, random, spontaneous notes* a teacher makes are usually anecdotes, capturing short vignettes or incidents. They record language and behaviors that are characteristic of a child or which seem significant. Sometimes we do not recognize a pattern of significance until we put together anecdotal notes over time.

Facial expressions and body language are important clues in the observation record. Valley College, Campus Child Development Center, Los Angeles

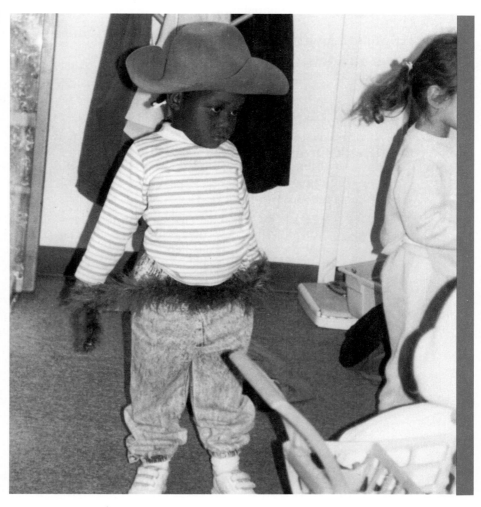

The *diary record* or *running record* is an observation covering a certain period, including all that can be recorded in that time interval. *Time sampling* records are observations repeated at intervals. *Event sampling* might take place at certain types of activity, such as observations of a transition time or of children's skill in making parquetry designs or mastering a computer activity. At one center teachers made special observations of the last hour of the day when there seemed to be more accidents and crying. By collecting clues from these records they introduced changes that made the end of the day a safer, more positive time as the children prepared to leave the center.

Still another form of recording behavior is the *sociogram*, which helps teachers to visualize a child's social relationships with other children and with adults. The use of a *video camera* provides yet another way of observing what is happening.

Informal, Spontaneous Anecdotal Notes

Reports of Single Incidents

May 12   Bruce, constructing a building, tried to enlist the help of Marvin, saying in a "bossy" tone, "You can be a roof helper," and then turned to me, "You are so tall you can help with the roof."
— K.R.

▶ *Comment and Interpretation*

In this short anecdote we catch a glimpse of Bruce's social skills. He enlists help from another child as well as an adult to reach his goal. We see his reasoning process, that the teacher's height will enable her to reach the roof.

Oct. 6   As I came out onto the playground, Joe ran up and asked me demandingly, "Tie my shoe!" I bent over and did it for him. Off he ran, and then Betsy, who had been sitting on the step, watching, said quietly, "Wait." She reached down, carefully untied her shoelace and stuck her foot out, asking me with a little smile, "Tie mine, too." We smiled at each other, and off she went.
— K.H.

▶ *Comment and Interpretation*

One is struck by the unself-conscious way in which Betsy asked for a share of the teacher's time. The teacher seemed willing to accept her request and give her an extra bit of attention. It appeared to satisfy Betsy, and she moved away into activity rather than just sitting. It would be worthwhile to observe Betsy further to see whether she may be an "easy" child who is not getting much attention, or whether she has a real problem with jealousy or with finding her place in the group. At least she is showing that she has ways of coping with the situation.

Ten-minute Running Record

10:30   Billy is kneeling in front of a low blackboard, carefully drawing diagonal lines of scallops, pursing his lips as he draws. Kim comes up, kneels beside him,

The observer records children's actual words, captures details or interactions, and follows an episode from beginning to end. Valley College, Campus Child Development Center, Los Angeles

and draws a heavy dark line through his scallops, then sits back with a pleased expression. Billy looks at her in surprise and then back at the board. He picks up the eraser and carefully erases both lines. He appears to ignore Kim and begins to draw scallops again, tracing the lines of the previous scallops, which are still faintly visible. As he draws the fourth scallop, Kim reaches out and draws another dark line intersecting the scallops. Billy sits back on his heels and looks at the board, but not at Kim, frowning slightly. Then he reaches forward and erases the board, glancing at Kim. He begins to draw the scallops again, this time looking at Kim each time he makes one. Just as he begins the fourth, again Kim reaches out and scribbles over his drawing. Billy turns to her, raises his hand with the eraser over his head, and then lets it fall. He turns back and uses the erase to erase the board very thoroughly.

10:38 Billy draws a line down the center of the blackboard, saying firmly as he finishes, "There," and pointing to the side nearest Kim, "Use your own spot." He sits quietly back on his heels and says with determination, "I'm going to be a good boy." Kim, bringing her eraser across the entire board, says, "Now we got to race." Billy says, as though to himself, "I don't care." Then he asks Kim, "Do you want to erase your name?" "OK," Kim answers. Billy draws a "B" on the board.

10:39 Just then a teacher calls to Kim to tell her that it is her turn to have the swing. She jumps up and runs off. Billy goes back to work on his scallops. When he finishes he leans back on his heels and, with apparent satisfaction, says, "There's my monster."

Comment and Interpretation

The observation seems complete, giving details that enable us to visualize what has taken place. The descriptive phrases that are used—"looks at the board, but not at Kim," "diagonal lines of scallops"—are objective and free of interpretation. The impressions are clearly labeled as "with determination" or "with apparent satisfaction." We have an objective picture of Kim's and Billy's behavior, relatively unclouded by what the observer thought.

Billy seems wholeheartedly involved in his own purpose. He copes with Kim's interference in an unusual way. First, he tries to ignore it almost as if she isn't there. As she persists, he repeats his attempt until it obviously is unsuccessful. He seems to feel like hitting her with the eraser, but he controls the impulse. It appears that he feels better after he drains off some of this feeling by erasing the board vigorously.

Then Billy moves on to another level of coping. He divides the space, one side for Kim and one for himself; he probably hopes he will be undisturbed. His internalized adult conscience comes out in the words, "I'm going to be a good boy." It seems that he is trying to exorcise the monster with these often-heard words. Kim, however, is operating on a different level. She seems to feel aggressive and competitive, or perhaps she is making a social approach. She suggests a race. At this point Billy tries to persuade himself that he doesn't care. This device does not seem to work with Kim, and he then comes up with a remarkable solution. He decides to give her something to erase, her own name, a wonderfully positive suggestion. It is in line with her interests at the moment. The "B" he draws is the first letter of his own name, probably the only name he knows how to write. As she has been intent on destroying his product, erasing the "B" seems significant. When Kim leaves at this point and Billy is able to finish his drawing, it becomes a "monster." It seems to satisfy him.

Billy's control over his impulses seems to be very strong. His strengths lie in his ability to put his feelings into words and finally to express them in his drawing. "I'm going to be a good boy" is not an easy thing when one is with others who have not internalized this concept. It leads him into some unusual problem-solving actions: dividing the board with Kim and giving her something to erase. These actions may demonstrate his capacity to cope with a situation on a high level and, later, his capacity to use drawing as an avenue for expressing the feeling that he has not allowed to come out more directly.

How effective Billy's defenses are, where they will lead him, and what they really mean to him can only be understood after further observations. Billy is the third child in a family of four children. One suspects that he has had a lot of help in coping with the interferences of a younger sibling. What help does he need in the center?

Kim, the minor character in the drama, also needs to be considered. She has been thwarted in carrying out a purpose. She wants to swing, and she has had to wait for a turn. She begins to frustrate someone else, teasing and annoying Billy, but not in an unfriendly way. She is apparently an active child; she does something rather than wait. She is sociable, and she turns to another child rather than to an object. She tries actively to get Billy's attention. In making a line through his drawing, she is also probably draining off some of her frustration. Kim is persistent, but she is not concerned with trying to be a "good girl." She, too, can make a suggestion. Her suggestion, "We got to race," is a vigorous, competitive one, but she is flexible. She accepts Billy's different suggestion about erasing her name instead. She quickly returns to carry out her original purpose when the teacher calls her.

Teachers may conclude that Kim's behavior is a reminder that any child who has to "wait" may need some of the teacher's help. To be at loose ends, frustrated in immediately carrying out a purpose, is not easy for a child. As teachers, we need to be alert to the child's need for a suggestion about what to do while waiting. Perhaps the waiting time can be used for a conversation with the child. At least we need to keep an eye on what the child does in the waiting period. Kim needed help in coping with her problem. She put a burden on Billy in this case.

Contrast in Observations

Just as detectives look for clues in trying to reconstruct a scene and solve a mystery, let us look for clues to understanding a child as we observe and record behavior. What clues do we look for? How well does the description of the child's actions enable us to get a vivid impression of what the child may be like? Is the record objective, as a camera might capture it, rather than subjective? Are impressions clearly labeled as such? Is the record free of obvious bias? Is the setting or the circumstance included when these play a part in the child's responses? Are clues included about how the child feels? How much can we learn from a record?

Here are three records of the same incident made by different observers. What does one learn about Jasmine from reading each record?

Observation 1

Jasmine helped the teacher set up the cots for nap time. She got her basket of bedding from her cubby and made her bed. The teacher helped her straighten the sheet. She covered herself with the blanket and went to sleep.

▶ *Comment*   In this record we have a sparse account of what Jasmine did. There are no details about the way in which she helped the teacher, how she seemed to feel about helping, or about the way she managed making her own bed and settling herself for sleep. Jasmine might have been any child. There are no clues to help us see Jasmine as an individual. What is she like? We do not know from the record.

Observation 2

Jasmine seemed to enjoy helping the teacher set up the cots for nap time. She had no trouble getting the legs of the cot into position and putting the cots in place. When she had finished helping the teacher, she went to her cubby and got her basket with its sheet and blanket and doll. She had a little trouble getting her sheet on the cot because she had it going the wrong way. The teacher helped her, and soon she had her sheet just the way she wanted it. She got her doll and blanket, crawled into bed, and pulled the cover over herself. She fell asleep quite fast.

▶ *Comment*

This observation tells us more about Jasmine, but details are missing. Some statements are subjective, for example, "Jasmine enjoyed helping the teacher." What did Jasmine do or say that made the observer reach this conclusion? The clue is missing here. Jasmine "had no trouble with the legs of the cot" is not a description of Jasmine's behavior. It suggests she is a competent child, but next we find she "had a little trouble" with her sheet and needed help. Did Jasmine ask for help? Was she aware the sheet was on the wrong way? Many of the clues are missing. We still do not know much about the child who is Jasmine.

Observation 3

Jasmine is helping the teacher set up cots while the rest of the children listen to a story. Jasmine walks purposefully, attending to her task with a happy expression on her face. She seems to feel important and confident, as though helping the teacher were something very special. Jasmine carefully pulls the lightweight cots out of their storage corner without bumping the wall. She proceeds to open the cots and secures the legs by applying a little pressure. She sets up three cots in their places, adjusting the positions slightly until she looks satisfied.

Jasmine is now ready to make her own bed. She gets a basket from her cubby, which has her sheet, blanket, and doll. She carefully places the basket on the floor next to her cot. She puts the blanket and the doll on the cot next to her cot and starts spreading the sheet with deliberate movements. As she pulls the sheet to one end of the cot, she sees that it is not covering the other end. She goes to the other end and pulls the sheet so that it covers that end, and again she notices that the sheet is not covering the far end. Again she goes to that end and pulls the sheet toward her. She repeats the same actions, apparently unaware that the sheet is on the wrong way. Lynn, the aide, comes over. She points out that there is a long and a short side to the sheet as like there is to a cot. Jasmine looks at her with a puzzled expression and continues to pull on the sheet. Lynn puts the sheet on the right way, unobtrusively holding one corner so that it will stay in place as Jasmine smooths it out. Jasmine has a satisfied expression now with her cot making. She grabs her blanket and doll from the other cot, hastily opens the blanket, which is slightly rumpled by now, and quickly crawls in under it. She cuddles up with her doll, puts her thumb in her mouth, and closes her eyes. In no time she is sound asleep.

▶ *Comment*

Here, in a much more detailed account, we see Jasmine as an engaging individual. The observer gives us clues to Jasmine's feelings in recording her "purposeful walk," the expression on her face, her careful efforts with the cots. These all suggest a child who is feeling important and confident, enjoying what she is doing. She is likely to be an observant child, too, as shown by the way she imitates the teacher's actions and later notices that the sheet does not fit. The observer is careful to label impressions by using such words as "seems to feel."

The bed-making experience is recorded in detail with descriptive words such as "carefully places the basket" and "deliberate" movements. Jasmine's persistence is apparent in her efforts with the sheet. She does not appear to expect help. She looks puzzled at Lynn's explanation about the sheet. Jasmine's change of pace from deliberate to hurried may be a clue to her feelings. She hurries to get into bed, cuddling her doll and sucking a comforting thumb. She may be somewhat upset about the sheet even though Lynn had helped her succeed. She falls asleep almost immediately.

We know much more about Jasmine than we did from the first two records. Observation 3 is full of rich, descriptive details. There are still questions to ask, and they can be answered by further observations as we begin to understand this child. It would help if the record included the child's age and the length of time of the observation.

Becoming a competent observer takes much practice. It is a skill well worth the effort if one is to understand and guide young children.

Assessment and Evaluation

What does the teacher do next to weave the collected information into an assessment? What are the purposes of evaluating children's progress?

The NAEYC defines assessment as "the process of observing, recording, and otherwise documenting the work children do and how they do it, as a basis for a variety of educational decisions that affect the child." Assessment serves several purposes: (1) to plan instruction for individuals and groups and for communicating with parents, (2) to identify children who may need specialized services or intervention, and (3) to evaluate how well the program is meeting its goals. (NAEYC, 1991. *Guidelines. . .*) We can expand the idea of assessment to include our observations of children's social, emotional, and motor development as well.

In their observation notes teachers have been describing children's current learning and behaviors. Now they can demonstrate how each child and the group of children have changed over a period of months. Teachers can plan learning activities tailored to the needs and interests of children, making curriculum truly relevant to these children at this time. The use of evaluations and assessment tools provides valuable information for parent conferences as well as for boards and funding sources.

Teachers, especially beginning teachers, may feel that assessment activities are the responsibility of the head teacher, director, or principal. However, teachers are a most important element in the process since they

From their observation records teachers can tailor learning activities to the needs of children.
Child Development Laboratory, California State University, Chico

are the people who know best how children are progressing and how the day-to-day program is functioning.

How can we put together our various observations of a child to make a helpful overall picture? We begin with written observations gathered by teachers. We also have information from parents, both written and conversational. Beginning with 3-year-olds, teachers can save in folders some examples of children's work, possibly paintings, drawings, or dictated stories. In some centers teachers make checklists of behaviors to help them focus on goals they have for these children. Others use tracking sheets as records of where children choose to play and participate. Videotapes of children in various activities can be reviewed with staff as another tool. Finally, teachers merge all of these components into comprehensive evaluations of children's development. (Bank Street College, 1991, November. *How do we know our children are learning? Bank Street looks at assessment through curriculum.* Pre-conference session at NAEYC Annual Conference, Denver, CO)

The director and staff plan for children and families, based on observations and assessments.
Migrant Head Start, Chico, California

Standardized screening tests should be used only with greatest caution, and only as a first step in further diagnosis of suspected conditions for which a child could receive special help or services. Programs such as Head Start are able to use the services of professionals who come to the center to do speech and language, hearing, vision, developmental, or motor skills screening. Other kinds of standardized testing for young children should be avoided.

Here are some questions to use in evaluating a center's assessment procedures, as posed in NAEYC's *Guidelines for appropriate curriculum content and assessment in programs serving children ages 3 through 8.* (NAEYC, 1991e, pp. 34–35)

1. Is the assessment procedure based on the goals and objectives of the specific curriculum used in the program?
2. Are the results of assessment used to benefit children, i.e., to plan for individual children, improve instruction, identify children's interests and needs, and individualize instruction, rather than label, track, or fail children?
3. Does the assessment procedure address all domains of learning and development—social, emotional, physical, and cognitive—as well as children's feelings and dispositions toward learning?
4. Does assessment provide useful information to teachers to help them do a better job?
5. Does the assessment procedure rely on teachers' regular and periodic observations and record-keeping of children's everyday activities and performance so that results reflect children's behavior over time?

6. Does the assessment procedure occur as part of the ongoing life of the classroom rather than in an artificial, contrived context?

7. Is the assessment procedure performance-based, rather than only testing skills in isolation?

8. Does the assessment rely on multiple sources of information about children such as collections of their work, results of teacher interviews and dialogues, as well as observations?

9. Does the assessment procedure reflect individual, cultural, and linguistic diversity? Is it free of cultural, language, and gender biases?

10. Do children appear comfortable and relaxed during assessment rather than tense or anxious?

11. Does the assessment procedure support parents' confidence in their children and their ability as parents rather than threaten or undermine parents' confidence?

12. Does the assessment examine children's strengths and capabilities rather than just their weaknesses or what they do not know?

13. Is the teacher the primary assessor and are teachers adequately trained for this role?

14. Does the assessment procedure involve collaboration among teachers, children, administrators, and parents? Is information from parents used in planning instruction and evaluating children's learning? Are parents informed about assessment information?

15. Do children have an opportunity to reflect on and evaluate their own learning?

16. Are children assessed in supportive contexts to determine what they are capable of doing with assistance as well as what they can do independently?

17. Is there a systematic procedure for collecting assessment data that facilitates its use in planning instruction and communicating with parents?

18. Is there a regular procedure for communicating the results of assessment to parents in meaningful language, rather than letter or number grades, that reports children's individual progress?

We can sum up the process of assessing and evaluating children's progress by a reminder of the importance of acquiring observation skills, which serve as the foundation for all assessment. Assessment benefits the child and the family, but let us remember that assessing and evaluating children's progress also benefits the teacher. Tangible evidence is gathered that demonstrates how well she has done her job as a professional teacher.

Chapter Overview

Skills in observing and recording young children's behavior provide valuable information to assist the staff in planning. Various types of observation records have been discussed with an emphasis on anecdotal note taking. The three example observations demonstrate the need for specific details in gaining an understanding of behavior. Finally, assessment procedures have been listed. Assessment and evaluation show the importance of developing observational skills.

Projects

1. Observe one child for a ten-minute period, keeping a record of what the child does and says. Comment on what you have learned about the child or what questions the observation has raised.
2. Select a piece of play equipment and record how children use it through a period of twenty minutes. Summarize your observations. What values can you see demonstrated in this equipment?
3. Observe a child for an hour in a center. Write a description of how the child interacts with other children, other adults, and with materials in the classroom. Include specific details of what you saw.

For Your Further Reading

Observing

Almy, M., & Genishi, C. (1979). *Ways of studying children: An observation manual for early childhood teachers.* New York: Teachers College Press. As well as providing techniques for skillful observation, this book discusses the meaning of child study for teachers, its theory and history. Includes bilingual children, culturally diverse children, and children with disabilities.

Bentzen, W. R. (1985) *Seeing young children: A guide to observing and recording behavior.* Albany, NY: Delmar. Helpful for observing children from birth to age 8; includes observation methods, forms, and ethical considerations.

Boehm, A. E. & Weinberg, R. A. (1987). *The classroom observer: Developing observation skills in early childhood settings.* (rev.) New York: Teachers College. Revision of 1977 edition; emphasizes diverse early childhood settings. Especially helpful with the current emphasis on basing assessment on systematic observation.

Cohen, D., Stern, V. & Balaban, N. (1983) *Observing and recording the behavior of young children.* (3d ed.) New York: Teachers College Press. A classic little book; useful and practical tips with illustrative anecdotes. See also Carlevale, J. M. (1985) *Observing, recording, interpreting child behavior: A workbook.* (2d ed., rev.). West Greenwich, RI: Consortium Publishing. (Accompanies Cohen, Stern, and Balaban, *Observing and recording the behavior of young children*, 3d ed.)

Assessment

Bredekamp, S. (1990). Achieving model early childhood programs through accreditation. In Seefeldt, C. (1990). *Continuing issues in early childhood education.* Columbus, OH: Merrill. Pp. 301–309. A brief description of the accreditation system of the National Academy of Early Childhood Programs. Helpful point-by-point comparison of accreditation with licensing. Discusses relationship of public school programs for 4-year-olds and the possibility of accreditation to ensure quality programs.

Hrncir, E. J., & Eisenhart, C. E. (1991). Use with caution: The "at-risk" label. *Young Children,* 46(2), 23–27. Deals with the difficulties of identifying children who need early intervention without using damaging labels. Urges three cautions in using the "at-risk" label.

Kamii, C. (Ed.). (1990). *Achievement testing in the early grades: The games grown-ups play.* Washington, DC: National Association for the Education of Children. A powerful "rethinking" of assessment through inappropriate standardized testing, and why achievement testing should stop. Deals with the dilemmas for teachers and principals. Suggests positive assessment approaches in early literacy and mathematics.

Leavitt, R. L., & Eheart, B. K. (1991). Assessment in early childhood programs. *Young Children,* 46(5), 4–9. A practical guide to effective assessment by providers in family day care and centers. Briefly discusses information parents provide, written observations, organizing collected information into a comprehensive assessment of a child, and how to use the completed assessment in program planning.

Meisels, S.J. (1989). *Developmental screening in early childhood: A guide.* (3rd ed.). Washington, DC: National Association for the Education of Young Children. Includes NAEYC's position statement on standardized testing. Offers help on how to select appropriate screening tests and methods and how to conduct an effective early childhood screening program. Includes sample forms and parent questionnaire.

National Association for the Education of Young Children. (1988). Position statement on standardized testing of young children 3 through 8 years of age. *Young Children,* 43(3), 42–47. Takes a strong position that information about children obtained from tests must be used only for improved outcomes for the children. Gives seven guidelines plus helpful definitions of terms.

National Association for the Education of Young Children (1991). Position statement: Guidelines for appropriate curriculum content and assessment in programs serving children ages 3 through 8. *Young Children* 46(3), 21–38. The second part of this position paper gives detailed guidelines for appropriate assessment of young children. Principles include using assessment for planning instruction, communicating with parents, identifying special needs children, and for program evaluation. Suggests questions to ask in evaluating and ways to implement the guidelines.

Pellegrini, A.D., & Glickman, C.D. (1990). Measuring kindergarteners' social competence. *Young Children,* 45(4), 40–44. Urges assessing children's social competence by using a combination of behavioral observations of peer interactions in free play, peer nominations, and teacher ratings. Suggests that peer relationships are accurate predictors of future components of social competence.

Seefeldt, C. (1990). Assessing young children. In Seefeldt, C. (1990). *Continuing issues in early childhood education.*

Columbus, OH: Merrill. Pp. 311–330. A comprehensive look at approaches to assessment that focuses on the individual, including observation and assessment that requires standardized testing, such as intelligence, achievement, and diagnostic instruments. Includes interesting history of the approaches and concludes with the purposes of assessment.

Initial Support Through Guides to Speech and Action

Trains (*boy, 3 years, 7 months*)

In this chapter the beginning teacher turns to relationships with children in guiding them with words and actions. You will learn:

▶ How we make constructive use of our feelings of inadequacy
▶ How we gain support for ourselves through learning guidance principles
▶ A language used in guiding behavior: guides in speech
▶ A behavior "language" used in guiding behavior: guides in action.

CRITERION: Staff use positive techniques of guidance, including logical or natural consequences applied in problem situations, redirection, anticipation of and elimination of potential problems, and encouragement of appropriate behavior rather than competition, comparison, or criticism. Consistent, clear rules are developed in conjunction with children and are discussed with them to make sure they understand. Staff describe the situation to encourage children's evaluation of the problem rather than impose the solution. (NAEYC, 1991a, *Accreditation Criteria* . . . p. 17).

We have described the center itself. Now we turn to the question of how we will fit into a center as teachers. What guides are there to speech and action? How can we best meet the demands made on us while we increase our understanding?

Feelings of Inadequacy

Each of us responds somewhat differently to the experience of beginning to work with children. Some of these responses may interfere with what we do, while others may be helpful.

As mentioned in chapter 1, accepting initial feelings of uncertainty and discomfort in the center is a necessity. Too frequently we only increase these feelings by struggling against them, making it more difficult to develop constructive responses. Sometimes we try to defend ourselves against feeling inadequate in a new situation by plunging into action as though to take our minds off the way we feel. We may do unnecessary things like talking to children when talking serves no useful purpose. We may offer help that is not needed or try to start activities that have no real place at the moment in the child's pattern of play. Sometimes we may defend ourselves against feeling inadequate by withdrawing and taking no action at all. Sometimes we may fight against the necessity for direction by being critical of the direction given; at other times we may seek reassurance by trying to be completely dependent on instructions, insisting that these be specific and detailed so that there is no room for uncertainty.

These adjustments or defenses are part of a resistance to change that all of us feel and that is sometimes a protection and frequently a limitation on growth. Growth can be an uncomfortable process. But our growth is rewarding and satisfying when we have mobilized our resources and reduced the conflicts that interfere with growth. Instead of spending energy trying to deny feelings, we can make constructive use of them.

Guides Give Support

When one feels inadequate, one needs support of some kind. What are the supports available in the situation? What help can one get from the experienced teacher? What help can one find in one's own experiences in related situations, in books, or from discussion? In any new experience we begin to gain confidence when we assemble the useful, appropriate supports and build a framework in which to operate.

In this chapter we will list techniques and principles that can be depended on as guides to action. These can be applied in an increasingly individual way with added experience. The success of some of these techniques depends in part on the relationship built up with individual children. Time is required to build as well as to understand relationships, but during the process these "rules" will give clues to appropriate action. In time, with experience and increasing insight, each of us will make our

"Teacher, I don't want him on here!" When and how should a teacher intervene with words or actions? Valley College, Campus Child Development Center, Los Angeles

own generalizations and add new interpretations. There is always more than one "right" way.

Set down alone, these statements may seem somewhat like letters in an alphabet. Only when they are combined by experience into larger units will they have meaning. At this point they must be accepted as part of the alphabet that goes to make a "language" used in guiding behavior.

Fifteen points can serve as guides to speech and action in the beginning when the situation is unfamiliar.

In Speech

1. State suggestions or directions in a positive rather than negative form.

2. Give a choice only when you are prepared to leave the choice to the child.
3. Use your voice as a teaching tool. Your words and tone of voice should help the child feel confident and reassured.
4. Avoid trying to change behavior by methods that may lead to loss of self-respect, such as shaming or labeling behavior naughty or selfish.
5. Avoid motivating a child by making comparisons between one child and another or by encouraging competition.
6. Redirect the child by suggesting an activity that is related to the child's purposes or interests whenever possible.
7. Give a direction or suggestion at the time that it will be most effective.

In Action

8. Avoid making models in any art medium for the children to copy.
9. Give the child the minimum help, thus providing the maximum chance to grow in independence; but give the child help when needed.
10. Make your directions effective by reinforcing them when necessary.
11. Learn to foresee and prevent rather than mop up after a difficulty.
12. Define limits clearly and maintain them consistently.
13. Be alert to the total situation. Use the most strategic positions for supervising.
14. Make health and safety a primary concern at all times.
15. Increase your own awareness by observing and taking notes.

Guides in Speech

1. State suggestions or directions in a positive rather than a negative form. A positive suggestion is one that tells a child what to do instead of what not to do. If a child has already done, or is about to do, something that should not be done, then the child needs help in getting another, better idea. We give this kind of help by directing the child's attention to what we want done.

It has been demonstrated experimentally that directions stated in a positive way are more effective than the same directions given negatively. This can be subjected to proof informally in many situations. A teacher in one center demonstrated it when she was finding it difficult to weigh the children. Reacting to the unsteadiness of the scale platform, most of the children reached for support, grasping the equipment. When the teacher asked them not to touch anything, she had very little success. She changed her negative direction to a positive one by saying, "Keep your hands down

Teachers learn to foresee and prevent rather than mop up after a difficulty. Migrant Head Start, Chico, California

at your sides," and the children did just that. Telling them what to do, instead of what not to do, brought results.

A question is not a statement. We may find ourselves putting something in the form of a question instead of a statement because of our own uncertainty. We may say, "Don't you want to pull the plug?" when we mean that we want the child to pull the plug but we are not sure that we can persuade him to do it. What we should say is, "Pull the plug now and dry your hands."

A positive direction is less likely to arouse resistance than a negative one. It makes help seem constructive rather than limiting and interfering. Perhaps the child is doing something purposely to annoy us. By emphasizing the positive we reduce the attention and thus the importance of the negative aspect of his behavior. We usually help rather than hinder when we make a positive suggestion.

In addition, when we make suggestions in a positive way we are giving the child a sound pattern to imitate when directing friends. The child is likely to be more successful, to meet less resistance, by putting suggestions in a positive form. This is a good social tool. We can tell something about the kind of directions that children have received by listening to the kinds of directions they give in play.

More important still, by having clearly in mind what we want children to do, we can steer them toward certain behaviors with more confidence and assurance—with more chance of success. Our goal is clear to us and to the child. We are more likely to feel adequate and to act effectively when we put a statement positively.

To put directions positively represents a step in developing a more positive attitude toward children's behavior inside ourselves. Our annoyance often increases as we dwell on what the child should not be doing, but our feelings may be different when we turn our attention to what the child should be doing. We may have more sympathy as we try to figure out just what the child *could do* under the circumstances. It helps us to appreciate the difficulties the child may be having in figuring out a better solution.

An experienced teacher often will say, "Keep the clay on the table, not on the floor," thus letting the child know what to avoid, but the emphasis is on making it clear what to do. It may be wise to use only the positive part of the statement in the beginning. It is easy to slip into old habits and rely on the negative. Making only positive suggestions is a hard exercise because most of us have depended heavily on negative suggestions in the past and have had them used on us. It is worth correcting oneself whenever one makes a negative statement in order to hasten learning this basic technique. Every direction should be given in a positive form.

For example, the teacher will say:

▶ "Ride your tricycle around the bench,"
  instead of, "Don't bump the bench."
▶ "Throw your ball over here,"
  instead of, "Don't hit the window."
▶ "Leave the heavy blocks on the ground,"
  instead of, "Don't put the heavy blocks on that high board."
▶ "Give me the ball to hold while you're climbing,"
  instead of, "Don't climb with that ball in your hand."
▶ "Take a bite of your lunch now,"
  instead of, "Don't play at the table."
▶ "Take little bites and then it will all go in your mouth,"
  instead of, "Don't take such big bites and then you won't spill."
▶ "Play softly on the piano,"
  instead of, "Don't bang on the piano."

2. Give a choice only when you are prepared to leave the choice up to the child. Choices are legitimate. With increasing maturity one makes an increasing number of choices. We accept that being able to make decisions helps to develop maturity. But some decisions are beyond the child's limited capacities and experience. We must be careful to avoid offering a choice when we are not really willing to let the child decide the question.

Sometimes one hears a mother say to her child, "Do you want to go home now?" When the child replies, "No," the mother acts as though the child were being disobedient because he did not answer the question in the way she wanted. What she really meant was, "It's time to go home now." Questions like this mother's are most often asked when a person feels uncertain or wishes to avoid raising an issue. Sometimes asking a question is only a habit of speaking. But it confuses the child to be asked a question when what is wanted is not information but confirmation. It is important to guard against the tendency to use questions routinely. The circumstances should dictate when a question is legitimate.

Circumstances differ, but usually a young child is not free to choose such things as the time to go home or eat or rest. A child is not free to choose to hurt others or to damage property. On the other hand, children should be free to decide such things as whether to play outside or inside, which play materials to select, and when to go to the toilet.

Sometimes a child may be offered a choice to clarify a situation. For example, one child may be interfering with another's sand pies and the teacher may ask, "Do you want to stay in the sandbox?" A response of "yes" determines the response, for example: "Then you will need to play at this end of the box out of Bobby's way."

It is important to be clear in one's mind whether one is really offering the child a choice before one asks a question. Be sure that your questions are legitimate.

3. Use your voice as a teaching tool. Your words and tone of voice should help the child feel confident and reassured. All of us have known parents and teachers who seem to feel that the louder they speak, the greater their chances of controlling behavior. We also may have observed that these same people have more problems than the parents and teachers who speak more quietly but are listened to. A quiet, firm manner of speaking conveys confidence and reassures the child.

It may be necessary to speak firmly, but it is never necessary to raise one's voice. The most effective speech is simple and direct and slow. Decreasing speed is more effective than raising pitch.

It is a good rule never to call or shout across any play area, inside or outside. It is always better to move nearer the person to whom you are speaking. Children as well as adults grow irritated when shouted at. Your words will get a better reception if they are spoken quietly, face to face.

Speech conveys feelings as well as ideas. No matter what words they hear, children are probably very sensitive to the tone quality, for example, to a tightness in the voice that might reveal annoyance, unfriendliness, or fear. One can try for a pleasant tone, and one may find one's feelings improving along with one's voice.

The teacher sets a pattern in her speech, as she does in other ways. Children are more likely to use their voices in loud, harsh ways if the teacher uses her voice in these ways. Voice quality can be improved with training, and each of us could probably profit from speech work to improve our voices. A well-modulated voice is an asset worth cultivating.

4. Avoid trying to change behavior by methods that may lead to loss of self-respect, such as shaming or labeling behavior naughty or selfish. We need to learn constructive ways of influencing behavior if we are to promote sound personality growth. Neither children nor adults are likely to develop desirable behavior patterns as the result of fear or shame or guilt. Improvement will be more apparent than real, and any change likely will be accompanied by resentment and an underlying rejection of the behavior.

It takes time to learn constructive ways of guiding behavior. The first step is to eliminate destructive patterns. We must discard the gestures, the expressions, the tones of voice as well as the words that convey the impression that the child should feel ashamed. In passing judgment, we make the child feel a lack of respect. It is hard for a child to change behavior patterns without feeling self-respect. Young children are especially dependent on feeling that they are respected by others.

If, for example, we believe there are reasons why a boy behaves as he does, reasons for his patterns of reacting, we will not blame him for his behavior. We may see it as undesirable or unacceptable and may try to change it, but we will accept and respect him. We will not add to his burden by passing judgment. Labeling behavior, for example, by calling it "selfish," means we are passing a judgment that fails to take circumstances into account. It often prevents us from observing closely. It does not build self-respect.

The child will be helped if we accept him as he is and try to make it possible for him to find some success, rather than if we reprove him because he does not meet our standards. An example:

Mark, an active child with a short attention span who often acts destructively, sits down and starts to put a puzzle together. He whines when a piece does not fit in the first place he tries and throws the piece on the floor.

The teacher says, "Does it make you mad when it doesn't fit right away?" She puts into words the feeling he appears to have, thus indicating her acceptance of it and him. This helps him to relax.

She reaches down and gets the piece and passes it to him, and he completes the puzzle successfully. She says, "That's fine. You did it." She does not reprove him for throwing a piece on the floor or expect him to pick it up. He is not ready to meet such an expectation. It is more important for him to have some success. She helps him be successful and respects him for what he can do.

5. Avoid motivating a child by making comparisons between one child and another or by encouraging competition. Comparing one child with another is a dangerous way to try to influence behavior. We may get results in changed behavior, but these changes may not all be improvements. Some of these results are sure to damage the child's feeling of adequacy and his friendliness.

Competitive schemes for getting children to dress more quickly or to eat more of something may have undesired effects. Children who are encouraged to be competitive are very likely to quarrel more with one another. In any competition someone always loses, and this child may feel hurt and resentful. Even the winner may be afraid of failing next time, or may feel an unjustified superiority if the contest was unequal. Competition does not build friendly, social feelings.

Competition not only handicaps smooth social relationships but also creates problems within the child. True, we live in a highly competitive society, but young children are not ready to face much competition until their concepts of self as person have developed enough to withstand the strains and inevitable failures that are part of competition. Although constant success is not a realistic experience and does not prepare a child for what comes later, too many failures may create feelings of weakness and helplessness—poor preparation for a competitive world. For sound growth it is important to avoid competitive kinds of motivation until children have developed ego strength and can balance failure with success.

This raises a question about sound motivation. Do we really get dressed in order to set a speed record or to surpass someone else? Is it not true, rather, that we dress ourselves because there is satisfaction in being independent and that we complete dressing quickly in order to go on to another activity? There may be a point in spending time enjoying the process of dressing if there happens to be nothing of greater importance coming next. We may be better off when we get pleasure out of the doing a thing, not just in getting the thing done. It is wise to be sure that we motivate children in a sound way even though we may seem to move more slowly. We ensure a sounder growth and give them better preparation for the years ahead.

Children should not feel that their only chances for getting attention depend on being "first" or "beating" someone or being the "best." They should feel sure of acceptance whether they succeed or fail. One has only to listen to children on a playground to realize how disturbing highly competitive feelings are to them. Statements such as, "You can't beat me" or "I'm bigger than you" or "Mine is better than yours" increase friction and prevent children from getting along.

6. Redirect the child by suggesting an activity that is related to the child's purposes or interests whenever possible. We will be more successful in changing children's behavior if we attempt to turn their attention to an act that has equal value as an interest or outlet. For example, if a girl is throwing a ball dangerously near a window, we can suggest a safer place to throw it. If she's throwing something dangerous because she's angry, we can suggest an acceptable way of draining angry feelings—like throwing against a backstop or using a punching bag or pounding at the workbench. In the first case her interest is in throwing, and in the second it is in expressing her anger. Our suggestions for acting differently will take into account the different meaning in her behavior. We should always try to suggest something that meets the needs that the child's behavior is expressing.

Robby stands up in the sand and throws a pan at Leticia who is startled and cries. Robby has been playing in the sandbox for some time. The teacher assumes that

Redirect by suggesting an activity related to the child's own purpose.
Migrant Head Start, Chico, California

he has lost interest and needs a suggestion for doing something more active. She says, "Robby, Leticia didn't like that. If you want to throw something, there's a ball over there. Let's fix a place to throw." She turns a barrel on its side and suggests to Robby that he try throwing the ball through the barrel. He tries it and is successful. They throw it back and forth. Another child joins and takes the teacher's place in the game. It involves a great deal of running and chasing, which both children enjoy.

If a group is running around wildly after a long period of quiet play, its members may need a suggestion about engaging in some vigorous and constructive play like raking leaves. Their needs will not be met by a suggestion about sitting quietly and listening to a story. The meaning of their behavior lies in a need for activity. On the other hand, if they are running around wildly because they are fatigued by too much activity and stimulation, a suggestion about listening to a story will meet their need for rest.

Effective redirection often requires imagination, as in the following example where the teacher gave a suggestion that captured the interest of these children.

Donnie and Niko are at the top of the jungle gym and notice a teacher nearby who is busy writing. They shout at her, "We're going to tie you up and put you in jail." They have a rope with a heavy hook on it. Donnie climbs down with it, saying, "I'm going to tie you up." He flings it toward the teacher and stands looking at her. She says, "You don't quite understand what I'm doing here, Donnie, do you? I'm writing down some things I want to remember. I wonder if you could use the hook to catch a fish from the jungle gym. It would take a strong man to catch a big fish from the top of that jungle gym." He picks up the rope and climbs up the jungle gym and the teacher ties a "fish" to the hook. The boys have fun pulling it up and lowering it for a fresh catch.

Effective redirection faces the situation and does not avoid or divert. The teacher who sees a child going outdoors on a cold day without a coat does not help by saying, "Stay inside and listen to the story now." She is avoiding the question of the need for a coat. She helps by saying, "You'll need a coat on before you go outside." In another situation, suggesting a substitute activity may help the child, as in the case of two children wanting the same piece of equipment. The teacher helps by saying to one, "No, it's Bill's turn now. You might rake these leaves while you're waiting for your turn." Redirection should help the child face the problem by showing how it can be met, not by diverting the child.

7. Give a direction or suggestion at the time that it will be most effective. The timing of a suggestion may be as important as the suggestion itself. Through experience and insight one can increase one's skill in giving a suggestion at the moment when it will do the most good. When a suggestion fails to bring the desired response, it may be due to the timing.

Advice given too soon deprives the child of a chance to work things out. It deprives him the satisfaction of solving his own problem and may very well be resented. A suggestion made too late may have lost any chance of being successful. The child may be too discouraged or too irritated to be able to act on it.

Help at the right moment may mean a supporting hand before the child loses his balance. It may mean arbitration before two boys come to blows over a wagon or suggesting a fresh activity before the group grows tired and disorganized. Effective guidance depends on knowing how to prevent trouble.

Douglas says to Javier, "There's Chandra. Let's hit her." They run over and hit Chandra and run away. The teacher comforts Chandra and goes after the two boys. They are already interested in digging and appear resentful that she interfered with their digging. If the teacher could have stopped them firmly and quickly as they started toward Chandra, she might have made it clear that she expected them to control their impulse and that she was there to help them control it. She might have asked them what other possibilities there were for action. They were more ready to learn the lesson before they hit rather than afterward. Timing is important.

Guides In Action

8. Avoid making models in any art medium for the children to copy. This may appear to be an arbitrary rule. We hope it will seem justified later. Of course, this rule takes away the teacher's fun of drawing a man or making little dogs or Santa Clauses out of clay for an admiring crowd of preschoolers. All this may seem like innocent fun, but we must remember that art is valuable because it is a means of self-expression. It is a language to express feelings—to drain off tension or to express well-being. Young children need avenues of expression. Their speech is limited. Their feelings are strong. In clay or sand or mud, at the easel or through finger paints, they express feelings for which they have little other language. With models to copy, the child may be blocked in using art as a means of self-expression, less likely to be creative and more likely to be limited to trying to copy. Art then becomes yet one more area in which the child strives to imitate the adult who can do things much better than he can.

Notice what happens to a group at the clay table when the adult makes something. The children watch and then ask, "Make one for me." It isn't much use to say, "You make one for yourself." They can't do it as well and they feel the adult is uncooperative. Most of them drift away from the table, the meaning gone from the experience. It is no longer art or self-expression.

You may see children cramped over a paper with a crayon trying to make a car like the one the adult made, or children who will not touch the paints because they are afraid that they can't "make something." They may well envy the joy of the freer child who splashes color at the easel, delighting in its lines and masses, and who is well content with the accomplishment. This child has had no patterns to follow.

The need for help with techniques comes much later after the child has explored the possibilities in different art media and discovered that these can be used as avenues of self-expression. Then the child will want to learn how to use the material to express better . . . but not to imitate better.

The skillful teacher will avoid getting entangled in "pattern making" under any guise. She may sit at the clay table, for example, feeling the clay, patting it, and enjoying it as the children do, but she will not "make" anything. It is possible, of course, for children to watch adults who have found in art a means of self-expression as they work in their favorite medium. This may be a valuable experience for the children. Being with an adult who is expressing himself through an art medium is valuable for any child, but it is a very different experience from having an adult draw a man or a dog to amuse the child. Avoid patterns!

9. Give the child the minimum, thus providing the maximum chance to grow in independence; but give the child help when needed. There are all kinds of ways to help a child himself if we take time to think about them. We can let a boy turn the door knob with us, so that he will get the feel of how to handle a door knob and will be able to do it alone someday. We can put a girl's boots on her while she sits beside us instead of picking her up and holding her on our lap, a position that will make it hard for her ever to do the job herself someday. Too many times the child must climb down from the adult's lap when she might have started on her trip to independence from a more advantageous position.

Giving the minimum help may mean showing a child how to get a block or box to climb on when he wants to reach something rather than reaching it for him. It may mean giving him time enough to work out a

Give the child the minimum help to provide the maximum opportunity for independence. Migrant Head Start, Chico, California

problem rather than stepping in and solving it for him. Children like to solve problems, and it is hard to estimate how much their self-confidence is increased by independent problem solving. To gather a child into one's arms to bring him in for lunch may be an effective way of seeing that he gets there, but it deprives him of the chance to take any responsibility for getting himself inside. It is important to give a child the minimum help in order to allow him to grow by himself as much as possible.

In leaving the child free to satisfy his strong growth impulse to be independent, we support his feeling of self-confidence. He says, "I can do this all by myself" or, "Look what I can do."

We must remember, however, that seeking opportunities to let the child do things independently does not mean denying requests for help. When a girl says, "Help me" as she starts to take off her coat, she may be testing the adult's willingness to help. The adult does not meet the test by replying, "You can do it yourself." The adult reassures the child by giving help freely, with a full measure of willingness, or, if the adult cannot help, by answering, "I'd like to help you but I'm busy just now," then giving whatever the reason for not being in a position to help. A boy may say, "Swing me," and he may be wanting assurance that the teacher really values him enough to do extra, unnecessary things for him. He seeks a relationship with the teacher. We should avoid giving unwanted help, but we should give the help that the child feels he needs.

10. Make your directions effective by reinforcing them when necessary. Sometimes a teacher must combine techniques to be effective. A glance at the right moment, moving nearer a child, a verbal suggestion, actual physical help, all are effective techniques.

A verbal direction, even though stated positively, may not be enough to get a response. "It's time to come in for lunch," may need to be reinforced to be effective. We need to add techniques in sequence until we get compliance. We must assume more responsibility at each stage in the sequence when the child avoids his responsibility.

The first stage may be to restate the direction, adding the reason for it. "Lunch is ready, and everyone needs to put things away and come inside." If there is no response, we may suggest active participation such as, "I'll help you put your wagon in the shed, and we can go in together." A conversational approach usually makes it easier for a child to cooperate and avoid a confrontation. Young children often get interested in the action and forget to be negative.

The next step may be to discover why the child is ignoring or refusing to comply. "What is the matter?" The child may have a reason that can be communicated. We can work together with the child in explaining or reassuring, but the necessity to go in remains. He may feel differently about going in for lunch, however.

If nothing reasonable emerges, we need to make the consequences clear to the child. In this case it will be "no lunch" and a hungry child, and we must make sure that the consequence follows. This is probably a child whose behavior should be discussed in a staff meeting.

The final stage in the sequence means that we must assume all the responsibility. We can bring the child in, picking him up or taking him firmly by the hand. Eating is up to him! This step should seldom be necessary. If it is a situation where there is any danger, of course, the teacher will immediately take over and act, explaining why later.

The sequence in using techniques differs by circumstances, but we need to remember that we have more than one tool to use. There is a reasonable sequence to follow when one gives a direction to a child. When children are playing together, some will respond to a direction more readily than others. A wise teacher approaches these children first when she needs to interrupt the play. Success with one child will reinforce our chances of success with the others.

Teachers and parents commonly use too many words in giving a direction or give two or three directions at once when one is enough. Anxiety and insecurity may take the form of oververbalizing, showering the child with words. Children develop a "deafness" on hearing too many words.

It is important to have confidence in the child's ability to respond to a reasonable request or direction, given once. It is better to use different techniques in sequence until one is successful. Reinforce when necessary.

11. Learn to foresee and prevent rather than mop up after a difficulty. Success in forestalling problems comes with experience. It takes time to learn what to expect in certain situations, or with particular children, or combinations of children.

Learning to prevent problems is important because, in many cases, children do not profit from making mistakes. For instance, a girl who approaches others by doing something annoying may only learn to feel that people don't like her, and, in time, this may become a reality. She may learn acceptable ways of approaching others if the teacher, knowing her behavior with groups, suggests suitable approaches to her as she is about to approach a group. The teacher may say, "If you'd like to play with them, you might knock first" or, "Ask Michael if he needs another block." The teacher may move into the situation with the child to provide more support, or to interpret the child's intentions to the group, or even to help the child accept failure and find another place with a better chance of success. Waiting until the child fails may prevent learning anything constructive—the child may only retreat.

Sometimes children tell us what they are going to do. In these cases we need to listen and prevent what may be undesirable, rather than wait until the damage is done when little chance remains to learn from the experience.

12. Define limits clearly and maintain them consistently. There are some things which must not be done. There are limits beyond which a child cannot be allowed. It's crucial that the limits are necessary and clearly defined. Much of the difficulty in disciplining children arises from confusion about the limits. In a well-planned environment there will be few "no's," but they will be clearly defined. The child will understand them, and the adult will maintain them.

We often overestimate the child's capacity to grasp the point of what we say. Our experience is much more extensive than his. Without realizing it, we take many things for granted. The child lacks experience. If he is to understand what the limits are, these limits must be clearly and simply defined for him.

When we are sure that a limit is necessary and that the child understands it, we can maintain it with confidence. It is easy to feel unsure or even guilty about maintaining limits. We may not like to face a child's unhappiness or anger. Our own feelings bother us here. We may be afraid to maintain limits because we were overcontrolled, and we turn away from the resentment and hostility that limits arouse in us. Because of our experiences we may not want to take responsibility for controlling behavior.

Gradually we should learn to untangle our feelings and handle situations on their own merits with confidence and without hesitation.

The adult must be the one responsible for limiting children so that they do not come to harm or do not harm others or destroy property. Children will feel more secure with adults who can take this responsibility. They will feel freer because they can depend on the adult to stop them before they do things they would be sorry about later.

13. Be alert to the total situation. Use the most strategic positions for supervising. Sometimes one will observe an inexperienced teacher with her back to most of the children as she watches one child. The experienced teacher, even when she is working with one child, will be in a position to observe at a glance what the other children are doing—alert to the total situation.

Turning one's back on the group may represent, consciously or unconsciously, an attempt to limit one's experience to a simple situation. It is natural that one should feel like withdrawing from the more complex situations or that one should take an interest in one particular child because other children seem more difficult to understand. It is a natural tendency, but one should guard against it. It is important to develop skill in extending one's horizons. Observation of the total situation is essential to effective guidance. It is essential if the children are to be safe. Safety requires alert teachers who will see that all are supervised.

Enrichment of experience will come when a teacher is observing all the children, not just one child. The teacher who is reading to children, for example, may encourage a shy boy to join the group by a smile, or she may forestall trouble by noticing a child who is ready for a change in activity. She may encourage him to join the group before his lack of interest disrupts others' play.

Sitting rather than standing is another technique for improving the effectiveness of supervision. One is often in a better position to help a child when one is at the child's level. Children may feel freer to approach the adult who is sitting. It also makes possible more unobtrusive observation.

In a group containing many adults, the adults should avoid clustering, for example, near the entrance, in the locker room, or around the sandbox. Clustering calls attention to the number of adults present and may increase any tendency children have to feel self-conscious or to play for attention. Too many adults in one place may also mean that other areas are being left unsupervised.

Where one stands or sits is important in forestalling or preventing difficulties. A teacher standing between two groups engaged in different activities can make sure that one group does not interfere with the other and so can forestall trouble.

"Remote control" is ineffective control in the center. Stepping between two children who are growing irritated may prevent an attack, but it cannot be done if one is on the other side of the playroom. Trouble in the

Safety is a primary concern at all times. Be alert to the total situation.
Valley College, Campus Child Development Center, Los Angeles

housekeeping corner, for example, may be avoided by a teacher who moves near quietly, as tension mounts in the "family," and suggests a solution. Her suggestion is more likely to be accepted if her presence reinforces it. Trouble is seldom avoided by a suggestion given at a distance.

Choose the position for standing or sitting that will best serve your purposes. Study a diagram of the center where you are teaching, and check the spots that are strategically good for supervision. List places where close supervision is needed for safety, such as at the workbench.

14. Make each child's health and safety a primary concern at all times. The good teacher must be constantly alert to the things that affect health, such as seeing that drinking cups are not used in common, that disposable towels are used, that toys which have been in a child's mouth are washed, that the window is closed if there is a draft, that jackets or sweaters are adjusted to changes in temperature or activity.

Being alert to safety means observing and removing sources of danger such as protruding nails, unsteady ladders, or boards not properly supported. It means closely supervising children who are playing together on high places or children who are using such potentially dangerous materials as hammers, saws, and shovels. The point is familiar but clear-cut and important: The skillful teacher never relaxes her watchfulness.

15. Increase your own awareness by observing and taking notes. Underlying all these guides is the assumption that teaching is based on ability to observe behavior objectively and to evaluate its meaning. As in any science, conclusions are based on accurate observations. Jot down notes frequently, statements of what happens, the exact words a child uses, the actual sequence of events. Make each note at the time of the event or as soon after as possible, always dating each note. Reread these notes later and make interpretations. Skill in observing and recording is essential to building understanding. Improve your ability to select significant incidents and make meaningful records.

Chapter Overview

This chapter provides the guides to speech and action necessary for positive classroom management and helping the young child know what is expected behavior. This lies at the heart of good teaching and interaction with the children. The teacher must work at observation techniques, be able to reflect on past performance, and change when change is needed.

Projects

1. Observe and record ten positively stated directions you heard a teacher use with a child. Indicate the effectiveness of each statement you recorded, giving the reasons why the statement seemed effective.
2. Observe and record five questions asked by the teacher. Classify the reason for asking a question as (1) to get information about a fact, (2) to discover an opinion or preference, (3) to suggest a possibility, (4) to clarify a situation, or (5) for another purpose. How effective was the question in each case?
3. Listen to the quality of the voices around you. What feelings do the tones seem to express when one pays no attention to the words spoken? Note the differences in pitch, in speed, and in volume in the teachers' voices. Report a situation where you feel the tone of voice was more important than the words in influencing the child's behavior.

For Your Further Reading

Clewett, A. S. (1988). Guidance and discipline: Teaching young children appropriate behavior. *Young Children 43*(4), 26–31. Tackles the issue of "time out" and offers teaching alternatives and prevention ideas in common problem areas. Concludes, however, that effective planning for curriculum, schedule, room arrangement, and supervision may not be enough.

Faber, A., & Mazlish, E. (1980). *How to talk so kids will listen and listen so kids will talk*. New York: Avon. An enthusiastic action approach to communicating with children and helping them solve their own problems. Offers a rich variety of guidance techniques.

Gordon, T. (1989). *Teaching children self-discipline: At home and at school*. New York: Times Books. Strategies for discipline that influence children to be self-responsible, self-disciplined, and respectful of other's needs. Makes a convincing case for how traditional rewards and punishments have negative results in children. Promotes ways to develop democratic relationships.

Honig, A. S. (1987). *Love and learn: Discipline for young children*. Brochure #528; single copies $0.50. Washington, DC: National Association for the Education of Young Children. Brief presentation of positive discipline that works.

Hymes, J. L. (1981). Teaching the basics: Good behavior. In Hymes, J. L. *Teaching the child under six* (3rd ed.). Columbus, OH: Merrill Publishing Co. pp. 131–154. A wise presentation of several approaches: how to improve the setting to promote good behavior; improving children's understandings of rules; working on children's feelings; how to proceed when children still misbehave.

Lickona, T. (1983). *Raising good children: Helping your child through the stages of moral development*. New York: Bantam. Ten excellent guidelines for moral development, carried through the stages by children's developmental ages, leading to becoming responsible people. Emphasizes love and respect and importance of attachment. Helpful listing of children's books.

Reynolds, E. (1990). *Guiding young children: A child-centered approach*. Mountain View, CA: Mayfield Publishing Company. A practical guidance approach based on problem solving, derived from the work of Carl Rogers, Haim Ginnott, Thomas Gordon, Jean Piaget, and Rudolf Dreikurs. Includes active listening, negotiation, limit setting, environmental modification, and reinforcement and strokes.

Riley, S. S. (1984). *How to generate values in young children*. Washington, DC: National Association for the Education of Young Children. Qualities like integrity, honesty, individuality, self-confidence, and wisdom are learned by children through countless interactions, through play, making decisions. In examples from early reading, bedtime, allowances, security blankets, discipline and television, this book offers a helpful guide to speech and action.

Spock, B., & Rothenberg, M. B. (1992) (rev.) *Dr. Spock's baby and child care*. New York: Pocket Books. This classic guide, updated to include contemporary issues in children's lives such as day care, teen pregnancy, and single parenthood, still offers excellent approaches to guidance.

Using Discipline: **Setting Limits**

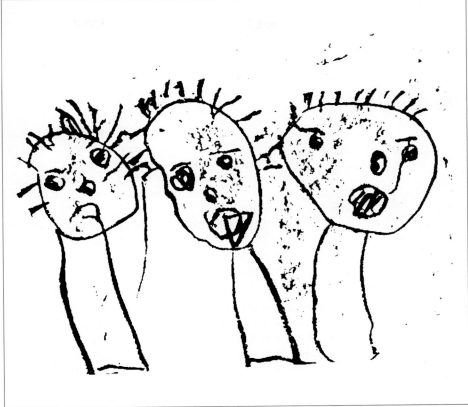

Three naughty girls (*girl, 3 years, 6 months*)

This chapter explains seven ways to set limits with positive results by exploring:

▶ What is discipline?
▶ What is punishment?
▶ What are some ways I can effectively help children develop self-control?

CRITERION: Staff do not force children to apologize or explain their behavior but help children recognize another child's feelings. Staff abstain from corporal punishment or humiliating or frightening discipline techniques. Food or beverage is never withheld as a discipline device.

Guidance techniques should be nonpunitive and accompanied by rational explanations of expectations. Limits are set for children but the environment is arranged so that a minimal number of *no's* are necessary, particularly for very young children. (NAEYC, 1991a, *Accreditation Criteria* . . . , p. 17).

Discipline

No subject is likely to concern a parent or teacher more than discipline. Normal, healthy children misbehave at times. Their behavior must be controlled for their own good as well as for the good of those around them. Adults must make decisions about the actions to take when a child's behavior is unacceptable or unsafe for himself or others. Discipline is a necessary part of guidance.

Some adults see discipline as synonymous with punishment. What is discipline? What is punishment? What are some essentials for sound discipline?

Defining Discipline

Discipline refers to actions adults take to help a child change his behaviors. Adults identify for him what kinds of behavior are acceptable to the people whose approval he wants and help him understand the possible consequences of his behavior. Discipline may involve stopping a child from a certain action and taking responsibility for helping him change his behavior.

Our feelings probably matter more than the methods we use in discipline. If we expect that children will sometimes misbehave, disrupt a story period or the play of other children, or destroy and defy, we are not surprised by their actions. We find it easier to respond in ways that help the child. We are helped, too, if we understand that it is often not our failure that has brought about the behavior, but that it is a result of the ordinary conflicts in growing.

Growing up is a complicated process that takes time. Children have a right to a certain level of irresponsibility during the process. If the adults around them are loving and firm and permit only what does no harm and produces no real anxiety, children will learn to master their impulses. We must have confidence in children and in ourselves. If we lack this confidence, we may respond to the misbehavior in a punishing way that can be very damaging.

Defining Punishment

Punishment refers to the actions taken by adults to change children's behavior by making them suffer physically or emotionally. Young children often do not understand why they are being punished. They may be confused about which behaviors are acceptable. As a result, punishment may leave them feeling angry, resentful, and guilty. They may only learn that they are "bad." Such feelings contribute to self-doubt, and the child who lacks confidence is less ready to assume responsibility for self-control.

We know from research that punishment, when it is used at all, must follow misbehavior closely; it must be appropriate in severity, and it must focus on the specific behavior. A child on an excursion who runs away from the group, even going into a street, must be dealt with promptly. The child must immediately be taken back to the center, even if it means the entire group goes back. The child must understand that the excursion is postponed until the unacceptable behavior changes to acceptable.

Effective consequences include restrictions in space, such as where the child can play or be, and restrictions in use, such as what can be used. Consequences should not include restrictions in activity, such as being made to sit on a chair. A child's thoughts during these times are likely to be of questionable value.

Some Essentials for Sound Discipline

In infancy and early childhood, normal, healthy children use all kinds of behavior to test the world. They need to discover how the framework of their world will stand up to what they can do to it. They need to find firmness and strength and love in the adults around them. Not all adults can stand up against such testing. An adult who refuses to allow a testing behavior gives a child little chance to discover what is acceptable and what is not. The child does not learn what may happen as the result of misbehavior. The adult who lets a child do anything he pleases, on the other hand, gives this child little chance to learn about acceptable limits. "Testing out" behavior leads to learning when the discipline that is used is sound.

Parents or teachers who discipline strictly or even harshly and those who avoid any disciplining are not likely to help children in learning to control their own behavior and to show consideration for others. As a result these children may become unhappy, unloved people. Children are helped when adults act with firmness, love, and the tolerance that comes with confidence and a sense of responsibility.

The word permissive is sometimes used to describe a kind of nonguidance that permits children to do anything they want to do. Allowing a child to act impulsively without guidance is neither realistic nor helpful to self-regulation. This kind of care-giving does not help the child control impulses. Such behavior by an adult can be a sign of irresponsibility or ignorance.

An environment that permits, freely and generously, all legitimate activity for a child at his particular stage of development is not a permissive environment. It is a supportive and encouraging environment.

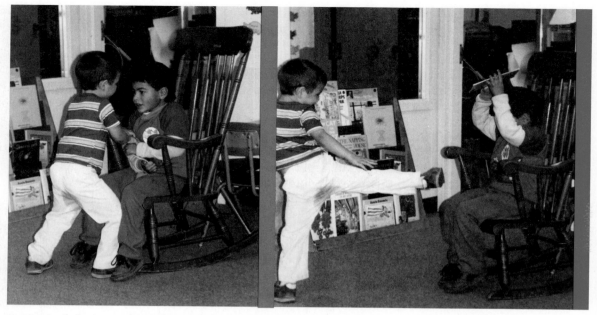

Aggressive behaviors seen on television influence how children handle conflicts. Valley College, Campus Child Development Center, Los Angeles

Changing Patterns or Standards

We live in a society that is not, on the whole, a giving one with children. The emphasis in childrearing is frequently on restriction: not touching, staying dry and clean, and being quiet. Human relationships often receive less consideration than do material objects. The child's needs to assert himself and find avenues of autonomy, initiative, and self-expression are often not accepted. The child may suffer a debilitating loss of self-confidence as a result of such patterns. As we shift to a more giving attitude, we should not bear a burden of guilt when we sometimes act in a way that is not giving. In changing our patterns of discipline it becomes all the more important to remember that limits have a positive value if they are appropriate for the child and are wisely maintained. Sound discipline promotes healthy social, emotional, and cognitive growth.

Ways in Which the Adults Help the Child Develop Self-Control

Accept Children's Need to Assert Themselves

Young children are in the process of becoming independent persons. They have urges to assert themselves and thus prove they are independent. At times they will assert independence by not doing what they are told. They are testing what it is like to be an autonomous person. The urge to assert oneself is important and necessary to healthy development. Children need to feel that it is possible to assert themselves safely, just as they also need to find that they can live with restrictions and limitations. The kind of discipline they receive will determine how well they learn to be assertive, as well as how they learn to limit their own behaviors. For example, as an infant, a child may have closed her mouth tightly, refusing the food her parent offered. Instead of interpreting this behavior as defiance, the wise parent waits, giving her time to assert her independence, knowing that she will soon be ready to continue with the feeding.

Take Action When Action is Needed

We may have to *restrain* a child who is about to hurt another by holding him with firmness. In taking action we respond as a confident authority. Although the child may be angry with us at the time, he ultimately will feel safer and less anxious. We can acknowledge his feelings by saying, "I know you are angry with me, but I cannot let you hurt John." Understanding and sympathy can accompany firmness. We should never act aggressively toward the child or try to lower his self-esteem by calling him not nice, bad, or naughty. When he can listen, we explain why the behavior is not permitted and what other action he might take to channel his feelings more constructively. We act as responsible adults who can help him learn to control his impulses.

Accept the child's right to assert himself, as this "boss" does.
Migrant Head Start, Chico, California

We may need to *remove* a child from a situation that is too difficult for him to manage acceptably on his own. For example, a boy who keeps disturbing the play of other children in the sandbox must play somewhere else. We should isolate a child only when he cannot control his own behavior. Such behavior may be due to fatigue or over-excitement. We should be honest with the child about the reasons for his separation from the group. We want him to view the time away from the group as a relief, rather than a punishment. He can have an opportunity to play alone quietly with something he enjoys until he feels ready to be with others.

We may need to *deprive* a child of an object or from participating in an activity as a consequence of his behavior. A child who knowingly uses a hammer in the wrong place should be deprived of the hammer for a time.

Set Reasonable Limits

There are not many prohibitions in a favorable group environment for young children. The important limits relate to safety, general welfare, and the protection of the rights of others. These limits must be clearly defined and consistently maintained for each child.

Set reasonable limits appropriate to the child's age.
Migrant Head Start, Chico, California

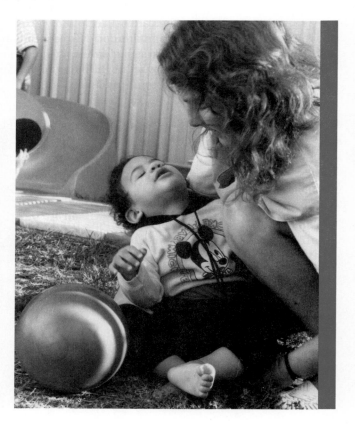

For example, children are not permitted to leave the premises. Teachers put this in a positive way by saying, "Stay where the teacher can see you, so she can keep you safe." If a girl does go beyond the limits of the play yard, for instance, she meets with disapproval and suffers a consequence, such as being restricted to a specific area in the yard. We explain the reasons why her behavior must be limited; however, we know that she does not fully understand why the act is dangerous. We also know that her control over her impulses is too weak to be reliable at all times. We must be responsible to watch and take care of her. She usually obeys us, because she trusts that we care about her and set limits for her protection. She needs the support of our limits.

Children often need help in respecting the rights of others, such as the right to keep possession of an object while using it or the right to be free of disturbance in carrying out an activity. For example, two 3-year-olds playing in the sand may come to blows over the possession of a spoon. The teacher steps in, putting her arm around the one who has taken the spoon by force and saying, "No, Bill was using the spoon. Please give it back to him. I will help you find another one." She may add, "Hitting hurts. Next time, ask him to give you the spoon when he finishes using it." If there are tears, she comforts the one who is crying and says, "I'm sorry you were hit. It hurts, I know." As a teacher observes the children, she may be able to step in with a suggestion before the hitting occurs and prevent the struggle.

Learning to control impulses is difficult for the child. Time and experience with both freedom and control are necessary if the child is to learn self-control. The teacher needs knowledge about how all children learn and develop, as well as insight about the individual child. This understanding and insight will grow out of many careful observations of a child and of children, as they work and play together.

Use Timing and Time Effectively

There is a right moment for stepping into a situation if guidance and redirection are to be most effective. The new teacher will find it helpful to observe experienced teachers, making notes when possible, and thinking over what observations as well as relating those observations to personal experience. The impulsive child, for example, will need help more quickly than the placid or slow-moving child.

Every child needs the opportunity to help himself as much as he can, even in settling disputes. The teacher must study each child until she can decide the timing of assistance and what help will be most useful. Children's temperaments and styles differ, as do the kinds of help they require and can accept. The guidance must fit the child at a specific moment. The teacher's relationship with a child will be a factor in determining when to step in to prevent a conflict that is beyond a child's ability to manage. Success in timing of help comes with experience and reflection. New teachers will make mistakes in judging when to intervene. Risking errors is a part of learning to teach.

A child sometimes just needs time to accept directions. When we say to him, "You will need to put your boots on before you go out. The grass is wet outdoors this morning," we do not have to see that he marches right over to his locker to put on his boots. He may have to protest a bit until he convinces himself that here is a demand with which he must comply. We may have to stop him if he starts to go outdoors without his boots, but we give him time to accept the limit and then comply or stay inside.

A conversational approach may help. Eric is outside playing in the sand and has pulled off his shoes and socks. A teacher decides it is too cold outdoors for bare feet. She goes over to Eric and sits on the side of the sandbox quietly. Then she says, "It feels good, doesn't it, Eric?" and she smiles, enjoying it with him. "I wish I could let you play in your bare feet in the sandbox, but I think it is too cold to be outdoors without your shoes on. You'll have to put them back on this time. When the weather is warmer, you can take them off outside." She adds, "I used to like to be barefoot when I was a little girl. Now I'll help you put your shoes on." Together they get the shoes back on while Eric tells her about what he was doing. Eric is a very independent child who has often resisted directions. Because his teacher takes

"I had it first!" Learning to respect the rights of others takes a long time. Valley College, Campus Child Development Center, Los Angeles

time to enjoy the moment with him and let him know she understands, Eric is able to accept the necessary limit and cooperate. There was no need for the teacher or for Eric to act quickly in this situation.

Develop Skill in Defining and Explaining Limits

Every teacher needs to develop skill in using language that the child can understand, as she explains the behavior expected of him. The teacher first explains clearly what *can* be done before defining what *cannot* be done in a specific and concrete way. It takes practice to use language effectively with young children as well as an understanding of each individual child's stage of development.

When a child hits another child, for example, the teacher must intervene and must also help the child who was hitting to understand the reasons for the intervention. She must explain how the other child feels (hurt and unhappy) and how she feels (disapproving) about this behavior. She also should make a positive suggestion about what can be done in the situation. "Next time *tell* him what you want" or, "Next time tell him you want him to move his truck." In some situations the teacher may state the consequences if the child continues this behavior. To a child who is throwing sand, she may say, "You will have to leave the sandbox unless you stop throwing sand."

The teacher may help two children who are in conflict by interpreting the actions of each, thus helping them begin to think about behavior rather than to act on impulse. Children can begin early to understand that there are reasons why people behave as they do. Guided by a teacher, 4- and 5-year-old children often benefit from discussing the reasons why a conflict occurred and what might be done at another time. Talking over problems is an important step in learning about social relations for 4-year-olds. Children need to learn to become aware of their own feelings as well as those of other people.

The Physical Environment and the Schedule

Careful planning of the environment and the schedule will often prevent the occurrence of conflicts or issues and reduce the need for discipline. Adequate and well-arranged space, where supervision is easily managed, will promote positive relationships among children and enable them to work and play together with a minimum of conflict. Making available a wide variety of carefully selected materials will also help reduce conflict, because the teacher has planned something to interest each child. When conflicts are frequent in any particular area, the teacher should observe carefully and try to determine if a different arrangement of space or equipment might create a more favorable situation.

Keeping the subgroups small is another preventive measure. A rule of thumb is that the number of children in a subgroup should be about the same as the age of the child, that is, three 3-year-olds, four 4-year-olds, and so on. When planning options, there should be about twice the number of work and play spaces as children. Small groups give each child an opportunity to participate and receive needed help from a teacher or another child. Such planning minimizes the potential for conflict.

A schedule that calls for little waiting by children reduces the need for discipline. Sometimes moving snack time to an earlier hour or making group times shorter can reduce stress. Children can take much more responsibility for their behavior if the environment and events are planned to meet the changing needs of individuals and the group.

Model Acceptable Behavior

The word discipline derives from the word disciple or follower. It suggests an important element in self-control, that of following an example. The child wants to be like the adults who are important to him. Teachers are important people to children. If the teacher is calm, speaks quietly, and manages her feelings acceptably in difficult situations, she gives the child a positive example to follow. If she can meet frustrations without piling up feelings of irritation, if she can respond to defiant behavior without anger, she gives the child a model for dealing with his own feelings and with similar situations he will face.

Children in a group are aware of how the teacher responds to a disruptive child. If that child is handled with firmness and understanding, other children are reassured that the teacher is trustworthy. They learn about limits of behavior, and they see a demonstration of an appropriate response. Anger should not be met with anger. It can be coped with reasonably and channeled in constructive ways.

Even the most competent teachers are not always successful models. Everyone has stress to cope with at times, so we should try to understand our own needs and meet them. For example, we can try to avoid fatigue. Rested, satisfied people are more likely to model acceptable behavior. There will be times when stress will cause us to be less sensitive to and thoughtful of others or to respond with irritation. This is a time to model ways to accept responsibility for our behavior and to apologize. Children are remarkably resilient and forgiving.

Chapter Overview

Using discipline and setting limits are part of teaching. The emotions centering around changing behavior are complex. Values and prior experiences influence the teacher's choices in handling children. By accepting the child's need to assert himself, by taking action when action is needed, by setting reasonable limits, by using timing effectively and by defining and explaining limits, the teacher helps the child learn expected group behavior. Careful planning of the environment and the schedule of the day as well as modeling acceptable behavior is necessary for positive classroom management.

Projects

1. Observe and report a situation in which a limit was set for a child's behavior. How did the adult define the limit? How did the adult maintain it? What was the child's behavioral response? How do you think he felt about himself in the end?
2. Report a situation in which the statement of a limit was well-timed. Why did you feel the timing was good? What was the result?

Report a situation in which the timing was poor or the teacher failed to maintain the limit set. What was the result?
3. Observe a teacher in the classroom or outdoors and describe the behaviors modeled for the children. Comment on what you saw the teacher do or say that provided children with a positive role model or a negative role model.

For Your Further Reading

Baumrind, D. (1972). Socialization and instrumental competence in young children. In W. W. Hartup (Ed.). *The young child: Reviews of research* (Vol. 2). Pp. 202–224. Washington, DC: National Association for the Education of Young Children. A classic study examining—longitudinally—authoritarian, permissive, and authoritative parenting practices and their outcomes in the children. Important perspective for teachers.

Brazelton, T. B. (1984). *To listen to a child: Understanding the normal problems of growing up.* Reading, MA: Addison-Wesley. A positive approach to help adults understand how children's developmental needs are revealed through common behaviors such as fears and tantrums. All of Dr. Brazelton's books reflect a warm, compassionate approach.

Haswell, K. L., Jock, E., & Wenar, C. (1982). Techniques for dealing with oppositional behavior in preschool children. *Young Children, 37*(3), 12–18. Also in J. F. Brown (Ed.). (1982). *Curriculum planning for young children.* Pp. 221–227. Practical helps in developing techniques for dealing with negativism.

Honig, A. S. (1985). Research in review: Compliance, control and discipline (Parts 1 & 2). *Young Children, 40*(2), 50–58; 40(3), 47–52. Very interesting reviews of studies of compliance and cooperation. The first deals with secure attachment as a predictor of compliance and the influence of settings such as a supermarket. The second looks at effects of group programs on compliance and recommends adult methods for promoting cooperation and compliance.

Marion, M. (1987). *Guidance of young children.* (2nd ed.). St. Louis, MO: C. V. Mosby. Deals with short-term goals (how to control children's behavior on a daily basis) and long-term goals (teaching self-control and developing caring, cooperative, competent people). As well as dealing with control and aggression, the book discusses prosocial behavior and positive self-esteem, always based on understanding theoretical approaches to guiding children.

Soderman, A. K. (1985). Dealing with difficult young children: Strategies for teachers and parents. *Young Children 40*(5), 15–20. Reviews the issue of individual temperament, which affects others' reactions to children. Offers positive strategies to replace those often used with difficult children.

Stone, J. G. (1978). *A guide to discipline.* (rev. ed.) Washington, DC: National Association for the Education of Young Children. An NAEYC classic, now revised, intended for teachers, caregivers, and parents. Filled with practical tips on helping children toward self-discipline as well as what to do in difficult situations.

Teaching Strategies Need a Theoretical Base

Tree (*boy, 4 years*)

Now that you have been introduced to the center and to guiding the children, you may have questions about the foundations of your work with children. This chapter explores:

▶ The work of three people whose thinking contributed greatly to our work: Freud, Erikson, and Piaget

▶ Twelve basic beliefs held by knowledgeable professionals in quality programs.

Observations of the behavior of young children hold more meaning if we see behavior not as an isolated incident, but as one related to a stage in the individual's total development. We can recognize, for example, that the 2-year-old who refuses our proffered hand on a steep slope is exercising an urge to be independent. Her behavior is evidence of an achievement in a growth process. The 2-year-old who always clings to our hand may be revealing a blocking in her growth. A group of 4-year-olds arguing in the housekeeping corner are using language as a tool to work out compromise. A year or so earlier the same children would probably have been pursuing their own purposes in parallel play and might have resorted to blows to settle a conflict.

Three People Whose Theories Have Influenced Early Childhood Education

Sound teaching strategies need to be based on a framework of theory about human growth and development. Among the many investigators in the area of child growth and development we have selected three whose thinking has contributed to our understanding of human behavior: Sigmund Freud, Erik Erikson, and Jean Piaget. Many other investigators have, of course, made important contributions, but they have not developed such comprehensive theories. The theories of these three men were based on careful observation of human behavior, much of it done under natural rather than laboratory conditions.

Contributions of Sigmund Freud

The theories of Sigmund Freud have greatly influenced our understanding of personality development. His work in the late nineteenth and early twentieth centuries has become part of our thinking about personality. It must be remembered that his work reflected his time and place, although it has been criticized today as sexist. Even if some of his concepts are considered dated, Freud was a germinal thinker who gave us the concept of the unconscious, that great reservoir of universal feeling within us that we can never be aware of directly but which influences what we do.

Freud's work with disturbed adults convinced him of the great significance of the individual's earliest experiences in determining later attitudes and behavior. He described the early stages in young children as the oral, the anal, and the phallic, with their respective sources of excitement and satisfaction, followed by a latency period lasting until adolescence. He pointed to the male and female components in the personality of every individual and the process a child goes through in establishing his or her sexual identification.

Freud developed the method known as *psychoanalysis* for gaining insights into the defenses built up by an individual that block the creative use of energies. Psychoanalysts working with disturbed young children have used *play therapy* as a method of treating children's emotional disturbances. Play therapy is based on the principle that in play children often reveal indirectly or symbolically the conflicts they are feeling. Among these therapists is Anna Freud, the daughter of Sigmund Freud, who has made important contributions to our understanding of children.

The process of discovering and accepting one's gender, according to Freudian theory, takes place in the first years of life and becomes the basis for normal sexual adjustment. In the beginning, all infants relate closely to the primary caregiver. Later, the infant moves toward identification with the parent of his or her own sex. The struggle of the male child to shift identification from the mother to the father is known as the *oedipal conflict* and is most acute in the third, fourth, and fifth years. We see boys of this age asserting themselves in vigorous, aggressive ways, imitating males and needing to have their father's attention and approval.

Young boys in families where the father is absent may have a serious problem; they have a real need for contact with a man from whom they can learn male attitudes and behavior. Centers should have men as teachers and caregivers to meet this need, either as regular staff members or as volunteers. The staff in centers for young children may be predominantly female, but it should not be exclusively so. Girls, also, need contacts with males in order to develop their femininity. Girls shift to a new relationship with their mothers, that is, identifying with the mother as a female. The shift to identifying with the same-sex parent is more gradual for girls than for boys.

In the center we observe the interest that children have in each other as they use the toilets together and observe differences in the sexes. A girl may be interested in the boy's penis and wonder why she lacks one. All children are interested in the subject of babies and where they come from. They have many misconceptions that can slowly be cleared up by offering the appropriate roles in their sociodramatic play, as they seek to discover more about what these roles are like in the grown-up world.

Contributions of Erik Erikson

Erikson, a student of Freud, suggested in his theory that the stages one goes through in life are centered on each person's relationship to the social environment. Erikson called his theory the psychosocial theory of human development. His interest in personality development led him to observe people in different cultures. From these experiences he formulated a theory of stages in personality growth that spans an entire lifetime.

Each stage has a major *task* that needs to be resolved in a manner that enhances social and emotional development and leads to successful entry into the next stage. According to Erikson, a task consists of resolving in a favorable direction the conflicting impulses that characterize the stage. For example, Erikson says that at first the infant must establish trust in the world in order to move successfully to establishing feelings of autonomy or independence, the next stage. Establishing trust for a baby means the infant can expect someone to come when he is hungry, tired of being in one position, cries, is wet, or needs to be comforted. The infant wakes in the morning with a certain expectation that someone will take care of him. If this expectation is not met, trust is thwarted.

For each positive need being asserted, there is a negative force that must be resolved in order to proceed to the next higher stage. The task of establishing a large measure of trust rather than mistrust is not completed in the first months of life, but its most significant growth takes place during this period. We will consider the crises and tasks of the preschool years as Erikson has outlined them.

Personality Tasks in Childhood as Formulated by Erikson

TRUST VERSUS MISTRUST   As we have said, the first and most basic task in healthy personality development is achieving a sense of trust that outweighs the sense of mistrust. In the first year or more of life the infant needs to feel that the world is a trustworthy place and that he himself is trustworthy. This sense of trust will grow out of the experiences the infant has with the mother or primary caregiver and later with other significant people. Out of many experiences of having basic needs met, being fed when hungry, being kept warm and safe, and being handled with loving care, the infant begins to trust the world. This feeling enables him to meet the new, the unexpected, the frustrating experiences that come later. Because of these good experiences, the individual learns to trust his own capacity to cope.

The importance of good early mothering and its influence on personality development has been studied further by D. W. Winnicott (1974), an English pediatrician who later became a psychoanalyst. Winnicott pointed to the importance of a mother's adaptation to her infant in the first weeks and months when, by her sensitive management, she adapts completely to the

The infant's sense of trust grows out of his many experiences of having his needs met, like being fed by this preschooler when hungry. Migrant Head Start, Chico, California

infant at first and then gradually withdraws this complete adaptation as she senses that the infant is ready to tolerate delays and frustrations—in other words, when the infant has developed sufficient trust. By presenting the world "in small enough doses," she enables the infant to build a sense of trust over mistrust, which is the cornerstone of a healthy personality.

All through life we continue to need experiences that contribute to our feeling that the world is a place where we can feel comfortable and trust ourselves. But the crisis point for the development of this trait falls in the earliest months of life. The infant needs protection then from experiences that produce a mistrust that may overpower him. Separation from the care-taking person, for example, may overwhelm an infant even when it is brief. It may seem an eternity to him because of his undeveloped sense of time.

Mutual adaptation is an important element here. As the months go by, the infant under favorable circumstances builds up a large "bank account" of trust to draw upon. The mother (or other caregiver) can then expect the infant to adapt to her needs and the needs of others. In doing this she shows her trust both in the infant and in the infant's growing capacity to delay satisfaction.

Infants differ in their responses. Temperamental differences are evident. Some seem to trust easily and others find it more difficult, but it is the parents' or caregiver's sensitive management that enables each to succeed in developing a healthy balance of trust over mistrust. We can see the results in children's behavior when they reach nursery school age. The task of continuing to build trust remains important throughout the preschool period. In fact, all our lives, as we suffer disillusionment, we need at times to restore our faith in ourselves and in the trustworthiness of others.

AUTONOMY VERSUS SHAME OR DOUBT   The second task in healthy personality growth is that of developing a sense of autonomy outweighing the sense of shame or doubt. Already toward the end of the first year we can see evidence of the child working on this task. It becomes the major task of the second and third years. The mother or other caregivers must be sensitive to the child's great need to assert independence at this time. It is the "Me do it" stage. Permitted to "do it," the child has the chance to begin to take steps in organizing himself or herself as a learner. It is the age of "No" and frequent "contrariness," but out of this is born an independent individual capable of feeling, "I am someone."

Mutual adaptation is again important here, if this task is to be accomplished with sufficient autonomy to balance the necessary dependence and doubt. It is a period when discipline should be mild and reserved for the most necessary points. If we can accept the self-assertion, we find the child usually does what we want because he can feel that he is deciding to do what we have asked. Giving the child choices, avoiding confrontations, and

Developing a sense of autonomy, this toddler climbs on the table to play. Migrant Head Start, Chico, California

introducing a play element all work better than creating issues at this stage. In this way we are protecting the child in the task of beginning to feel, as an autonomous person, "I am, and I am important and powerful." Feeling autonomous is better than feeling helpless as one faces life.

INITIATIVE VERSUS GUILT   The third task in personality growth as outlined by Erikson is developing a sense of initiative outweighing the sense of guilt. It is the important personality task of the child of three, four, and five years, although we see many signs of initiative earlier. In this stage the child is more actively exploring and investigating. The child is beginning to ask questions, to think new thoughts, to try out all kinds of things—in other words, to take the initiative. The child also is developing a conscience, a sense of being responsible for actions as an autonomous person. A conscience is necessary and valuable, but it should not carry too heavy a load at this point in healthy personality growth. A 4-year-old can easily feel too guilty for some transgression or guilty for the wrong things. It is important that the sense of initiative, of being able to forge ahead and try, should outweigh the fear of wrongdoing. Understanding guidance is needed in this period if the child is to emerge with a large measure of initiative outweighing but still maintaining the capacity for guilt.

In this stage the child has an urge to make and to do things. It is a creative period in personality growth. A 4-year-old helping to carry blocks back to the shelves may suddenly discover the interesting patterns the blocks make as they tumble from the wagon or the way in which the blocks can be stuffed into the holes in the fence . . . and so begins a new and imaginative form of play. The child may need a reminder about the job at hand and perhaps some help in getting on with the task. We can give these with an appreciation for what he has discovered and for the excitement he feels for his discovery. Life should be made up of such experiences in discovery when one is 4.

This period is important for intellectual development. The groundwork is being laid for the child's learning in school. With a firm foundation of trust and a sense of being an autonomous person, he exercises initiative, taking hold of experiences as they are offered and making something of them.

The child uses all of the senses as he explores and discovers and makes things happen. It is a period of learning by doing. Initiative thrives on opportunities for play in a favorable environment. Of course, unfinished business will be left over from the earlier stages for almost all children. We need to give help with all of these tasks if sound personality growth is to continue, but the major task of the period is to encourage and support the child's sense of initiative.

INDUSTRY VERSUS INFERIORITY   The fourth task in healthy personality growth, the development of a sense of industry outweighing the sense of inadequacy or inferiority, is the important task of the school-age child. It continues to adolescence. At this stage the healthy child sees himself as a worker and a learner. Games with rules, skill in sports, and group activities become important. He is a schoolchild ready to accomplish learning under favorable circumstances. He is in the intellectual stage of "concrete operations," to use Piaget's words.

As we work with children, we will keep in mind these personality tasks and the help we may be able to give children in order that the crises may be resolved in ways favorable to healthy development. We will adapt our methods so we can support the balance of trust over mistrust, the balance of autonomous feeling over doubt, and the balance of initiative over guilt. We will value the child's developing sense of industry over inferiority as he becomes more of a learner and worker.

Contributions of Jean Piaget

Jean Piaget, a biologist, became interested in observing the behavior of his own children and devoted himself to studying their behavior. He was interested in how children learn, and he continued his work by observing and interviewing many children. He developed a theory about how children reason and learn. He was well known in Europe before he was "discovered" by American educators in the late 1950s.

Construction of Knowledge

Piaget concluded that young children learn by constructing their own knowledge. They do this by moving from one level of understanding to another, correcting earlier inaccurate perceptions. *Constructivism* is central to Piaget's theory. He felt that knowledge is not taught but must be constructed through an active mental process. Learning does not entirely depend on maturation, which is a biological process. It comes from within if it is true understanding. In constructing knowledge, children move through different stages. In the first stage, for example, the child constructs physical knowledge out of her experiences with objects. She constructs knowledge or "learns" about objects and their properties. The more experiences she has with objects, the more she "learns." Her learning is an active mental process. It is not taught but has been constructed by the child.

Social-conventional knowledge is another type of knowledge. Communication with others, either through body language or oral communication, is part of this knowledge. We might note that the child structures the ac-

As *she builds, this girl constructs her own knowledge of balance, height, weight, size, and stability.* Bakersfield College, Bakersfield, California

quisition of language without being "taught." Logical-mathematical knowledge, another type, is constructed by the individual in a later stage of development.

We can help the cognitive or constructive process by providing activities that stimulate thought, the discovery of the properties of objects, and the putting of objects into relationships. Among activities that do this are block building; painting; playing with sand, water, and clay; and pretending.

On the basis of his detailed observations of children, Piaget has described the stages children go through as they construct knowledge. Central to these stages is the concept that the child constructs knowledge through assimilation and accommodation. The "taking in" (assimilating) of information complemented by an intellectual reorganization (accommodating) when previous information does not "fit" with what is "known" is one way of explaining the construction of knowledge.

Stages in Constructing Knowledge

SENSORIMOTOR STAGE (BIRTH TO TWO YEARS)   The construction of knowledge for the infant begins with the ability to act on the world through the senses and the reflexes, which slowly are replaced by purposeful coordinated motor skills. In this time frame the infant or toddler is looking, listening, touching, smelling, tasting, and moving in response to stimulation of her senses. She learns in sensorimotor ways. Thought consists of patterns of action or sensorimotor schemata. These schemata are ways of behaving that she can apply to a variety of objects or situations, behavior like grasping, shaking, banging, and even sucking.

As previously stated, the infant develops these schemata through *assimilation,* or taking in of sensory impressions, and through *accommodation,* or modifying action patterns to fit changes in the situation such as a rattle presented in a different position. She comes to "know" an object like a rattle by having different experiences with it, fingering it, mouthing it, banging it. Through all these experiences she stores up impressions and nourishes this zest for exploring.

During this stage she becomes aware of *object permanence.* She begins to look for the rattle she has dropped and realizes it still exists even when she no longer sees it. Her mother is somewhere even when not within sight. The mother is important to the infant because good relationships with her, her attention and care, enable the infant to feel enough trust to reach out for new experiences. The mother's interest and encouragement support learning and may be as necessary for learning as the experiences themselves.

PREOPERATIONAL (TWO TO SEVEN YEARS)   This is the age of the use of symbols. Evidence of this advancement is seen in the latter part of the first year as the infant begins to use language. For the preoperational child language now opens the door to symbolic thought. One of the most interesting aspects of symbolic thought is the imaginative play that is now possible for the young child. A block can become a car or an airplane, and fastening a scarf around one's shoulders turns one into Superman. Pretending is a major part of this symbolic thought process. Having a real experience and then representing that experience in dramatic play becomes the major thrust of the preoperational child's play.

In the preoperational stage the child continues to construct physical knowledge, but she now constructs much more social-conventional knowledge. She is introduced to the give and take of play and involvement with others and begins to understand what is expected in these encounters. She becomes aware that people respond differently to her ways of behaving. Egocentrism is evident. The preoperational child is at the center of things and everything revolves around her wishes and desires. It is a long, slow process to go from "mine" to "ours."

Steps in a Preoperational Child's Perceptions

The preoperational child perceives differences, but it is some time before she can grasp logically that an amount is the same whether it is in one piece or divided into parts. Piaget calls this the *conservation of matter* and says that children at the preoperational stage of development are nonconservers. The child "centers in" on one aspect and is unable to consider such aspects as reversibility. Young children have no problem with the concept of big or small, but most cannot yet arrange objects in a serial order from largest to smallest. Classifying objects presents problems in that the preoperational child has a difficult time remembering the rule that is required to be consistent in grouping objects.

In the preoperational stage the child continues to construct knowledge out of her experiences. She reconstructs her thinking to fit a new level of understanding. For example, she may know that a dog and a cat are "animals." Her concept of animal at this point may be of something that has a furry feel, that runs around, that makes a variety of sounds. Then at the center she meets the large, hard-shelled turtle. It has a very different feel. It moves very slowly or hardly moves at all and does not make any kind of noise. She is told that it is an animal, too. She must "accommodate" these perceptions, changing her concept of "animal" to include this new dimension. She learns by making mistakes.

Speech Assists Learning

The development of speech gives the child a new tool for remembering and storing impressions. The child can begin to learn from the experience of others when it fits into what has already constructed from personal experience. She can understand simple explanations if they are put in terms of what is already known. She asks questions and seeks answers to "why?"

but continues to assimilate and accommodate, to adapt what she perceives or experiences to new patterns of action.

Understanding Numbers

Reaching a level of competence in a field of thought seems to depend on having completed necessary experiences. The young child may know how to count to ten or twenty, but she may have constructed a true concept of numbers only as far as four. She has internalized her knowledge only that far. Most 3-year-olds and 4-year-olds are not yet able to match the saying of the number in one-to-one correspondence with pointing to each object in a group that is being counted even though they can successfully say the numbers in counting. Understanding what the numbers actually represent is a long slow process that will take time and experience to master.

Piaget outlines four stages in how the child and the adult construct and reconstruct knowledge. This text deals with the first two of these stages: *sensorimotor development* and *preoperational thought*, which encompass about the first seven years of a child's growth and development. *Concrete operations* and *formal operations* are the other two stages in Piaget's theory of how the intellect unfolds.

Young Children Are Active Learners

Piaget's work has value for teachers because he has shown "the fundamental connection between action and learning and the extent to which true learning is dependent on the activity of the learner. 'Activity' is no fanciful addition to the curriculum to give children more enjoyment (although it does) but the necessary element in all learning. Piaget has helped us to understand what we mean by activity, by revealing its role in the genesis of mental structure and therefore of 'mind itself.'" (Brearley & Hitchfield, 1966)

Concerns Regarding Cognitive Development

We believe that young children must be active in any learning process. It is a process of constructing knowledge based on incomplete experience, making errors, and constantly reconstructing with added experience. Piaget calls this constructing knowledge from within. It is a thinking, not a passive, process. Neither is it a matter of giving correct answers. As Piaget has pointed out, knowledge does not develop from "all wrong" to "perfectly correct." Teachers should take into careful account the knowledge children have constructed from previous experience.

As teachers we may know that a certain procedure is useless or even harmful to a child's learning, but we may be required to use such a procedure by pressure from politicians and a public interested in what they consider correct answers or the call to go "back to basics." We need a rigorous scientific, explanatory theory about how to construct knowledge in order to explain and defend our practices. Constance Kamii (1985), whose early childhood research focuses on learning, feels that educators are now in a position to make a statement about teaching as a profession using a scientific basis and specific objectives. Our goal in the future should be to "prepare people who have the knowledge and the originality to build a far better world than we ever imagined." The teaching profession itself should be engaged in a reconstruction of teacher education. Children deserve this effort from the teaching profession.

Basic Tenets in Early Childhood Education

The overall goal of early childhood education is to provide a child with an environment that will promote optimum development at a time when growth is rapid and the child is most vulnerable to inappropriate experiences and deprivation of appropriate experiences.

All aspects of growth are considered in a quality program: physical development; the development of social relationships, or the capacity to enjoy and get along with other people; emotional development, including confidence in and understanding of oneself as a person and growth in ability to express thoughts and feelings and to manage impulses; and intellectual, or cognitive development, including language competency, nourished through guidance in a stimulating environment.

Some of the basic assumptions and tenets underlying a program:

1. Every child is an individual
2. The genetic constitution and the environment together determine the course of development of an individual
3. Intelligence develops as it is nurtured
4. All aspects of development are interrelated
5. Growth means change
6. Growth takes place in orderly sequences or stages
7. Play is an important avenue for learning and for enjoyment
8. Attitudes and feelings are important in learning and in healthy personality growth
9. Behavior is motivated by extrinsic and intrinsic factors
10. Understanding, responsible guidance is necessary
11. The development of a young child suffers if there are deficiencies
12. A healthy environment is the right of every child

1. Every child is an individual with an unique rate and style of learning and growing, patterns of approach to situations, innate capacities. Genes and experiences make every child unique. A child's family experience is different from that of any other individual, with its strengths and its vulnerabilities. Some of these differences may seem "deficiencies" if aspects fail to fit the expectations of a particular situation. A child from a Spanish-speaking home, for example, may seem "backward" compared with children in an English-speaking group. We need to accept each child as an individual in his own frame of reference and values, without employing any limited or preconceived standards. A child skillful in cooperation with others may not be successful in competitively motivated situations; a child with manual skills may be considered "deficient" in an academic setting. To do justice to individuals we need to broaden our horizons to include respect for the strengths of individuals.

Every child needs experiences adapted to his individual needs, with respect for his individuality. For example, in Chapter 1 Juan waits and watches before entering an activity, while Alicia plunges into new experiences without waiting to watch what others are doing. Guidance for children takes into account their differences and their varying backgrounds of experience.

2. The genetic constitution and the environment together determine the course of development of an individual. We may say that the genes determine the limits of development and the environment determines how much of what is possible will be achieved. A normal person born with the capacity for developing speech does not learn to talk unless he is with people who use speech. The kind of language learned and how well that language is used depend upon the speech he hears.

A normal person is also born capable of a range of feelings. What he will feel, his biases and prejudices, his loves and hates, grow out of his experiences. In the center, we influence the direction and the extent of development in the children we teach.

3. Intelligence develops as it is nurtured. Cognitive development depends on adequate and appropriate physical, mental, and social nourishment supplied by the home, the school, and the community. The "critical period" for nurturing intelligence seems to occur early in life. The individual needs a range of suitable experiences and opportunities to act on these. He needs to feel secure and valued by people who also value learning.

Intelligence is not just a single entity, although it is part of the whole child. There are varieties of intelligence. Among the children we meet in the center, there will be some who have been nurtured intellectually and others whose nurturing has been inadequate. Making up for deficiencies may be an important part of the program for many children. Play, both the informal and the more organized types, is significant to intellectual growth.

4. All aspects of development are interrelated—physical, social, emotional, and intellectual. The child develops as a whole, with each area influencing and being influenced by what takes place in other areas.

*All aspects of develop-
ment are interrelated:
cognitive practice,
shared experience
with work, and lan-
guage skills.
Migrant Head Start,
Chico, California*

In planning a program, we consider the child as a whole, not just one aspect of development. For example, in planning equipment for developing
body skills we are also interested in how these build self-confidence and
increase opportunities for contacts with other children and add to the
child's knowledge of physical forces.

5. Growth means change. Changes take place not only in a child's
height and weight but also in his capacities and characteristics. Changes
often are accompanied by conflicts or disturbances until a new equilibrium
is reached. During these periods of change the child is likely to respond
well to appropriate guidance or help. Our role is to influence growth
changes in positive, healthy directions, physically and psychologically.

Children's behavior changes as circumstances change. When a child is
tired or ill, for example, he behaves differently than when he is rested or
well. When we say that a child is "dull" or "lazy" or "selfish," we are reporting judgmentally only what we interpret at the moment. In time, or under
different circumstances, or in someone else's view, the child might be de-

scribed very differently. We change, too. With more experience and more understanding, we perceive different meanings in children's behavior.

6. Growth takes place in orderly sequences or stages, with each successive stage depending on the outcome of previous stages. No stage can be skipped without handicapping the child. Rates of growth differ for individual children, but the sequence of stages is uniform. A child sits up before walking; he scribbles before writing. Age gives only a general indication of what to expect because children differ in the time they take to complete a stage, but not in the order in which the change takes place. For example, most 6-year-olds and some 5-year-olds can tie shoe laces, but very few 4-year-olds can.

Having time to complete each stage, with a variety of experiences appropriate to the stage, enables the child to leave one behind and move on, fully prepared for the next. Pressure or "nudging" to move on before a stage is completed inhibits sound growth, just as blocking the forward movement does.

In every stage certain aspects of development are "critical," most vulnerable to deprivation, and most likely to benefit from optimum conditions. Severe protein deficiency in the diet of the 1- to 2-year-old child, for example, will impair physical and intellectual development, but the same deficiency may have only a temporary effect on an adult. Between six months and twelve months, the infant is at a critical stage in the development of a feeling of trust. He is more disturbed by an extended separation from the mother at this point than he will be later.

7. Play is an important avenue for learning and for enjoyment. Children learn through active experiencing in play, using all of their senses; through doing things to and with materials; through representing concepts in play, rehearsing roles, and thus clarifying them. Children test out, explore, discover, store up impressions, classify, organize, assimilate, and accommodate to experience.

Discovery and mastery are part of play, as are sustained attention and effort, the characteristics needed in learning. Play calls for initiative, imagination, purposefulness. It calls for motor skills and for social skills. Beginnings of symbolic thinking occur in play. Play with other children is considered essential for healthy personality development. The values of play are increased by informed guidance and a wide variety of appropriate materials and equipment, as well as space and uninterrupted time.

8. Attitudes and feelings are important in learning and in healthy personality growth. The child's attitude toward self is an important factor in her learning and mental health. If she is to develop well, a child needs to feel that the significant people around her like her and believe she is an able person. A positive self-concept enables the child to use her capacities well.

Becoming aware of one's own feelings and those of others and finding avenues for expressing feelings in constructive and creative ways are

Play is an important avenue for learning and enjoyment in motor skills and taking turns.
Santa Monica College, Child Development Center, Santa Monica, California

other important aspects of learning. They can be fostered by understanding guidance. Self-control results from being aware of one's impulses and having avenues into which negative impulses can be channeled. Imagination and its expression in art and language and its use in problem solving can also be stimulated through a favorable environment.

9. Behavior is motivated by extrinsic and intrinsic factors. Extrinsic forms of motivation consist in giving attention, approval, or reward for a specific behavior or in withholding attention, in disapproval, or in punishment to reinforce behavior or to make it more likely that the child will repeat or desist behaving in some way. The effectiveness of the reinforcement will depend in part on the relationship between the child and the one who reinforces. Personal relationships play a large part in motivation.

Intrinsic motivation comes from inside the child, arising out of her curiosity, drive for competence, and experiences in finding satisfactions or in not finding them. In using a hammer or a saw, for example, the child may persist because she has an end in mind or because she finds satisfaction out of the increasing competency she feels in doing the job.

Timing of reinforcement and type of reinforcement used at any point are important. The child who is doing something because she wants to does not need reinforcement in the same way as a child who is doubtful about herself and her ability. The first child may want to be sure of the teacher's interest; the second child is dependent on the teacher's external reinforcement.

10. Understanding, responsible guidance is necessary if the child is to develop to full potential. In the early years the child needs caregivers who like her, who are generous and warm in feeling, who can assume responsibility for setting limits, who are informed and resourceful in providing a favorable environment, who enjoy learning themselves, who can feel respect for the child as well as for themselves, and who can communicate with children. Learning is personal for the child and is influenced by relationships with those who provide for and guide her. Personality development depends, too, on personal relationships with caregivers who serve as adequate models for the child.

Parents are the child's most important teachers. Teachers need to work with parents. Teachers and parents learn from each other. Early childhood education programs respect the parent-child relationship. Teachers have responsibility for interpreting programs to parents as well as understanding the expectations of the parents about the education of their own child.

11. The development of a young child suffers if there are deficiencies in nutrition and health care; in attention and loving care; in opportunities for play which nourishes social, emotional, and intellectual growth; and in richness and variety of appropriate firsthand experiences. Some apparent "deficiencies" are only differences in experience, such as those in language competency in which English is not the first language. When real deficiencies do occur, they can best be compensated for by going back and supplying what was lacking in earlier stages, giving the chance for sound growth to take place, rather than pushing a child on to the next stage.

12. A healthy environment is the right of every child and the first responsibility of the community, the state, and the nation. A healthy environment provides adequate health care, food and shelter, and community services including schools and services that offer support to families. It includes a family life free from excessive burdens of economic insecurity, deprivation, and discrimination, and with adequate provision for satisfaction and stimulation for all members of the family. A child development center is one of these community services. It contributes to the child and the family at a critical time.

Chapter Overview

In this chapter we have explored three major theories about how children develop, Freud focusing on the psychological needs and drives, Erikson focusing on psychosocial development, and Piaget focusing on the intellectual unfolding of the child's mind. The basic tenets, as outlined here, provide a fundamental philosophy of early childhood education. Let us keep in mind that Piaget's preoperational child is the same child Erikson describes in the stage of developing the sense of initiative outweighing the sense of doubt and guilt. She is the child Freud describes in the process of discovering and accepting her sex and moving toward an identification with the parent of the same sex. She is the child we meet in centers for 2-, 3-, and 4-year-olds.

Projects

1. Prepare a written or oral report on Sigmund Freud, Erik Erikson, or Jean Piaget.

To prepare your report include:

A. The bibliographical source for your report.

B. A brief description of the historical period in which the theorist lived or lives, and the forces that influenced him.

C. Some highlights of the person's life.

D. Two or three major ideas and/or contributions made by the person.

E. A closing statement or reaction to the person's ideas.

2. Using the format of the basic tenets in this chapter, write a statement of your personal philosophy of early childhood education.

For Your Further Reading

Braun, S. J., & Edwards, E. P. (1972). *History and theory of early childhood education.* Worthington, OH: Charles A. Jones. A well-known book that traces evolution of early childhood education in western civilization. Discusses theorists from Plato to Piaget.

Cleverley, J., & Phillips, D. C. (1986). *Visions of childhood: Influential models from Locke to Spock.* New York: Teachers College Press: Analyzes the theories of education of the most influential theorists in early education, including Freud, Piaget, Marx, and Dewey.

Elkind, D. (1967). Piaget and Montessori. *Harvard Education Review.* 37(4), 535–545. Discusses three original ideas about child behavior that ``Piaget and Montessori arrived at independently but share in common.'' Both of these innovators reflect great empathy for the child in their observations and subsequent teachings, providing bases for teaching strategies.

Erikson, E. (1963). *Childhood and society.* New York: W. W. Norton. A book with an indelible impact on thinking about eight stages of psychosocial development and emerging ego qualities from each stage. Every early childhood teacher needs to be familiar with Erikson's developmental tasks.

Kamii, C. (1985). Leading primary education toward excellence: Beyond worksheets and drill. *Young Children,* 40(6), 3–9. Makes a strong argument against pressure to produce higher test scores and use of workbook drills, which are erroneously based on ``what did not work before'' in education. Defines constructivist teaching and learning and pleads for reform in teacher education to include Piaget's theory.

Peterson, R., & Felton-Collins, V. (1986). *The Piaget handbook for teachers and parents: Children in the age of discovery, preschool-3rd grade.* New York: Teachers College Press. Presents Piagetian theory through many real-life examples, which makes the understanding of children's cognitive development understandable to students, teachers, and parents.

Schweinhart, L. J., Weikart, D. P., & Larner,

M. B. (1986). Consequences of three preschool curriculum models through age 15. *Early Childhood Research Quarterly, 1*(1), 15–45. Examines the fifteen-year outcomes for children who at ages 3 and 4 were in quality programs using curriculum from the High/Scope, Distar, and traditional nursery school models. Curriculum models made important differences in aspects such as delinquency, family relations, and jobs.

Tribe, C. (Comp.) (1982). *Profile of three theories: Erikson, Maslow, Piaget.* Dubuque, IA: Kendall/Hunt Publishing Company. Simple presentations of the three theorists, in outline form. Helpful for beginning students in understanding the essence of each theoretical approach.

PART THREE

Guidance in Experiences Common to Everyone

Helping Children Adjust to New Experiences

Fun to go to the store, (*boy, 4 years*)

In this chapter you may learn about yourself as you consider:

▶ How children respond to new situations in a variety of ways
▶ How we give support in new situations to children and parents: Steps in beginning a group situation
▶ How we support children: Steps in meeting many other new experiences.

CRITERION: A process has been developed for orienting children and parents to the center which may include a pre-enrollment visit, parent orientation meeting, or gradual introduction of children to the center. The transition from home to center can be a difficult one and must be planned. There are numerous methods of orientation for both children and parents. The criterion does not require that one particular method be implemented but it does require that an orientation for both children and parents be provided. (NAEYC, 1991a. *Accreditation criteria* . . . , p. 26)

CRITERION: Staff are flexible enough to change planned or routine activities according to the needs or interests of children or to cope with changes . . . or other situations which affect routines without unduly alarming children. (NAEYC, 1991a. *Accreditation criteria* . . . , p. 24)

We All Know What It is Like to Be in a New Situation

We suggested earlier that one of the first steps at the center was to accept the feelings we had because the situation was new for us. We may have tried to defend ourselves against the inadequacy we felt because we were new. Some of our defenses may have handicapped us in learning. We needed to learn to feel comfortable about being new in the situation. We felt competent as we mastered the new situation.

Children face feelings similar to those of the adult when meeting new situations, such as entering a center or accepting the approaches of unfamiliar people. They may try to defend themselves against uncertainty and fear by inappropriate behavior, rejecting the strange people, crying, or withdrawing. Because we know what it is like to feel new and strange, we may find it easier to understand the behavior. We may be better able to help as they try to cope with a new experience.

Each Child Has Characteristic Patterns of Responding to New Experiences

For the child, as for the adult, new experiences call forth defenses, tendencies to retreat, or to explore. What the child or the adult does will depend on his or her individual makeup and experiences.

What kind of adjustment is a "good adjustment"? Fear is obviously very limiting to any learning. Desirable behavior includes the capacity to pick out familiar elements in the situation, the ability to relate the known to the unknown, and a readiness to accept differences.

Each Child Brings the Past to a New Experience

What lies behind differences among children in their adjustment to the same situation? We can be certain that the same situation does not seem the same to all children. Individual differences in responsiveness to stimulation are present at birth or soon after. One infant may be more disturbed than another by a sudden, loud noise or a difference in the intensity of light. Later, new people, places, and events will have different meanings for each child depending on the sensitivity that is part of individual temperament.

Each child brings his own experiences to a new situation. These experiences have prepared him differently. It does not matter if we do not know specifically what these experiences have been as long as we accept the child's behavior as having some meaning. Being taken to a new place may mean pleasant possibilities to one child and disturbing possibilities to another.

The many daily experiences a child has are of more importance in influencing adjustments than any single disturbing event. It is desirable, therefore, for the child's daily life to contribute to feelings of security and adequacy. We are not likely to gain strength by being hurt; we are certain to acquire scars.

A child's "defense" in a new situation may be to begin each day alone, observing. Valley College, Campus Child Development Center, Los Angeles

A child who is forced into making adjustments for which he is not ready is less prepared for future experiences. He may try to conceal his feelings, as is sometimes the case with the child whose mother declares, "He doesn't mind being left anywhere." The strain this child suffers may be evident only in indirect ways, as in a loss of creativity, an inability to play, greater dependence, or increased negativity. Too many experiences of feeling strange or frightened add up to a total that may be disastrous for sound adaptation.

Entering a center means that the child must leave the familiar home and depend on adults other than parents. It means finding a place for himself in a group of other children about the same age. There are new toys, different toilet arrangements, new rules. He meets a variety of responses from other children, some of them apparently unreasonable responses. The child must trust the new teachers to understand him and keep him safe.

Children's feelings of confidence in themselves will be strengthened if they can make adjustments successfully. For many children, attending a

Some children need solitude for a while when they are in a new situation. Private spaces help. Valley College, Campus Child Development Center, Los Angeles

center confirms a feeling of trust in others and in themselves that has already been fostered in home and neighborhood. For other children, entering a center gives them a valuable opportunity to work through earlier fears and take steps in building feelings of confidence and trust. They feel competent as they master the new situation with a sense of "I can do it!"

What makes a child ready for group experience? Why do some children enter eagerly and others hold back? What can we do to reduce the difficulties to manageable proportions for each child?

Children who are cared for by loving people feel safe, secure, and friendly. There are many reasons why one child may not feel as safe as another. Frequent moves, long or extended separations from parents, or many changes in caregivers may interfere with a child's feelings of security. Separations coming at sensitive times in development are likely to make it harder for children to develop a sense of trust.

It is important to reduce the stresses of entering a center. The experience should add to, rather than threaten, the child's feeling of trust and security. Safeguards include avoiding starting the child in school shortly after major family changes such as a new baby, a family move, or the mother starting to work. It is better, when possible, for the child to enter the group well before such changes occur. If it is necessary for a child to enter a center under unfavorable circumstances, he must be given more time and support by the staff in making the adjustment. Parents can help prepare the child by talking about the center and describing what it may be like to enter a group.

Entering a Center is a Significant Experience for a Young Child

The transitional process from home to school confronts a child with three milestones: a new environment, a new teacher, and new children. As a child enters a center, she faces two tasks: First, she must feel secure enough to meet the new situation, rich with possibilities for learning and social contacts but full of the unknown. The second and perhaps more significant task is one inherent in growth itself. The child must resolve the conflict inevitably felt when entering something new and strange. The conflict to be resolved in this case is lessening the close dependency on parents or other caregivers in order to live in the world of the center. In going forward she must leave behind a measure of dependence in order to take a step toward independence. She must resist the desire to cling to the relationship with the parent, which has been the main source of satisfaction and security until now. She must act on the wish to separate herself and be ready to explore new relationships that may also prove to be sources of satisfying experiences.

For children who have found their sources of satisfaction in a number of other people, such as children from large extended families, there may be less conflict. These children have already found security in a variety of relationships and have less need to hold on to dependency. There are children, too, who have not known closeness to any one person and who do not appear to need much support. They have needs that are likely to come out later in other ways. For the child from a small family with mainly positive relationships there may still be some degree of conflict to resolve as she enters a group and leaves the family for even a short time.

Each Child Has Strengths and Vulnerabilities

In meeting these tasks, each child brings different strengths and vulnerabilities. A child's inborn temperament will affect the intensity of responses. One child may respond quickly, delighting in the new environment, while another responds more slowly and cautiously. Differences in cultural patterns may mean important differences in how children approach new situations. All children will come with their own expectations about the center and with their own special interests.

Relationships with the Caregiver and Teacher Are Important

Relationships with the mother or primary caregiver will probably have the most effect on the way the child proceeds toward independence. If the parents have helped the child develop a sense of trust, they will have satisfied in large measure the pressing dependency needs of infancy. The child is now free to move on to develop new relationships that will meet new needs.

The teacher plays a significant role because of the help she gives the parents as well as the child. They both face a new kind of experience. The teacher can support the parents' desire to leave the child free to separate as well as support the child's desire to move toward independence. Many parents will feel successful in their parenting if the child achieves these tasks comfortably.

It is not simple for a teacher to move with certainty because each child and each parent will differ in what he or she brings to the situation and expects from it. In addition, the teacher may be handicapped by set patterns in the way school entrance is handled, or by personal fears, or the need to control, or the way his or her own dependency needs have been met. As the teacher develops in sensitivity and skill, satisfaction will come in helping children and parents work through the problems of separation. It is here that the center can make one of its most significant contributions, one that will be of value in future separation experiences.

The Process of Giving Support to the Child and Parents

How does the teacher proceed in helping the child face separation and an experience with groups of other children? How does he or she help parents face separation from the child? We will suggest a series of steps that may be taken to help a child enter a group successfully.

We recognize that, in many situations, the steps will necessarily be condensed or changed. When parents' employment, transportation, or cultural reluctance prevents them from spending time at the center during the child's first week, teachers must devise flexible ways to meet the child's needs. The steps suggested here recognize the need for such alternatives. Perhaps teachers can arrange parent-teacher meetings in small groups, teachers' visits to homes, permission to call a student parent from classes or a parent from the nearby business to the on-site center. Attending the center for an hour with mother, father, other relative, or caregiver may be the best that can be managed as a first step.

The child must have some trusted person staying with him for at least part of the first day. No young child should ever be left at a center without any preparation. Ideally the first day should be shorter than a usual session. Attending for only part of the time for the first week may help the child adjust more easily and save time in the end.

Step 1: A Parent-Teacher Meeting

A conference between the teacher and parents or caregiver is a necessary first step. The teacher explains the policies of the center and makes clear the matter of fees, health regulations, hours, and steps in admission. In

A child new to a center may need to be cuddled on a teacher's lap at times.
First Step Nursery School, Santa Monica, California

funded programs for low-income parents the teacher may determine the family's eligibility at this conference. She tells them something of the program and their part in it. She encourages questions and discovers some of the parents' expectations. At this first meeting parents are asked to fill out a developmental history and home information form including the child's interests and skills. An important part of the conference will be a discussion of the steps to be taken in enrolling the child. It is essential for the parents to understand that someone well known to the child must be there for the child to turn to or be on call during the first days at the center.

The teacher will point out that the child needs to feel that his parents are glad to have him go to the center and that the center is a good place to be. The teacher may suggest ways the parents can talk to the child about what to expect. If parents are clear about such matters as toileting, eating, and napping and the few rules that apply to the center, they are more likely to be able to help the child understand what the center is like. Eventually the child can feel, not that the parent is leaving him, but that the parent is letting him do the leaving.

Step 2: A Visit to the Center

The next step is to give the child some concept of what the new experience is like through a visit to the center. The child needs a picture in his mind when hearing the word "center" or "school" or "day care." He needs to be anticipating what lies ahead in as realistic a way as possible. The first visit will be short, perhaps an hour, with the parent or caregiver staying with the child. The teacher will decide with the parent the most convenient time of day for the child to visit, for it is important to give consideration to the family's schedule. In some centers this may be a special "pre-session" or center visit just for new children. For example, in campus child-care centers a pre-session visit can be arranged before the student parents' classes begin. Every child should visit the center with a parent or main caregiver before entering.

Children will differ in the way they use this visit. If other children are present, the child can watch, possibly make contacts with others, and participate if ready. A few may make contacts while others will watch. Some may return to familiar play materials that they enjoy, seeming to pay little attention to other children around them. Some may dart from one area to another, barely engaging in any activity for even a brief time. Whether visiting with other children or not, children become familiar with aspects of the physical setup. They feel more at ease when they know the center has toilets for children, that food will be available, that there is a special place for their personal belongings. They get an idea about climbing or the housekeeping corner, areas where they can explore or where they feel secure.

The teachers have an opportunity to become acquainted and to take a step in understanding what each child's needs and interests are likely to be. They will add to their understanding of each child by observing each one in this new situation. Seeing a child's interest in something, a teacher may place this material within reach. If he watches another child painting at the easel, the teacher may walk nearer and say a few words about the paint and the colors. He or she may encourage him to try it but does not push him into activity. The child may find the book corner, and together they may share a brief story. If he is more interested in watching what other children are doing, the teacher may comment on what is happening, mentioning the children's names. Some children may be made anxious by too much attention from the teacher until they feel more at home. The teacher can limit help to a reassuring smile and an encouraging nod, and be ready with more active help later.

When a new child visits an ongoing group, he holds a special place as a visitor. Other children have a chance to become aware of the "new" child. They may become aware of "newness" and the fact that there are steps in proceeding from being "new" to feeling familiar and at home in a group. A wise teacher uses the opportunity to support growth in individual children already in the group and may say, "Remember when you were new and visited?" She may recall some special incident and add, "Now you know where things go and what we do. You have friends." In this way she points out and strengthens the movement this child has made toward independence and greater security.

There should be opportunities to develop a relationship with a teacher. Through observation and interactions with the child during the first visit, the teacher makes an effort to establish a relationship. The teachers' task is to help the child discover a teacher as a person who is there to be depended on and who cares for and about him. It is important for the teacher to spend time with the child or to be available. The teacher reminds the child of her name and that she will be there every day. The child needs a person he trusts and to whom he can turn, if he is to make the adjustment in a constructive way.

In yet a different arrangement for a visit to the center, the teacher may plan to bring perhaps four or six children together for an hour with their parents. Another group can come at another hour to go through the same process, and in a few days several such groups may come together to become a larger group entering the program. In this way, each child begins in a small group first and is with familiar children when entering the larger group. Some programs, including Head Start, provide home visits when a child begins school.

A clear understanding about the length of time the child is to stay helps in the adjustment. The wise teacher will have a clear understanding with the parent about how long the child will stay on the first day. More than a half-day spent in an environment that demands so much responsiveness may tire a child who has never been in a group situation. Some children can, of course, stay longer, and many children will wish to do so; but there are advantages in setting a definite length of time for the first visit.

During these first days it is important for the child that a parent come without bringing other children in the family, if possible. Entering school is a significant event in the life of the child and parents. If the parents are free to give the child all their attention, they may reaffirm for their child a sense of being valued. This attention may be especially important if other children at home, other family events, or work have been taking much of the parents' time. Setting aside this special time together at the center helps the child to realize that the parent cares at this moment of beginning a new experience.

The parents' feelings influence the child's adjustment. The way the parents feel about sending the child to school will have a profound effect on how the child adjusts. If parents feel reluctant, unsure, or overanxious, they hinder the child's ability to meet the new situation and grow more independent. Both parents and teacher may not realize how completely a child senses what they may be feeling.

There are many reasons why parents may feel ambivalent. They inevitably feel some conflict between wanting to hold on to the child, to prolong dependence, and at the same time wanting the child to be outgoing and independent. If the mother is returning to work after being at home with her child, she has a feeling that she might miss some important accomplishments like a baby's first step. She might even feel competitive with the teacher, if for example a toddler were to call the teacher "Mama." The teacher needs to be ready with reassurance to strengthen the parents' acceptance of what the center offers and confidence in the child's readiness.

Parents who are employed may not be able to take an entire day away from their jobs. In this case the teacher has a special responsibility for meeting the child's need for closeness and reassurance. Much will depend on the child's own capacity to cope with change and how well the parents have prepared the child.

During the first visit the accompanying parent can help the child by saying, "I will be right here. I am staying with you. I won't leave." It is helpful to find a chair where the parent can see and be seen easily by the child and stay there, but not push him away with words like, "Why don't you go play with the blocks or with the girl over there?" It is the teacher's, not the parent's, responsibility to encourage the child to move from the parent. The parent expresses pleasure in whatever he has done on his own. If he is hurt or rebuffed by another child, the parent gives the comfort needed, but also accepts the incident as part of the reality of existence with others, trying to set an example for the child. The parent should show confidence in the child's ability not to be upset just as she will not be unnecessarily upset herself.

The teacher finds ways to help both the child and the parent. The teacher is the one to take the responsibility for helping the child to participate when ready. The teacher is alert to the need to give support in the efforts the child makes to move toward independence. When he does leave his parent, the teacher stays nearby to give the protection needed at first. By staying nearby, the teacher is demonstrating to both child and parent that she is there to look after him. This makes it easier for the parent to permit the child to participate.

Parents respond in different ways. Some parents find the time spent at the center interesting; others are restless. If the parents are interested, they will find it easy to respond to the child's request to come and look at things; but they also need to make the child feel that it is his center. They look at what the child shows them, but avoid trying to point out many things. The teacher, meanwhile, looks for ways to help the parents appreciate the significance of what is occurring. When possible, the teacher can sit with the parent, pointing out and explaining what is happening. Questions can come up informally, like, "How do you discipline the children here?" or, "I've been wondering about her speech; do you think it is coming along all right?" Some people have had little background for understanding the development of children. They may not know what to look for in the center. Their questions may surprise the teacher. Parents are almost sure to be interested if they are helped to see the significance of the children's play. The teacher and the center may open up possibilities to parents for growth in understanding that will be valuable through the years.

Step 3: Attendance with Gradual Increase in Separation

The next step for the child is to begin the process of having the parent leave her or of having the child be able to do the leaving. The point to keep in mind is that her trust in the teacher and interest in the program itself are the sources of support that will enable the child to be successful in staying at the center with confidence and a sense of achievement.

This next step may be for the child to attend the center for part of several sessions with the parent gradually leaving for longer periods each day. Perhaps the child must begin regular attendance immediately, but the parent can remain in the morning for a half-hour and return a bit early at the end of the session. The center's way of helping with this step must meet the needs of individual parents and children and not be a set routine for everyone.

Some children are helped to make the adjustment if they bring something from home to keep with them at first. While it may not be the usual

A new child finds a safe place and a comforting thumb to observe group time. Valley College, Campus Child Development Center, Los Angeles

practice of the school to encourage children to bring their own toys, it may be desirable during the initial adjustment period. It is unlikely that the child will be able to "share" this possession if she is depending on it for support, and she should be protected against having to do so. A simple explanation by the teacher such as, "Mary is new here and needs to keep her bear. Later, when she knows us better, she may let you play with it, too," will serve to deepen understanding by both children. It is important for a new child to know where the special place is for a sweater, change of clothing, blanket, or bag of comforting possessions. She needs to know that the teacher will protect her belongings.

Some parents overestimate their children's capacity to adjust. One cannot depend on a parent's assurance that "She'll be all right without me; I've left her lots of times." This may be a child who stands quietly and withdrawn, the very child who needs the parent most because she can not express her insecurities. She may already have had too many experiences of being left. Entering the group experience with the parent or caregiver may mean the chance to overcome some of the past, to reassure herself in the present situation that this trusted person really will stay. This may be the feeling that she needs to be free to explore and enjoy the new setting.

The tendency on the part of some parents to expect too much of their children in the ease of adjustment probably indicates how universally adults fail to realize what is involved in learning and growing. We are not accustomed to observing behavior for clues to feelings. We look for what we want to see and not for what is really there.

It is usually necessary for the teacher to take an active part in helping the child separate from the parent. It is not enough to wait for parent and child to sound totally ready to make the separation. Some sensitive teachers, concerned about forcing the issue, lose sight of growth potential in the child. They fail to pick up the clues she offers for her readiness to move toward independence, provided she has some help. Prolonging dependency in the new situation may interfere with growth toward independence, which is the task at hand developmentally. The skillful teacher will help the child reach the goal in the shortest time possible.

The parent helps with her understanding. As soon as the parent and teacher agree that the child is feeling comfortable at the center, the teacher can help the parent prepare the child by saying something like, "Today I am going to do some errands while you are here. I will be gone a little while, and when I get back, I'll see what you are doing." If her response is, "I don't want you to go," the parent may answer, "I won't go for a while, not until I know you are ready. I will tell you and I'll only be gone a very little while." The parent never leaves without telling the child.

The teacher can prepare the child for what she already expects by saying quietly, "Your mother is going now, Aleta. She will be back very soon," or "at lunch time," or "after work," or whatever is truthful. With the teacher there the parent can say good-bye to the child and leave for the agreed-upon time. In a day-care situation, the first shortened separation may be for part of a day or by the parent returning early at the day's end. In a half-day program the parent may be able to return in an hour. If the child's readiness has been estimated correctly, the teacher will be able to help the child with her sense of loss. One child may stand at a window, waving and watching the parent leave. Another needs to be encouraged into a favorite activity. One teacher walked a sobbing girl about the center after her mother left for the first time. As they came by the dress-up corner the child exclaimed through her tears, "Bracelets! Bracelets!" and broke into a smile. She was ready to play, adorning her arms with many bracelets.

When the parent returns, she will speak to the child and stay for a while, giving the child time to show her the toys and activities, perhaps to climb for one more time, before they leave together. The parent is showing the child the pattern that she will follow. She goes, but she comes back. The child is discovering the satisfaction of feeling more and more comfortable about being able to stay at the center and in this way looks forward to returning.

Some children may cling to one parent but more easily allow the other to leave. Arranging for a grandparent to bring the child and stay for a time may help the handling of the separation. A Head Start child may say good-by when the bus or van comes to the home. In all such arrangements it is most important that the trust-building steps be followed. The goal is for the child to feel secure as the separation is made.

If after some weeks a child seems to be finding the separation very difficult, the teacher may consider arranging to visit the home. A brief home visit from the teacher may bridge the distance between center and home in the child's eyes and help build confidence.

At this step in the separation process, parents may want information about what to expect as well as the teacher's reassurance. The teacher may prepare parents by reminding them, as one center does, "Your own child's adjustment will be unique, and individual, not quite like anyone else's. What is 'normal' falls in a wide range from no apparent stress to dramatic behavior problems. Adjustments and readjustments may crop up for months, not just for the first week. At home or at the center your child may cry or cling when you leave, observe for a long time, play near but not with other children, regress with thumb or 'blanky,' need a special hat or 'costume,' or refuse at school to eat, use the toilet, remove his jacket, or wear a name tag. Or he may smile and wave good-bye happily!" (Child Development Laboratory, 1991. *Parent Information Handbook.* Chico, CA: California State University, Chico)

Parents may be anxious about their part in the adjustment process. It is important to talk with the teacher about any concerns the parent may have.

Step 4: Full-Time Attendance

The 4- or 5-year-old child will probably be able to feel safe at the center more quickly than the 3-year-old. The older child has had more experience and more time to develop confidence. Few 2- or 3-year-old children reach this step of comfortable full-time attendance in less than a week. Some take much longer.

Sleep disturbances, toilet accidents, and increased negativity may result from trying to move too fast for the child. Good adjustment requires time, and relapses are less likely if the adjustment has not been either hurried or unduly prolonged.

Sometimes the struggle to separate may be extended because a parent finds it hard to leave the child, rather than the other way around. The parent may lack confidence in herself, the child, or the center. It is important that the teacher be aware of the point at which the separating has "bogged down" and that the child is ready to stay. The teacher needs to take positive steps in this case to resolve the conflict by talking with the parent, indicating that it appears the child is ready to stay without the parent. The teacher will listen to the parent's feelings about the process and ask what behaviors the parent is seeing at home. They plan together how this next step may be accomplished. The teacher acts with kind firmness and confidence in carrying through the plan. She may need to hold the child in her arms when the mother goes, giving her time to cry, putting into words the fact that she knows she wants her parent and that she will be back. Then the teacher will help the child find a place in the center, sitting near her, watching with her, possibly finding a familiar toy.

Mentioning teachers' or children's names and describing what they are doing may help. One child exclaimed, "Too many teachers!" The understanding teacher replied with outstretched hand, "Oh, too many teachers you don't know. Let's walk around and learn their names." This proved to be just what was needed for the child to relax and enter into the day's activities.

It may happen that a child in the process of separation will revert to an earlier level of dependency—wanting a parent again. A parent may question whether the child was disturbed by some event at school, or the teacher may ask if anything occurred at home. It is important that the child's real needs be accepted and met. The teacher may need to be available again to spend time with the child, or the parent may need to be willing to stay at the center for a short time. Usually it does not take long for her to become independent. Again, the teacher helps by accepting her and by giving all the support possible to her desire to be more self-sufficient.

We have described steps that are suited to the needs of a child in entering a group, whether all day or part time, center or family day care, Head Start or preschool. The optimum procedures are not always possible. But in every case both parent and teacher should recognize the importance this experience holds for a child. They should give the child as much support as possible as in coping with the new experience.

If the step of moving toward independence and away from dependence on the parent is taken so that it does not produce more anxiety than the child can manage easily, she is free to enjoy and profit from the group experience. The child gains in self-confidence and feelings of mastery.

Different Children Make the Adjustment in Unique Ways

Here are some examples of the ways in which some children make the adjustment to entering the new group experience.

An Infant Starts at a Small Family DayCare Home   Mark accompanied his parents to work until he was 6 months old. Now his parents needed to locate care for him. He had been a smiling, sociable baby, but he had begun to show signs of anxiety about strangers, new faces and places. His mother visited several family day-care homes to find a warm, nurturing place for him.

On his first day at Yvette's, Mark soberly looked around. His mother cuddled him on her lap while she explained his routine. She planned to stay for an hour so the baby could observe with her. When she left for work, Mark was in Yvette's arms. He leaned back and stared at her. Shortly after his mother left, he began crying. He cried harder and harder until he was in a frantic state. Yvette carried him around with her and tried to comfort him with diaper change, bottle, pacifier—no improvement. Finally she put him in a crib, patted him, and talked soothingly to him. After some deep sobs Mark abruptly fell asleep. He slept for three-and-a-half hours, very unlike his usual one-hour morning nap. His mother arrived at noon, breast fed him, and took him with her.

The next three days were similar. Mark looked around at the new surroundings and the other children, cried hard for a half-hour, tired himself out, and slept until lunchtime. He reluctantly accepted a noon bottle from Yvette. By the end of the week he allowed her to put him down on a blanket near the other children where he could watch them, and he rewarded Yvette with a wide grin. In the next few weeks Mark became more comfortable and slept less. Some days he still cried a little while, but he greeted Yvette each morning with smiles and began to be entertained by the other children. However, he clung to his mother even more insistently in any other new situation.

His parents were surprised at his difficult start in day care. He had previously been around many caring people outside his own home. His parents were confident they had chosen a nurturing caregiver. Perhaps his normal developmental awareness of strangers and new situations at six months caused his strong reactions. He solved his problem by sleeping for long hours. Another infant might have stayed awake and fussily demanded to be held. His parents wondered if Mark would have adjusted more easily if they had started him a month or two earlier. They were pleased and relieved when he finally made the adjustment.

A Toddler Begins a ParentChild Program   Jena and her mother arrived for the first day at the recreation department's "Mommy and Me" program. Parents and toddlers met twice a week for one-and-a-half hours in the community center for a planned program with a trained teacher. Jena had always been a clinging, fearful child; her mother hoped this program would help her become comfortable with others. Since parents remain with the children for the entire session, Jena would not have to separate from her.

For four sessions Jena sat on her mother's lap or stood next to her, arm wrapped around mother's leg. As other toddlers and mothers sang songs and did finger plays, tried the sensory materials, played with toys together, or tentatively explored other children, Jena whimpered, "Up, up," insisting on being carried. Her mother consulted the teacher about whether they should withdraw. She said Jena cried every morning, not wanting to come. "It's so hard. It isn't worth it. The other children are enjoying it," she sighed. The teacher reassured her that Jena was observing the others and probably would warm up soon.

One day Jena turned on her mother's lap to face the teacher as she sang "Open Shut Them" with the group. Jena barely opened and closed her fingers and "gave a little shake." Later at home her mother overheard her singing little parts of the song.

Jena's continued growth from that beginning was slow but steady. When the eight sessions ended, she had progressed to playing with toys on the floor next to her mother. One day Jena and another child had a wordless tussle over a doll. Jena's mother and the teacher were delighted that she started to assert herself with another child.

Her mother enrolled Jena and herself for another series of the playgroup sessions. After several talks with the teacher the mother became more accepting of her child's slow-to-warm temperament. She stopped thinking something was "wrong" and became comfortable with giving Jena much time to make transitions to new situations.

Integrating a Preschooler with Special Needs   Zachary, just 4 years old, arrived for his first visit with his father at the campus children's center, which was not in session this day. He had an unusual visual handicap in that he could see in part of his field of vision but not at all in several visual areas. The family was financially eligible for the center, but the parents and teacher needed to determine whether Zachary's special needs could be met by being enrolled there. He had been at home with his mother who now also would be in school. The parents hoped to enroll him five mornings a week.

As his father and the teacher walked around the center with Zachary, he bumped into a door and a cabinet. He quickly recovered by peering at the offending object with his head tilted, while his father anxiously described what it was. As they arrived in the playground, Zachary broke loose from his father's hand to run to the climbing equipment. In his clumsy eagerness to climb up a slanted board, he slipped off and bumped his head, crying. His father hugged him, saying, "That's okay, little guy. Now let's find something to play with besides climbing." "NO!" Zachary shouted and ran back to try a ladder.

For the remainder of the hour's visit he insisted on trying every piece of climbing apparatus. He slipped a number of times. The father's worry showed plainly as he kept trying to divert his son to another activity. The teacher demonstrated to Zachary how to use his hands to feel the ladder or climbing box or steps, but the father seemed not to notice. Zachary refused an invitation to have a snack and would not go back into the classroom to see the little toilets or his cubby space. Soon it was time to go. The father said, "I don't think this will work for Zachary. It doesn't seem to be safe for him. I'd be worrying about him all the time."

The teacher asked the father if they could try another visit the next day during the group presession with six children and parents. She suggested that it would be important that the mother attend, too. She reassured him that his son made a fine start. He looked dubious. After they left, she admitted to another teacher that while she believed Zachary could learn to manage in the center, she was concerned that he would need a teacher all to himself for some time, a "guardian angel." The center had many daily changes in adult helpers; could this work for Zachary?

His mother proved to be much more at ease with his unskilled fascination with climbing and his frequent falls. It was the father who was overanxious. Zachary was enrolled. Both parents arranged to spend extra hours in the center as volunteers, and the center assigned aides to help Zachary learn to get around, using his sense of touch as well as his residual vision. Six weeks later he looked very competent. Both parents smilingly told the teacher, "We learned so much from watching him here and seeing how you deal with him. We just didn't realize how much he can do for himself. We all have grown."

A Child Who Makes a Smooth, Uneventful Entrance   Annie, at age 3, had been familiar with the center since she was born because her two older brothers attended the program. She announced cheerfully to her grandmother as they approached for their visit, "You don't need to stay. I'm going to paint a picture and eat lunch." Her grandmother explained how it was going to work: a visit today at which grandmother would stay, next week staying most of the day, mother or father would pick her up a bit early after work, and so forth.

Annie did indeed enthusiastically paint at the easel, eat a snack, use the toilet, climb, ride a trike, and play near two other girls in the housekeeping corner. She asked the teacher, "What's your name again?" When it was time to leave after an hour, she refused. "You go away. I stay." Grandmother looked at the teacher helplessly. The teacher began to explain to Annie, who burst into tears. "No, no, I stay here!" The teacher picked her up to carry her to the door, saying, "You don't want to leave; you like it here. You can come back Monday. I'll see you when you come back."

The next week Annie ran in the door, calling out, "I came back!" Grandmother stayed for an hour over Annie's protests. When she left, Annie waved good-bye through the fence. Annie's father arranged to leave work early at the end of the day to visit and have Annie show him her favorite activities before they left for home.

Her entrance into the program appeared unusually smooth. It is of interest to note that a month later, when Annie missed a week because of illness, she had a somewhat difficult time returning. "I don't like naps," she proclaimed. "I stay with Grandma." The teacher and grandparent arranged to repeat the usual beginning steps, which Annie hadn't seemed to need earlier. Soon Annie was running in the door in the morning with her accustomed smile and a hug for the teacher.

Here was a child who could handle new situations with ease. She could put into words what she wanted and how she felt. The careful teamwork between teacher, grandparent, and parents added to the secure feelings she already had about herself.

New Experiences Need to be Handled Thoughtfully

Entering a group situation like a center is a big adjustment, but it is not the only new situation the child may face. New people, places, and events, wherever they are encountered, need to be handled thoughtfully. They may build up confidence or decrease it. When children go on walks they may see unfamiliar or even frightening things. A trip to the fire station may mean strange noises and unfamiliar people as well as the sight of the huge fire engine itself. One child may be able to watch the fire engine comfortably while holding an adult's hand. Another may need the safety of being held in the adult's arms. The arrival of a cow and calf at the center may be observed fearfully from a distance by some of the children. One gradually approaches the large animals, while another leaves to go indoors. Children need the reassurance of knowing that they can leave the situation whenever they want with the support of a teacher.

The necessity of keeping each new experience within the level of the child's ability to participate without anxiety means that at least two adults must go on any field trip to all but the most familiar places. On a trip to a farm, for example, a child may show signs of fear about going inside a barn. An adult will need to stay outside with him, accepting the fact that he is not ready to go inside. They can have a pleasant time together outside the barn. Later the child may want to go inside. With the fear accepted and with time to proceed at his own rate, the child will gain self-confidence as he succeeds in handling the fear. If he is pushed into entering while still afraid, he may only learn to conceal fear or to depend on adult support for all frightening situations. If anything startling happens while he is in the barn, such as a cow mooing, he may panic because of the feelings of fear released by the sudden noise. The child may become more afraid and lose confidence.

Children are continually meeting novel situations that must be assimilated into their previous experiences. For one child it could be an ambulance demonstration in the center's playground; for another it could be finding a dead bird while taking a walk. In one center a woman came for four days in a row to demonstrate Hawaiian hula dancing. The first day no child approached her, but a small group solemnly watched from far away. By the fourth day several children danced freely with the visitor, laughing and talking with her comfortably.

It is important that teachers respect children's reluctance and fears and help them to cope gradually. Teachers show respect for fears by words showing they understand: "The fire engine is so big; it scares you" or, "You were startled when the cow mooed; you want me to hold you."

The Adult's Feelings Influence the Child's

The attitude of the adult influences the child. In any emergency it is imperative that the adult meet the situation calmly for the sake of the child. A group of 4-year-olds was visiting the fire station one day when the alarm sounded. One of the firefighters directed them calmly, "You all stand right against the wall and watch this fire engine go out." His composure steadied everyone. In a matter of seconds all were against the wall, and the truck pulled out before the line of wide-eyed children. It was the best trip to the fire station they had ever had. The reports of bombings in World War II showed that children reacted in the way the adults around them reacted. If children were with calm people, they were not likely to be upset even when the situations were terrifying. Children became hysterical for much less cause when they were with hysterical people.

In planning any experience for children the teacher must first be familiar with it herself. If the event is to be a field trip, she should have made the trip so that she can prepare the children for what they may expect. She will also prepare the adult at the field-trip site for what young children are likely to be interested in. If the event is to be a visitor to the center, she will prepare both the children and the visitor in the same way. It helps children to go over the planned event in words so that they have a framework into which to fit the situation. The use of pictures, books, and even videotaping of the field trip or visitor serve as preparation and review. Another way children "review" experiences is through opportunities for dramatic play. These activities will help to place the new experiences among "known" things.

It is important to talk to the volunteers, parents, and community helpers about what will help children enjoy the trip. Not all adults understand the needs of young children. For example, on a visit to the center by a police officer in his patrol car, he may startle children by turning on the siren unexpectedly. An observant firefighter asked, "How old are these children? Oh, they're about the right age to talk about 'stop, drop, and roll.'" He was able to adapt his explanation to the understanding of his young audience. Ambulance personnel are likely to understand the importance of overcoming children's fears and of seeing them as helpers. They tend to be appropriate in their explanations and warm and friendly to the children. People who work with animals can usually be counted on to be gentle and quiet and to help rather than hinder the children's pleasure in the experience.

We have described new situations that are planned, like a child entering the program, field trips outside and visitors within the familiar setting of the center. In addition, many surprising events occur spontaneously in children's lives that can make them apprehensive. The same principles we have discussed apply for teachers and parents to help children feel supported and confident as they face the unexpected.

A child witnesses an accident on the way to the center; sirens wail as police and ambulance arrive at the scene. A utility truck stops outside the center to tear up the street; the loud jackhammer causes several children to run away and cover their ears. A child arrives one morning with an arm in a cast; others wonder, "Is her arm broken off in there?"

Teachers must act during or after the frightening situation, not having had the opportunity to prepare before the event. Setting up dramatic play opportunities, physical holding or touching while explaining and reassuring, and stating children's real feelings are equally helpful whether the new situation to be faced is planned in advance or happens unexpectedly.

Observing a Child Meet a New Experience Gives Us Insight into His Feelings

Observing the way children explore the world outside the center or new experiences introduced into the center is one way to become aware of the children's behavior patterns. Some children go out to meet the new with confidence. Others are disturbed by the smallest departure from the familiar; this is seen most often in 2- and 3-year olds, who feel most secure when their routine remains consistent. Opportunities offered to children must be adapted to what they are ready to accept. Some adults need assistance in discovering this developmental appropriateness.

When a child stops to watch something, the wise adult will wait. It is a sign that the child is absorbed in the new, attempting to relate it to what he can understand. He may or may not ask questions. Moving on before he is ready will only mean leaving behind unresolved ideas. The habit of exploring the new fully is a sound one and builds feelings of adequacy.

In the first few months of attendance most children need to be limited to the center itself before going out on any trips. There are many new people, objects, places, and events in the school. By watching, questioning, and participating, the child becomes familiar with the new, whether it be an empty wasp's nest brought in by the teacher, a visitor cooking a food of her ethnic background, or a parent sharing his occupation. When a child repeats an activity over and over, he is assimilating it, making it his own. He is adding to his feeling of being an adequate person as he masters the activities in the environment. He feels competent.

CHILDREN HAVE DEFENSES WHEN THEY FEEL UNCERTAIN Children, like adults, have defenses that they are likely to use when they feel uncertain because of the new and strange situation. When children feel unsure of themselves, they may withdraw or retreat from any action and play safe by doing nothing, thus avoiding the risk of doing the wrong thing. This behavior is a type of denial, like turning one's back on something.

Sometimes a child who feels strange and uncomfortable will suddenly begin to bid for attention or act "silly," as though seeking reassurance by surrounding himself with attentive adults. Another child may be aggressive. He may bully others as though to prove to himself that he is big and strong and not as weak and helpless as he fears. These children are doing something active about their problem. They give us an opportunity to help them with it.

CHILDREN NEED HELP WHEN THEY ACT DEFENSIVELY It is not uncommon to see a child who has been frightened by something startling or unusual to turn and hit a companion with almost no provocation. In this way he releases the uncomfortable feeling of fear. The adult's role is to help the child face the feeling and find an acceptable outlet for it. Fear is a less uncomfortable feeling when one is not ashamed of it. It may help if the teacher can say, "Lots of people feel afraid when they hear a big noise like that. It's all right to be afraid." The other child will need some explanation such as, "I think he hit you because he felt afraid. I'm sorry." This kind of handling will help each child to understand why people behave as they do.

Often children will actively reject a situation or some part of it because they feel strange and insecure. In a laboratory school or a parent cooperative the number of adults present may overwhelm a new child. He may meet a friendly advance from an adult with the words, "Go 'way, I don't like you." It is like getting in the first blow when you are expecting the worst. For the child's sake it is important to recognize the real feeling behind these words, to understand its meaning as, "Go 'way, I don't know you." It usually is better to retreat until the child has had more time to make an adjustment. It sometimes helps for a teacher to put the child's feelings into words.

It is important to be able to identify children's defenses and to help them make adjustments that are really appropriate to the situation or to help them discover how to release their disturbed feelings in acceptable ways. It is equally important to see that children have experiences in which they feel adequate, so that they will have less need for defenses. When adults can do these things, they offer real help to the child.

Chapter Overview

This chapter has provided a great deal of information concerning a child's entry into a center, a family day-care home, and a parent-toddler class and mainstreaming a child with special needs into the classroom. Steps have been outlined for enabling a child to make a smooth entry into the world away from home. Emphasis has been placed on the sensitive handling of new beginnings for both child and parent in order to promote a healthy emotional adjustment. Support ideas have been provided to enable the parent to deal with the variety of emotions that are a part of this separation.

Projects

1. Locate a place in your community where you can observe young children facing a new situation: a playground, fair, petting zoo or making a first entrance into a center or school. Observe specific behaviors of several children that give clues to their underlying feelings. Observe what adults say and do in response. What are your conclusions about unhelpful responses and helpful ones?
2. Observe a parent-child-director interview where the child is going to begin a center

experience. What does the director say or do to help the parent and child feel comfortable? Describe the child's behavior in this new experience.

3. Interview a director about a child's entrance procedures to the center. What are the steps in the process? What role does the parent play?

For Your Further Reading

Balaban, N. (1985). *Starting school: From separation to independence.* New York: Teachers College Press, Columbia University. This book for professionals also appears in a version for parents. Very comprehensive and helpful to both groups.

Bowlby, J. (1975). *Separation anxiety: A critical review of the literature.* New York: Child Welfare League of America. Relates observations of children to traditional theory, proposing that separation anxiety, grief and mourning, and defense are phases of a single process.

Bowlby, J. (1982). Attachment and loss: Retrospects and prospect. *American Journal of Orthopsychiatry, 52*(4), 664–678. A summary of Bowlby's important contribution to our understanding of attachment and separation.

Dunn, J. (1977). *Distress and comfort.* The developing child series. Cambridge, MA: Harvard University Press. Readable, helpful book on the topic, referring to research, and giving practical suggestions. Raises questions of temperamental differences, importance of early exchange between parent and infant, and cultural differences.

Gottschall, S. (1989). Understanding and accepting separation feelings. *Young Children 44*(6), 11–16. Full of examples of teachers helping children act out anger and anxiety through symbolic play. Includes tips on sensory reassurance, use of stories and books, and working with parents.

Jervis, K. (Ed.). (1985). *A guide to separation: Strategies for helping two to four-year-olds.* Los Angeles: Edna Reiss Memorial Trust. Begins with John Bowlby's theory explaining separation anxiety. Goes on to discuss the separation and attachment process as children start to group programs out of the home. Warm, readable suggestions for parents and teachers.

Jewett, C. L. (1982). *Helping children cope with separation and loss.* Harvard, MA: Harvard Common Press. Outstanding book dealing with stages of coping with losses of many kinds: divorce, moving, death, hospitalization, military service, and finally, letting go and moving on.

Kleckner, K. A., & Engel, R. E. (1988). A child begins school: Relieving anxiety with books. *Young Children, 43*(5), 14–18. In addition to the "gradual start" process advocated in this chapter, this article proposes additional help to the young child through advance preparation using books. Annotated bibliography of children's books that deal with separation.

Ziegler, P. (1985). Saying good-bye to preschool. *Young Children 40*(3), 11–15. Adults prepare children for beginning attendance but may not see the importance when a child leaves day care or preschool during the year or to enter kindergarten. Suggestions for involving parents and preparing for school-leaving by means of curriculum, books, and planning together. Useful list of children's books.

Helping Children in Routine Situations

Street (*girl, 3 years, 6 months*)

In this chapter you will become more at ease as you help children become comfortable with:

▶ Toileting
▶ Mealtimes
▶ Rest and sleep
▶ Transition times

CRITERION: Routine tasks are incorporated into the program as a means of furthering children's learning, self-help, and social skills. Routines such as diapering, toileting, eating, dressing, and sleeping are handled in a relaxed, reassuring, and individualized manner based on developmental needs. Staff plan with parents to make toileting, feeding, and the development of other independent skills a positive experience for children. Provision is made for children who are early risers and for children who do not nap.

. . . Young children gain a sense of their own identity and self-worth from the way in which their bodily needs are responded to and satisfied. As much as possible, personal care routines should be determined by the individual child's needs and rhythms. (NAEYC, 1991a. *Accreditation Criteria . . .* , p. 25)

Staff conduct smooth and unregimented transitions between activities. Children are not always required to move from one activity to another as a group. Transitions are planned as a vehicle for learning. (NAEYC, 1991a. *Accreditation Criteria* . . . , p. 24)

We have seen how new experiences can contribute to building confidence and security in a child if we respect the child's level of readiness for the experience. The need to understand the child's readiness for an experience is as important in everyday events as in new or unusual ones. Daily events may contribute to feelings and set patterns in ways that influence growth even more significantly than do the new or the unusual.

Routines such as toileting, resting and sleeping, dressing, washing, and eating are everyday events. They serve as a framework around which the child's day is organized. They satisfy biological needs and are closely tied to her interest in her body. The child gains assurance from knowing there are familiar aspects of the day that can be anticipated and understood. They enable her to get a sense of the passage of time and of order in life. These routines are also part of the procedures or rituals of individual families and their cultures.

Toileting

Some of the best opportunities for teaching young children occur in the toileting situation, for elimination is a significant part of the young child's life. It is one about which feelings are sure to be strong. It offers the possibility for growth in autonomy and mastery.

For the child, toileting is associated with many intimate experiences with parents or caregivers, with their care of her, with efforts to please them, and perhaps with conflicts over their attempts to train her. Toileting may even be related to the child's ideas about good and bad behavior. One mother used to leave her child at school with the admonition, "Be a good girl today." What she really meant by these words was, "Stay dry today." This kind of morality is confusing.

When children enter a center at about 3 years of age, they have probably only recently been through toilet training. They may not have emerged from this period unscathed. Many children now enter group programs at ages of 1 to 2 1/2. Teachers of toddlers must assume more responsibility for the accomplishment of toilet training than teachers of 3- to 5-year olds. We will suggest ways to help teachers foster children's feelings of mastery and comfortable acceptance of the elimination process. A child's behavior tells us something about what the experience means to her, whether at 2 or 4 years old.

TRAINING FOR TOILET CONTROL MAY AFFECT MANY AREAS OF BEHAVIOR   Excessive negativism is one common result of toilet training that is not based on a child's readiness. The child who says "no" to everything and who looks on contacts with adults as possible sources of interference and restriction may have acquired this attitude during toilet training. A most resistant, hostile child in one center had been subjected to an early, rigid period of toilet training. She defied adult suggestions and could not share with children. The quality of the relationship she had with her earnest parents can be pictured in the note her mother sent one day: "Pearl has refused to have a bowel movement for four days."

If the child has been forced to achieve bowel and bladder control before she is ready, her "control" may include the inhibition of spontaneity and creativity in many areas. We see some children who were trained early to stay "dry and clean" and who are now unable to use play materials in creative ways. They can not enjoy play in mud and wet sand, use finger paint, or savor the ordinary joys of childhood and the social contacts that occur in such sensory play.

According to pediatrician T. Berry Brazelton (1984), this kind of early pressure for toilet control has decreased dramatically in his thirty years of practice. However, some parents still feel pressure from so-called experts to train early with reward or punishment and may feel like failures if the child is not successful.

The child whose parents have treated the acquiring of toilet control in the same way as any other developmental step, such as walking or talking, is likely to be a comfortable child. After the child has started walking, she may show an interest in the toilet and in imitating the behavior of the

Toileting is a significant part of the young child's life.
Jean Berlfein

people she observes there. Parents encourage her efforts and make it easy for her to use the toilet in the way they do. They can show the same satisfactions in her success here as they do in other developmental accomplishments. They should be ready to accept any resistance as a sign that the child is not ready yet and drop their efforts for a time. They should not make an issue of learning toilet control any more than they would of learning in other areas. When there is no undue pressure, the child usually begins to take on the patterns of adults some time between the ages of eighteen and thirty months.

ADULT ATTITUDES AND STANDARDS MAY COMPLICATE THE TOILETING PROCESS Parents may give a great deal of anxious attention to the child's elimination. They may undertake training early, in a determined way, to prove themselves good parents. They may impose standards about toilet behavior before the child can understand them. Separation of the sexes, demands for privacy, and disapproval of many kinds of toilet behavior have little meaning to the young child. These standards may add feelings of fear or guilt. It becomes hard for healthy attitudes to develop under these circumstances.

Parents should examine their own feelings of pressure from society for early toilet training, according to Brazelton. "Success in the toilet area should be the child's own autonomous achievement, not success by the parent in choosing the right technique to 'train' him. Unless he feels it is something he wants to achieve, parental efforts will always be seen as pressure." (Brazelton, 1984, p. 37)

CHILDREN GAIN FROM INFORMED HANDLING OF TOILETING AT THE CENTER The important thing for us to remember as teachers caring for young children is that the children come from homes with many different beliefs and practices about toilet control. Some children will have healthy, matter-of-fact attitudes with no doubts about their ability to handle the situation competently. They will expect to meet friendly, accepting adults and will not be disturbed about toilet accidents. Other children will be tentative and insecure. They may be upset by failures to control their elimination. Some will use the toilet situation to express their anxieties or defiance. Some will not be able to use the toilet at the center until they feel comfortable there. They must be helped according to their different needs. All of them will gain from informed handling of toileting at the center.

If the handling is to be sound, the children must meet adults in the center who are themselves comfortable in the situation. To feel comfortable is not always easy, for many of us have had experiences in our past that have included being ashamed or embarrassed about the subject of toileting. Being with children and adults who have matter-of-fact attitudes will often help us free ourselves from conflicts generated by our own experiences.

The interest that children show in toileting can be seen in the frequency with which it appears in their dramatic play. Again and again they will act out with their dolls what is for them the drama of the toilet. This play is a desirable way of expressing any conflicts they may feel and making them seem more manageable. The center designed to meet children's needs will provide bathroom fixtures including toilets among the doll house furniture and dolls.

WHAT THE ADULT DOES ABOUT TOILET ACCIDENTS IS SIGNIFICANT   Toilet accidents are likely to be common in the child's first weeks at the center and may indicate the strain felt in the new situation. The child is reassured when she realizes that she does not need to fear having an unplanned movement. Confidence is gained when friendly, accepting adults help her if a urine or bowel accident occurs.

Another child may react to the new situation by withholding urine and feces. She may be unable to use the toilet for some time. This behavior may be an indication of feelings. It is hardly necessary to say that no pressure should be put on a child to use the toilet until she is ready.

Sometimes a child who has been attending the center and successfully using the toilet will suddenly have a series of accidents. These accidents may be a sign of emotional strain or impending illness and should be regarded as a significant symptom. It is helpful for the teacher to talk with the child's parent to try to discover any possible sources for the changed behavior. We should not increase the strain by disapproval.

It cannot be emphasized too strongly that adults' matter-of-fact attitudes about toilet accidents is exceedingly important. If a child knows that accidents are not condemned, she feels much freer and safer. She can proceed to acquire control at her own rate and to feel pride in achievement.

While we can show pleasure in successes, we must not value success too highly. If success is overemphasized, the child may also overemphasize the occasional, inevitable failures. Under no condition should a child be made to feel disapproval or shame for her toileting behaviors. It is the child's feelings about success or failure that must be considered, not the parents' or society's.

TOILET PROCEDURES THAT ARE CONSTRUCTIVE   The physical setup plays a part in building positive feelings. If the toilet room is a pleasant, light, and attractive place, the child is more likely to feel comfortable there. Small toilets are desirable because they make it easier for the child to manage independently. If they can not be obtained, a step can be placed in front of the toilet and a hinged seat provided to make the opening smaller. A door to the room or in front of each toilet can be a handicap. It may interfere with the children's self-help efforts and the teacher's ease of supervision.

Interest in the plumbing usually rises to a peak around the age of 4. Observation of the toilet while it is being flushed, with discussions about water pipes, sewer systems, and destination of the products of elimination, are of absorbing interest. These discussions have value. Attempts to hurry children out of the situation or to discourage curiosity will make it harder for them to develop a healthy attitude. The wise adult will be prepared to spend time and feel comfortable in the toileting area with children.

Children from about the age of 3 can be expected to handle their clothing independently at the toilet if they are properly dressed. Some parents need to be urged to dress children in self-help clothing such as pants with elastic tops. Boys can be reminded to raise the toilet seat before urinating. Children can be expected to flush the toilet. The teacher might say, "Now it will be fresh for the next child." When an occasional child refuses to flush it, we can safely assume, as we can with any refusal, that there is some meaning behind it. Children are sometimes frightened by the noise and movement of water in a flushing toilet. They will be reassured in time as they watch others. Their refusal should be respected.

Hand washing should be expected after toileting. "Children must be educated by staff members concerning hand washing procedures, use of running water, soap, rubbing, and single use of disposable towels." (NAEYC, 1991a. *Accreditation Criteria . . .* , p. 55) It is a desirable habit, and a child usually enjoys the washing process. Hand washing is necessary before food preparation or eating. Children pattern their judgments after what they see. Often their hands look clean to them. If the teacher washes her hands

"Smooth and unregimented transitions" include handwashing before food preparation or eating. Migrant Head Start, Chico, California

and tells the children it is important to wash hands after going to the toilet as well as before eating, they are likely to follow her example.

In the center boys and girls use the toilets freely together with an adult present. Children usually are very accepting of this arrangement. They value their ability to manage toileting independently more than they are concerned about who else is using a toilet. If an occasional child seems surprised or uncomfortable, the teacher can explain, "Here all children use the toilet together." Adults sometimes ask, "But won't this practice make it harder for a child when she has to learn a different custom?" The teacher may reply that children are able to accept the custom that is appropriate for the time and place. Toileting on a picnic differs from that at home. Boys accompany their mothers into public restrooms when they are young but learn to make a distinction when they are older. Patterns of behavior differ with age, gender, and society. The child learns to accept differences.

ACCEPTANCE OF CHILDREN'S INTEREST IN EACH OTHER PROMOTES HEALTHY ATTITUDES   Sound handling of toileting includes a matter-of-fact attitude in situations in which children show an interest in each other at the toilet. Children need a chance to satisfy their curiosity about bodies and processes. The center offers casual opportunities for this healthy curiosity. Girls will be interested in the fact that boys have penises and stand when they urinate. Boys may wonder if girls used to have penises. A girl who has no male family member at home may want to watch boys urinate until her interest is satisfied. It may help if the teacher verbalizes in some way, such as, "Bill has a penis. He stands up at the toilet. Boys stand up, and girls sit down."

Psychiatrists tell us an important factor in sexual adjustment is the acceptance of one's gender. In the toileting situation a boy may feel important because he possesses a penis. Sometimes a girl will try to imitate the boy by attempting to stand—with not very satisfactory results! She learns from her own actions, and no comment is needed. Girls may need help in feeling that being a girl is desirable. The teacher may remark, "Mothers sit down, too" or, "Boys have a penis, and girls have a vagina."

ESTABLISHING TOILETING SCHEDULE   When a very young child enters the center, the teacher soon discovers how frequently she needs to go to the toilet by talking with her mother and by observing her behavior. The teacher can establish a schedule to fit the child's rhythm by taking most of the responsibility at first, saying, "Time to go to the toilet now," and attempting to time these interruptions to a shift in activity. In this way the teacher will avoid building resistance. If the teacher is pleasant and friendly, the child will welcome this opportunity for adult contact and attention. A new child may adjust more easily if the same adult helps her each time. She feels secure more quickly and may begin to come to the same teacher when she needs to go to the toilet.

As a next step the teacher might ask the child, "Do you need to go to the toilet now?" rather than simply stating that it is time to go. This question begins to shift responsibility to the child. If the number of toilet accidents shows that she is not ready to take this much responsibility, the teacher can go back to the earlier stage. Many factors change a child's rhythm, such as cold weather, excitement, or drinking more liquids than usual.

A set schedule for going to the toilet has the disadvantage of not meeting individual needs or changing needs. Nevertheless it is possible to have a framework within which to expect toileting, and this routine simplifies management. If we remember that the goal of any toileting schedule is to help the child go to the toilet when she needs to, and not when the teacher wants her to, we can devise a schedule that will be flexible. Younger children will need reminders at the normal transition times in the day, such as snack time, lunchtime, and before and after rest time. The more mature children, those who have taken responsibility for their toileting, will follow their own schedule; but the teacher will find it wise to suggest toileting before lunch or before taking a walk.

EXAMPLES OF PROBLEMS IN THE TOILET SITUATION Let us consider some specific problems that may arise.

Duncan, a 4 1/2-year-old, was a joy to have in class. He enjoyed all that the center had to offer. Duncan's mother spent a great deal of time in Chicago on business, and much of Duncan's life was spent with a housekeeper. Duncan flew to Chicago one weekend with the housekeeper to visit his mother and on the return trip was told by the housekeeper, "If you're not a good boy, I'll flush you down the toilet." Duncan came back to school and refused to use the toilet and instead had soiled pants every day. He would use the toilet at home but only if he didn't have to flush it. His mother returned, discovered what had happened and had the housekeeper apologize and tell Duncan, "I would never really do that." However, the damage was done and Duncan had a very real fear of the toilet and the flushing sound. The teacher felt that Duncan, perhaps, could be helped by a story about Jose, a *persona doll*[1], who was frightened when the gardener mowed the lawn. It turns out that Jose was afraid of the noise the lawn mower makes. The teacher stopped at this point and asked the other children if they were ever afraid of any sounds. The vacuum was mentioned and one child volunteered that he got scared when his dad yelled. The teacher said through Jose, the persona doll, that Jose sometimes is scared when the toilet flushes. The other children agreed that they were, too. She suggested they form a delegation to help Jose get over being scared of toilet sounds. Later, after group time when the children had become busy in other parts of the room, the teacher approached the table where Duncan was sitting and asked if anyone wanted to be part of the delegation to help Jose. One child eagerly said yes and another said, "Me, too," and Duncan excitedly said he wanted to be a part of the delegation. The teacher offered the doll to Duncan and he clutched it to his

---

[1]Persona dolls were created by Kay Taus at Seeds University Elementary School, UCLA. She uses dolls to help children connect to the stories that she tells. For further description see Derman-Sparks, L., and the A.B.C. Task Force (1989), p. 16.

chest. "Which toilet would you think Jose would be afraid of?" she asked. Duncan spoke up, "That one," pointing to one of the three small toilets. They looked in the toilet together, and the teacher asked, "What would fit down the toilet?" They all agreed that Jose was too big and they further agreed that they wouldn't fit, either. The teacher flushed the toilet several times, and the delegation with Jose watched closely. Later the teacher and Duncan came back with the doll, and she was able to get Duncan to flush the toilet using Jose's hand. She talked confidently about what happened. This was all it took for Duncan to get over this scary experience. Needless to say, his mother was truly grateful.

 Maria, a 4 1/2-year-old, was a delightfully imaginative child. She loved music and often played and sang at the piano or danced when music was played. She was friendly with other children and enjoyed homemaking play in the dramatic play area. She was curious about many things, played actively outdoors, and enjoyed expeditions outside the center. However, she responded to adults in a very negative way. She resisted suggestions and was likely to become self-conscious and show off. At the table she seemed to concentrate on behavior she knew would not be acceptable, like putting her fingers in the food, throwing it, or running away from the table. She found rest difficult. She was wet several times a day and consistently refused to go to the toilet. She always changed her underpants immediately, leaving the wet ones on the floor in the toilet room. Her mother reported that she had been toilet trained early and then suddenly began wetting again within the last year. They had "tried everything" to make her stop, even shaming her and making her wear diapers. At first she would stay wet, but they had succeeded in impressing on her how "dirty" that was, and now she wouldn't stay in her wet clothes a minute.

It was easy to see where Maria's negativism came from. It seemed likely that she was an able child trying to assert herself. The methods of training and disciplining that her parents had used with her more docile older brother had only increased her resistance. She was defiantly insisting on being independent.

Since Maria was out to defeat "bossing," it seemed evident that pressure for conforming to standards, no matter how desirable the standards, needed to be reduced before she could be expected to change. The whole matter of toileting was dropped at the center. No comment was made on her need to use the toilet or her wet clothes. It was hard for her parents to accept the idea that she must be convinced that she could be wet if she chose before she could accept adult standards. However, they were cooperative and intelligent; somewhat reluctantly they followed the teachers' suggestion of saying nothing, perhaps because they had tried everything else. It was several months before Maria began using the toilet at the center. It might have happened sooner if her parents could have been more wholehearted in turning the responsibility completely over to her. Whenever she felt dominated, Maria would revert to a series of wet pants. It was the area in which she felt she could win in the battle to assert her independence. When left to accept things at her own rate, she was an unusually social and capable child who thoroughly enjoyed the activities available.

A child does not always express resistance to pressure as directly as Maria. In a less friendly and understanding home a child may have to conceal his feelings of resentment.

Jethro was a little over 4 years old. His mother reported that she had felt that "the sooner I started him on regular toilet habits, the better." She began when he was 6 months old, and he responded "perfectly." Now, however, Jethro often sat passively instead of playing. He chewed on his blanket, sucked his finger, and was very inactive. His mother said, "He doesn't enjoy anything that I can see."

This child did not feel strong enough to protest in a direct way as Maria was able to do. With many other strains in his life added to the pressure to be clean, his position was far less favorable. He was dry but not free. Spontaneity and the ability to play were sacrificed to conformity.

Mealtime

Eating is also important in the development of feelings and behavior. When children enter a group they come with a long past as far as eating goes. They have had many experiences with food. These experiences have been satisfying in varying degrees. The child's attitude may consequently be favorable or unfavorable toward the meal situation.

ADULT BEHAVIOR AND ATTITUDES INFLUENCE THE CHILD From the beginning the child is affected by the way adults act and feel about his eating. The infant's hunger pangs are an individual matter and usually do not fit into a regular schedule. They are acute and distressing to him. If they are not relieved by food, he is miserable and helpless to meet his own needs. Even being awakened to be fed constitutes an intrusion that may be annoying to a baby. The more experienced parents are in caring for children, the more likely they are to trust their child and feed him when he indicates he is hungry. This experience may account in part for the easier adjustment that is frequently seen in later children in families.

Today most mothers leave the hospital one or two days after the birth of a child. The newborn infant may have been put to the breast soon after birth, and the mother may have been able to feed the infant according to his needs. She was also able to meet the infant's need for close bodily contacts and her own need to know the infant and care for him.

BASIC ATTITUDES APPEAR IN THE EATING SITUATION From the child's behavior in the meal situation at the center we can get clues to his feelings and to the kind of adjustment he is making. Appetite is a sensitive index to emotional adjustment. Maria, who resisted efforts at toileting, also defied every convention at the table. This behavior was part of her effort to assert her right to be independent. It is important, not only from the standpoint of nutrition but also from that of personality development, that the child's behavior at mealtime be managed with understanding.

EATING WITH OTHERS The ordinary, healthy child enjoys eating. Unless unpleasant experiences have been connected with food, the child enters

Foods familiar in a child's culture, such as tortillas, rice, beans, and fruit, help him to feel comfortable.
Valley College, Campus Child Development Center, Los Angeles

the group ready to enjoy mealtime. He usually has a conservative attitude about food and prefers those foods already known. He has his likes and dislikes and probably has not done much eating with groups outside the family. At first a new child may be distracted from eating by having other children around. The implements, the dishes, even the chairs are likely to be different from those used at home. He will probably meet quite a few unfamiliar foods. The expectations of the adults may be different, too. There is a great deal to adapt to in the new eating situation.

GOALS FOR MEALTIME AND SOME WAYS TO SUPPORT THE CHILD'S LEARNING   Just as there are goals for learning in other opportunities provided, there are goals for mealtime. We want the child to continue to enjoy food, to learn to like a variety of nutritionally desirable foods, and to practice acceptable ways of eating and behaving at the table. Achieving these goals will take time. Pushing or forcing a child is almost sure to lead to problems.

ENJOYMENT OF FOOD   The teacher should start by making sure that the child enjoys the meal. Parents can indicate what the child likes and dislikes, and the staff can try to make sure that some familiar, well-liked foods are served. This is especially important with children in an ethnically diverse group, for whom foods of their own cultures mean security. Familiar foods may make the difference between a child's eating or not eating adequately at the center.

There are individual differences, too, in the amount of food that children eat. Some children eat much more than others. The same child will eat different amounts on different days or may eat a great deal of one food and very little of another. It is a good thing if we avoid any preconceived notions about what or how much a child needs; then we will find it easier to accept the fluctuations in appetite common to all children.

The best practice is to serve very small helpings and leave the children free to take as much more as they want. A child is likely to eat more when served small helpings rather than large ones.

Children should have the right to refuse a food and to make choices, but the main meal should precede dessert, and at least some of the main meal should be eaten before the dessert. Drinking milk should be encouraged, though teachers should be alert to possible milk-related allergies. With a good mealtime atmosphere, a skillful teacher helps the child live up to her expectations most of the time.

TABLE MANNERS   Finger foods, such as toast sticks and carrot sticks, should be served often. Green beans, for example, are often more popular than peas because of the ease with which they can be eaten as finger food. We are primarily interested in nutrition and only secondarily interested in table manners at this point, although table manners are not neglected. The teacher models good manners and gives approval to the child who says, "Please," or uses utensils properly.

A child will usually continue to use fingers at times long after beginning to use a spoon. He may revert to an earlier level when he is tired or not feeling well. If we believe that it is important to enjoy food, we will not interfere. Gradually he will depend more and more on a spoon and fork. The kind of manners acquired in the end will depend on the example set by the adults around him and not on how much pressure they have exerted to meet their standards. On the other hand, a child's interest in food will be adversely affected by their pressure. We need confidence that the child will acquire the eating patterns of those around him when ready, just as he acquires their language.

MEALTIME PRESSURES   If we move too fast in teaching manners, we may interfere with the child's appetite. Being "messy" with food normally precedes being neat in eating. We remember a 3-year-old who ate like an adult, but who ate practically nothing at the table. She ate between meals when she did not have to conform to the very high standards expected of her at home and the pressures to eat more than she wanted.

Introduce new foods gradually and do not expect the child to learn to like too many foods at one time. Extending food horizons too rapidly does not bring good results in most cases. As he watches others enjoy different kinds of foods, the child will be ready to try them.

How a child feels influences appetite. There are important emotional factors and emotional consequences to what we do in the eating situation. A secure child may be able to accept a variety of new foods more easily than a less secure child who may need to cling longer to familiar foods, as in other things, to gain reassurance. The emotional balance of the insecure child may be threatened if pushed into eating too many new foods.

FEELINGS AND APPETITE   What the child eats often will depend on who is offering the food. Infants seem to be sensitive to the likes and dislikes of the person feeding them. They also are sensitive to other feelings in the person feeding them. A baby make take a bottle well or accept cereal when the person who gives it is relaxed and enjoys the feeding. He may refuse the same food if it is offered by someone who dislikes the "messiness" of eating and is tense and uncertain in her relationship with the infant. Some children eat very little when there is a new teacher at the table but will taste new foods or eat everything on their plates when the familiar teacher is there with whom they feel safe.

Because feelings and appetite are so closely related, we must recognize that any emotional disturbance will affect the appetite. We all probably have had the experience of losing interest in food for a time because of upset emotional balance. The child suffering from anxiety or some other emotion may have little appetite even though he may be physically well. When the emotional problem is solved, appetite will respond to the normal demands of a growing organism.

Attacking the loss of appetite directly may do a great deal of harm. The immediate effect on the child may be vomiting or storing food in the mouth. The more serious and lasting result may be a strong aversion to food. Being made to eat when one is not hungry is a very unpleasant thing. If eating is to be a pleasant experience for the child, we will avoid forcing in any way.

Frequent demands to be fed may be regarded as part of a pattern of dependence. Perhaps the standards for eating behavior have been set too high. Often a child will ask to be fed when he grows tired because of the demand on his coordination that eating makes. As motor skills improve, he will need less help. Sometimes a child asks to be fed because he wants to find out if the adult is willing to help, to be reassured about the ability to get help when wanted.

ENJOYMENT OF EATING   There are many direct and indirect ways to help a child enjoy eating. Bright-colored dishes, flowers, a neatly laid table, all add to the child's pleasure and interest in food. Food that "looks good," with a contrast in color, is important. Chocolate pudding, for example, usually disappears faster than colorless pudding.

Children's tastes differ from adults' in that children usually do not care for very hot or very cold foods. They do not like mixed flavors, either. A casserole or loaf may be unpopular even though each individual flavor in it may be relished separately. They care less for creamed foods or sauces over foods than adults do, which can be a welcome advantage to a busy cook. Strong flavors or unusual textures in a food are usually less acceptable to a child.

Children usually enjoy foods they have helped to prepare. Many centers include cooking activities as a regular part of their curriculum. Children who cut up raw vegetables for a mixed salad and sample the vegetables as they prepare them are more likely to eat the salad for lunch. The use of "real" cooking utensils like knives with cutting boards, graters, food mills, egg beaters or blenders, and even electric skillets and hot plates provide learning as well as enjoyment. Children learn about safety by using unsafe things. It goes without saying that an adult is needed in these preparations.

A child will enjoy eating more when comfortable at the table. He needs a chair that will permit feet to rest on the floor and a table that is the right height. He needs utensils that are easy to grasp. A salad fork rather

Learning takes place in figuring how many more cups are needed in setting the table.
Migrant Head Start,
Chico, California

than a large fork, a spoon with a round bowl, and a small glass add to comfort and pleasure. He also will enjoy clearing away his own dishes. A child is more comfortable if not crowded too close to others at the table. A name card at the table avoids uncertainty about where to sit and helps the teacher plan suitable combinations of children.

EATING WITH OTHERS   Companions can be distracting at times. Eating with other children is fun, and one good eater will influence others; but sociability may need to be kept within bounds by thoughtful spacing and placement of the children. The main business at the table is eating, although conversation has an important place.

The teacher may need to help children by influencing the amount of conversation. In the enthusiasm for communicating with others, a child may forget about eating. If he is a child for whom the teacher estimates that talking has more value at the moment than eating, she may give him time to finish later, as in the case of a shy, withdrawn child who is just "blossoming out" and needs to be encouraged to continue. A different child or a 5-year-old who is already socially skilled may need to be reminded at some point to "eat now and talk later."

TIME LIMITATIONS   Practical time limits inherent in the situation may determine how much time a child can be permitted to spend at the table. Eating should not proceed by a clock. Just as a "set" toilet schedule does not meet the needs of children, so a "set" length of time to eat can not mean the same thing to all children. Some are deliberate, and some are quick. These differences are reflected in the time they take for their meals. Meals are served because we need food, and we enjoy eating. There is no special virtue in eating to get through a meal.

SUGGESTIONS FOR SNACK TIME   Some centers have children taking care of their snack on an individual basis, the goal being to provide children with options to make choices and having a feeling of independence about fixing their snack. A picture reminding children about washing hands hangs near the table. A small table with four chairs is arranged and children understand that if a chair is available they can go in for a snack. Another small table with food laid out and small snack trays for assembling their food is provided. The child prepares the food, puts it on the tray, and takes it to the table, sits down with a friend and eats. Afterwards, the tray is sponged off and napkins discarded. The snack area is open during the "work time," which is about an hour and a half. Occasionally, all the children will have a special snack together.

Rest and Sleep

Rest is something children need but often resist, both at home and at the center. Many children find it hard to settle down for a rest or nap because it comes as an interruption in play. It may hold special difficulties when children are in a group and distract each other. The teacher must feel very sure that rest and sleep are important if this conviction is to be communicated to the children.

Every program should include a rest or quiet period if the children are to avoid getting overtired. In a morning program rest may be before snacks or before lunch. There may be music to listen to or the teacher may read a story. Sometimes a child will need an extra rest. There may be a quiet corner with a cot or pillows in it for use when a child wishes to rest.

In the full-day program a nap will follow lunch. The children may be expected to leave the table, go to the toilet, brush their teeth, and go directly to rest, or they may have a period of quiet play until the whole group is ready for rest. The schedule will depend on the physical arrangements of space and on the number of staff. It is desirable, but not always possible, for children to rest in a room other than the room where they have played actively. Whatever the arrangements, the children should sleep or rest on comfortable cots or mats with a sheet and with adequate covers.

The teacher can set the stage for naps by seeing that the room is in order and everything is ready for rest. By darkening the room she creates an atmosphere that suggests rest. She will move quietly herself and speak in a low voice. She will make her expectations clear—that is, expects the children to come in quietly, remove their shoes and perhaps other garments, and settle down without disturbing others. Her expectations will be reasonable. Each child will be given time to settle down, with perhaps a whispered word to a neighbor. A child may bring a favorite toy, perhaps, or a picture book to help relax. Children who do not fall asleep can rest quietly for at least half an hour. Many children will sleep for about two hours after an active morning.

A rest period usually proceeds most smoothly when the children know the teacher well and have confidence in her. The children are more likely to be restless if the adult is new and strange to them or if there are too many adults present. The new teacher must accept the children's restlessness and not let it disturb her. The experienced teacher will give the children time to settle down in their own ways. Teachers are often tired by the time a rest period comes and may be eager to get the children settled. They may find themselves pushing the children into resting. A more relaxed teacher will be better able to help children make the transition from wakefulness to sleep.

DEPENDENCY NEEDS ARE GREATER AT REST TIME   One can expect the child to make demands on the teacher at rest time because resting is closely associated with experiences with her parents and their care. The child's need for them may come closer to the conscious level. She reverts to earlier dependencies. She may want the teacher's attention or may want to have a blanket straightened just to have some contact. Failing to get attention, she may be noisy, which is another way of getting attention. She may be less able to bear the teacher's disapproval at rest time than at other times.

At rest time children are likely to be jealous when the teacher's attention goes to other children. The teacher must be able to make each child feel that there is enough attention for all. If an individual child needs extra attention, she will make it clear to the others that this child needs particular help today. Children can accept this fact; each child has needed special help at some time. Prolonged back rubbing is not a desirable way to give attention because it interferes with real resting. For some children back rubbing may also cause them to rely on someone helping them to sleep rather than falling asleep on their own. The confident, nurturing person will be most successful in helping the children relax and perhaps sleep.

INDIVIDUAL NEEDS DIFFER Children who fall asleep will probably sleep for varying lengths of time. Upon awakening, each child can get up quietly and put on the clothing removed earlier. Here is an opportunity for children to grow in independence, with the teacher giving only the help that is needed.

After resting, some of the older children who do not take naps have an opportunity for play in small groups before the younger children are up. The teacher may use the period to provide these children with individual learning opportunities and attention. There may be opportunities for trips that are not appropriate for younger children or for games and "work" periods that challenge these children.

The teacher will want to consult with the parents about the child's patterns for resting and for naps at home. Knowing what is customary at home will help adapt the center's schedule to the child's needs or to allow the ritual that helps her rest, as she tries to help develop good patterns for rest and relaxation in the group setting.

We have discussed some of the meanings that toileting, eating, and resting may have for children. We have indicated some of the problems that arise in connection with these routine activities and how the teacher facilitates learning. Now we will look more closely at transition points in the day's program and the meaning these hold for children and for teachers.

Transitions

Many of the difficulties a teacher faces occur during transitions, the times when the teacher interrupts children's activity to direct them into a routine activity. Children may delay, resist, or defy directions. Their behavior is appropriate to their developmental level. They need to assert themselves to test how independent they really are. Everyone finds it hard to leave an enjoyable activity, but it is often necessary to do so.

*Children enjoy helping
with transition activities
such as sweeping sand off
the sidewalk.*
*First Step Nursery School,
Santa Monica, California*

Clean-up time is a transition period that often presents difficulties. Children do not always feel ready to put materials away and help with straightening the playroom. It is a challenge to the teacher to devise ways of helping them feel and act like independent, responsible people at this point. The teacher sets an example with her own actions. She reinforces whatever steps the children take in helping by her attention and approval. As the teacher and children work together, they talk about what they are doing or about the day's events. Sometimes singing together, or making up games will lighten the task. Some children will give more assistance than others, but the teacher makes no comparisons.

Some of the problems that arise in connection with routine activities may be related to the physical surroundings. A crowded locker area creates problems when children are putting on their outdoor clothing. Cots set up in the playroom may make resting more difficult. Changing the physical environment may help. Sometimes changing the schedule itself,

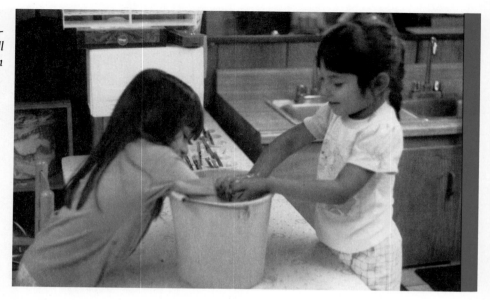

the time or the sequence as well as the physical arrangements, may reduce any difficulties that may have arisen.

Young children are always learning, both from planned and unplanned activities. Transitions between activities should be integrated into the program as learning opportunities. The emphasis is on procedures that will help prevent problems and conflicts. Teachers will plan carefully for transitions. They will give children advance notice of the coming change, and they will make the transitions gradual. They will encourage the children to help during the transition, although any waiting should be short. Lining children up is not a developmentally appropriate practice. Young children are placed in positions that invite classroom management problems when they are made to wait in line.

IT IS IMPORTANT TO RESPECT CHILDREN'S NEEDS TO FEEL INDEPENDENT   Children find great satisfaction in doing a task unaided. Shoes laced in irregular ways, a shirt on backwards and hands only partly clean may be sources of pride to a child because these accomplishments were achieved independently. The drive to be independent, which every healthy child feels, may come up against one of our own needs—the need to help. This need is especially strong when we feel least sure that we can help. By doing things for a child, we try to prove to ourselves that we are in fact competent, able, and needed. The child's dependency on us reassures us that we have a place in the center.

Watch what happens in the locker area. The unaware teacher steps in and expertly buttons the button the child has been fumbling with intently.

She takes the child's coat from its low hook and holds it for him. Then she may be surprised when he runs away instead of putting it on. In the washing area she may put the plug in the sink when he is ready to wash his hands, push up his sleeves, and hand him the soap. She deprives the child of many opportunities to perform tasks that can be done for himself. She is acting out of her own need to help. If she is to handle her feeling about wanting to help, she must be aware of this feeling as well as aware of the values for the child in being independent. Keeping his need in mind, she will plan the situation so that he has a maximum opportunity to do things independently. She will refrain from helping him needlessly.

Chapter Overview

In this chapter we have seen the need for positive experiences centering around toileting, mealtime, rest and sleep time and transitions. Recognition of the child's important need to be autonomous and the likelihood that adults will sometimes offer unnecessary help is evident. Adults must still be ready to accept the fact that at times the child does need to be dependent on them. Erikson makes it clear that no development is completed at any one stage; we carry on to the next stage the uncompleted tasks of earlier stages. A child may ask for unnecessary help because of wanting reassurance that he can still be dependent if he wishes. It may be important to help a child with a coat if he asks us, or to tie his shoe when we know he can. In routines we must be certain only that we do not deprive the child of the opportunity to be independent when ready.

Projects

1. Observe children during the following transition times. Note the different responses shown by the children and discuss the possible inferences.

   A. Toileting
   B. Mealtime
   C. Nap time
   D. Story time
   E. Indoor to outdoor time
   F. Outdoor to indoor time
   G. Clean-up time

2. Observe a transition period and record the behavior of the children. What differences in individual needs do you see? What help does the teacher give? What goals does she seem to have in mind?

For Your Further Reading

Alger, H. A. (1984). Transitions: Alternatives to manipulative management techniques. *Young Children.* 39(6), 16–25. Also in J. F. Brown (Ed.). (1984). *Administering programs for young children.* Washington, DC: National Association for the Education of Young Children. Classroom management at times of arrival, group, clean-up, meals, toileting. Emphasizes learning and appropriate expectations for children.

Brazelton, T. B. (1984). *To listen to a child:*

Understanding the normal problems of growing up. Reading, MA: Addison-Wesley. Warm, helpful discussion of topics like bedwetting, feeding, and sleeping problems.

Cherry, C. (1981). *Think of something quiet: A guide for achieving serenity in early childhood classrooms.* Belmont, CA: David S. Lake Publishers. Chapter about rest times in centers is especially helpful. Deals with helping children under stress and learning relaxation techniques. Teachers will welcome ideas on creating environments that can relax children.

Cooper, T. T., & Ratner, M. (1974). *Many hands cooking: An international cookbook for girls and boys.* New York: Thomas Y. Crowell in cooperation with UNICEF. Attractive, colorfully illustrated recipes from many countries, simple enough for young children to make.

Davidson, J. (1980). Wasted time: The ignored dilemma. *Young Children, 35*(4), 13–21. Also in J. F. Brown (Ed.). (1982). *Curriculum planning for young children,* pp. 196–204. Washington, DC: National Association for the Education of Young Children. Poorly planned transition times may waste as much as an hour each day for children in waiting and boredom. Examines causes; offers ideas for enrichment of routines and transitions.

Ferber, R. (1985). *Solve your child's sleep problems.* New York: Simon and Schuster. Widely admired by parents, this book can also help teachers who find sleep routines with young children difficult. The author is perhaps the foremost researcher in children's sleep problems.

Hendrick, J. (1988). Handling daily routines. In *The whole child* (4th ed.). pp. 48–72. Columbus, OH: Merrill Publishing. This helpful chapter introduces the daily schedule, discusses arrival and departure issues, and outlines nutrition guidelines. Discusses toileting and rest routines.

Rothlein, L. (1989). Nutrition tips revisited: On a daily basis, do we implement what we know? *Young Children 44*(6), 30–36. The charts alone make this article a must-see: guide to nutrients, foods to include daily, healthy snack suggestions, how to introduce new foods to children, guides for food preparation activities with children, children's cookbooks.

Wanamaker, N., Hearn, K. & Richarz, S. (1979). *More than graham crackers: Nutrition education and food preparation with young children.* Washington, DC: National Association for the Education of Young Children. This best-seller is more than a cookbook, though it does contain recipes that children love. Features ideas for teaching children about good food while they cook.

PART FOUR

Understanding Behavior

The Early Childhood Education Movement: Key to Understanding

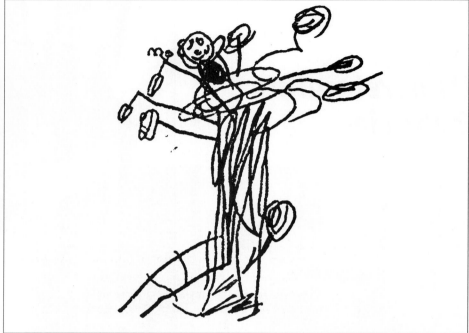

Peter in an apple tree, (*boy, 3 years, 7 months*)

In this chapter you will gain a historical perspective of the early childhood field:

▶ Before the twentieth century
▶ Early twentieth century innovators in Europe and America
▶ Important milestones: the Lanham Act, the space age, Head Start, The National Association for the Education of Young Children.

To understand the early childhood program and the philosophy behind it, we must see it in relation to twentieth-century social change. The roots of the movement are deeply embedded in the past, but the role of education has expanded, attempting to adapt to the needs of those who are coping with profound social changes.

One of those changes concerns women in today's world. More and more women of all classes are employed. Families are smaller. Men are sharing more of the home responsibilities, while women are moving toward a more equal status in the business and professional world as well as in the general labor market.

Quality child-care centers assume new importance under these conditions. Parents who work outside the home need adequate care for their young children while they are at work. There is evidence, too, that all children can benefit from some group experience outside the home by the time they are 4, and almost all parents can use the support that a good child development center can offer.

History of the Development of Early Childhood Education in the Twentieth Century

By the late nineteenth and early twentieth centuries there had been a growing interest in early childhood education. Among the people who contributed to earlier thought and the literature in Europe was John Amos Comenius (1592–1670), who is credited with writing the first illustrated picture book for children. Comenius advanced the concept that early learning determines what a person will become. Jean Jacques Rousseau (1712–1778) expressed the idea that childhood was a separate state from adulthood. His novel, *Emile*, outlines how children are to be raised and educated. For Rousseau, the child should grow up whole and free and able. He saw no use in verbal instruction and instead advocated allowing children to solve the problems of living through their own experiences.

Johann Pestalozzi (1746–1827) might well be considered the pioneer of early childhood education with the school he established in rural Switzerland. He took in poor children and orphans, caring for them as well as educating them. Friedrich Froebel (1782–1852) opened the first kindergarten in Germany in 1837 and was influenced by Pestalozzi's work. Froebel is known as the "father of the kindergarten." He valued the child as a child and saw play as serious and significant. He viewed the child as a unique, creative, and productive person who learned through playful activity. Froebel wrote that "play is the highest phase of child development." (Braun & Edwards, 1972) He laid an important foundation for what would be a later concept—the child-centered school.

At the turn of the century, G. Stanley Hall and John Dewey were among the important American educators who were writing and teaching. Dewey stressed the need for firsthand experiences for young children, as Froebel had done. To test his educational ideas Dewey established a laboratory school at the University of Chicago in 1896.

Following the work of Hall, Arnold Gesell made detailed observations of growth and development in the 1920s and 1930s. He outlined norms for physical development. Gesell felt that the first six years of life were the most important for physical development. His normative approach gained great popular acceptance.

John B. Watson, the founder of behaviorism, also had a tremendous influence on child-rearing practices during the 1920s and 1930s. His behaviorist theories about habit training were at variance with other researchers in the field. After World War II Benjamin Spock's book, *Baby and Child Care*, did much to counter the effect of some of Watson's theories.

The first nursery school was established in 1911 in England by Rachel and Margaret McMillan. The McMillans had worked with children in health clinics in the London slums and wanted to prevent the physical and mental illness they found so prevalent there. The nursery school program they planned included opportunities for children to learn to care for themselves and to assume responsibility for some "housekeeping" chores. It also had some activities in learning language, colors, and forms and in reading, writing, arithmetic, and science. Grace Owens, a contemporary of the McMillans, believed that the needs of 3- and 4-year-old children could be met best by programs that provided large blocks of time for play and other unstructured activities such as art, woodworking, and water and sand play. She thought reading, writing, and arithmetic should not be introduced to 3- and 4-year-old children.

About the same time that the McMillans and Grace Owens were opening nursery schools in England, Maria Montessori was working with retarded children in Italy and later teaching children in the slums of Rome. She developed sets of materials that were self-correcting, needed little supervision, and could be used in a sequence from simple to complex. Montessori was interested in children's intellectual development and adopting good work habits. Many of her special materials are still widely used in early childhood and primary schools.

In the 1920s Susan Isaacs in England had a program for a small group of children, largely from professional families, for the purpose of learning about the development of young children. She provided the children with a rich variety of practical materials and encouraged them to explore these in their play. She kept full notes of her observations. She studied social, emotional, and intellectual aspects of development and interpreted her observations with insights from Freud's and Piaget's theories. Her goal was the development of the whole child.

One of the first nursery schools in the United States was the Play School, founded by Caroline Pratt in 1913. It was later called the City and Country School and was directed by Harriet Johnson with the assistance of Lucy Sprague Mitchell. This school was the laboratory for the Bureau of Educational Experiments, which later became the Bank Street College of Education in New York City. Caroline Pratt designed the unit floor blocks used widely today in nursery schools and kindergartens.

About the same time Hull House, the settlement house founded and directed by Jane Addams in Chicago, opened a nursery school for children of the area's large immigrant population. It was used for observing children by students from the National College of Education as part of their teacher training program.

Although the public showed little interest in educational programs for young children, after World War I two nursery schools opened in the Chicago area. One was in the Franklin School in a poor socioeconomic area and the other in the Winnetka School in a well-to-do area. These schools existed in part because of Rose Alschuler, a benefactor interested in children and their welfare. She gave generously of her time and money to help maintain the best possible educational programs in both settings.

In 1922 the Merrill Palmer School in Detroit opened a nursery school under director Edna Noble White. She brought two nursery school teachers from England to teach there in the first years. The nursery school served as the laboratory for students interested in preparing for parenthood or teaching. It was used by students from colleges across the country who came to learn about the development of young children. At the same time, a day nursery was opened in Boston that later became the Ruggles

Unit blocks, found in all centers, were invented by Caroline Pratt. Valley College, Campus Child Development Center, Los Angeles

Street Nursery School under the direction of Abigail Eliot. The programs of both these schools were influenced by the English nursery schools.

State universities and some private colleges began establishing laboratory nursery schools in the 1920s. In the late 1920s a Rockefeller foundation grant made possible the opening of nursery schools for training and research in the Universities of Minnesota, Iowa, and California at Berkeley.

Some private nursery schools were opened in the 1920s such as Broadoaks, established in Whittier, California. Dorothy Baruch, the director, wrote one of the early books in the 1930s for students and parents, *Parents and Children Go To School.* Broadoaks later became Pacific Oaks College for teacher training.

During the 1920s and 1930s the nursery school movement flourished, but little attention was given to improving the standards of day care in public or private schools. University research in child development was the major contribution during this time. Examples include The Iowa Child Welfare Research Station, The Fels Research Institute, and the Gesell Child Guidance Clinic.

Lawrence K. Frank was active in promoting the field of child development and parent education throughout the 1930s and after. He thought of child development as multidisciplinary and believed it should draw from anthropology, biology, sociology, medicine, psychology, and psychiatry in order to understand the development of the individual.

During the economic depression in the early 1930s the federal government authorized establishing nursery schools to provide care for children 2 to 5 years old from low-income families. The schools were established under the Works Progress Administration (WPA) (later the Work Projects Administration) to provide jobs for unemployed people. Unemployed professional people, such as high school or elementary school teachers and social workers, attended short training courses at colleges or universities with laboratory nursery schools before they began teaching. A consultant from each state visited each WPA school, giving in-service training. In addition to nursery school the programs included health care and well-balanced meals with menus prepared by nutritionists. The federal government covered most of the costs. These programs generally were of positive benefit, lessening the strains of the Great Depression for families and individuals. Establishment of these schools funded by the government also raised the hope that nursery schools might become a permanent part of the educational system.

The Lanham Act

A change came with the outbreak of World War II. The WPA-funded programs ended, and unemployment almost disappeared. The federal government met the changed situation by passing the Lanham Act. This act provided funds to establish schools for the care of young children whose mothers entered war-related industries. Some Lanham-funded centers were sponsored by war-related industries and some by community agencies. These centers varied in their standards.

One of the most successful centers was in the Kaiser Shipyards in Portland, Oregon. Two well-planned buildings were constructed at the entrances to the shipyards. This program met the child-care needs of mothers who worked there. At the peak of the war as many as five hundred children a day were cared for in a twenty-four-hour program six days a week. The centers had nurses on duty around the clock to meet the health needs of infants and children up to school age. Hot meals that could be taken home were available at a modest cost.

The two Lanham centers sponsored by Kaiser were under the direction of Lois Meek Stolz, with James Hymes as manager of the Child Service Department for the two Kaiser shipyards. (Hymes et al, 1978, p. 28) All of the teachers were college graduates, some with more experience in nursery school teaching than others. Many of the staff members subsequently became leaders in the early childhood field. While the Lanham schools were closed abruptly at the end of the war with funding withdrawn by the federal government, many of the teachers continued teaching in other schools throughout the country. Day-care centers, nursery schools, and parent cooperatives as well as teacher training programs in colleges and universities gained because of these teachers and because of the equipment the government sold to institutions at minimal cost.

Public awareness of the nursery school movement and early childhood education grew steadily through the 1950s. Parent cooperative nursery schools and parent education programs gained in popularity. Research in the 1950s continued to support the significance of early childhood education for later school performance.

Sputnik May Have Influenced Early Childhood Education

The Russian success with Sputnik in 1957 caused many Americans to fear that the United States might be falling behind in its educational program. A prevailing attitude was that if we had educated our children better, we would have been first. Mathematics and science education as well as early childhood education were proposed as the answer to our failure to be first in space. Pressures developed to teach reading, writing, and arithmetic at the kindergarten and nursery level, a return to academic "basics" in education that has created problems ever since.

As we have emphasized throughout this book, the kind of "basics" we promote are the foundation for learning that we know from research and experience. These "basics" are based on a manipulating objects, discovering, and relating to people, all under the guidance of understanding adults. Pushing a child may actually restrict his learning.

Head Start

In the 1960s the federal government again began supporting programs for young children. The Economic Opportunity Act in the Lyndon B. Johnson administration was designed to attack poverty through a number of community action programs. This *War on Poverty* included provisions for educational programs to give children from families below the poverty line learning opportunities to prepare them for school. Head Start, as it was called, began with a summer program in 1965. The following year Head Start became an all-year program providing a preschool experience for 4- and 5-year-old children. Professionally trained people administered the teaching program, and community groups participated by providing space and services. There were medical and dental services, social services, balanced meals, and parent education programs. Volunteers were encouraged. The goal was and remains an effort to help the family.

Head Start has maintained its political popularity. It has been widely recognized as one of the most cost-effective and successful federal programs for children. "A review of research on Head Start shows that Head Start children performed as well as or better than their peers when they began school. Head Start children had fewer grade retentions and special education placements, lower absenteeism, fewer cases of anemia, more immunizations, better nutritional practices, and in general, better health. For Head Start parents, the studies show improved parenting abilities, increased positive interaction with their children, and increased involvement in their communities.... Every dollar invested in high-quality preschool programs saves six dollars in lowered costs for special education, grade retention, public assistance, and crime later on. Children who participate in such programs are more likely than their peers to be literate, employed, and enrolled in postsecondary education.... They are less likely to be school dropouts, teen parents, dependent on welfare, or arrested for criminal or delinquent activity." (Children's Defense Fund, 1990, p. 47) Head Start has received federal funding more continuously than any other program for children. "The ground-breaking federal programs Congress approved and funded FY1991—the Child Care and Development Block Grant and the 'At-Risk' Child Care Program—will give the states new money to help low-income families pay for child care." (Children's Defense Fund, 1991, p. 44)

It is estimated that by 1995 about 65 percent of all women with a child under 6 years of age will be working outside the home. Most of these women need child care for their young children. Fifty-four percent of all Head Start families are headed by single parents. (Children's Defense Fund, 1991, pp. 42, 43)

The National Association for the Education of Young Children

In 1929 a group of nursery school teachers and college teachers of child development formed an association. They decided that this association would be open to anyone working in a field related to young children, including educators, social workers, nurses, doctors, psychologists, therapists, and parents. The group called itself The Association for Nursery Education and was renamed in 1964 to become the National Association for the Education of Young Children (NAEYC). In 1991 it had a membership of approximately 75,000 with 380 Affiliate Groups throughout the United States. NAEYC offers professional development opportunities designed to improve the quality of services to children from birth through age 8. Membership services include the journal *Young Children*, books, brochures, videos and posters, an annual conference, a celebration of the Week of the Young Child, membership action grants, insurance plans, and public policy information. NAEYC administers a national, voluntary accreditation system for early childhood centers and schools and offers a centralized source of information sharing. For membership information, write to NAEYC, 1834 Connecticut Ave., N.W., Washington, DC 20009-5786.

Chapter Overview

The history of the development of early childhood education in the twentieth century demonstrates the social changes that have taken place affecting young children and their educational experience. From Comenius to Gesell we have witnessed the dedication of men and women who attempted to improve conditions for young children. We have seen the rise of laboratory nursery schools beginning in the 1920s and still providing a rich setting for continued research. The 1930s found the federal government providing some care for children from low-income families through the WPA. World War II saw enactment of the Lanham Act, which provided day-care centers for children of women working in war-related industries. However, the greatest event was the enactment by the federal government of Head Start in 1965. Finally, the professional organization for early childhood professionals, NAEYC, has taken its place in the history of the early childhood movement.

Projects

1. Select an individual, an organization, or agency and report on its contribution to the field of early childhood education.

2. Develop a time line showing the major changes that have occurred in early childhood education from Plato to Head Start.

For Your Further Reading

Berrueta-Clement, J. T., Schweinhart, L. J., Barnett, W.S., & Weikart, D. P. (1984). *Changed lives: The effect of the Perry Preschool Program on youths through age 19.* Ypsilanti, MI: High/Scope Educational Research Foundation. Every early childhood educator and child advocate needs to be familiar with the now widely known findings of the Perry Preschool Program, showing clearly that quality preschool experience for at-risk children is cost-effective to society.

Chattin-McNichols, J. P. (1981). The effects of Montessori school experience. *Young Children, 36*(5), 49–66. Reviews many studies comparing Montessori programs to other models; shows in which areas Montessori programs exceed or are inferior to other approaches.

Hymes, J. L., Jr., with Ginsberg, S., Stolz, L. M., & Goldsmith, C. (1978). *Early childhood education: living history interviews. Book 2: Care of the children of working mothers.* Carmel, CA: Hacienda Press. The article by Lois Meek Stolz, the first president of NAEYC, tells about the Kaiser Child Service Centers during World War II, which she directed. These two centers had a lasting effect on early childhood education and care in post-war years.

Hymes, J. L., Jr. (1991). *Early childhood education: Twenty years in review: A look at 1971–1990.* Washington, DC: National Association for the Education of Young Children. The final report in a series of reviews of highlights in early childhood education of each year since 1971. Chatty, full of facts, names, dates, and history. Fascinating.

Rousseau, J. J. (1974. Reprinted from 1933). (B. Foxley, Trans.) *Emile.* London: J. M. Dent & Sons. (Also published by New York: Teachers College Press, W. Boyd, Trans. & Ed., 1962). An influential novel on child rearing and education, first published in 1762. Sets forth an entire view of education that may persist today, in that Rousseau believed society was inherently corrupt and education should evolve from the child's immediate contact with the world of nature.

Spodek, B. (1985). Early childhood education's past as prologue: Roots of contemporary concerns. *Young Children, 40*(5), 3–7. Explores recurring themes in early childhood education, including school entrance age, kindergarten and early reading, preschool as a social change agent, and concepts of knowledge.

Young Children. (1990). Celebrating Head Start's 25th Anniversary. *Young Children 45*(6), 22–52. Four articles by Lombardi, Pizzo, Mallory & Goldsmith, and Greenberg, reviewing Head Start's 25-year history from the view of participants, and projecting new directions.

The Role of the Teacher

Miss Annie in school (*girl, 2 years, 6 months*)

In this chapter you will be able to look at yourself as you learn about:

► The teacher's contribution to the child's personality development
► The teacher as a model for actions, attitudes, suggestions, language, and meeting frustration
► The teacher's attitudes toward racial and social justice
► The teacher as facilitator of decision making
► The teacher's role in encouraging self-expression
► The teacher as a time planner
► The teacher's role in using authority
► The teacher's relationships with parents.

RATIONALE AND CRITERIA: . . . Optimal development in all areas derives from positive, supportive, individualized relationships with adults . . . Staff interact frequently with children. Staff express respect for and affection toward children by smiling, touching, holding, and speaking to children at their eye level throughout the day, particularly on arrival and departure . . . Staff are available and responsive to children; encourage them to share experiences, ideas, and feelings; and listen to them with attention and respect . . . Staff speak with children in a friendly, positive, courteous manner . . . Staff equally treat children of all races, religions, and cultures with respect and consideration . . . [and] provide children of both sexes with equal opportunities to take part in all activities. (NAEYC, 1991a. *Accreditation criteria* . . . , p. 15, 16)

In a center for young children the teacher has a stimulating and challenging role. No two days are ever the same. All children have their own individual needs. Childhood is a period when learning is more rapid than it ever will be again. Basic personality patterns are being established. There is an excitement about learning, and the environment is one in which everyone is learning, both children and teachers. The teacher may get tired or discouraged at times but will seldom be bored. The rewards are the growth and the changes observable in the children.

The teacher's goal is to help each child grow as a person, gain the ability to enjoy and profit from opportunities for learning, and develop his or her potential as an individual and a member of a group.

In this chapter we will look at the teachers as people, their skills and the quality of the relationships they have with children. In Part Five we will consider ways in which teachers may facilitate learning.

The Teacher Plays an Important Role in the Child's Personality Development

The teacher's relationship with the young child will influence both his learning and development as a person. What the teachers are like as peo-

The teacher makes a learning experience from children's curiosity about the human body.
Child Development Laboratory, California State University, Chico

ple may be more important than what they teach. What teachers are like determines to some extent what the child is able to learn under their guidance.

Learning is very personal for young children. They learn through experiences with people who are significant in their lives. The first attachment bonds are with parents, their first and probably their most important teachers. From them a child learns many things such as language and patterns of behavior. He also begins to learn to trust people and himself, the first task in personality development, according to Erikson. The development of a sense of trust must outweigh mistrust if the child is to achieve healthy personality development.

The teacher's first task when a child enters the group is to start building a trusting relationship. Most children entering a center already will have a measure of trust in adults and are ready to begin to relate to the teacher. The teacher needs to show that she is trustworthy and reliable. In some cases the teacher may need to help restore a sense of trust in a child who has not succeeded earlier in building much trust.

The next task in the development of a healthy personality is the achievement of a sense of autonomy or independence outweighing the sense of dependency. The teacher will give the child many opportunities to be independent, to do things his way, to make choices. She will encourage him to master skills like climbing, riding a tricycle, fitting puzzles together, or building with blocks. By her approval and encouragement she helps him see himself as someone able to do things independently while still using the help that may be needed for success. The teacher is in a position to add to the child's confidence and self-respect because of the trusting relationship they have built together.

The teacher also plays an important role in helping children with the third task in personality development: encouraging a sense of initiative that outweighs feelings of doubt and guilt. Children need to feel free to explore, discover, imagine, and create without being afraid of making mistakes. Developing initiative is the most significant task of healthy 3-, 4-, and 5-year-old children. They are active and eager to explore, make discoveries, and play with their peers. They are also beginning to develop a conscience and feel a sense of responsibility. At this age they sometimes feel too responsible for what happens because of their inexperience. It is very important that the teacher or the parent be aware of children's feelings. The adult needs to make the situation clear to children and not add to a burden of guilt feelings. The adult should define what is acceptable and what is not acceptable, so children can grow in understanding. The teacher in the center will provide many opportunities for children to explore their interests, enlarging and enriching them and will give them many opportunities for experiences with peers. The teacher also will make sure that children have opportunities to create with materials and with words and in play with others, such as in dramatic play. At the same time, the teacher makes sure throughout these explorations to keep children safe, so that trust and confidence are not damaged.

The Teacher Accepts and Respects Each Individual Child

A good relationship between a teacher and child makes it easier for the teacher to discipline in constructive ways and easier for the child to respond in desirable ways. The teacher will be friendly and firm in setting realistic expectations for behavior. She helps the child face the consequences of behavior without resorting to punishment that stirs resentment but not repentance.

The significance for children in having a teacher whom they like and who, they feel, likes them is tremendous. Young children see the world subjectively and are influenced by their relationships with people even more than adults. Children are influenced, too, by the teacher's expectations. They tend to behave and achieve accordingly. They need a teacher who appreciates their strengths and who helps them make the best of their capacities.

We must remind ourselves that a child's environment presents both favorable and unfavorable factors. Deprivation of some kind can exist in almost every background. While one child may have experienced poverty in material things, he may be rich in personal relationships. Another child may have had poor personal relationships, even though he has lived with material abundance. All children have had some favorable experiences

The teacher models curiosity and "Let's find out" attitudes with her visiting tortoise.
Child Development Laboratory, California State University, Chico

from which they draw strength. It is important that a teacher respect and make use of these strengths.

We are responsible as teachers for accepting and respecting each child as another important human being who is trying to cope with difficulties, find satisfactions, and learn. Every child is worthy of the best we have to give.

The Teacher Helps Children Face Failure in a Positive Way

The teacher gives approval and attention to the child when he achieves or behaves acceptably but can also accept his failures and try to turn these to constructive use. The teacher may say to the child at the workbench, "Next time hold the hammer this way, and it may be easier to make the nail go in straight." In saying this the teacher helps the child look for causes, consider what has happened, and improve performance. Errors become a means of learning and not just a failure. The child gains a new perspective and approaches situations more positively.

Sometimes the teacher will say, "I wonder why that happened," when she thinks the child is ready to discover the remedy or reason. This encourages a "problem-solving" attitude, which is very necessary in learning. If the child is successful in finding the reason, new confidence is gained in his own capacities. He may discover that the block tower fell down because the base was not broad enough, or because it was not on a level surface. It often is easy for a child to want to blame someone or to blame himself when something fails to work out. All children can learn to take a less personal way to face failure and can learn to look for reasons.

The Teacher Serves as a Model for Children

The children in a group will imitate their teachers' actions and attitudes, which become part of what young children learn. Children sometimes mirror the teacher in unexpected ways. A teacher, looking around the playground one morning, was puzzled to see two boys with jackets thrown over their shoulders. She suddenly recalled that she herself had been wearing a jacket thrown over her shoulders whenever she had a short time to spend outside.

Because children imitate so readily, teachers must be careful not to set models in areas where self-expression is the goal, as in art and music.

The Teacher Serves as a Model in the Way Directions or Suggestions are Given

The teacher accustomed to guiding children by positive directions, telling them what they can do or may do, sets a model for children to use as they play or work together. Positive statements are more effective than negative ones. They make it clear to a child what the child can do or should do. They help children succeed. If children are with teachers who use positive

The teacher encourages sensory exploration and learning by providing water play.
Migrant Head Start, Chico, California

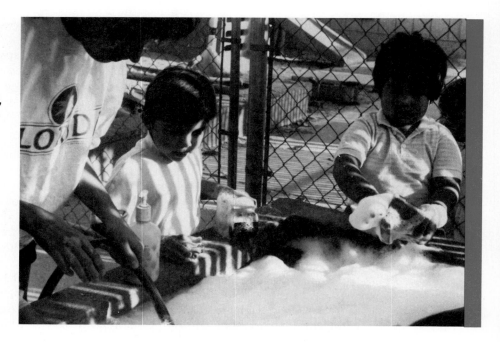

rather than negative statements, they are likely to imitate the teacher's way of giving suggestions. If we listen to these children as they play together, we may be surprised at how often we hear positive directions given. They have gained an important skill in social relations.

In the following situation the teacher emphasized what she felt was the correct response.

Pat, Tyrone, and Felicia were playing with picture lotto under the direction of their teacher. Pat was the first to complete his card. He excitedly yelled, "I win. I win." The teacher, wishing to emphasize the positive rather than the competitive element, said quietly, "You covered your card. Yes, you covered your card." She suggested to Pat that he might help Tyrone and Felicia to cover their cards. Pat was delighted to do this, and his help was accepted willingly. The lotto game was very popular. When it was brought out the next day, Pat happened to be the first to cover his card again. This time he yelled, "I covered my card. I covered my card."

The teacher's role in modeling is a powerful force in shaping behavior. In fact, this teacher was surprised at the power she had in changing the child's language.

The Teacher Serves as a Model in Meeting Frustration

The teacher sets an example for the children in the way she meets the frustrations that are an inevitable part of teaching. If she accepts this state of affairs, she helps children build a concept of how to live with frustration. One does not need to lose faith in oneself or in others but can have patience and confidence that the next time will be better.

If the teacher can leave the children free to doubt and question and sometimes not to respond to her suggestions, she is helping them, too. There is uncertainty, and there is flexibility. Both serve constructive purposes. The children can build more trust in themselves as well as in the teacher when frustration and doubt are accepted and acceptable.

The Teacher Needs to Face Attitudes Toward Racial and Social Changes

We have become a multiracial, multicultural society. The old inequalities of sex, class, and economic condition are no longer acceptable. Racial and cultural biases are not acceptable. The teacher needs to understand these changes and needs to be aware of personal biases.

All of us have some biases from the past. These may lie deeper than we realize, but it is important for the teacher to model attitudes that are as free from biases as possible. Every individual has the right to expect to be accepted and judged on his or her own worth.

In most groups in a center there will probably be children of more than one nationality—African-American, Asian-American, Native American, Latino. They may come from families with different cultural patterns or structures. The teacher can better understand these children if she learns as much as possible about the ethnic and cultural backgrounds of the children in the group. The teacher may find it possible to attend celebrations or festivals arranged by one of these groups. She can learn from talking with parents or other people belonging to the cultural group. She may find that some of her own attitudes are changing, revealing an unknown bias. The children may look, speak, believe, and behave differently from the teacher's expectations. The teacher may find herself responding negatively to a child or expecting poorer achievement from a child who does not use correct English or does not behave in ways she thinks appropriate. Many apparent "deficiencies" in children may be simply a difference in cultural background and experience. The teacher may misunderstand the meaning of the child's behavior until she understands more about the culture he comes from, just as the child or the parent may misunderstand the teacher's.

Attitudes of acceptance and understanding may not be enough to overcome all discrimination and bias. The teacher needs to promote positive attitudes of acceptance in children toward persons of all colors, languages, and cultures. All racial slurs and stereotypes that perpetuate attitudes of discrimination must be stopped. In Part Five we will consider ways the teacher may help young children in this area.

Families represented in the groups may include many nontraditional occupations. It is acceptable for women to enter the same range of occupations

Teachers offer choices and use language as they serve snacks to infants and toddlers. Migrant Head Start, Chico, California

as men in most cases. The old sex-role stereotypes are changing. Men and women share the tasks at home. More women work outside the home. Children of the single or divorced parent, the career mother, the large extended family, the blended family, and the traditional family may all be represented in the center. Teachers need to be aware of these changes and to respect them. Their relationship with the children and the families is the same. Each is an individual to be accepted and respected.

The Teacher Gives Children Opportunities to Make Decisions

Making decisions for oneself is a part of taking responsibility for one's behavior. In guiding children we look for situations where they can make their own decisions. We give a child a choice whenever choices are possible. We look for alternatives where a child can select what he prefers to do. In many matters the child is not yet ready to make judgments, but there are other situations where he can make decisions. These opportunities are important for growth in autonomy. If we give the child a choice or ask for an opinion, we must be sure that it is a legitimate choice or question. If we ask, "Are you ready to go now?" or, "Are you through painting?" we must be in a position to accept the answer. Here are two examples of a situation that often occurs. (Note the different ways in which two parents manage the same situation.)

Henry is a somewhat immature little boy. His father comes in and says to him, "Are you ready to go?" "No," Henry says sturdily. His father answers, "Well, even if you're not, you're going anyway. Put your things away and come along." His smile relieves his words, but the words suggest a reason that Henry remains immature. He is treated as a much younger child. One senses that he feels helpless.

Dick, the same age as Henry, says to his mother when he sees her, "I don't want to go home." His mother answers with a smile, "I know you like it here and you want to stay, but we have to go now. We'll be back in the morning." Her words show that she accepts his feeling. It isn't difficult for Dick to leave.

There is, of course, a danger in giving the child responsibility or authority for which he is not ready. We must remain the confident authority, while we present the child with reasonable alternatives from which to make his own choices.

The Teacher Provides Many Opportunities for Exploring and Learning

The teacher creates a physical, social, and emotional environment that invites learning through exploration and discovery. She encourages children by the questions she asks and by her own zest for finding out about things. She encourages individual initiative and supports the excitement of discovery, an excitement that begins in early childhood and should be preserved through life.

Here is an example of learning by discovery in a group of 4-year-olds; it would not have taken place without guidance from the teacher. A potential conflict, with the teacher's help, became a social studies investigation.

In a block scheme a boy had built a fish store. . . . Every time [a girl] went to his store to buy fish, he closed it. Finally, in great irritation she yelled at him, "You can't do that. A store has to sell—that's what it's for, stupid." The teacher approached the children and entered the conversation, first by listening and then by asking, "Can you go shopping in a store any time you feel like it?" Discussion led to the following conclusions: (1) you do not shop late at night because you have to sleep; (2) stores do have hours for shopping to which people must pay attention. . . . It was decided that the boy and the girl plus two other children who had joined the discussion would take a walk around the block with the teacher in order to find the answer to her question, "How do you know when a store opens and when it closes?"

They returned from their trip and as they entered the classroom, their newly gained information exploded: "It's on the door," "It's not the same for all the days," "They have a sign." Information was explored and shared. Signs went up on several buildings posting store hours. One child posted times for visits to her house, fixing the hours around the baby's sleeping schedule. (Cuffaro, in Hirsch, 1984. pp. 69–87)

It is worth noting the way in which the teacher guided this opportunity. She "entered the conversation, first by listening and then by asking." She took time to find out what the argument was about and then asked the right question. She guided the discussion and supplied information that the children did not have by making a suggestion about how to find out. The children returned from their trip excited by their discovery. The results of what they learned appeared in many forms, even the imaginative one of posting a schedule for visiting. It was a social studies and language opportunity with meaning for the children. They gained information and, more important, they had models for problem solving and answering questions. One talks over the solutions to a problem; one investigates; one reorganizes one's ideas. Learning can be exciting!

THE TEACHER PROVIDES OPPORTUNITIES FOR SELF-EXPRESSION

An important part of teaching young children is helping them become competent in expressing thoughts and feelings. Language is an important means of expression. A child needs to be able to put thoughts and feelings into words in order to have satisfying social relationships. Teachers must be aware of the many ways in which the excitement of language can be developed.

There are other avenues of expression. For the young child, art media offer important avenues for expressing feelings and for communicating. Art media such as paint, clay, pencils, and marker pens are used freely when they are available. Construction with blocks, manipulative toys, and wood are other ways of expressing ideas and concepts. Body movements and dance are also forms of expression that children enjoy.

The teacher gives praise and encouragement by describing the child's art. Migrant Head Start, Chico, California

All of these avenues of self-expression should be developed in a program for young children. We will discuss the skills needed by the teacher to encourage expression of thought and feeling in Part Five.

The Teacher Provides Many Opportunities for Experiences with Peers

The social environment created by young children playing and learning together is enhanced when the teacher sets the stage for it. As children play with each other they begin to define relationships, sometimes taking on the role of leader, sometimes of follower. These roles tend to change depending on what the child brings to the activity. A block-building project may find one child directing the others to bring the long blocks from the shelf and the children following these directions, delighting in the camaraderie of belonging to the project. Another time the leader in this activity enjoys the role of being the follower. The teacher observes and rearranges either the structure of the setting or the relationships in the group depending on what will most benefit children's play together.

Young children often need to be taught how to interact with others in a friendly and acceptable manner. Some children need to learn how to be a part of a group of peers and how to enter the group. Emily, a 4-year-old starting nursery school for the first time, didn't know how to enter the group. She would pick up a handful of sand and throw it at other children as she entered the outside area of the school. Some children ran when they saw her coming; others ran and told the teacher. Emily needed help in entering the group. The teacher first made sure that Emily was met at the gate when arriving and later added another child to the welcoming committee. Slowly Emily began to move into the group.

As children go through their day, talking, playing, and working on projects, the teacher plays an important role in helping them having meaningful experiences with each other: that of watchful observer, mediator, and comforter when social situations break down.

Planning for the Use of Time

There will be a structure in the schedule the teacher plans. Some events occur every day at regular times, such as snack time, mealtime, rest time. Other events will change with the seasons or with children's shifting interests. The teacher will make sure that opportunities for art, music, and science experiences are always available along with reading to the children, looking at books, and storytelling.

The teacher also will plan for blocks of uninterrupted time to give children the chance to develop and complete their projects. Dramatic play lends itself to acting out many themes. Block building may become more and more complex when there is enough time. Dramatic play themes and block play may develop over many days with changes in the themes in play and increasing complexity in building structures. Some activities

The teacher plans for comfortable time structure through the day and the week. She helps with good health practices. Migrant Head Start, Chico, California

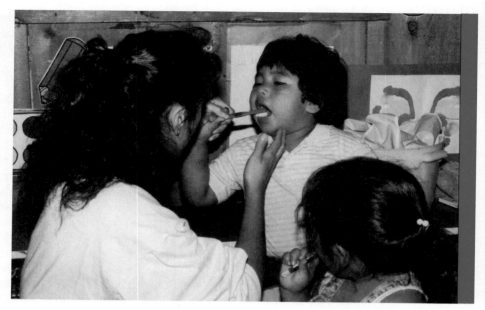

soon end. Successful completion of a project gives children a feeling of accomplishment. When a child or a group of children finish a project, they understand something about beginnings and endings and something about efforts that bring results. One can move on to new projects.

The sense of completion comes after many repetitions. Maria loved to play with puzzles. She fitted them together time after time, and each day she returned to the puzzles. The satisfaction she felt was apparent in her expression of delight. She concentrated on her task. It took some time before she moved on to new activities. Other children may find satisfaction in fast-moving dramatic play in small groups. The play evolves and calls for resourcefulness. The play changes each day. All children need blocks of uninterrupted time if they are to carry on self-initiated activities in which the teacher plays only a supporting role.

There often will be situations in which time runs out. Children terminate their play because it may be time for lunch or a scheduled activity. The teacher helps children if she gives them the reason, for example: "I'm sorry, but it is time now to get ready for lunch. There is no more time for painting." By stating the reason, the teacher helps children learn that there is a structure in a day and a limit to time. The teacher will avoid saying, "You've played with blocks long enough now." This statement adds nothing to children's understanding. It is misleading and suggests that they have no control over time and what they do in it.

A teacher needs to be sensitive to the times when activities should be terminated because of fatigue, lack of interest, or impending trouble. The activities initiated by adults should be short. In one school a young volunteer brought his guitar for a song period with the children. They were delighted and almost all of them gathered around. The opportunity to have a man in the teaching role was new to these children. He adapted his songs to their level, and they participated eagerly as he taught them the words. He continued with song after song, enjoying their close attention. By the time he stopped singing, some of the children were very tired, although only a few had left the group. The children could not settle down for a while after he left. Several children cried, and others were disorganized before they became involved in other activities. Several shorter sessions would have benefitted the children much more than the one long session.

The Teacher's Role in Using Authority

"You're the boss of the whole school," Shana remarked to the teacher as they sat eating lunch together, and she added with deliberation, "Last year the school was all the bosses itself." Shana had evidently been trying for some time to figure out who was "boss" at the center. Her parents were still trying to show her who was "boss" in their house. She must have been puzzled about the center situation, until she selected the teacher as the source of authority.

For many people, as for Shana, the confusing problem of authority remains throughout their lives. As children these people have been made to feel that the role of boss is the most important one. When they are grown, they struggle to do some bossing themselves or to resist being bossed by others. This struggle interferes with their solutions to other problems. They hurt themselves and often the people they love in their efforts either to boss or to resist bossing.

Discipline that leads to a struggle over who is going to be "boss" is damaging to a child. It does not help children respect themselves or others. Like Shana, people who have met this kind of discipline have little concept of what it means to be a responsible member of a group. They are not ready for the self-discipline that democratic living demands.

Authority takes many forms. Some people have experienced authority mostly as a succession of commands or "don'ts." They associate authority with punishment. All of us at some time have met with authority that was needlessly harsh, restrictive, and not based on respect for individuals.

Children develop best when they experience authority based on love and a caring attitude. This kind of authority enables a child to feel safe and free to be herself. Then the problems of authority can be worked out in a way that has positive values.

Our Own Feelings Are Important When We Use Authority

If the authority we experienced as children was mainly reasonable and sympathetic, we will be able to exercise authority ourselves with more confidence and with more respect for individual needs. Our goal is to help children to take more and more responsibility for their own behavior, that is, to be their own authority. To prepare them for this role we must be clear about our feelings on the subject. We must be aware of the adaptations we have made. Our feelings about these adaptations will facilitate or interfere with the exercise of discipline that benefits the child.

When a child defies us, for example, how much threat do we feel from the behavior? Are we secure enough to see the child's defiance for what it represents to the child rather than what it means to us? Do we face this behavior by overreacting, because we identify with the rebellious child or because we feel a threat to our own autonomy? Can we be responsible adults, no longer little and helpless, who can support a child in the struggle for independence while maintaining necessary limits for behavior? Can we be confident, responsible authorities capable of acting with respect and understanding? Let us look at two teachers whose feelings made it difficult for them to exercise authority.

Sally had difficulty helping the children in her class control their behavior. The children often lost their control and engaged in a great deal of destructive behavior. She was a sympathetic person with insight and at times was skillful in turning the group's energies back into constructive activities. After they had overturned the furniture, for example, the children usually did complex block building. They often were creative and played well together, but some of the timid children in the group suffered. They were frightened by their own anxieties after participating in or watching an episode of uncontrolled behavior.

Sally had never been able to accept discipline herself. She had grown up as an only child in a strict household. She conformed outwardly but expressed her resistance in indirect ways. She was never on time; she never quite finished a task; she was absent-minded. As soon as she was grown, she left her home. In her work with children she was determined that they should not suffer from the "boss" type of authority, as she had. Because she had not experienced authority as a help, she found it difficult to use it constructively, with her group. A sensitive, creative person, she gave her group freedom but was not able to meet their needs for the support of limits in their out-of-bounds or destructive behavior.

Regina bitterly resented the way she had been treated at home as a child. She too often experienced a form of discipline that served only as an outlet for hostility and aggression. Her feelings against authority were very strong. She could not limit the children in her group because she would have disliked herself too much for doing it, or she might even have disliked the children for "making" her act that way. She was thus unable to discipline in a constructive way.

It is true that aggressive feelings may come out in the use of authority. People may punish because they wish to hurt; in punishing they may pour out their aggressive, hostile feelings. At times all of us release feelings in inappropriate ways and with the wrong person. When we face the hostile, aggressive feelings we inevitably have, we are better able to cope with them and find appropriate and constructive avenues for their expression. We can keep or direct them where they belong, and they need not spill out in inappropriate places. We can act with confidence when the limits we impose are meeting the child's needs rather than serving as an outlet for our own feelings.

When we enforce a standard of behavior that interferes with a child's impulse to act as she wishes, we may expect the child to be angry with us or at least to feel resistant or resentful. She has every right to feel this way, but she does not have the right to act out these feelings if the action hurts herself or others. We are acting responsibly when we stop this type of behavior.

It is important that we not deny her feelings and help her express them. We can say, "Tell me about it." Expressing a feeling in words helps drain off some of the anger. The child is then better able to listen and talk things over with the teacher. She can take a step toward identifying and understanding feelings. This step leads to better control over impulsive behavior. With her feelings identified and "off her chest," the child is ready to channel her energies more constructively. Having a sense of humor and imagination helps in these situations.

We have a right to our feelings, too. In the center a teacher may say to a child, "I feel very cross when you do. . . ." Her words help the child to perceive the teacher's feelings and understand the impact of the behavior on another person. We ourselves get angry or annoyed at times, and we must acknowledge our negative feelings and cope with them. It may often help to talk over the kinds of feelings we have with our colleagues or others who can reflect on them with us. As we share our feelings, we may discover new aspects of ourselves as teachers. We may feel more self-respect, and perhaps we can manage our feelings in more mature ways as we work with children.

The child is less bewildered when the feelings she arouses in others are identified directly. Putting feelings into words makes them more manageable. If we as teachers face and manage our own feelings, we help create the kind of climate in which a child can learn to recognize feelings in herself and others and learn to cope with them in ways that are constructive and even creative. She will then be less afraid of her own feelings and those of others.

The Role of Guilt

Feelings of guilt are a necessary part in changing behavior. We must feel sorry about our behavior if we are to make any real change. We can only be truly sorry because we care. Fear of punishment does not make this kind of change in a child. As the child develops trust and a sense of autonomy and moves on to the stage of initiative, daring to do things on her own, she begins to feel a sense of responsibility for her acts. Doubt and the fear of being wrong bring feelings of guilt. Her conscience is developing. But she is inexperienced, and too often feelings spill out over too many actions. The child who said, "I didn't do it" when her mother crashed the car into a tree was feeling responsible in some way. A measure of guilt may be the first step in changing behavior, but a heavy load of guilt is damaging for a child. She may feel so much guilt that her impulse controls break down. She may no longer care about the consequences of her actions. Authority that relies on increasing a child's guilt may have serious effects on personality development. As adults we should avoid adding to a child's burden of guilt and shame by the way we use authority, just as we do not interfere when a child must face reasonable consequences and feel guilt that is within her capacity to bear if she is to learn.

The Teacher's Role with Parents

The relationship between the teacher and the parent or caregiver is an important one for both. The teacher needs to learn about the child from the parent. The parent needs to share with the teacher information about the child, the child's needs, and what the parent's expectations for the child as the child enters the group. The teacher needs also to know more about the parent's point of view, for parent and teacher must work together for the good of the child.

As discussed in Chapter 9, in the first interview the teacher will explain the steps taken for the child in entering. The teacher will outline the program and the center policies, answer any questions the parent may have, and encourage the parent to visit, and feel welcome at any time to talk with her again. It is important to begin to develop a relationship of confidence so that the parent feels trust in the teacher, and the teacher begins to understand the parent and her reasons for entering the child in the program.

Parents may be anxious or uncertain about the separation. They may have little understanding of what the center is really like. Parents may not be in touch with present practices in the care and education of young children. The early childhood education movement is relatively new. Many questions are sure to arise, and the teacher should welcome then, listening carefully and thoughtfully to understand the meaning of the question fully. The teacher is responsible for helping the parent feel more comfortable and satisfied about having the child in the center. The teacher may be able to make some changes if they are needed while still maintaining the standards of the program. She accepts and respects the parent's viewpoint.

The teacher's relationship with the parents is a professional one in which the teacher offers knowledge and experience in the interest of the child. It is not a social relationship as with personal friends. The teacher treats all information the parent gives as confidential. It is never discussed with anyone outside the staff. Confidentiality is the first tenet in professional ethics and must be strictly observed.

When there is a relationship of trust between teacher and parent, both find themselves learning and growing in understanding young children.

Chapter Overview

The teacher of young children needs to be interested in understanding people, experiences, and events, rather than in passing judgment on them. The teacher also needs to be sensitive and responsive, able to "listen with the third ear" to what the child may be trying to say through behavior. The teacher should know the satisfactions of learning and be able to appreciate the child's accomplishments in mastering each stage in development. With the help of such a person the child can grow comfortably as a whole person.

The child also needs a teacher who can communicate, both in language and in expression and gesture, with a smile or a nod, as well as an approving word. The child needs a teacher who is aware of his or her own feelings and is able to express feelings as well as ideas in constructive and clear ways. The child needs a teacher who values spontaneity and yet can maintain an orderliness in activities and in the setting. The child needs a teacher who is imaginative and resourceful and who has a sense of humor. We are reminded in this chapter that few of us show all these qualities in all situations. We have our weaknesses as well as our strengths, but we grow and change with experience.

Projects

1. Describe a teacher from your past. What were his or her strengths? What grade were you in? What do you remember learning in the class? Draw a diagram of the classroom as you remember it.
2. Observe the teacher in a nursery school or day-care center and record incidents in which he or she did any of the following:
   A. Created a climate for discovery
   B. Extended and enriched an interest or purpose initiated by a child
   C. Allowed time for a child to complete a task
   D. Played a supportive role in building a child's self-confidence
   E. Helped a child to solve a problem for himself
   F. Helped two or more children to cooperate.

For Your Further Reading

Beaty, J. J. (1991). *Preschool appropriate practices.* Fort Worth, TX: Harcourt Brace Jovanovich College Publishers. How the teacher's role differs from the traditional in a self-directed learning environment, as she provides appropriate learning materials and supports children in their learning. Detailed suggestions for ten activity centers in the classroom.

Greenberg, P. (1989). Learning self-esteem and self-discipline through play . *Young Children 44*(2), 28–31. Examines what the adult is "teaching" as children play: perspective, communication with words, helpfulness of adults, self-esteem and self-discipline. Through play the child learns about art, science, math, language, how the world works, and more.

Jones, E. (Ed.). (1977). *Dimensions of teaching-learning environments: Handbook for teachers.* Pasadena, CA: Pacific Oaks College. Significant findings from classroom research on dimensions such as soft-ness/hardness, simple, complex, and super units of materials, intrusion/seclu-sion, enrichment/simplification of the en-vironment. How teachers can analyze the teacher-learning environment, including free play and teacher-directed time.

Jones, E. (ed.). (1978). *Joys and risks in teaching young children*. Pasadena, CA: Pacific Oaks College. Unusually valuable contribution in chapter, "The invisible child," as well as others on emergent cur-riculum and teachers' roles.

Katz, L. G. (1984). The professional early childhood teacher. *Young Children, 39*(5), 3–10. Defines the professional teacher, the nonprofessional, and the un-professional teacher, and how each would handle a specific problem situa-tion in a center. Challenges teachers to look closely at what is being taught by teachers and learned by children.

National Association for the Education of Young children. (1987). Ideas that work with young children: Child choice—An-other way to individualize—Another form of preventive discipline. *Young Children, 43*(1), 48–54. Lively article on importance of choice in young children's learning. Discusses five reasons for au-thentic choices by children as they move around the room, choosing their own toys and educational materials. Deals with le-gitimate boundaries provided by adults.

Phyfe-Perkins, E. (1981). *Effects of teacher behavior on preschool children: A review of research*. Urbana, IL: ERIC Clearing-house on Elementary and Early Child-hood Education. ED211 176. A brief summary of research findings on direct teacher effects and indirect teacher ef-fects. Supports the belief that behavior of adults in early childhood settings does indeed have an impact on children.

Platt, E. B. (1992). *Scenes from daycare: How teachers teach and what children learn*. New York: Teachers College Press. Describes how children work at making sense of their world and what is growth-promoting teaching. Deals with specifics of what happens to young children in day care.

The Role of Play

CHAPTER 13

I like to play with my friends (*girl, 4 years*)

In this important chapter you will explore the most enjoyable aspect of children that we can observe—their play. You will learn about:

▶ The values of play
▶ How children learn through play with other children
▶ How children use play in finding their places in a group
▶ Dramatic play, a special way to gain insight
▶ Coping with aggressive feelings through dramatic play
▶ Expressing many feelings through play
▶ Fantasy in dramatic play
▶ How group games develop from dramatic play.

IMPORTANCE OF PLAY: Children's play is a primary vehicle for and indicator of their mental growth. Play enables children to progress along the developmental sequence from the sensorimotor intelligence of infancy to preoperational thought in the preschool years to the concrete operational thinking exhibited by primary children. In addition to its role in cognitive development, play also serves important functions in children's physical, emotional, and social development. Therefore, child-initiated, child-directed, teacher-supported play is an essential component of developmentally appropriate practice. (Bredekamp, 1987, *Developmentally Appropriate Practice*, p. 3).

The whole panorama of life is lived over again in the play of children. If there is any way of gaining knowledge particularly suitable to this stage of development, it is in the play they spontaneously devise but which needs nevertheless an attentive teacher for its support and nourishment. (Biber, 1967)

The Value of Play

From infancy on, all healthy children enjoy play. Play is at the heart of any program for young children.

Susan, not quite 3, was in the kitchen with her mother who was preparing for a tea party. "You may put the cupcakes on this big plate," said the mother in answer to Susan's wish to help. Pleased at the task, Susan carefully placed the cakes one by one on the plate until it was covered. Then she faced a dilemma. There were several cup cakes left but there was no space left on the plate. She stood looking, uncertain and thoughtful, and then she began placing each remaining cupcake exactly on top of one of those already on the plate. Susan exclaimed with delight, "Look, caps!"

Play makes a major contribution to the physical, social, emotional, and intellectual development of children. Children explore, discover, and learn in play. They make contacts with others in play and begin learning about relationships with their equals.

Children Play For Many Reasons

Children play because it gives them pleasure, as was the case with Susan's delight with her creation of "caps." They play because they have an urge to explore and discover. The infant discovers her fingers at one stage and spends time moving them and gazing at them intently. The preschool child is absorbed as she pours water into the sand, watching how it runs down the channels she has dug. Children also play because of an urge to master a skill or solve a problem. A toddler will return again and again to a stairway, climbing up and coming down until she does it easily. Another child will persist in riding a tricycle until she rides with skill. Children play to make friends, for it is one important way that young children form relationships. Play also serves as a means of mastering the emotional problems that inevitably come with growth. It is essentially creative, involving all of the child's capacities.

Children Play to Master Feelings

"In the preschool years play is the child's principle means of solving the emotional problems that belong to development." (Winnicott, 1957) Children have many fears, the fear of being left or deserted, the fear of being hurt and helpless, and sometimes the fear of their own violent impulses. Children use play as a way of reducing and gaining mastery over these

Wearing a hard hat and pounding vigorously on hard plaster helps this boy to feel powerful.
Bakersfield College, Bakersfield, California

fears and anxieties. As we watch children at play we observe how often they take the role of the one who punishes and controls and who does the going away and leaving. By reversing roles they are helped to deal with their feelings in these situations. We also see this in the frequency with which "doctor-nurse" play appears when a child has had a painful experience with doctors or a hospital.

Play also is a way for children to handle the problem of being "little" in a world of big people. In play they can identify themselves with "big" roles and lessen the inevitable frustrations of growth. Notice which child wears the helmet or goggles. It may be a child unsure of a place in the group. Children may use gun play or "super hero" play to help them feel big and powerful. Whatever we may feel about the use of guns and this kind of play, we need to accept the fact that it meets a need for the child. More free of fear or anxiety, children can go on to master other problems with more confidence.

Children Play to Make Contact with Others

It is in play and only in play at first that children make contact with other children. Through play with others a child begins to be aware of the feelings of other children. She is better able to understand that others may be sad, happy, afraid, or frustrated, or that they may want to possess or be first. These feelings are not hers alone but belong to others as well. They can be dealt with in an outer world and managed with help.

In playing together, children share ideas and extend the range of one another's experience. They make friends through play. In their dramatic play they re-create and rehearse roles and seek to understand better their common problems in family life. Play with other children seems to be essential to healthy growth.

Children use play as a means of reducing their fears, anxieties, and aggressive feelings. Spontaneous dramatic play, alone or more often with others, fosters imagination, resourcefulness, and reasoning. Play brings its own reinforcement, and the child puts wholehearted effort into it. Healthy children in favorable environments spend a great deal of their waking time in play.

In our sometimes compulsive society play is often not respected, because it does not seem directly productive. Yet the creative achievements of scientific thought depend on sustained attention and imaginative ways of perceiving and dealing with reality, the very qualities that appear in children's play. We need to appreciate the tremendous significance of play for children. Teachers who observe children as they play can gain important insights into what children are thinking and feeling. Children need teachers who value children's play.

In this chapter we will consider the ways in which play contributes to social learning and personality development. In later chapters (17–20) we will discuss ways in which play fosters learning in a variety of areas: motor, language, music, art, mathematics, and the sciences.

Early Play

The beginnings of play appear in infancy when the baby starts to be aware of people and objects. First she plays with her fingers, and later with her toes. We notice the concentration that goes with any satisfying play activity. As coordination improves, she fingers an object, bangs it, grasps it tightly, only to let go when another attractive object presents itself. She is learning about the "me" and the "not me," about objects and their qualities and what she can do with them. She smiles, and her parent or other caregiver responds. There is mutual play between them as the adult is caring for her. She is learning about relationships.

The playful modes of responding begin early in the games parents play with infants, such as in peek-a-boo and dropping and picking up objects as well as in smiling, repeating sounds, and bouncing on the knee. These are games that have no rules. They are forms of relating to people, of finding mutual responses, and of playing together. These kinds of responses will be elaborated later in play with other children.

Infants explore objects and toys; they begin to explore each other. Santa Monica College, Santa Monica, California

Playful Behavior Depends on a Capacity to Trust

Being able to play freely implies a sense of trust. Building a sense of trust, as Erikson points out, is the first and most basic task in healthy personality development. Its foundation is laid in the child's early experience in being cared for by a loving, responsive caregiver.

Parents or caregivers who are reliably present when the infant needs them and who can regulate their giving to her needs, who see and respond to her as an individual, enable the move into spontaneous playfulness. She can test and discover the enlarging world. She can become involved in relationships with other people. Playing is a sign of health, made possible by a favorable environment.

As a toddler the child still plays best in the presence of an adult whom she knows and can trust. Even 3-year-olds who are playing together need a responsible person readily available, someone on whom they depend but not someone in a "managerial" capacity. The adult's role is to provide the setting and to assist by enriching and extending the play as needs are observed, giving guidance and the techniques for play.

Transitional Objects

Sometime during the first year most young children find a favorite object, perhaps a cuddly toy or a blanket to which they become attached. It

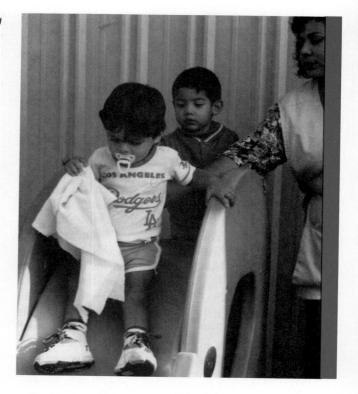

Infants and toddlers may find comfort in transitional objects like the pacifier and "lovey." Migrant Head Start, Chico, California

becomes their first possession and serves as a comforter, a defense against anxiety. It seems to represent the early security of contact with the mother. It stands in place of the parents as a symbol to tide the child over when they are not present or when the child is under strain. This transitional object has properties for the child that ordinary objects do not have, standing as it does between the inner world of feeling and fantasy and the outer world of realities to be faced. Possessing this object, she is freer to proceed with playing. We see the use made of such a symbol by children who bring an object from home in order to make the adjustment easier as they enter a group. We need to respect the special qualities with which such an object is endowed. The attachment weakens as the child becomes more secure and is involved in a wider variety of play relationships.

Settings for Play

We discussed some of the equipment and materials needed for a favorable play environment in Chapter 4. We also considered the adequacy and use of space and time provided for play. There should be spaces where one child or a small group of children can play without being disturbed, open spaces for activities like block building, space where buildings can be left and worked on over time, outdoor space that is full of variety and interest. Every group can use supplementary "bits and pieces" or "junk" as well as the standard equipment and raw materials that have many uses. A schedule should provide both flexibility and a framework for ordered activities. All of these considerations promote a rich play experience.

Children need to play often with materials in what appears to be random play, "messing about," before they can use the materials to the best advantage in problem solving. It is a kind of "as if" or "what if" exploration of the materials in play to discover what their possibilities are before they can make use of them. Watch a child at play and observe how he tries possibilities, finds new uses for objects, arranges, combines, pretends, and through these activities comes to understand more about the materials.

The teacher's "ingenuity and resourcefulness in providing the necessary equipment must be combined with understanding of the value of different forms of play, e.g., dramatic, creative, free, organized, and constructional." (Winnicott, 1957) All of these forms of play have a place in a center for young children.

Play Is Action Oriented

Play is self-initiated with motivation for involvement coming from the child. It is usually spontaneous, with action rather than outcome the challenge. Young children's play may begin as a make-believe astronaut preparing for an adventure in space, change to a person putting out a fire, and end in making roads in the sandbox for cars. In this example we see play focus on active participation rather than leading to some planned conclusion. The play may give the child a sense of mastery and self-worth because the child is in control of the action.

Play Contributes to Cognitive Growth

Often skills are practiced during play that enhance cognitive growth. As children build with blocks they solve the problems of bridging, enclosure, and patterning. As they play in the sand they discover that dry sand has different properties from wet sand. As they add water to their paint pot, they discover the paint runs on the paper. These open-ended materials require no right answers and involve creative thinking. They facilitate greater thinking processes.

Relationships in Groups: Living and Learning through Play with Others

Children's relationships in a center will differ from their relationships at home because the group in the center consists of contemporaries. Playing with a group of equals is significantly different from being a member of a

Thoughtful selection of equipment such as two-seater tricycles promotes social cooperation.
Migrant Head Start, Chico, California

family. We can add to our understanding of what relationships mean to each child as we observe them in their group living.

Readiness for Social Experience

Readiness for social experience with groups will depend on the child's earlier experiences in the family and the kind of group the child enters. If the adults the child has known at home have enjoyed play with him and have treated him with respect, the child is more ready for experiences with other adults and for the give and take of play with others. If the child has felt secure at home in possessing love that has seldom been withheld, he will have confidence when entering a group. If the child has experienced a conditional kind of love ("Mother won't love you if . . . "), he is likely either to make heavy demands for attention in a vain search for satisfaction or avoid or resist contacts with others. This child is fortunate if he enters a group where the teacher has the understanding, the patience, and the time to help him feel respected and valued.

Children are individuals, and they reveal some of their differences in play. The same solution has different meanings for each child. Here is an example:

 Patty and Lois had been playing house together when they decided to take their babies for a walk. They each pushed their doll buggies to the far end of the playroom. Lois looked back and saw two boys in their playhouse. "Someone's getting into our house," she said anxiously. Patty turned around. "Oh, we have company,"

she exclaimed joyfully and hurried back to welcome the boys. Patty expects friendliness, while Lois seems to expect nothing but trouble.

Children May Gain a More Realistic Concept of Self Through Group Play Experience

One of the most significant values for the child in being a member of a group of equals lies in the chance to find out more about what kind of person he really is through his play experience. He has an opportunity to build a more realistic concept of himself as a person apart from being a member of a family.

In the family group each member is valued or should be valued because he or she belongs to that particular family, regardless of what he or she may be or do. We do not need to prove our worth in order to belong to the family. In a group of contemporaries, on the other hand, the place each one of us holds depends more on our skill and what we have to offer the group. We must measure ourselves against others who are like us, finding our strengths and facing our weaknesses, winning some acceptance and meeting some rejection. When we experience success, it is based to a great extent on achievement. The limitations we face are likely to be real rather than arbitrarily imposed. A favorable family situation helps us to feel secure, but experiences with our own age group help to develop an awareness of ourselves and of social reality that family experience alone cannot give. Playing with age-mates provides this self-awareness.

Discriminations of any kind have an effect on the development of the sense of self. When our position in the group does not depend on our worth to the group or the contribution we bring, we are likely to build a distorted sense of self. We may fail to value ourselves or others. The distortions about self that result from discrimination and prejudice are reflected in a loss of potential contributions to society and in diminished individual growth.

A realistic sense of one's individual identity, of who one is, is important to everyone. For example, the child who is challenged by being different from the mainstream in the classroom may have problems with other children understanding this difference. Negative values are attached to some human differences. Helping the child with a special need to accept his own identity is necessary in order to deal with the inevitable questions that arise from being different. The teacher plays an important role in creating a climate of acceptance of differences. She is careful to not deny the difference by saying, "He is just like you," because this confuses the child who is trying to cope with the difference that is so obvious. The blind child is blind, and this must be explained in a way young children can understand. The African-American child has a different skin color, and again the teacher works at helping the young child understand the difference. Children notice how adults treat differences, so one begins by modeling behavior one wants children to copy. Encourage children to talk about differences.

When appropriate, offer children experiences with adults who are different. Help children explore differences openly. Two books that have suggestions for classroom activities are *Alike and Different: Exploring Our Humanity With Children*, edited by Bonnie Neugebauer, and *Anti-Bias Curriculum: Tools For Empowering Young Children* by Louise Derman-Sparks.

Self-Confidence Through Play

Besides building a more realistic picture of who he is, the child begins to feel less helpless and little in a group of other children. In the world of adults the child really is helpless. When playing in a group of children he is among equals. He may feel able to act in ways that he would not dare to on his own.

It may be difficult for teachers to accept group defiance unless they appreciate what it may mean to the child. A small group of 4-year-olds, for example, may climb to the top of the jungle gym when they are told it is time to come inside. They are playing a new role, doing the thing they may have wanted to do many times in the past. They are no longer helpless children, dragged away from play by a powerful grown-up. They are powerful people, high above the adult, asserting themselves in their play.

The teacher in such a situation does not need to panic or feel threatened in her authority, although it is easy to have this feeling. She can

"Get off! You are in my way." Children learn to handle property rights disagreements with words.
Jean Berlfein

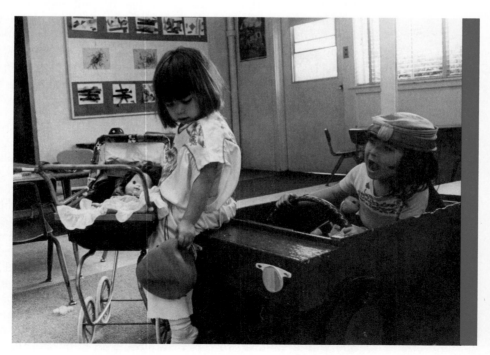

allow them their brief moment of power in their play. Inside themselves, they know they are children and she knows that she is an adult, responsible for bringing them inside. She may perhaps manage the matter playfully, pretending they are spotters for people from outer space, or she might say, "I'm ready to pull you home in the wagon," or she might seriously discuss with them, "I wonder why it is that you don't want to come in now?" To this question she might receive replies that give insight into how things look to them and what they dislike. Teacher and children will learn from this method of resolving the situation to their mutual satisfaction. Everyone is the better for reaching a solution together.

Children Find that They Can Share Attention and Like Teachers

Children in groups have the opportunity to face and manage the feelings they have about wanting a big share of the adult's attention. Sharing the teacher's attention with others is less difficult than sharing the attention of one's mother. If the teacher gives her attention freely and generously when children request it, she helps them feel that there is enough for all. They are less likely to feel deprived at the times when they cannot have attention. They are more likely to be satisfied. It may be easier to learn this lesson in a center group than at home.

The teacher helps a child feel secure by giving freely what he may need in the way of attention and materials for play. The child who experiences a generous giving by the teacher will be more likely to give freely to others.

The Teacher Helps with Techniques for Getting Along in Play

We can help children by suggesting good ways of approaching others or by helping them to understand the feelings that lie behind the social advances of other people, however clumsy these may be.

An approach is usually more successful if the child has some suggestion about what she might be or do or if she makes some contribution to the play in progress. A straight request such as, "May I play with you?" is often doomed even if it is accompanied by the adult word "please." Adults offer more help if they can suggest something specific to the child that she might be or do. If the child is rejected in one role, she can always find another role or a different activity to suggest. This way there is more protection against failure.

Sometimes the teacher may need to enter the play, taking a role herself, to help the less skillful child and withdrawing when no longer needed. She may demonstrate a technique by saying the words for the child, "Doctor, I think my baby needs a shot," to help carry on "doctor" play. She may forestall difficulty by suggesting, "There will be more room for the building over there," when two builders are encroaching on the territory of others.

Children are often very realistic and successful.

Terry calls to Tommy, "Say, Tommy, you'd better let Doug play with us because he won't let me have the rope unless he plays, and I want it."

Possessing something desired by others is as much of a social advantage at 3 as at 33. A wise teacher may utilize this fact in helping the shy child. Letting the child introduce a new piece of equipment or bring something from home for the group may help her feel more accepted and give her added confidence. Obviously, such a technique should not be depended on too heavily or for too long, but it can sometimes be the basis for a social start.

Offering something in return for something else one wants is a successful device. Some children have amazing skill in making a second object desirable when they want the first. Even secondary roles can be made attractive by an imaginative child.

 Regan wanted to join the group playing police officer mounted on tricycles, but there were no other tricycles. Terry encouraged her to join anyway, saying, "You can be a walking policeman, Regan. They have walking policemen. You can play if you are a walking policeman." He made it sound worthwhile, so Regan became a "walking policeman."

Terry is already a master at working out compromises. On another occasion he was busily building with blocks when Regan wanted him to play house with her again. He satisfied her by saying, "I'll live over there with you, but I'll work here. And I'm working now." He went on with his building. Terry has had many successful experiences of getting along with others. He has confidence, and his confidence shows in the way he meets his problems.

As we listen to children in their play, we find that they approach others in friendly ways far more frequently than we may have been aware. We may not have noticed their consideration for each other, because our attention is more likely to be directed to the times when they hit or grab. We will find, too, that there is more friendly behavior in a group where the children receive courtesy and consideration from the adults.

Children in Groups Learn about Sharing and Taking Turns

Children often need help from the adults in learning about property rights and "taking turns." Playing in a group of equals provides many opportunities for learning in this area.

Equipment at the school does not belong to individuals but to the group. No child feels as threatened by a sense of loss when she shares group objects as she might in sharing things that belong to her personally. Two simple principles can be established to cover most situations. First, when a person is through using a piece of equipment like a tricycle or swing, it "belongs" to the next person who may wish to use it. One does not continue to claim a thing one is no longer using. Second, after one has used a piece of equipment for a time, one may have to let someone else use it even though one has not finished; but one can expect to get it back again.

"Here, want this one? You can have a turn." Children learn negotiation and sharing through play. Child Development Laboratory, California State University, Chico

When we teach children about "turns" we must be sure to follow through. If a child gives up a swing so another child may have a turn, we must see that the first child gets it back afterward if she still wants it. Even if she isn't standing there waiting, it may be wise to say, "Tony, Rachel has had her turn now and you can have the swing again if you wish." This clarifies the concept and prevents the child from feeling that taking turns really means losing something.

Michelle and Davy, a pair of 4-year-olds, were playing with boats in a large pan of water where there were also two play turtles. Michelle had a boat but wanted a play turtle. She picked up the turtle that Davy was playing with. "Hey, that's mine," said Davy, and he quickly grabbed it back.

The teacher accepted his assertion of his right to the turtle, but she commented to Michelle, "It's hard to want a turtle and find that someone else is playing with it."

Davy then turned to Michelle and said, "Here, this one will be for both of us. I'll share it with you," and he shoved it across to her. It often happens that the child who can assert himself freely can also share easily when he perceives the situation. He can feel good about sharing.

Special Cases Arise Under This Concept of Property Rights

Since property rights are considered very important in our society, the child must begin early to learn about possession. At home she discovers that some things are not hers to touch. Wise parents help her accept this fact by giving something that is hers when they take away something that she can not have. They teach her that some things are hers and do not insist that she share the things that are hers until she is willing and ready to share. They will find that the child can share first with people she knows and likes and then slowly can broaden the ability to share in most situations.

An interesting situation is sometimes created by the children themselves. An aggressive child may prefer a certain piece of equipment. Almost before the teacher is fully aware of what is happening, she may establish that it is "hers," and the other children, fearing her attack, may prefer to leave it for her and give up their turn with it. The teacher must be alert to such situations and protect the other children in their right to use all equipment equally.

Kevin, whose aggressiveness was making him unpopular, preferred a red tricycle. With his usual lack of awareness of the needs and feelings of others, he proceeded to take it when he could. It became important for the teacher to accept responsibility for maintaining the right of others to use the coveted red tricycle. It was important because Kevin needed to have other children feel friendly toward him. No one in the group was more eager to be liked. It was also important for the teacher to watch this situation because the other children needed to be successful in standing up for themselves in the face of Kevin's threat.

Enrique was a quiet, thin child who stayed aloof from the children and the teachers. One day he discovered the large red wagon. It may have been like one he had at home. Whatever the reason, he began to play with it almost exclusively and could not bear to share it. The teacher felt that it was important to protect Enrique in his use of the wagon for a time. She helped the more secure children find a substitute whenever possible and allowed Enrique time to grow more sure of himself at school before she expected him to take turns with the wagon.

Children Adjust to the Group Through Play

Children Find Their Place in the Group Step by Step

In the center most children have temporary or shifting relationships with other children. Two children may play together for a morning or for a few days, drawn by a mutual interest in digging a hole, playing firefighter, or setting up housekeeping somewhere. Then each will have an equally close but short-lasting friendship with someone else. But even in these shifting relationships there are likely to be certain children who are consistently antagonistic to each other or attracted for reasons we may not fully understand. We can help children better if we are aware of their feelings of liking and not liking, so that we can be careful to use the one wisely and not to add to the other.

Rivalry Creates Problems

One of the least helpful things the teacher can do is to encourage direct competition among children. Competitive situations breed ill will. Comparing children, holding one up as an example to others, is unfair to all because of the hostility it arouses. "See who will finish first" or, "See how much faster Rachel is dressing" or, "See how quiet Tony is"—all of these comments are likely to make children like each other less. They make others appear to be rivals or competitors rather than friends.

Teachers must be aware that young children, in part because of their dependency, will compete for their attention. Comparisons increase rivalry. They should be very careful to do nothing to increase jealous feelings. These feelings can cause real unhappiness. Often a child will misbehave at rest or at the table because he wants the attention that the teacher is giving another child. The teacher must be ready to reassure him with a word or a smile that she cares about him, too.

Close Friendships Are Often a Source of Strength

Sometimes children discover one particular friend, and from this close friendship they develop confidence and assurance. There is nothing much better at any age than having a special friend. The confidence and assurance that comes from feeling that one is liked by an equal, sought after, and depended on make possible a great deal of development. Such friendships are worth encouraging, even though at one stage they may mean that the pair excludes others. The friendship is likely to lead later on to a growth in friendliness. As friends, they can show consideration for each other's feelings.

 Stephen and Francisco were friends. Stephen ran out to the playground one day carrying a firefighter's hat and yelled, "Francisco, here's a fire hat. Put it on fast." Francisco replied, "I don't need it. I'm an astronaut." Then he added, "But I'm your friend," and the two ran across the playground together. In rejecting the hat, Francisco was careful not to let his friend feel rejected.

 Mickey can assert himself but remain friendly. Lisa had bumped her truck into Mickey's dump truck. Angrily he said, "Hey, you can't bump into my truck. I don't like that; you can't do that," and almost in the same breath he added, "But you're a nice girl," and he blew her two kisses!

Children who are not aggressive may still fail to find close friends. Beth was not aggressive at all. In fact, she sought affection from children and adults. She would run after any teacher saying, "Lady, I love you." In spite of Beth's words her relationships with people were superficial and lacked warmth. Beth had not received the love she needed from her parents. The quality of the relationships each child has experienced at home influences and limits the kinds of relationships he is able to establish outside the home. Sometimes a teacher can supply the child with a relationship sufficiently warm to make up for a deficit so that the child can achieve an adequate measure of social satisfaction.

If we were to sum up our goals as we work with children in groups, we might say that they all lead in the direction of helping the children like each other more rather than less because of what we do. We might use this as a yardstick. Will the children like each other better if we do this? If children are friends, they will find it easier to get along. If the techniques children use are constructive, they will find it easier to live with others.

As teachers we may have to redirect children as they try to unload hostility onto other children.

 Amy and Stevie were washing their hands side by side. Amy carried a heavy load of hostile feeling and was always attacking others. She said, "Stevie's a bad boy." The teacher replied casually, "Oh, he's my friend, and you're my friend. Isn't it nice that I have two friends?" Stevie beamed, and Amy picked up the idea with, "and Keosha's your friend and Mike and Jim." "Yes," said the teacher, "there are lots of friends here."

Isolation Should Not Be Used as Punishment

We sometimes see a parent or teacher isolating a child as punishment for not getting along with others. We have come far enough in our discussion to be aware that punishment may be undesirable because of the resentment and hostility that may accompany it. While the child may not repeat a particular act after being punished, he is not likely to feel more friendly toward others or to get along better with them because of it. Isolation or being made to sit on a chair deprives him of the chance to have other, and perhaps better, experiences. It also labels him as "bad" in the eyes of the group and thus adds to his difficulties in getting along with others.

Isolation may be desirable when it is used with a child whose difficulties are the result of overstimulation and fatigue. In this case, the teacher may accept the child's need of a simpler environment. She will try to achieve it without giving a feeling that isolation is a form of punishment. She may suggest a story alone or a walk, or she may put him in a room with a favorite toy for a time, explaining that he will get along better with the others after a quiet time. She may remove a child who is disturbing other children to a place where he can be free to do as he wishes, but she will not do it as punishment for failure.

 Judy is a tense child, very jealous of her twin brother whom she feels her parents prefer. She has trouble getting along with other children because she seems to see them as rivals. She put it this way to the teacher one day.

JUDY: "I want to be a wicked witch."
TEACHER: "I wonder why you want to be a wicked witch?"
JUDY: "Because they cause spells on people."
TEACHER: "You mean there are really too many people around and you would like to get rid of them."
JUDY: "Yes, there are too many, and I'm going to be a witch and get rid of them."

ited only by the imagination of the children themselves. Guided by an observant teacher, dramatic play situations can contribute significantly to the children's learning.

CHILDREN USE DRAMATIC PLAY AS A WAY OF COPING WITH AGGRESSIVE, DESTRUCTIVE FEELINGS As mentioned earlier, children are helped to deal with their feelings by reversing roles. Here is an example of a child's play that reveals his efforts to master conflict by reversing roles.

David, a 3 1/2-year-old, is playing by himself with small doll figures and furniture, while the teacher sits nearby. He talks to himself as he plays. A comfortable, happy child, his words nevertheless reveal something of the conflict all children feel during the socialization process. He puts the smallest doll in a bed, saying, "She has to stay right in her bed. If she makes a noise, I'm going to spank her little bottom— spank her little bottom—spank her little bottom." He turns to the teacher. "She's a nasty little girl because she got up and made a noise, didn't she? She's a nasty little girl. She has to go sound to sleep." He turns back to the doll and continues as if two people were talking together. "Quit doing that. I'm just going to stay downstairs all day. Shut up. It's not daytime. It's still nighttime. I want to stay up all day. Do you want to peepee or not? You're not going to peepee. Stay right in your bed."

In his play David appears to be coping with feelings of resentment about the inevitable issues in conforming to adult standards and resentment of being little and unable to express his feelings. David's parents were comfortable and friendly people. It is unlikely that they were severe in their discipline. This may have made it possible for David to play out this drama. A child from a less favorable background might be unable to express the resentments that all children experience in the process of growing up. David is probably reassured by the teacher's presence, although she makes no comments. He feels her acceptance. She is there to help him if the play should become too disturbing.

In discussing this issue of expressing resentments one parent described her doll play as a child. She could remember spanking her doll and saying, "You must eat all of your spinach," even though she had no recollections of her parents spanking her and making her eat foods she disliked. In fact, she recalled her childhood as one of happy family life. Yet she distinctly remembered being quite punitive with her dolls.

In dramatic play children often act out aggressive, destructive feelings. It is important to accept them in play, being sure only that the children are safe and that the impulses are under control and kept on the pretend level. An adult may need to remain near to "steady" a group that is acting out negative feelings, as in a war game or a fire play. It is important to the children to know that they can stop or that they will be stopped before they do real harm. Without this help the play may not serve the purpose of draining hostility and keeping it within manageable proportion. It may only increase the anxiety of some children about their ability to handle their impulses. As adults we should not hesitate to make a suggestion, redirect, or limit play that we can see is going "out of bounds."

In redirecting play, we do not want to deny expression to negative feeling. We must avoid an adult tendency to want only "good" behavior. Here is an example.

Genny, Leah, and Ryan are pretending they are lions. Leah, an inhibited child, says, "I'm a good lion." Ryan says, "Don't eat me up." Lions seem to fascinate him because of their dangerous possibilities. Leah changes her role. It's safer. "Don't eat me up," she says. Genny boldly says, "I'm a mean lion," and chases Ryan. Then she stops and asks him, "Are you a mean lion?" When he answers, "Yes," Leah feels braver and says, "I am, too." "Pretend you can't get us," says Genny. Ryan answers with, "I'm going to eat you up." Unfortunately, at this point a teacher steps in and tells them to be "good lions," and they drop the lion play. It no longer serves a purpose for them. Leah, who has conformed to high standards of good behavior and has paid a price in loss of creativity, had just reached the point of joining Genny and Ryan in daring to be a "mean" lion. The teacher's words close this avenue of escape from adult demands for Leah. It is interesting to get further insight into what Leah is seeking by watching her subsequent play. A few minutes later she climbs up high in the jungle gym and says, "This is dangerous."

Play that individuals and groups repeat is almost sure to have meaning for them. We need to try to understand this meaning if we are to offer sound help. It is probably neither accident nor perversity that makes a child knock over things or throw them down. We must remember that she has tumbled many times. She has been startled, and perhaps hurt, by falling in the course of learning to walk. She may recover some assurance by making other things fall and thus reduce the threat that falls hold for her. We know that children are frightened by sudden, loud noises, and yet as soon as they are able, they pound and bang, making all the noise they can. In this way they may be better able to handle their fear. Because they can make noises themselves, they are less disturbed by noise.

Being little and often helpless, and being unable to comprehend fully what is taking place, inevitably creates some degree of anxiety and resentment in every child. Life becomes more manageable for the child because she can escape at times into play.

MANY KINDS OF FEELINGS ARE REVEALED IN PLAY   It is always interesting to note what children consider funny. Understanding humor is one clue in understanding the kind of adjustment a person is making. Children's dramatic play often has a humorous quality, but underneath the humor may lie disguised meanings. We must be aware that feelings of many kinds are likely to be expressed under the acceptable guise of a joke.

One child tickles another with a leaf that he is carrying. They both laugh, for his gesture expressed friendliness. Another child tickles a companion with a leaf, and the child objects. She senses the attacking quality that exists under the apparent playfulness of the gesture and resents it.

Simon, who is struggling to establish a masculine role in the world, is making a mask at Halloween. He says, "I want a man witch. I don't like girls." His father is a withdrawn person, defensive and aloof. His mother clings to Simon and is overdirective and possessive. But Simon is valiantly making the effort to identify with male things, even male witches. At times he dresses up in skirts and then tries to defend himself by rejecting all girls. His conflicts are revealed in his play.

It has been clearly established that dramatic play has therapeutic value for children. We need to recognize this fact. Such acceptance does not imply that teachers are in a position to undertake play therapy in the more technical sense of the term. In the center, however, children need to have plenty of opportunity to play out feelings, try out roles, clarify concepts through spontaneous dramatizations, and thus benefit from the therapeutic values of dramatic play.

Through dramatic play the child may also communicate feelings and ideas. With only limited ability to express herself in language or words, she uses actions to represent in symbolic ways what she is feeling and thinking. The child's struggle with jealous feelings after the arrival of a new baby, for example, may be expressed in destructive behavior with some object that is used as an outlet. An apparent fascination with covering up objects may be a communication about concern over the disappearance of people important to her or with finding an answer to something hidden. We should look carefully at play behavior that occurs repeatedly and try to understand what the child may be trying to tell us.

CHILDREN WHO ARE UNABLE TO PLAY   Sometimes we find a child who seems unable to enter into play, whether on her own or with others. She is likely to lack a basic sense of trust in some respect. She may be overwhelmed by the anxieties or the anger she feels.

Brandon, whose parent sometimes acted with violence, shouting, or throwing objects, was unable to engage in much play at home or at school. In the center his play was limited to riding a tricycle around in circles or just watching other children. He seldom explored materials, and he had not developed much speech. He seemed to feel the world was a dangerous place. He trusted no one, including himself. His teacher's first task was to establish herself as a reliable person who accepted him in every way, whatever he did. After many weeks he began, hesitantly, to play near other children when his teacher was with him. Then he began to use materials more aggressively and to act out some of his fears. Before many months, he was playing with other children although he needed "his" teacher with him at first. He had learned to trust in this situation and had begun to reach out to play with others. He also began to communicate with speech.

Some children lack social competence. They are unable to recognize an invitation to play. They miss the signals sent out by the other children to join in an experience. Adults in the center can help by saying, "Kerry wants you to hold the doll while she sets the table," there by putting into words for the child what the expectations for behavior are.

Alertness on the part of the adults in the center about temperamental differences such as children who are "slow to warm up" to a given situation is important, too. Allowing the child to watch for a while before moving into the play is more successful than pushing a child to join in. Centers will have a full range of temperamental styles represented from the bold active child to the timid withdrawn child. Working in harmony with the child's given temperament is far more successful than trying to change the child to meet teachers' expectations for behavior. (Chess & Thomas, 1987)

There are times in the lives of all children when they may not be free to play because they are overwhelmed by the new, the strange, or the feared. Children may become overwhelmed at times of illness, accidents, death, or family problems. Demands to perform beyond their ability or teasing can overwhelm them. It is important that all children who can not play or whose play is disorganized and aggressive find a trustworthy, reliable adult in their center. They need a teacher who will not push them to be busy, but rather one who will take time to build a trusting relationship and will help them find ways to cope with their particular stresses.

Fantasy and Imagination in Dramatic Play

Young children often confuse fantasy with reality. What they think seems true to them, whether or not it is true in reality. Children need help and time to make the distinction between reality and fantasy without having to reject their fantasies. They have a right to imagine and to create fantasies as well as a need to learn to identify reality.

Angelo is at the table playing with the clay. He rolls it with a rolling pin and pats it. He talks softly to himself. "Is that a birthday cake? Where are some candles?" He reaches and gets some cut straws and places them on the playdough. He then turns to a teacher sitting near and says, "I don't want to sing." The teacher assures him that it is all right to have a birthday cake and not sing. He blows two very hard puffs and says, "I blew it out," adding, "Where is the knife?" The teacher hands the knife to him. He says, "A really birthday because I'm cutting the cake. It must be real because I'm cutting it. I blew out the candles and I'm cutting it."

TEACHER: "You pretended to blow out the candles, didn't you?"
ANGELO: "Yes, but I'm really cutting it." He hands the teacher a piece, and he keeps a piece."

TEACHER: "You really cut it, but we'll have to pretend to eat it."

ANGELO: "Yeah." A slight frown comes across his face. He runs across the room to Jamie, who is building with blocks. "Superman, I cut the cake for you. I pretended it was my birthday."

Jamie smiles but makes no comment. Angelo runs back to the table, picks up the clock, and runs to Jamie with it.

ANGELO: "See what I got for my birthday?"

JAMIE: "Why?"

ANGELO: "Because it's my birthday, and it's brand new."

JAMIE: "Not your birthday."

ANGELO: "I pretended. I made a cake."

Angelo, like most 3- and 4-year-old children, is coping with the problem of the real and the pretend and is well on his way to finding pleasure in both. He makes the distinction when he says, "I cut the cake. I pretended it was my birthday."

It is sometimes a struggle for children to get the real world and the world of magic into their proper places. A child is fortunate who has help from a parent or a teacher in learning this. Imaginative tales can be valued for what they are, delightful figments of the imagination, a method of escape we can all profit from at times. It is fun to make up stories, but one should be clear about the differences between the "pretend" and the factual. Occasionally one meets a child who makes few contacts with other children and who seems to use fantasies repeatedly as a way of avoiding reality. The child who consistently escapes into fantasy is a child in need of professional help.

Self-Initiated Sociodramatic Play

At ages 4 and 5, children spend more time in the kind of play called sociodramatic by Sara Smilansky, who studied children's play in Israel and the United States. In dramatic play a child pretends to be someone else. He plays a role imitatively, and he may play alone. In sociodramatic play there must be at least one other role player, and the children interact with both words and actions in their make-believe. (Smilansky, 1971. In Engstrom, 1971.

In this episode we find three 4-year-old girls playing in a house made of two small screens covered by a blanket.

KIM: "There is a lion outside the house. We are frightened so we stay in."

BARBARA: "Yes, and we have to take care of baby sister, too, or else the bad lion will get her."

Kim comes out of the house. She finds another child, Bonnie, standing near the tent. Kim goes up to her, takes her hand and says, "You are a bad lion. You frighten people, so they lock you up in a cage. Now you go to your cage." (Pause.) Leads Bonnie to the other room, saying, "Come, I will make you a cage." She puts four long blocks together and tells Bonnie, "Now you get in there. That's your cage." Bonnie stands in the enclosure and Kim goes back to the house. She says, "The lion is locked in the cage, so we are safe."

In the meanwhile, Barbara, still in the house, says to Nancy, "Now you better listen to your big sister like a good girl or else the lion will catch you. Mommy will be back home soon." Kim, returning home, calls out to Bonnie from inside the tent, "You have escaped from the cage. You have unlocked the cage and you have escaped."

As Bonnie walks toward the tent, Kim shouts to the others. "The lion has escaped, the lion has escaped." They all three scream and shout.

KIM: "I must call the zoo and tell the manager." She picks up the telephone and calls. "There is a big lion escaped from the zoo and he is frightening us. Please get him, will you?" She puts down the receiver.

BARBARA: "Now they will come and get him and put him back in the cage, Ha! Ha!" Everything quiets down and the play shifts.

NANCY: "I am the mother."

KIM (pointing): "No. You (Barbara) are the big sister and you (Nancy) are the little sister. You are 8 and she is 5. You better mind her while I go out." She goes out for a few seconds and comes back.

KIM to BARBARA: "Did she (Nancy) mind?"

BARBARA: "No, she was a very bad girl."

KIM to NANCY: "Mommy is not mad at you, but next time you must mind."

NANCY: "I will."

Kim goes out for a few seconds and returns.

KIM to NANCY: "Did you do what mother said?"

NANCY: "Yes."

BARBARA: "I know. When you go somewhere like downtown, we could play ring around roses."

KIM: "But be careful, big sister, because she is only 3 and she might fall down and get hurt."

KIM to NANCY: "You didn't behave and we spanked you—not real hard—I'll show you how—it doesn't hurt, does it?"

NANCY: "No—but don't spank too hard, OK?"

KIM: "And then you played with the telephone."

BARBARA to NANCY: "You better not. You are too little to play with the telephone."

KIM to NANCY: "You were playing in the street and we caught you."

NANCY: "I have to go out to pick berries."

KIM: "No, because you fooled us." Pause. "Why do you have to pick berries?"

BARBARA: "I want to call Grandma." Picking up the telephone receiver. Dials 1, 2, 5, 8. Puts down the receiver. "I called but the line is busy."

BARBARA: "I am going to pick berries."

KIM to NANCY: "You also go to pick berries. When we are not looking."

KIM: "We must sleep now. Curl up, honey."

Nancy walks out on tiptoe. Suddenly Kim and Barbara rush out shouting. "Where is she? Where is she?" Both of them run out looking for Nancy. Barbara finds Nancy behind the door and shouts excitedly, "Here she is, Mom—hurry, Mommy." Barbara and Kim hold Nancy's hands on either side and drag her into the house. Kim pretends to lock the door of the house and tells Nancy, "You have been a bad girl. Now you have to stay in all day."

Here we see the children's concern about misbehavior, fears, playing in the street, running away, and taking care of siblings. They cope with the problem of being little and the temptations they face by creating a "bad lion" and dealing with him. They practice being the punishing parent themselves. They show well-informed solutions such as telephoning the zoo director to come and get the "escaped lion." The maternal role is an important one as they reflect a benign discipline and take care of baby sister.

All the elements of sociodramatic play are seen in their imitative role play, imaginative make-believe substituted for real objects, three players, and much verbal interaction. (Smilansky, 1971) Sociodramatic play builds confidence as they master the situations they create. They re-create their world, but this time they are in control.

The Beginnings of Group Games Develop Out of Dramatic Play

We see the beginnings of group games developing in children's spontaneous play, forerunners of the more organized games they will enjoy later. Four-year-olds enjoy very simple activities in groups. four or five children and a teacher may join hands in a circle on the grass in "ring-around-a-rosy, and we all fall down" with appropriate action. Marching becomes a group activity with a variety of instruments in the band and frequent changes of leader. We need to guard against too much patterning, or we may lose the spontaneous development of group feeling that holds much value for children.

Chapter Overview

Playing is a creative experience, an act of the imagination, and one that can be enjoyed alone or shared. We have seen that the values found in play can help children establish relationships with others. Self-confidence is gained as children learn skills for getting along with others in play. Spontaneous, playful behavior is a source of satisfaction and relief. Winnicott writes, "It is in playing and only in playing that the individual child or adult is able to be creative and to use the whole personality, and it is only in being creative that the individual discovers the self." (Winnicott, 1971) Play brings the inner world of feeling in touch with the outer world of shared reality. Play leads to the integration of personality. Play is the way a child begins to make sense of the world.

Projects

1. Observe a group of children playing and record an incident:
   A. in which a child seems to be discovering something about the nature of the world while playing
   B. in which the child seems to use play as a way of mastering an anxiety, fear, or conflict
   C. in which the child is re-creating a role in the world around him
   D. in which the child is discovering what other people are like

2. Describe the closed play materials, that is, those that require attention to constraints for a correct solution, such as puzzles, geoblocks, and lotto. Describe the open play materials that have no one particular "right way" to play (i.e., blocks, paints, clay, housekeeping).

3. Write a report about the value of play in young children's learning. Investigate the authors included in "For Your Further Reading" for references.

For Your Further Reading

Cherry, C. (1976). *Creative play for the developing child: Early lifehood education through play.* Belmont, CA: Fearon Pitman. Begins with developing a philosophy of play, then discusses physical and human influences on the play environment. Like the author's useful books on creative art and movement, this book offers detailed, practical ideas on facilitating play in many areas of the program.

Garvey, C. (1977). *Play.* The developing child series. Cambridge, MA: Harvard University Press. A basic, readable book that starts with the question, "What is play?" and then examines play with interaction, objects, language, social interaction, rules, and ritual.

McKee, J. S. (Ed.). (1986). *Play: Working partner of growth.* Wheaton, MD: Association for Childhood Education International. Interesting articles on aspects like learning through make-believe, role of teachers in play, and play with children who have special needs. A particularly helpful chapter describes play materials for children from birth to age 10.

Rogers, C. S., & Sawyers, J. K. (1988). *Play in the lives of children.* Washington, DC: National Association for the Education of Young Children. Helpful introduction to stages of play, what children learn through play, and how adults can encourage it.

Sawyers, J. K., & Rogers, C. S. (1988). *Helping young children develop through play: A practical guide for parents, caregivers, and teachers.* Washington, DC: National Association for the Education of Young Children. Covers play with each age group: infants and toddlers, preschool, and school-age children. Gives practical suggestions.

Strom, R. D. (Ed.). (1981). *Growing through play.* Monterey, CA: Brooks Cole. Many short articles on significant aspects of play. Chapter 2, "Playing alone," (pp. 35–57), consists of sections on dominion play, solitary play, and a child's need for privacy.

Trawick-Smith, J. (1988). "Let's say you're the baby, OK?" Play leadership and following behavior of young children. *Young Children, 43*(5), 51–59. Defines play leadership; discusses skills of effective leaders as well as characteristics of three kinds of unskilled leaders. Concludes with suggestions for teachers to enhance both leading and following behaviors.

Winnicott, D. W. (1971). *Playing and reality.* New York: Basic Books. Emphasizes the importance of children's self-initiated dramatic play in helping the child understand reality and its relation to creative thinking in adult life. Useful for those familiar with Winnicott's earlier writing.

Feelings of Security and Confidence

Snail and his house (*boy, 4 years*)

This chapter explores the teacher's feelings and children's feelings of confidence, including:

▶ What makes children feel secure and confident?
▶ How can we recognize children's feelings to help them feel secure?
▶ How do we accept children's feelings?
▶ How can we help children gain confidence through expressing feelings?
▶ How does my teaching help children gain security and confidence?

CRITERIA: Staff are available and responsive to children; encourage them to share experiences, ideas, and feelings; and listen to them with attention and respect. (Criterion A-2) . . . Staff speak with children in a friendly, positive, courteous manner . . . (Criterion A-3). Staff equally treat children of all races, religions, family backgrounds, and cultures with equal respect and consideration . . . (Criterion A-4). The sound of the environment is primarily marked by pleasant conversation, spontaneous laughter, and exclamations of excitement rather than harsh, stressful noise or enforced quiet . . . (Criterion A-7). Staff assist children to be comfortable, relaxed, happy, and involved in play and other activities . . . (Criterion A-8). (NAEYC, 1991a. *Accreditation criteria . . .* , pp. 15, 16, 17, 18)

"Look here, teacher, I'm bigger than you think. I'm going to have a birthday soon. Let me do this by myself," said Katherine to a well-meaning adult who was trying to help her.

Katherine's words remind us of how often adults handicap children by acting as though children were unable to meet situations. A child has a difficult time developing confidence when surrounded by people who "help" all the time. Children often are more competent than we think. Katherine was able to express her self-confidence as a person able to do things, but most children lack not only this verbal ability but also the feeling itself.

As adults, most of us probably wish that we had more self-confidence. We realize that we are likely to do a thing better when we feel confident than when we are afraid of failing. We realize, too, that we get more pleasure out of doing something when we feel adequate and are free from anxiety. For all of us, feelings of insecurity and a lack of confidence are handicapping. The person who has self-confidence may enjoy undertaking something entirely new, but many people are not free enough of self-doubts to consider the unfamiliar a challenge to them.

Security refers to the feelings that come with having had many experiences of being accepted rather than rejected and of feeling safe rather than threatened. Security results from a person's having had positive relationships with people. Confidence refers to the feelings of cheerful assurance that an individual has, related to the individual's self-concept as the kind of person able to meet and overcome challenges. This concept, too, grows out of responses from others. Security and confidence are closely related. Secure children dare to be themselves. They play with materials and use the equipment in appropriate ways. They play with other children as well as alone. As we work with children, we will seek ways of strengthening their feelings of confidence and security.

Foundations for Feeling Secure and Confident

Feelings of security and confidence develop from the way the infant's basic needs are met: experiences with feeding and, later, with toileting; the kinds of responses received from other people; and the satisfaction found in exploring the world. Out of these early experiences, the child builds a feeling of trust in the world, her first developmental task. Having learned to trust others, she is ready to trust and have confidence in herself. The

Being fed by her mother, this infant learns to trust and to feel secure. Santa Monica College, Santa Monica, California

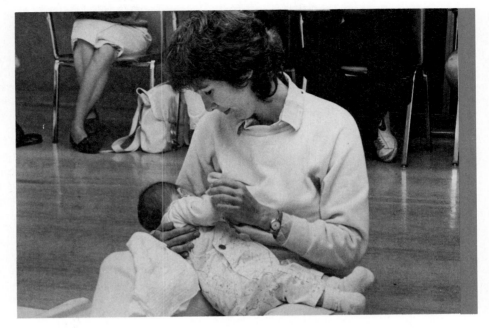

attitudes and feelings of her parents are the most important factors in building confidence because she depends largely on them to satisfy her basic needs.

If the child's first experiences have made her feel secure and confident because her needs were satisfied, if she has obtained positive responses from people, and if she has had satisfying sensory experiences, then a firm foundation for confidence and security has been laid. If, on the other hand, basic needs have not been met and if she has failed to get response when she needed it, the child has already experienced insecurity and felt inadequate. If she constantly heard the words "no" and "don't" when reaching out for experience, she has already grown to distrust her own impulses. The world does not seem to be a place where she can feel safe, and she builds a picture of herself as a person inadequate to cope with problems. She may begin to think of herself as a person who is likely to do the wrong thing.

Children Are Influenced in Their Feelings by the Attitudes of Adults

Children tend to behave as they feel they are expected to behave or according to the concept of self they have built from people's responses to them.

Paul, a 3 1/2-year-old, thinks of himself as a boy who gets into trouble. As he and his father came into nursery school one morning, his father remarked, "See how nice and quiet this place is until you get here!" What is a boy like who hears words such as these? He is a boy who is noisy, defiant, and difficult. He lives up to the picture his father paints.

Eric, a 4-year-old, was brought by his mother to the center and she explained to the teacher as Eric stood beside her, "Perhaps he'll learn to ride a tricycle here. He doesn't know how yet. He just tries for a minute and then gives up." It was not surprising that Eric lacked confidence, did not persist, and was unfriendly with both children and teachers.

Ella, a 3-year-old, was timid. She didn't join other children in play, but she did like to paint. She was at the easel painting carefully around the edges of the paper when her mother came for her one day. Her mother saw the picture, and she said half-scornfully, "Nobody paints like that!" How can one have much confidence if one is considered a "nobody"? Ella didn't expect to have an important place in the group.

Keisha, a 3-year-old, was new in the center, eager for experiences but lacking in skills. Climbing fascinated her. One day she tried very hard to climb a tree even though she was afraid. With help from the teacher, she finally managed to reach a high limb. Delighted, she called out to everyone, "Look, I'm up here as brave as ever." We see in this incident the element of healthy personality development. Keisha sees herself as brave. She has made an effort and mastered a difficult feat. She wants to share her delight. She is sure there will be someone who cares.

Children who have confidence and do not feel helpless have less need to fight against adults. They can accept adults without feeling threatened by them. Some children, on the other hand, never develop sufficient confidence to defy adults but remain anxious and dependent on them. They are "good" children but not happy or emotionally healthy. It takes insight to perceive that resistant behavior may mean growth for the child as a person. It takes insight both into the child's behavior and into our own behavior. It takes skill, too, to guide a child so that the values of this stage are retained and, at the same time, safe limits and a respect for the child are maintained.

To understand children who are in this phase of development we must understand our own feelings. Because most of us have many areas of insecurity, we may find it hard not to feel threatened by resistance. The adult who meets children's attacks with, "I won't have that" or, "You can't get away with that," reveals herself as an adult who is defending herself against feeling helpless rather than as one who is helping the resistant child.

Leighton and Kluckhohn (1947) make an interesting comment on the attitudes that appear in another culture. They describe the way the Navaho treat young children: " . . . the Navaho toddler is given self-confidence by being made to feel that he is constantly loved and valued." Would Ella and Eric have behaved differently if they had lived under conditions in which they were "constantly loved and valued"? Many children in our culture are "constantly loved and valued," but many others are treated as "nobodies," like Ella and Eric, even though there is no conscious intent on the part of adults to treat them this way.

We live in such a competitive society that it is often hard for us to recognize the values that may exist outside of achievement. Parents feel the pressure for accomplishment. They want children who will learn to write their names or who paint good pictures. They push their children, even toddlers. Children who have been pushed through a developmental stage frequently have to go back and experience it again before they are free to go on or secure enough to develop further.

Adults May Make Children Feel Guilty

Children sometimes find it hard to develop self-confidence because they feel they are to blame for things that happen. A child may enjoy an activity, such as playing in the mud or exploring a dresser drawer, only to find that what she has done is considered unacceptable by the adult. With little basis for real understanding of adult values and with a great need to please adults because of her dependency on them, she comes to feel uncertain about herself and her behavior. Many times she thinks that mistakes are much more serious than we really consider them, and she suffers from a heavy load of guilt. When we blame the child for what she does not understand or understands only in part, we damage her feelings of confidence and trust in herself.

By making events conditional on a child's good or bad behavior, we may increase her sense of uncertainty and lack of confidence. She may feel responsible for events that have no connection.

 Betsy said, "Next week if I'm a real good girl, know where we're going? To the beach!"

Let's hope that her parents were not "too busy" or "tired that week" and that nothing interfered with their plan. Children who can bring about a trip to the beach by being good can also cause calamity by being bad.

 Pam arrived at nursery school one morning and didn't see the ducks. She was very interested in them and inquired anxiously, "I can't see the ducks." Then she added, "I made a noise. Do ducks get headaches?"

Pam has evidently had to bear a feeling of guilt for causing headaches. Without enough experience to correct her concepts, the child is the victim of her misapprehensions. We may not suspect a child's real feelings or the heavy load of guilt she may feel for events.

Adults May Be Afraid of Spoiling Children

Sometimes adults are afraid to accept children as they are and to meet their needs because they are afraid of "spoiling" them. They needlessly deny and interfere with children because of ignorance of the growth process. They make it hard for the child to think of herself as adequate. "Spoiled" children are, in fact, those who get attention when the adult wants to give it rather than when the child needs it. They are those children who are subject to inconsistent interferences rather than being given the support of consistent limits by parents willing to take responsibility for limits. Flexible handling that allows the child to live on her own level tends to build secure feelings in the young child rather than "spoil" her. It reduces to a minimum the denials and interferences that are likely to shake a child's confidence. It accepts her as she is. It helps her feel adequate.

Adults Can Be Caring without Spoiling

Children need limits. Adults who let a child do anything she wants are avoiding responsibilities. These limits sometimes can be set at quite different points. One person will not interfere with a child or stop her in what she does unless sure the child's action will result in undesirable consequences. The child is thus free to explore and experiment with materials, to act in all kinds of childish ways, and to learn for herself. Another adult will interfere or stop a child unless sure that what the child is doing is desirable. There is much less room for the child to discover and to try out ways of acting under this method. The first person's attitude is "caring," in contrast to the second person's restrictive attitude.

By caring we do not mean indulgence. Instead, we mean leaving children free to explore, to discover, to create and to find their own way within acceptable limits. That extends to a generous quality in giving to the child, not a meager giving: "Of course you can," rather than, "I guess you can, but I wish you wouldn't"; or, "Take all you need," rather than, "Don't take much"; or, "There's plenty for everyone," rather than, "No one can have more than one piece." When we give generously, children grow less anxious. They need less.

Children are not helped to build confidence by parents who are indulgent, who give in to them rather than face the unpleasant behavior of a thwarted child. Children are more secure if there is no lack of firmness when firmness is needed. Both parents and child need to learn to face unpleasant realities in constructive ways, rather than avoid facing them.

Adults Need to Be Secure People

A secure adult is relaxed, comfortable, giving, feeling no need to make demands on others. Secure people are likely to create the kind of environment in which it is easy for the child to think of himself as an adequate person. Mike, for example, has lived with comfortable parents. He is free of defenses. He looks at the puzzle he worked the day before and says, "That one was hard for me. And today I'm going to do one that's even harder." He is a secure child, able to try new things and eager to learn.

Insecure people are often defensive and demanding, likely to set standards that the child can meet only with difficulty, if at all. They are likely to be very concerned with what other people say about them as parents. Many reasons may explain why parents have a hard time feeling secure. They may be handicapped by economic insecurities, tensions, and conflicts in the world, or by inadequate housing, limited community resources in health and recreation, or by an education that offers little guidance in understanding parent–child relationships. Paul's father, who speaks in a belittling way to his son, is typical of many parents. He wants to be a successful parent, but he lacks experience and preparation for the role. Like many people, he values success and is striving for it professionally. His concept of a successful parent is one whose child behaves like an adult. He feels he has failed to achieve this goal with Paul. His love for the child is hidden under his constant criticism. He is not a secure parent. He makes Paul an insecure child.

By the time the child reaches 2 or 3, feelings of security and confidence should outweigh those of mistrust and doubt. The child may have come from a home where the parents are too insecure themselves to be able to accept immaturity. Clear evidence exists that the quality of the experience a young child has with parents is far more important than the amount of time spent together. (Stevens & Mathews, 1978) A mother or father who enjoys spending time with the child can contribute greatly to the enrichment of the child's development, even though the time they have to spend with each other is limited. Both boys and girls profit when the father enjoys being with his young children. He brings a different quality to the caregiving than the mother. It also seems true that parents who find satisfactions in their own lives, at work and at home, are likely to give a child the freedom and the encouragement needed to develop her own interests. The satisfied parent is likely to provide many of the experiences that will enrich the child's intellectual development and increase self-confidence.

Recognizing The Child's Feelings

How do we recognize a child's feelings? How do we identify feelings so that we may help a child?

Children reveal their feelings through behavior. Sometimes they do it openly and directly, and they act as they feel. Sometimes their feelings come out in ways that are more difficult to identify. We must learn to understand their feelings; then we can recognize how plainly they speak to us through behavior.

The first step in understanding the meaning of behavior is to be able to look at the way a child behaves without feeling a necessity to change his behavior. We must learn to look at behavior as it is rather than in terms of what we want it to be. We are likely to confuse the meaning of a child's behavior with our own feelings if we try to judge it or if we decide that the child should or should not be behaving as he is.

Cues in Nonverbal Behavior

We have already pointed out how children differ in the kinds of adjustments they make to new situations. These differences have meaning. Adults who wish to understand a child watch carefully how he responds in a new situation. They do not decide how the child should respond and try to force that pattern of response on him.

Children reveal characteristic attitudes in everyday, familiar situations, too. These cues may be seen in such things as the way the child walks and runs and holds his hands or his facial expressions and posture. Posture is, of course, influenced by constitutional and environmental factors, but over and above these, reflections of the child's emotional patterns

A distressed child can gain feelings of security from the teacher's comfort. The child regains control with help. Santa Monica College, Child Development Center, Santa Monica, California

can be seen in his muscle tensions. One child's hands are relaxed, and another's are tense and constantly moving. One child clutches our finger tightly as we walk along, a sign of the need for support and the intensity of feelings. Another lets his hand lie limply in ours, suggesting perhaps the nongiving quality of his relationships with others, in contrast to the warm, responsive grip of still another child who welcomes closeness without clinging to it. These bits of behavior are all cues that help us understand the child's feelings.

Sometimes a conflict the child is feeling is expressed in the movements of his hands, as in the case of the child who is watching finger painting. He may stand at a distance, wiping his clean hands on his shirt or wringing them together, showing us the conflict he feels between the wish to put his hands into the paint and the force of the restriction not to get dirty.

Cues in Speech

Voice quality and language offer cues to feelings. The quality of a child's voice may be strained and tight, or relaxed and easy. It may be loud and harsh, or soft and faint, or confident and well-modulated. Even the amount of speech may indicate the extent of the child's assurance or hesitation. One child talks very little; another chatters almost constantly. These extremes may be reactions to strains and pressures that are making them feel less confident and less secure than they should feel. Insistent, needless questions are sometimes a symptom of insecurity, a seeking for reassurance more than for any specific answer. Too often these questions meet an impatient rebuff, not calculated to satisfy the need they express.

Spontaneous singing usually indicates confidence and contentment. The child who sings at play is probably comfortable, and it is worth noting the times and places when singing occurs spontaneously. We can learn from this behavior in what areas or on what occasions a child feels secure.

The child who asks the teacher, "Do you want to go outdoors with me?" may really be saying, "I'm afraid to go out by myself. It would help if you wanted to go with me." The teacher needs to understand the meaning behind what the child says.

The child who says happily, "Isn't this going to be a good gate? I'm building it all myself," is telling us something about the comfortable feelings he has about himself. This same boy's father once remarked, "I think he's one of those fortunate people who like themselves." The child liked himself—and everyone else; he was one of the most likeable children one could meet. He had been "loved and valued" in his family.

There is a real consciousness of an emerging self in these words of Katherine—the same Katherine who is "bigger than you think"—when she says, "I'm different from all the other people. When other people laugh, I don't, even if it's silly." Katherine feels secure enough to be different.

Cues in Behavior

Children who feel insecure are likely to face a new situation or a difficult problem by defending themselves. They may retreat, avoid the activity, resist, or attack. Their defensiveness may make it difficult for them in the situation. Children who feel secure, on the other hand, do not feel the need to defend themselves. They are free to look for ways of coping with the situation. They often seek new experiences.

Three-year-old Ralph bursts into tears when someone knocks against the tower he is building, and then he hits frantically at the offender. He has little confidence in his ability to cope with interference.

When people lack confidence in themselves, they may act defensively. Janet, who is new in day care, cries when the teacher asks her to be quiet at rest time. She is too insecure to accept any indication that she is behaving unacceptably. The teacher's suggestion that it was time to settle down and rest would have helped a child who felt at home in the school. The

This girl's self-esteem and pride of achievement show in her face.
Migrant Head Start, Chico, California

comfortable child can cope with demands. The insecure child tries to defend against them.

Sometimes we meet a child who is unable to accept comforting even from a familiar teacher. This child may not welcome a friendly pat, or may avoid an expression of closeness such as a hug. He often is an insecure child who may have found relationships unreliable and unsatisfying. Only slowly does he come to trust adults. Occasionally we find a child striving for autonomy who resents comforting. He has developed patterns for finding his own way and sees the adult's approach as encroaching on his independence. Only by careful observation can we determine each child's needs.

The secure child finds it easy to be friendly. He can share with others because he does not fear loss. He does not need to defend his rights. The insecure child can not afford to share. His problem is not one of selfishness or unfriendliness, but one of degree of security. We need to handle the real problem, not the symptom, in such cases.

Sometimes the Cues Are Indirect

Peter, a 3-year-old, had a hard time separating from his mother when she started to leave the school. He cried and protested. His mother was distressed and felt she could not leave him. One day he had this conversation with his teacher as she was helping him get ready to go home:

PETER (half-teasingly): "Miss Williams, will my locker be here when I come back?"
Miss W.: "Yes, Peter, it will be right here waiting for you."
PETER: "If my locker starts to run away, will you hold it?"
Miss W.: "Yes, I'll hold it tight and tell it to stay right here because Peter is coming tomorrow."
PETER: "You just hold it. I want it right here."

As the teacher thought about the conversation, she felt that in an indirect way Peter was telling her that although he wanted to run away and go home, he wanted more to stay at school. He needed more help from her in resolving the conflict he felt in separating from his mother. He wanted his teacher to "hold" him, like the locker.

She telephoned his mother and suggested that the mother try leaving, even though Peter protested, for Peter really was enjoying school and might be ready to stay by himself. The mother left him the next day, a bit reluctantly, for he was crying and struggling. Almost immediately he relaxed and was ready for play under the watchful eye of his teacher. She had given him the help he wanted.

Alex, a 4-year-old, shows us what a name tag can symbolize to a child. He was proud of the name tag he wore and reminded the teacher to put it on each morning. One day one of the teachers reproved him for something he did. Alex said nothing, but a few minutes later this teacher observed that he had taken off the name tag. She felt it was as though he did not want his name to be associated with misbehavior. He could remove his guilty self by removing the tag.

Thumb Sucking May Be a Symptom of Insecurity

One may see a child sucking a thumb at rest time, or when the group is listening to a story, or even during a play period. Like all behavior, thumb sucking is a symptom and may indicate a need in the child for more reassurance and greater security. It may be a difficult world for him because of expectations to be more grown-up than he is ready to be. He may be expected to be quiet, to inhibit impulses for touching things, to take over adult ways of behaving at the table or in social situations, to comprehend and maintain the rules for property rights. The strain of living up to all these demands or of failing to live up to them may be so great that the child seeks an infantile source of comfort—turning to his thumb as a refuge.

The child is telling us something through thumb sucking, and we need to understand. Adults should not increase strain by taking away this avenue of comfort but should try to make his life simpler and more comfortable. They should try to reduce the child's tensions and offer a greater opportunity for feeling secure and adequate, so that he may seek other kinds of satisfactions.

 Mary Lou Took Her Own Thumb Out of Her Mouth   Three-and-a-half-year-old Mary Lou sucked her thumb most of the time at the center. She was timid and often held onto the teacher's skirt with her free hand. She didn't venture into activity with other children or even play alone actively.

Mary Lou was the oldest of three children and had always been a "good" girl, according to her mother. She had been easy to care for and could even be depended on to watch her little sister while her mother was busy with the baby. She seemed content with little to do and never disturbed the younger siblings. It was not hard to imagine that Mary Lou had had very little chance to have the satisfactions that usually come with being a baby. She had grown up quickly, seeking approval by behaving in unchildlike ways.

She remained dependent on the teacher for many weeks, but her interest in the children was plain as she watched a group having fun together. Sitting close to the teacher, she sometimes became part of a group at the piano or at the clay table. She had a real capacity for enjoying what she was doing and a sense of humor that became evident as she felt freer to act. She thoroughly enjoyed the clay, the sandbox, and the mud hole in the playyard. She often played alone in the homemaking area after she felt more comfortable.

Later she ventured into more active play. She still stood watching activities with her thumb in her mouth part of the time, but she was busy in the sandbox or riding the tricycles more of the time. The most marked change came after she gained enough courage to use the slide. Sliding was a popular activity, and Mary Lou often would stand watching, but she resisted any suggestion that she join the group. At last on a day when no one else was at the slide, she tried it, with her favorite teacher near to hold her hand. It was an effort, but she succeeded and went down again and again. She waved gaily to her mother when she came that day and showed off her newly acquired skill. From then on she participated more freely in every group. Mastering the slide seemed to give her confidence. She even did a little pushing to hold her place in line at the slide and began to stand up for herself in other ways. She was active and happy. She rarely had time for her thumb. By the end of a year some of the adults had even forgotten that she used to suck her thumb. The fact that she no longer needed her thumb told a great deal about the change in Mary Lou.

All Nervous Habits Are Symptoms

Some children may express their tensions by biting their nails, twisting on their clothing, or sucking other objects. Masturbation is another means of finding satisfaction and a defense against strain. We may do a great deal of harm by attacking the symptom directly and denying the child an avenue of expression while he is still feeling tension and seeking relief and satisfaction. We need to look on all of these so-called nervous habits as symptoms of a cause that must be sought and treated before the symptom itself can be expected to disappear. Treating only the symptom may make some other form of expression necessary for the child and increase the strain he feels. Thumb-sucking may evolve into nail-biting or masturbating, for example, if the symptom and not the cause is attacked. All kinds of behavior have meanings that we cannot afford to ignore.

Accepting The Child's Feelings

In all of these ways, a child shows how she feels. After we have learned to recognize the child's feelings, we must find ways of adding to her security and confidence and reducing her insecurity. What are some of the ways we can do this in the center?

We Must Face and Accept Feelings If We Are to Help

The most important step is to make sure that we really accept the child's feelings and that we do not condemn or blame. Perhaps she feels afraid or angry or unfriendly. These may be feelings of which we do not approve, but approval and acceptance are different things. Acceptance means recognizing without blaming. It does not mean permitting the child to act out feelings as she may wish, but it does mean acknowledging that she has the right to those feelings without being ashamed. Our very acceptance often reduces the feeling and makes the child less defensive about the insecurity, fear, or anger. Instead of hiding feelings, she can bring them out where she, and we, can do more about them.

Accepting Our Own Feelings May Be Difficult

We usually find it difficult to accept feelings that we have had to deny in ourselves. As children we often felt jealous, resentful, or hostile, but we may not have been permitted any expression of these feelings. We had to act as though we loved a little sister, for example, and were willing to share our dolls with her, or we had to let the neighbor boy ride in our wagon because the adults insisted that children must be generous. Now we find it hard to accept the child who refuses to share her doll or who pushes another out of the wagon. We feel like punishing this child. This helps us deny that we were ever like this girl or boy. If we handle our feelings by denying them, we cannot offer help to children who face problems with their feelings.

Few of us will have escaped childhood without some areas of behavior we find hard to accept. If, on the other hand, we were helped to accept our real feelings when we were children, we will now find it easier to accept children as they show their feelings. If the adults with us when we were children said, "It's easy to get angry at someone who takes your things, I know," instead of saying, "She's your sister, and you must love her and share with her," then we would have felt understood and could have faced our feelings with this kind of support. It would have seemed easier to feel and act more generously. This is the kind of help we want to offer the children we care for.

It is important that we free ourselves of our old defenses. As adults we can now take the step of accepting the reality of any feelings that exist. All of us find sharing and loving difficult at times. Some jealousy is inevitable as children adjust to changing patterns in the family or at the center. It is not necessary to deny the existence of feelings. Hostile, aggressive feelings exist in all of us. Finding appropriate outlets is the task.

Acceptance Helps the Child

The child who refuses to share a toy is not helped by disapproval and shaming. Neither is the child who is afraid. These children need to be accepted as they are if they are to feel secure. There is always a reason for their behavior. As we work with the child who refuses to share a doll or who pushes a companion out of the wagon, we will accept those feelings and use the behavior as a cue to understanding. We will ask ourselves some questions. What kind of child is it who tries to keep the doll—one who craves affection and substitutes the doll for love? Does this child depend on possessing things to give feelings of security? How can we help?

We Can Voice Our Acceptance of Feelings

We can express our acceptance in words: "I know how you feel. It makes you cross because it's Timmy's turn on the swing and you want it to be yours" or, "You feel mad when your blocks tumble over" or, "You're pretty angry with me right now because I can't let you play outdoors." Words like these help if they express a real acceptance of the feelings that exist. They are different from words like, "You didn't mean to hit Bobby, did you?" that are untrue, as the child's reply, "I did, too," tells us. We must be honest and state what is true.

Expression Of Feelings Leads to Confidence

Feelings must be expressed in some way if we are to be secure and confident. If feelings are not expressed, they remain with us to be carried around until they come out unexpectedly in ways that may make us unhappy and less sure of ourselves.

Feelings are best expressed at the time they occur. The child who says, "I'm afraid," is already less troubled by the feeling of fear. The child who says, "I don't like you," to someone who frightens him may be managing the feeling better than the child who says nothing but then bursts into tears when the person tries to make his acquaintance. The child who is angry needs to do something about the feeling at the time, rather than keeping the anger hidden where it may come out in more damaging ways later; by that time, the anger may have grown.

When we can do something about the way we feel, we are more confident. Psychiatrists say the child who has been aggressive in his early years and whose behavior has been met with understanding has a better chance to make a good adjustment in adolescence than the submissive child. The aggressive child has done something about the feelings and has had an opportunity to identify them and learn how to manage them.

It Is Essential to Express Feelings in Words

When children can use language to release negative feelings, they have taken a step toward being able to control feelings. Their later responses will be more reasonable.

As adults, we often put our feelings into words to ourselves, silently, and then we know how we feel. We may feel even better if we can talk to a friend. Putting a feeling into words makes it clear to us, and thus it seems more manageable. It helps drain it. Knowing how one feels is tremendously important. It is a dangerous thing to try to fool ourselves about our feelings. We must understand and face our feelings if we are to be secure, comfortable people.

The child needs help in understanding what he feels and in putting his feelings into words. We should welcome verbal expressions, for this means a step in his growth. Children usually find it easy to talk things out directly, on the spot. They call people names or shout insults to one another. They may be using the best means of handling feelings that they have for they are not grown up people yet. They are controlling the impulse to hit or attack, and they are expressing, not hiding, their feelings.

 Sharona, a 4 1/2-year-old, shows what putting feelings into words can do for a child. Sharona had been in the center about six months and had been developing well. She was a friendly, active child who enjoyed play with other children, and she was eager and curious.

Then Sharona began to change. She had a worried look on her face. One morning she dictated the following journal entry to the teacher.

The Boogie Man and Mommy

The boogie man tried to get the mommy boogieman and the childrens. The childrens were crying. They were both sick. They were fighting. The brother was fighting with his sister. The mother was fighting with her husband. Then they were happy. That's why they were eating so much cookies. There's a horsie in her tummy.

The teacher showed Sharona's mother the Boogie Man story. "This doesn't surprise me at all. I can tell you exactly where that came from." Sharona's sister Jo, 16, had recently announced her pregnancy. The news had created tremendous tension and had divided the bicultural family. The mother, who had her first child at 16, understood Jo's need for a supportive family. But teen pregnancy was not an accepted practice in Sharona's father's culture. The father felt disgraced by his daughter. What was once a peaceful, loving household turned into a battleground. The father couldn't talk about his feelings, and he didn't want anyone else to, either. It wasn't until he saw Sharona's journal entry about the boogie man that he realized what he was doing to the family. Finally he could talk about the pregnancy. The teacher sharing this experience said, "I have never questioned that writing has a great capacity to heal the writer. But now the writings of a 4-year-old have healed an entire family." A.S.

Jill, a 4-year-old, had an experience in the doctor's office that left her frightened and upset. Her parents had comforted her as well as they could and tried to interest her in other things. Since they were disturbed themselves about the affair, they preferred not to talk about it. This occurred over a holiday and they did not mention it to the teacher when Jill returned to the center. The teacher noticed a change in Jill's behavior. She was quiet and passive. She clung to the teacher and cried easily. Her teacher felt sure that something was wrong and asked the parents for a conference. Gladly they told her about the incident. They, too, had felt that Jill was acting differently, and they were eager to help. The teacher pointed out that it was important for Jill to talk to someone about her fears. Jill's mother seemed understanding, although she felt it might be hard for her to talk with Jill about the matter. The teacher suggested that the next time Jill got upset and cried, her mother might tell her that she, too, had been upset in the doctor's office, that she understood how Jill had felt, and that it was good to talk about the matter.

A few days later the mother telephoned to report that she had had a talk with Jill the night before. The parents were preparing to go to bed and had found Jill still awake. She seemed unhappy. The mother had gone into the room and, sitting on Jill's bed, she had begun to talk with her about the frightening experience. She said that at first Jill did not seem able to put anything into words, but as they continued talking, she became freer and finally went over all the details. Her mother told Jill that whenever she felt unhappy and afraid, she could talk with her, that she would understand, for she felt the same way sometimes.

At rest time that day in school, Jill said to the teacher, "You know what happened? Last night I was unhappy, and I told Mummy." The teacher asked, "And Mummy understood?" "Yes," said Jill, "she asked me why I was unhappy, and I couldn't say, but she knew it was about the doctor." The teacher answered, "Mummies do understand and know, and you can tell Mummy when you feel that way again." Jill went on, "And she said that at night when I am unhappy to come and tell Mummy and Daddy, but I wasn't unhappy anymore. I was just a little unhappy, and now I'm happy." The teacher repeated, "Mummies and daddies do understand, don't they! You can always tell them."

That evening the teacher telephoned Jill's mother to tell her about the conversation. Jill's mother could hardly believe that Jill had repeated this conversation, even using the same words the mother had used to her. She realized it had made a deep impression on the child. She felt that she herself could talk to the child more easily now.

At the center and at home Jill's behavior began to change rapidly. She played and laughed that day, jumping in and out of a box with two other children. She began to assert herself more and to take her place in the activities of the center. She became more like her old self. It seemed wonderful to the teachers, too, that a conversation with a mother who understood could do so much to relieve a child. Putting her fears into words with the help of someone she trusted had drained much of the disturbing feeling and had left the little girl free to grow as before. Her mother had learned from the experience. It gave her confidence. She knew better how to help her child.

There Are Other Ways to Express Feelings

Crying is another good way to express feelings, yet many times we hear people tell a crying child, "That didn't hurt. You're too big to cry." Whatever the reason, the feeling of wanting to cry is there and needs to be accepted. Words like, "I know how you feel," when they are said by a person who really accepts the feeling, help a good deal more than words like, "You're too big to cry."

A young child may kick, bite, hit, or throw to express feelings. Our job is to help him use motor outlets in a way that will not hurt others. He may even need to be put by himself so that he can act in these ways without hurting anyone. An older child may be able to take a suggestion about using a punching bag. Vigorous physical activity, such as pounding or throwing a ball hard against something, will serve as an outlet.

If there is a warm, understanding relationship between child and adult, the child can accept many types of suggestions for releasing negative feelings. The teacher may be successful by saying, "You feel just like hitting someone, I know, but you must not do it. Try hitting the target over there with these beanbags. See how many times you can hit it. I'll count the hits." The child may be able to handle his feelings with the help of an understanding, accepting teacher. Our first job is to see that he does not use destructive outlets. Then we can direct him to outlets that are possible and acceptable.

Creative expression can be used to release feelings and make them more manageable. Finger painting, painting at the easel, working with clay, or playing in water, the sandbox, or a good old mud hole will help a child relax as he expresses feelings through these media.

Creative materials should be freely available to children because of their value in the expression of feelings. Adults use these same outlets. The child who has found he can turn feelings into such creative channels has discovered an outlet that will serve him throughout life. A child is more secure if many avenues of expression are open to him. He grows when he can express ideas and feelings through art. If he is denied self-expression because models are set for him, a valuable avenue for the relief of feelings is lost.

The Timid or Shy Child Can Learn to Express Feelings

We will often see a timid, child launch into unduly aggressive behavior as he begins to gain confidence. This may be the first step in gaining confidence. He must first express his feelings and find acceptance for them. Then he can proceed to modify them. The child who has been inhibited may express feelings in clumsy and inappropriate ways in the beginning. The first expression of feeling may seem exaggerated. This expression may belong at a much younger level than his present chronological age. With understanding guidance he will come through this stage quickly, but he must "live out," for however brief a time, a period of expression at the less mature level. He must try out being "bad" and discover that he is accepted and that his "badness" does not frighten the adult. It can be managed.

'Transitional Objects' Give Security

As we saw in Chapter 13, children sometimes use "transitional objects" to help themselves feel more secure and better able to cope with new or diffi-

Elements of "soft-ness" in a center lead to feelings of security: rugs, pillows, rocking chairs, laps, soft furry animals.
Valley College, Campus Child Development Center, Los Angeles

cult situations. For some children it may be a blanket they have had from babyhood. For others it may be a cuddly toy. Carrying it or knowing it is available may help the child weather the strains he feels. The object is a device for coping with a difficult world. It has symbolic value for the child.

Transitional objects help in the "weaning" process that is part of growing. They are useful in periods of change when the child must leave behind the old sources of security. They signal to us the child's need for support as well as the effort he is making to deal with change. One 2-year-old in a group could not part with his sweater for several weeks after entering the group. It may have represented his mother or home. He wore the sweater or carried it, and became very anxious if it was out of sight. The way a child uses a transitional object gives us insight into his feelings.

A Child Feels More Secure When Having Satisfying Experiences

Having his needs met applies to the child's experience in the center as well as to experience at home. If the center is providing satisfying, stimulating opportunities, it makes it easier for the child to be happy and secure. The whole program, including the equipment provided, will contribute to the child's feeling more secure and adequate. Learning opportunities adapted to the child's level of development, equipment that fits and makes it easy to solve problems, support from adults who understand his needs—all make it easier for a child to gain feelings of security and adequacy.

Most important, in the center the children are with others who are on about the same level of development. They can have fun doing things with other children. Among this group of equals they do not need to feel inadequate, for they can keep up. They can do things as well as many of the others. They gain strength from the feeling that they are like others, from being able to identify with people who are at similar stages of growth. Belonging to a group of equals constitutes one of the best forms of insurance against feeling little and helpless.

Children need to find teachers in the center who will accept their positive feelings. We must be ready to return their smiles, take their hands when slipped into ours, take them into our arms, or talk with them when they feel the need for closeness. We must respond to their warm, friendly feelings. If it is their need and not ours that we are meeting in responding, we can be sure that they are helped to be more independent by what we do. They will gain confidence as they feel sure of having a warm response from us when they want it.

Good *Teaching* Contributes To Development Of *Confidence*

By the techniques we use as teachers we will help the child grow more secure and confident. Let us take as an example the situation of a child climbing on the jungle gym and see what it may mean.

Goldie, who is almost 3, is just learning to climb; she cautiously and awkwardly manages to get halfway up in the jungle gym and then calls for help. "Help me! I want down!" An adult answers the cry by lifting her down. Goldie is on the ground, safe, but with all feeling of achievement lost! On another occasion a different adult comes to the rescue. She stands beside the child and says reassuringly, "I'll help you, Goldie. Hang on to this bar and put your foot here," thus guiding Goldie back to the ground. Once again safe, Goldie is elated. She starts right up again and this time reaches the top. When her mother comes, she can scarcely wait to show her this new achievement.

If, when Goldie starts to climb the jungle gym, her mother says in an impatient voice, "Come on, Goldie, you've had all morning to play. I'm in a hurry. You can show me tomorrow," Goldie may again lose the feeling of confidence. If her mother is eager to share the experience and watches her, exclaiming. "That's fine, Goldie, you've learned to climb way up high," Goldie takes another step in growing confident.

Chapter Overview

Let us review some of the things we have discussed to increase children's feelings of security and confidence as suggested in this chapter.

Accept children as they are, feelings and behavior, knowing that there are reasons for the way they feel and act. Recognize that hitting and other forms of motor expression of feelings are normal for young children. Stop unacceptable actions without blaming or shaming. We can expect children to change their behavior, but they have a right to their feelings. We want them to respect themselves and have self-confidence. We want children to feel that we have confidence in them.

Help children find acceptable outlets for their feelings. Help them put their feelings into words, not only as a way of identifying what they feel but also as a step toward control. Help them use many avenues for the expression of feelings, especially the creative avenues, but be sure that feelings are expressed. The really destructive feelings are those that have no recognized outlets.

Try to meet children's needs as they indicate what they are and leave them free to develop in accordance with their own growth patterns. Thus, we will give them confidence and the feeling that they are adequate persons. Refrain from "nudging" the child. Instead, try to understand him.

Acquire skills in handling the child that will increase their confidence, making suggestions in a positive way, reducing the difficulties of the situations they face, adjusting demands to fit their capacities, and forestalling trouble when possible.

Projects

1. Observe and record three situations in which the guidance given by the adult was directed toward helping the child feel more secure and confident. Estimate how successful it was.

2. Listen to the quality and pitch of the children's voices. List the names of children whose voices are high-pitched or strained, soft and indistinct, loud and somewhat harsh, and easy and pleasant. How would

you relate what the child's voice seems to reveal with what you know of the child's adjustment and her feelings about herself? Do the same with motor forms of behavior such as posture, hand movement, and body tension.

3. Make a list of emotionally loaded words sometimes used in describing behavior, such as "spoiled", "stubborn", "selfish". Indicate briefly how using such words may influence objective observation of behavior. Give an example of descriptive terms that might be used to describe the same behavior in the case of some of the words listed above.

For Your Further Reading

Briggs, D. C. (1970). *Your child's self-esteem: The key to his life.* Garden City, NY: Doubleday. Deals sympathetically with children's feelings; introduces skill of reflecting children's feelings. Includes section on developmental stages. Useful for parents and teachers.

Curry, N., & Johnson, C. (1990). *Beyond self-esteem: Developing a genuine sense of human value.* Research Monograph, Vol. 4. Washington, DC: National Association for the Education of Young Children. Chapters on developing a sense of self in infants, toddlers, preschoolers, and primary-age children; helpful implications for practitioners, age by age. Based on extensive references.

Hitz, R., & Driscoll, A. (1988). Praise or encouragement? New insights into praise: Implications for early childhood teachers. *Young Children* 43(5), 6–13. Distinguishes between praise and encouragement; discusses ineffective and all-too-common ways to praise; gives examples of encouragement.

Jalongo, M. R. (1987). Do security blankets belong in preschool? *Young Children* 42(3), 3–8. Discusses "transition objects" as sources of comfort for young children as they make changes from dependence to independence and make transitions from home to school. Examines how adults can respond helpfully; lists children's books about transition objects.

Warren, R. M. (1977). *Caring: Supporting children's growth.* Washington, DC: National Association for the Education of Young Children. One of the best little books on topics of accepting children, accepting parents without judgment, self-esteem, and mastery in emotional growth.

Werner, E. E. (1984). Research in review: Resilient children. *Young Children* 40(1), 69–72. Examines research and implications for teachers on how some children develop stable, healthy personalities and ability to recover despite life stresses. An important protective factor was the establishment of a close bond with at least one caregiver in the child's first year.

Feelings of Hostility and Aggression

Fire (*boy 4 years, 4 months*)

In this chapter you will consider a topic difficult for many people to handle, both for themselves and in young children:

▶ How are hostility and aggression related to our growth?
▶ What are some sources of hostile feelings in children?
▶ How can children express hostile and aggressive feelings?
▶ What is the your role as a teacher in meeting aggressive behavior?

DEVELOPMENTALLY APPROPRIATE PRACTICE: Adults facilitate the development of self-control in children . . . when adults treat them with dignity and use discipline techniques such as . . . redirecting children to more acceptable behavior . . . listening when children talk about their feelings and frustrations . . . guiding children to resolve conflicts and modeling skills that help children to solve their own problems. (p. 11). [Toddlers] need guidance in how to express their often intense and hostile feelings in acceptable ways. If [they] do not have the guidance of adults who understand and plan appropriately for them, they may experience severe stress and conflict. (p. 25). Adults recognize that most of the time when toddlers are aggressive, hurting or biting other children, it is because they lack skills to cope with frustrating situations such as wanting another child's toy. (p. 41). (Bredekamp, 1987). *Developmentally Appropriate Practice . . .*)

We can use the center as a laboratory to study hostile and aggressive feelings and try to understand them. Resentment and hostility expressed aggressively are evident in the behavior of children whenever the situation is not rigidly controlled by adults, whenever children are free to show us how they feel. An angry child may address the teacher as "You dummy," and this teacher will be the one in whom he has some confidence. This child is likely to be more polite to the teacher with whom he does not feel as safe. "We don't like you," sing out two children to a third. Occasionally, a chorus of "name calling" greets the visitor to the center. Some children do not reveal hostile feelings by such direct expressions, but they may have these same feelings anyway. We can learn to recognize their less direct expressions, too. We can learn how to prevent more hostility and aggressiveness from developing.

Hostility and Aggression Are Tied Up with Growth

A certain amount of hostile feeling in all of us results from the growing-up process. As infants we were helpless and often our needs were not met. We felt threatened by the greater strength of the people around us. There were many frustrations and interferences for us all. Frustrations breed resentment when the frustrated person is little and helpless.

Some aggressiveness is necessary, for growth itself is a going-forward process that demands it. Lawrence Kubie (1948, pp. 67–80, 88) states, "The acquisition of positive, self-assertive, commanding and demanding attitudes in the first two years of human life is an essential step in the development of every child." However, much unnecessary aggressiveness, as well as hostility, is aroused by some of the traditional methods of handling children at home and at school. Healthy aggression becomes unhealthy. Resentments develop that interfere with healthy growth. As our knowledge and understanding grow and we use better methods of guiding children in the growing-up processes, we will reduce the hostility and unproductive aggression in the world with increasing effectiveness.

Resentment Is Increased by Inconsistencies in Guidance

The amount of resentment and aggression as well as the amount of confusion and guilt over these feelings is perhaps greater when the child meets many contradictory expectations. The child at home is supposed to be obedient. On the playground he is expected to "stand up for himself" and come out ahead in competitive situations. The same behavior is wrong in one place and right in another. These inconsistencies make learning difficult and may increase the number of mistakes the child makes and the resulting guilt.

Children in our culture also carry a handicapping load of resentment when parental management is harsh and standards are rigidly or inconsistently enforced. Such methods may arouse hostile aggressiveness. We usually have refused to acknowledge the extent of these feelings and have gone on multiplying them—in children and in ourselves. The result is that they spill over in all kinds of unsuspected ways in our personal and group lives in rebellious, aggressive, or bullying behaviors. Few problems are more important than those of facing and reducing the hostility we feel.

Patterns of Violence in a Society Make Control of Aggression Difficult

Managing feelings of hostility and aggression in constructive ways is made more difficult for the child who is exposed to patterns of violence in behavior in the society. Children watch programs on television that are full of brutal attacks on people, cruelty, and disrespect for the dignity of human beings. The example set by these behavior patterns in television programs as well as their existence on the street makes it only too easy for children to follow these patterns themselves when their own controls break down. There are uncontrolled, violent ways of expressing the negative feelings within us, and there are more "civilized" ways that require understanding and control. Feelings must be expressed, but they can be expressed in words, in art forms, or in actions that do no harm to others.

Children Need to Express Hostile Feelings

It is safe to say that all children at times feel aggressive and hostile but that not all children act out these feelings. In the past we tended to give approval to the children who did not act out their negative feelings. From what we now know about mental health, we realize it is essential that feelings be expressed, and preferably on the spot if a person is to remain mentally healthy. The problem is to discover avenues of expression that are not destructive rather than to deny expression to these feelings. It is unlikely that we can have a peaceful world when individuals in it are carrying around a load of hostility with the added guilt of denying them. We must help children to face and express their hostile feelings.

It is worth quoting Kubie again (1948, pp. 70, 89):

Repeatedly in the early years of life anger must be liquidated at its birth or it will plague us to the grave. . . . If we are ever to lessen the neurotic distortions of human aggression, then it seems clear that the anger must be allowed and encouraged to express itself in early childhood, not in blindly destructive acts but in words, so as to keep it on the fullest possible level of conscious awareness. Furthermore such conscious ventilation of feelings must be encouraged in the very situations in which they have arisen, and toward those adults and children who have

These aggressive boys are playful—or are they? The girls aren't sure.
Migrant Head Start, Chico, California

been either the active or the innocent sources of the feelings. Only in this way can we lessen the burden of unconscious aggression which every human being carries from infancy to the grave.

Adults Must Accept Hostile Feelings in Themselves

The important job of parent and teacher, then, becomes one of encouraging expression of feeling in nondamaging ways and of diminishing the number of situations where negative feelings can develop. Our ability to do this will depend in part on our ability to accept our own feelings, or we will find ourselves meeting aggression with aggression and hostility with hostility. When a child calls us, "You dummy," we must be able to accept the child's feeling of anger without getting it tangled up with our own angry feelings. This will be easier as we realize that the words offer no real threat, as such words might have in the past or under other circumstances. We happen to be the recipient of anger and hostility at the moment, but these feelings have been generated by many factors, just as our own have been.

To the extent that we were punished or shamed for expressing our own hostile feelings, we may find it hard to accept that the child needs to express such feelings. If our own defenses against such feelings are strong or if we have permitted ourselves little expression, it may be difficult for us to permit expression for others. It remains important for us to achieve this acceptance if we are to be of help to the child.

Coping with Strong Feelings

Let us look at an example of the steps one child took to master his anxiety and resentment as he prepared himself to cope with a situation.

Tal attended a child-care center last year but only for five days. He had objected to going and had cried each day. His parents had not stayed with him, but the director had reported he was "a nice, quiet little boy." However, the parents learned that on the fifth day he had climbed into a chair and stayed in it all day, clutching his teddy bear. He had not eaten lunch or taken a nap. As he was a lively, active 3-year-old at home, the youngest of three children, they realized he had really been unhappy and arranged for his care with a caregiver in the neighborhood while they were at work.

They talked over plans the next year and decided to try the center again. Tal was now 4, and there was to be another teacher, whom they knew, in charge. Here is the father's report of what happened when he broached the subject to Tal:

Tal was eating his breakfast. He was in his usual exuberant mood while eating his cereal. He was dive-bombing his spoon into the bowl with appropriate sound effects.

"Tal," I said, "one of Daddy's friends is going to be working in the center you went to with Tommy. Would you like to visit her with me sometime?"

Tal stopped eating, his spoon poised in midair. His eyes grew wide with alarm. His body tensed and he almost visibly drew into himself. He continued to stare at me and his lower lip began to tremble.

"If you take me to that center again I'll throw a bomb at it and break it all up!" he blurted.

"We could go just for a visit," I said uneasily, not at all prepared for the impact the idea still held for him.

"They're bad there! Those children don't like me! That lady doesn't like me!"

"You liked Tommy. Didn't Tommy play with you?"

Tal was breathing heavily. After a pause he said, "Tommy could come to my house and play with me. I won't go there again!"

"You didn't like that center?"

"No! I will take my axe and chop it all up!"

"You don't want to go there again?"

He was a bit more relaxed. "No." A pause. "No. They don't have good toys. Or good boys and girls. Or good people."

"You didn't have fun there?"

"No." He became quite agitated again. Then, in a quiet voice, he said, "I'm tired of eating." He put down his spoon, climbed down from his chair and walked into our bedroom. He climbed into our bed and covered himself up.

I sat down on the bed beside him. "Pat me," he said.

I patted him and told him we would not visit the center until he wanted to and that I would stay with him while he visited when we did go.

"But not today?" he asked.

"No, not today," I agreed.

"Not for this many days?" He carefully arranged his fingers so that he could hold up three.

"Not for many days," I agreed.

He lay still for a moment. "I better finish my cereal," he said, throwing back the blankets. He climbed out of bed and went back to the table. "Not for many days," he said to himself as he climbed into his chair.

We see that Tal's first response is a rush of strong feeling. Then he mobilizes his forces and asserts himself. He attacks aggressively: "I'll throw a bomb at it and break it all up," and "I will take my axe and chop it all up." He will solve the problem by destroying it. Wisely, his father retreats. Tal then tries to think of reasons why going to the center must not happen. Not only is the center "bad" and the lady there "doesn't like me," but his friend could come to his house to play. His father puts Tal's feelings into words more directly. "You didn't like that center." His father states the heart of the problem. "You don't want to go there again." Tal seems a bit more relaxed as it is put into words by his father. He can count on his father's understanding. This time he is less negative.

His acceptance begins, but his appetite has gone. He goes to the most comforting place available and hides himself. His father is taken aback by the intensity of the child's feeling but appreciative of the difficulty of the problem the child must struggle with. "Pat me," says Tal, needing and able to use the support he knows an understanding father can give. Now the father suggests a compromise. We see the "mutual regulation," the working out of a problem together, which brings good solutions and good relations when there is understanding. Tal tests it: "But not today?" and "Not for this many days," holding up three fingers. When his father agrees. Tal's response is, "I better finish my cereal." He has coped with the situation actively and constructively. His self-respect and confidence remain. His father has stood by him in the steps he took to master his anxieties. One suspects there has been a mutual growth in understanding, and both will be able to meet the situation when the "many days" are over and it becomes a reality. They are better prepared eventually, Tal did enter as planned and he liked the new teacher. She was "good," and he made friends at the center.

Sources of Hostile Feelings

Let us discuss some of the common situations in which resentment is felt by children, how feelings develop in these situations, and how they may be liquidated.

Feelings of Jealousy

When a new baby arrives a sibling may feel jealous and hostile. Parents often reassure themselves that the older child "doesn't seem the least bit jealous." Yet it is inevitable that an older child will resent in some respects the coming of a new baby, however much she may also enjoy other aspects of the changed situation. Julia, a well-adjusted child, was not eager to receive a baby sister into her home. She was at the center when her grandmother came with the news of the arrival. After asking some questions, Julia said, "She won't come home today, will she?" When her grandmother affirmed this, she added, "I don't want her to," and returned to her play.

If parents ignore the child's jealousy, it may come out indirectly in her hugging the baby too roughly, in "accidentally" hurting it, or in an increased cruelty in her play with other children. These indirect ways are not so healthy as a direct expression in words. They are less understandable and less likely to drain the child's feelings of guilt and may even add a burden of guilt feeling. There is less need to be afraid of hostile feelings themselves than of what they do to us when we try to hide these feelings and thus lose control over them.

Resolving Hostile Feelings at the Center

When there is a new baby at home, the older child's feelings often spill out in behavior at the center. She will act them out in the doll corner, perhaps spanking the dolls frequently, smothering them with blankets, or throwing one on the floor and stamping on it. By releasing hostility, she can better face the real situation. A center should have some dolls that can stand this kind of treatment. A direct "draining off" of feelings in this way may be about the only means some children have of expressing the conflict they feel. Many parents do not, as Julia's parents did, understand and accept expressions of feeling.

Since our interest is in sound personality development, it is not hard to see how little real value there would be in emphasizing the proper care of dolls at this point. If one did insist that dolls were not to be treated in this way, one would block for the child this avenue of expression, leaving her in an emotionally dangerous situation. There might be a good deal of trouble ahead for her in the relationship with the real baby.

Rubber dolls and other rubber toys serve as a good medium for the release of aggressive feelings. They can be pinched and bitten with a good deal of satisfaction.

Jeremy, a 3 1/2-year-old, whose relationships at home had been tense and strained, had felt his position in the family threatened by the return of a father who was almost a stranger to him, and then even more threatened by the arrival of a new baby. His insecurity and hostility came out in the readiness with which he attacked and bit other children in the center. The teacher had to watch him constantly to prevent his attacking others. She found that she could substitute a rubber doll and that he seemed to find relief in biting it. Biting is usually done by a child who feels helpless. He can see no other way to meet his problems. She carried the doll in her pocket for a time so that it would be instantly available, and she gave it to him when she saw his tension mounting, saying, "I know! You feel just like biting someone. Here's the doll. It's all right to bite the doll." The least interference or the smallest suggestion of a rejection filled his already full cup of negative feelings to overflowing. He had to do something, and biting on the doll served to reduce the feeling to more manageable proportions. The teacher's acceptance and her understanding gave Jeremy confidence. The day came when he ran to her himself because he knew that he needed to bite the doll. He could recognize his feelings and handle them in a way that did not damage the other children. He began to have more success and find more satisfaction in his play. Steadily he had fewer hostile feelings to handle.

During this time, Jeremy also had been engaging in a great deal of aggression against the adults in the center. Faced with limiting his activity during the rest period, for example, he would lie on his bed and attack the teacher verbally, "cut her up, her legs, her head, her arms," and would sometimes "put her in the garbage can," or sometimes "put her in the toilet." His words revealed the extent to which he himself had been hurt and felt angry and fearful. Slowly, with many avenues of expression open to him, he released some of his resentful feelings, and the acceptance and success he had in the center helped him build other kinds of feelings. He discovered other kinds of relationships, and the warm, supporting relationship he had with his teacher left him free to find friends among the children.

The Necessity for Keeping Clean

Another source of resentment in children, in addition to changing positions in the family, lies in the demands made on them to "keep clean" and the fear and guilt they often feel when they yield to the impulse to play in dirt.

 Katy, a 3-year-old, was a child whose mother had emphasized cleanliness and proper behavior, including a strict toilet-training regimen. Katy showed as much hostility and resentment toward adults as did any child in the group at first. She refused requests or suggestions that came from an adult, even though they might be ones she really wanted to try. Her mother characterized her behavior as "just plain stubbornness." Their life together had been a succession of issues over one habit or the other. The following incident occurred after she had been at the center almost a year and had begun to participate in activities with confidence; at this point she was even affectionate with the teachers she knew, saying, "I like you," with real feeling. Even then she still grew disturbed and anxious when faced with a little dirt.

Katy happened to be on the playground with a student teacher. She was swinging. It was muddy, and as Katy's boots swept through the puddle under the swing, they splashed mud on her and on the teacher. Katy looked disturbed. "What will your dad say?" she asked the student teacher anxiously. The teacher assured her that he wouldn't say anything and that it was just an accident and couldn't be helped. But Katy answered darkly, "Oh yes, he'll say something."

She again tried swinging but once more they both got splashed. Katy said warmly, "I'm sorry," and she repeated, "What will your dad say?"

This time the teacher replied by asking Katy what she thought he would say. Katy answered, "He'll say you're all dirty and will have to clean up and take a bath," and then she added, "I'm going inside and stay in, if you don't mind." She went in and did not come outside again during the morning.

Even though she expected no punishment for splashing the mud in this situation, it was a "bad" thing to her. It meant disapproval from the adults on whom this insecure little girl had to depend. Standards for behavior were high and punishment severe. Her anxiety was apparent in her words and behavior. It was not hard to see why she had shown hostility and unfriendliness.

In this situation, a more experienced teacher not only would have recognized the extent of the anxiety the child was showing by her questions, but she also would have tried to help Katy put it into words so it might have become more understandable and manageable. She might have said, "Does your dad get mad when you're dirty? Mothers and dads often do, don't they, when children get dirty?" This might have given Katy the help she did not find in the student teacher's denial that her dad would be mad. Katy knew better about hers! It would have made it a common experience, easier to face. The teacher might have continued, "Sometimes it is all right to get dirty because we can get cleaned up afterward just as we can now. Sometimes it's even fun to get dirty. I used to like to myself," and this might have relieved the child. She might have been able to stay outdoors and have fun. She might have been better able to trust herself.

The Cue May Be a Small One

Sometimes it is harder to identify the feelings that lie behind words or actions. The child may be afraid to express her hostility or aggression openly. We have to find the meaning from a very small cue.

Kassi, a 4-year-old, had always been very "good." This meant that she was not able to be very expressive or creative. In the center she gradually began to find it possible to act with greater freedom. It was clear that she often wanted to act differently but did not dare.

One day the teacher observed Kassi carefully laying chairs on their sides on the floor. The teacher made no comment, not understanding the meaning of this behavior. The next day Kassi's mother asked anxiously about how her daughter was behaving. She was worried because Kassi had told her that the day before she had "knocked over all the chairs." It was then clear to the teacher that this careful laying of a few chairs on their sides was in reality an aggressive act for Kassi. It was as far as she dared to go in expressing her aggressive feelings, and she would have liked to have made it a much bigger act than it was.

Kassi needed to be helped to see that she could express aggressive feelings, that she could really be accepted as a little girl who had "bad" feelings as well as "good" ones, that there were safe limits at the center, too. Her parents needed to have more understanding of the importance of accepting all of Kassi's feelings.

Cody, a 3 1/2 year old, was very timid and showed much the same kind of need when he declared, "I'm going to make a lot of noise," and then took one block and carefully threw it on the floor. His parents approved of quiet boys. He had few opportunities to be noisy, and he was trying to show that he really dared to be the kind of person he wanted to be.

With children like Kassi and Cody it may be important to accept their "acting out" of feelings without limiting or redirecting them at first, provided the behavior does not harm them or others. When these children have an opportunity to convince themselves that their "bad" part is accepted, then they are ready to take the more constructive step of putting the feelings into words, of talking about the feeling as Tal did with his father about going to the center he had not liked. Then the children can begin to manage such feelings more acceptably.

Failure to Gain Attention and Response

Failure to get attention and response will arouse resentment and hostility in children, too, especially in insecure children who are seeking reassurance by getting attention. Their feelings are involved in a way that makes them sensitive to failure. Situations are constantly arising in which children want attention from the teacher or from other children, want to feel important and needed—and fail. They may be resentful and hostile as a result.

When the situation is competitive, there is more likelihood for failures. A child may want the teacher's attention and, not receiving it, may attack either the child, who she feels is a rival, or the teacher, who seems to be deserting her. Such a child needs to have her confidence built so that she will see others as less of a threat. She needs help in accepting and finding better outlets for feelings. When it is all right to admit wanting the teacher all to yourself, it becomes easier to work out a better solution than attacking others.

As teachers, we should be aware of the strong need most children have to feel sure of their place and to receive a share of our attention. When we give attention to one child, we need to remember that other children may feel left out. We saw an example in Betsy, who untied her shoe so that the teacher could tie it for her just as the teacher had done for another child. Not many children can deal with their feelings as directly as Betsy. They may need some help from us. A teacher may say, "I think you'd like me to do something with you sometimes. I've been doing a lot with Helen lately because she is new and isn't sure about what we do. Of course I like helping you, too. Remember when you first came and I had to show you what to do? Now it's different, and you sometimes help the new children." She can add, "But you tell me when you really want me to do something for you and I'll do it if I can." This attention helps a child feel sure that there is a place for her and that she can have attention, too.

'Nudging' and Harsh Methods of Control

Children who have been "nudged" from one stage of development to the next and who have had high standards set for their behavior may feel resentment that they can not express directly. One way these children may try to handle the feeling is by reproving others. They identify with the teacher to escape from the feeling of being helpless. Joshua, for example, has received a great deal of punishment from parents who have never heard of any methods of discipline except the "good old-fashioned ones."

Joshua and Larry were building a block tower to dangerous heights. The teacher warned, "Not so high." Joshua immediately turned to Larry and said severely, "The teacher said no more blocks, and when she says something you mind her." Thus he got rid of some of his resentment, but his "punishing" attitude makes it hard for any but the most comfortable children to play with him. Incidentally, in Joshua's behavior we see the quality of control that harshly disciplined people impose when they themselves are in power and the need they often feel to identify with the controlling authority. Children who are harshly punished often identify with the aggressor and become punishing people themselves.

Sam Wanted Desperately to Feel Big

Sam is an example of a child who had been pushed around in many ways without gaining much love from the adults in return for their heavy demands.

 Sam, a 4 1/2 year old, was expected to behave like a little gentleman when there were visitors at home, and he usually came to the center in his best clothing instead of dressing in play clothes like the other children. His speech was more like that of an adult—even his vocabulary of swear words. He was advanced in his development, but he was also burdened with tremendous hostility. It came out in the frequency and the cruelty with which he attacked younger children and animals and in his many verbal attacks against the adults when he discovered that these acts would not be punished. Instead of trying to identify with the teacher, he fought her on every occasion.

As the group was coming in from the playground one day, he savagely attacked a friendly little boy who got in his way. The teacher separated them quickly and firmly. Sam exclaimed, "That was fun." The teacher merely said, "It wasn't fun for Jim. It hurt him," and told Sam to wait outside. As soon as the others were taken care of, she returned and sat down beside him. They knew each other well, and she felt sure that he could accept her presence without feeling threatened.

"I wonder why it makes you feel good to hurt Jim and the other children," she speculated quietly, not knowing whether he could give her any clue. He immediately began a description of how his uncle had brought him a toy gun, and he and his "little friend" (an imaginary friend) could use it.

Again the teacher answered, "Sometimes it makes children feel big to have a gun and it makes them feel big to hurt someone. Do you ever feel that way?"

With apparent relief the child answered, "Yes." They discussed how people wanted to feel big and how sometimes it wasn't fun to be little. The teacher mentioned that being friendly sometimes made people feel big. Sam stuttered as he talked and was near tears, something that almost never happened with him. He seldom dared to relax his defenses enough to cry.

At last the teacher told Sam that it was about time for them to go inside. He said, almost crying, "I could stay out here until afternoon." "Yes," she said, "you could." She busied herself picking things up and then asked, "Well, now you can either come in with me or stay outside. I wonder which you are going to do?"

He got up and said rather sadly, "I don't know." At that the teacher knelt down and put her arms around this hurt, bewildered little boy, and for the first time he could accept her loving and nestled close against her, no longer "tough." She said, "I know how it is," and then suggested, "You might paint a big picture inside." He nodded and took her hand, and they went inside. He went straight to the finger-painting table where there was an opportunity for him to express more of what he felt.

Sam gained at the center and became better able to play with others. He was imaginative and resourceful and found a place for himself as his hostility decreased. When he left the center, he was a less hostile child but still needed sensitive understanding. Although his mother had gained insight into the child's problems, his father would accept none of this "sissy stuff" and continued to rely on repression and a generous use of the rod to bully his son into "good" behavior. It is interesting to note that when Sam was in high school some years later he excelled in athletics and became a person of importance there. He also received several awards for his artwork. He seemed to have found outlets for some of his earlier hostile aggressiveness.

To the Child, Even Friendly Adults May Seem a Threat

All children, to some extent, struggle with feelings of being little and helpless. Even friendly adults are so much stronger and more powerful than the child that they represent a potential threat. Children handle their feelings in different ways. When they are together in groups, they are quick to blame the adult for things that happen. We may overhear the following when Ricky comes on the playground and says to Nate, "Who covered up our holes?" "Oh, some teacher probably," Nate replies. Both boys are friendly with teachers, but they recognize in them the source of many interferences and frustrations as well as the source of needed support. They are glad to identify with each other against the teacher at times.

Craig gives us another amusing example. He happened to throw some sand, which got into Celia's eye. Celia had to go inside and have the sand washed out of her eye. When she came back on the playground, Craig was sympathetic and wanted to look in her eye. He said to her comfortingly, "I should have thrown it in the teacher's eye and then it wouldn't have hurt you, Celia."

As adults we are concerned with helping children to express these feelings in ways that will not be damaging and yet will serve to reduce them or turn them into constructive channels. We need to understand the possible avenues of expression.

Possible Avenues for the Expression of Feelings

Motor expressions, of course, offer the simplest, most direct means of releasing feelings for children. That is why hitting, pushing, and biting are common among young children. However, more acceptable forms of expression can be utilized instead. Pounding at the workbench, hitting a soft material like clay, using a punching bag, biting on a rubber toy, throwing a ball against a backstop, or even running and digging can serve as an outlet for feelings in ways that do no damage to anyone. Some children give vent to their resentment at adult interferences by the hard pats they give each piece of paper they paste or by pounding clay.

The skillful teacher will accept the feeling and put it into words: "I know you feel like hitting him because he has the tricycle you want." She will channel the expression into acceptable behavior. "When you feel like that, you can hit our punching bag or pound the clay."

Language Is Another Avenue for Expression

The crying child relieves himself of a lot of feeling; so does the child who hurls angry words at an offender. Young children may verbally destroy their teachers in all kinds of ways and tell them "to get dead." Such expressions relieve their feelings. They can see that it results in no harm to the teacher, who remains their friend. It is a satisfactory way for a child to "liquidate" feelings that might otherwise be a source of trouble. Later, as adults, these same children may use fantasy rather than speech and be helped in relieving serious irritations.

Art and Music Are Avenues, Too

Art and music are important avenues of expression because they may extend into the adult years and serve as a protection against the emotional

Dance is an avenue for expressing strong feelings.
Santa Monica College, Child Development Center, Santa Monica, California

load that adults must carry. If art is to have value as a release for feeling, the child must be allowed to use the medium in his own way. The child who paints the same motif or theme again and again is saying something about the way he feels through his pictures. He may do this through work with clay or music, too. We need to conserve the values of art as an avenue of expression of feelings. These values are lost if art consists of copying patterns or models.

How the Teacher Meets Aggressive Behavior

When feelings have many avenues of expression, they do not pile up and become so unmanageable. The teacher encourages expression even though he or she may face problems within the group situation. How can the teacher meet the needs of individuals and of groups?

The Teacher Helps the Children by Her Example

The teacher helps all children by remaining undisturbed in the face of aggressive behavior and not meeting anger with angry feelings in return. By the teacher's example, the children will find it less disturbing to meet the inevitable aggressions that occur in their world. Children who are most disturbed over being called a name may be children who have been severely reproved for name calling themselves. Adults have attached importance to this kind of behavior. Children are likely to meet some rejection and some angry responses wherever they happen to be. If their own aggressive behavior has been met casually, they will find it easier to accept unruffled the attacks they receive. They are less afraid and better able to take the world as it is. In responding to aggressive behavior, teachers can say, "We all feel this way sometimes." They are not upset by it because they do not accept it as a personal attack.

The Teacher Helps By Accepting and Interpreting Behavior

An important way to help is by interpreting to one child some reasons why another child is behaving as he is. The teacher may reassure the first child by saying, "He's calling you names because he's mad. It's your turn on the swing, and he wants it to be his. It makes him feel better to call you 'dope.' You don't need to let it bother you."

The teacher may help a child by showing him how to meet the rejection. "They want to play by themselves. It's all right. I'll help you find another place to play, and you can look for someone who does want to play with you." She does not say, "But you must let him play," to the angry child who has shouted at another child, "You go away!" The newcomer will not be likely to have a successful experience with a person who feels unfriendly toward him.

Some solutions protect the group while still respecting the needs of individuals. If the child who is excluding others is monopolizing the homemaking corner or the sandbox, the teacher can say, "It's all right if you want to play by yourself, but all the children use the homemaking corner or the sandbox. You can make a house over in this corner and leave the rest for the children who do want to play together."

The Teacher May Need to Help Hostile, Insecure Children by Giving Them Techniques for Cooperating

Children need protection when they are unsure and suspicious of others. The demands of group life are complex. Children who are hostile and lack social skills may not be able to play with more than one child at a time. They may need to exclude others. The teacher helps when she accepts exclusion and makes it possible for them to be successful at their level.

Helping an insecure, hostile child to be successful may mean reducing the difficulties he faces. He may need to play with just one child at a time or with materials that can be shared easily or in situations that make few

How should the teacher meet aggressive behavior? She can give techniques for cooperating. Migrant Head Start, Chico, California

demands for adaptation. It may mean suggesting a desirable way to approach others before he fails in his approach. The teacher may say, "You might get a block and help John build the road", or, when another child approaches, she may forestall failure by interpreting, "I think he would like to dig with you. I will help him find another shovel." Reducing the difficulty of a situation and forestalling and preventing failure are helpful techniques to use with children who find it difficult to accept others.

The Teacher Helps by Providing a Suitable Environment

In a physical setup designed appropriately for children, they will feel less hostility because they will meet fewer frustrations. They can get their own coats, find play materials within reach, solve their own problems in many ways, and submit to fewer limitations. The program as well as the physical setup can be designed to reduce, rather than increase, interferences and frustrations. If it is flexible and imposes only essential limitations, it meets individual needs in a way that minimizes hostility. Under this kind of program, teachers become people who help rather than people who interfere with the child.

The Teacher Acts with Firmness

Teachers help the aggressive, resentful child when they are confident and firm in their management. The child needs firmness, not punishment. He may want to feel that someone else is to blame, but his teachers will accept only his need to wish that this were so; they do not accept this as fact. They are sympathetic but firm in dealing with his behavior and facing the reality of the situation. They state it clearly for him. They have confidence that he will be able to face it, too. They try to help him deal with feelings directly, in a constructive way. Their firmness helps steady the angry child and reassure the insecure child.

Punishment does not help a hostile, resentful child. It only increases his burden of feeling. Firm action by the teacher may be essential so that he does not hurt others and thus add to his burden of guilt. For example, the teacher acted firmly with Sam, who used biting as a way of attacking. She knew she must prevent his biting children and help him use acceptable means such as biting on a small rubber doll, to feel relieved of a tremendous resentment and feeling of helplessness. If she had punished or rejected this child because of the biting, she might have offered no help. The already overburdened little boy would have had to find his way out alone or fail.

We should act promptly to stop some kinds of behavior, but we need not do this in a punishing way. We can remove a disturbing child from the group or hold him firmly, but we do not have to blame him for the actions. We do not try to make a child feel more ashamed or even to apologize. Making a child say, "I'm sorry", usually makes him say something untrue.

Vigorous physical activity like digging a hole provides for expression of feelings.
Child Development Laboratory, California State University, Chico

Truth is important. Later a child may say he is sorry when really feeling this way. Our responsibility is to help children find nondamaging channels to express resentment.

Some Children Need Special Help

A child seriously burdened with hostility may need to be assigned one teacher or an aide to help him manage his feelings. With this kind of individual help, he may be successful. A teacher reported this observation of a child who attacked others with little or no provocation. He had had a great deal of punishment and little real discipline. As he started to hit another child, the teacher caught his arm and held it firmly while saying, "You must feel very angry." He looked at her in surprise, without resisting, and then nodded in agreement. Suddenly he turned and hugged her. The teacher knew how he felt and he was safe. She returned his hug and added, "Next time you feel angry, I will try to help you."

The child who acts out hostility may be serving a function for the whole group. They learn what happens by watching this child and the way the behavior is handled. If it is handled firmly, without anger, all children feel more comfortable. They have more confidence that their own angry feelings can be managed, if not by them, at least by the teacher. The children are learning how to manage their feelings by observing each other and by responding to others.

There is often a "difficult" child in a group. Most children can be helped within the framework of the group to handle their hostile feelings acceptably. An occasional child may need individual therapy outside the group in addition to help within the group.

Participation in a Group Has Special Value for the Timid Child

The value of group participation for timid children is worth attention. Timid children are greatly helped to express their feelings by the safety they find within the group. The group offers an environment where it is easier for them to accept their own hostile feelings. These children will benefit greatly from the "freeing" of expression that comes in attending a good center. Children in groups may resort to verbal defiance of the teacher when there is some reason for resisting. They feel strength in being together, and this feeling is one of the values that group experience holds for them. With people their own age who also are feeling and expressing resistance, timid children are no longer so afraid of their feelings and behavior. They become healthier from the mental health standpoint and capable of achieving more emotional maturity, even though teachers may find them more challenging.

 Ben, a 4-year old, learned to express his real feelings. He was a quiet, timid child who remained dependent on the teacher for a long time after he entered the center. He usually found a place beside her when she sat down and often held onto her skirt when she moved around the school. When he played, he would select the small toys and take them into a corner. He was not active and vigorous and was never aggressive toward others. Slowly he began to join the other children in play and to identify himself with the group. He seemed pleased when they shouted names or chanted silly or "naughty" words. Finally he dared to express himself in this way, too. One day he was even a member of a group who defied the teacher from the safe height of the jungle gym.

A videotape taken at the center was shown one morning. A picture of Ben's teacher appeared on the screen. Laughing, Ben went up to the screen and slapped her image. The act may have symbolized the strength and freedom to be aggressive the child felt. With that slap he proved that he had left his dependence behind. He and the teacher were friendly with each other, but he was no longer tied to her skirt. Ben had known plenty of love at home but not much chance to express the resentments that he inevitably felt. As soon as he dared to be aggressive, to express what he felt, he became more active and social. He had no great amount of hostility to release. Soon he was able to maintain and accept the limits the teachers set for the group. He developed rapidly.

Chapter Overview

We may summarize what we have said about hostility and aggression by pointing out that adults must: (1) accept the existence of these feelings; (2) see that they are expressed in some acceptable way, but as directly as possible, so that the individual will be freed from the emotional load that she will otherwise carry; and (3) learn how to handle children without creating in them unnecessary feelings of hostility and resentment that make good social adjustment difficult.

Reducing the amount of frustration a young child has to meet, building up her feelings of security and confidence, accepting her as she is rather than "nudging" her into being something different, will help in solving the problems these negative feelings present to any individual or group of children.

Projects

1. Describe angry actions or feelings you remember from your own childhood. How were these feelings resolved?
2. Observe and record a situation in which a teacher helped an angry child put his feelings into words.
3. Observe and record two situations where a child faced frustration (was unable to carry out a purpose). How did she cope with the situation? What feelings did she express at the time? Later?

For Your Further Reading

Caldwell, B. (1977). Aggression and hostility in young children. *Young Children.* 32(2), 4–13. Comprehensive review of past and present thinking on aggression, with practical guides to decrease aggression and increase cooperation.

Caughey, C. (1991). Becoming the child's ally—Observations in a classroom for children who have been abused. *Young Children 46*(4), 22–28. In a special program for children who have been abused, how do children deal with their hostility and aggression? Discusses role of the teacher in providing for safe expression of anger and helping children feel in control of their world.

Carlsson-Paige, N., & Levin, D. (1987). *The war play dilemma: Balancing needs and values in the early childhood classroom.* New York: Teachers College Press.

Carlsson-Paige, N., & Levin, D. (1990). *Who's calling the shots? How to respond effectively to children's fascination with war play and war toys.* Philadelphia: New Society Publishers. Two thoughtful books look at the effects of proliferation of high-tech war toys on children's fascination with war play. A developmental approach to the possible role played by war play in children's gaining a sense of mastery over conflicts and aggression; discusses whether it should be allowed.

Honig, A. S. (1983). TV violence and child aggression: Research review. *Day Care and Early Education. 10*(4), 41–45. Simple summary of strong evidence from more than 2500 studies that watching TV violence later causes child aggression. Discusses differences between home or research TV viewing. Practical suggestions for parents and teachers.

Kemmer, E. (1984). *Violence in the family: An annotated bibliography.* New York: Garland. Useful references on family violence from 1960–1982, including many on child abuse.

McGinnis, K., & Oehlberg, B. (1988). *Starting out right: Nurturing young children as peacemakers.* Oak Park, IL: Meyer-Stone Books. Offers different view on how to handle the war play dilemma plus ways of promoting peaceful, nonviolent skills in children.

National Association for the Education of Young Children. (1988). Ideas that work with young children: The difficult child. *Young Children 43*(5), 60–68. Discusses many sources of a child's being difficult: temperament, disability, mental illness, retardation, catastrophic family lives, personality disorders, and finally those children made more difficult by classroom mismanagement. Presents guidelines for those who have the responsibility to help difficult children.

PART FIVE

The Program Evolves from Experiences

The Process of Learning in Early Childhood

Man and airplane (*boy, 3 years, 3 months*)

In this chapter you will explore children's learning, which illuminates the process of adults teaching as you study:

▶ The child as a learner or "knower"
▶ How young children are motivated to learn
▶ Readiness for learning
▶ Reading: a special kind of learning
▶ The characteristics of a good thinker.

DEVELOPMENTALLY APPROPRIATE PRACTICE: Curriculum planning emphasizes learning as an interactive process. Teachers prepare the environment for children to learn through active exploration and interaction with adults, other children, and materials. The process of interacting with materials and people results in learning. . . . Much of young children's learning takes place when they direct their own play activities. . . . Such learning should not be inhibited by adult-established concepts of completion, achievement, and failure. Activities should be designed to concentrate on furthering emerging skills through creative activity and intense involvement. Learning activities and materials should be concrete, real, and relevant to the lives of young children. (Bredekamp, 1987. *Developmentally Appropriate Practice . . .* , p. 3–4)

Now we will look more closely at the learning process itself and how young children are helped to develop sound strategies for thinking and reasoning.

The development of knowledge in the early stages of growth is personal. It depends on personal relationships between learner and teacher. Learning is done by individuals, not by groups. Children who have shared experiences may enjoy listening to stories in a small group or to music or poetry; but they do most of their learning as individuals, in different ways, at different rates, about things of immediate and personal interest. Just as they play first as individuals, then in parallel play, and only slowly in groups, so they grow through these same cycles in cognitive activities.

Without stimulation from the environment and encouragement from attentive adults, the child's more complex intellectual skills and competencies may fail to develop or may develop only in restricted ways. Too much inappropriate stimulation may be as damaging as lack of stimulation. The learning process is exceedingly complex.

The Child as Learner or 'Knower'

We must remember that the child has learned a great deal before she enters school. She has had many experiences and understands her world on the basis of these experiences. Our teaching must be based on a knowledge of and a feeling for her understandings. It is important for her not to skip any stages, emotional or intellectual, in her development.

Each child has her own pace and style of learning. Some children seem to learn best by watching. Some children learn best by manipulating and through trial and error. Some children stay with things much longer than others. The attention span is different for each child.

The young child, the "knower" we are concerned with, is still engaged in building a balance of trust in herself and others that will free her from too great mistrust and enable her to use her capacities. She is also still engaged in moving beyond infantile dependency and in achieving a greater measure of independence that will enable her to assert herself more actively in the learning process. Above all, she is engaged in using initiative, in exploring, discovering, imagining, and going on to the new and untried. Erikson's three personality tasks, building a sense of trust, a sense of autonomy, and a sense of initiative, continue to be essential in learning.

As a learner the young child continues to use all her senses as she did in the sensorimotor stage, gathering impressions of the world around her and acting on these impressions. But she also has moved into the preoperational stage described by Piaget. She is doing more organizing and classifying of these impressions. She sees similarities and differences, develops systems in her thinking, and tests her conclusions. She is developing concepts. In water play, for example, she is no longer content just to splash, enjoying the feel and sight of water, but she fills containers, pours the water, and watches what happens. She may put various objects in the

*A 2-year-old learner,
squeezing, spooning,
stirring.
Santa Monica
College, Child
Development Center,
Santa Monica,
California*

water; she finds an object that sinks and then tries to make others sink. She imagines and uses symbols in play. After she has seen a boat on the lake, she pretends a box is a boat as she rocks it or "fishes" from it. She rehearses and clarifies concepts in dramatic play. She accommodates to what she has assimilated in more complex ways. Her play reveals her progress. She makes things happen. If one block is not long enough for bridging a distance she finds the one that fits the space.

The young child is increasing her competence in language expressions as well, and this ability makes possible greater complexity in thought. Words help her recall experience and organize and classify perceptions. She can communicate better than when she was younger. Verbal expressions help to clarify her own ideas.

In a center the child also learns from being with other children and with the adults there. Children find out more about how others respond to approaches and what they can and cannot do. Children begin to identify with the teacher and learn from her. They "accommodate" to a greater range of social experiences. When 4-year-old Amy asks a visitor to her center, "Whose grandma are you?" she demonstrates her development of concept formation. No one told her that the visitor was a child's grandmother. From her experience she has constructed knowledge about adult women.

Some are teachers, some are mommies, some are grandmas. We are not sure what her classification scheme is but she evidently knows that adult women have different roles.

The Properties of Water: An Example of Implicit Knowledge and Explicit Learning

Margaret Brearley (1970) described the child's learning as developing from two sources: *implicit*, suggested but not clearly expressed knowledge, and *explicit*, clearly expressed, distinctly stated learning. We can understand implicit knowledge and explicit learning through the example of experiences with water. What explicit teaching may be done in this or in any other area of experience? It takes many years to reach an understanding of such a complex subject as the laws of floating bodies, but children begin to gain some of the necessary implicit knowledge through the daily experiences they have with water beginning in infancy. Children love to play in water. They are motivated for learning here.

Some Possible Experiences with Water

Bathing in water.

Washing one's face and hands, using soap, using water of different temperatures.

Turning the faucet on and off.

Pulling the plug in the basin, letting the water out, filling the basin.

Washing other things: doll clothes, a variety of fabrics or objects that feel different when wet, fabrics that are colorfast and those that are not.

Drying wet objects in sun, in shade, over heat.

Painting with water on different surfaces, seeing it dry in sun and shade.

Scrubbing table or floor, using wet cloth, mop, sponge. Wringing out cloth, sponge, or mop. Watching water being absorbed by blotter or sponge.

Flushing the toilet.

Pouring water, filling containers.

Using a hose to water plants, squirting streams of water.

Using a watering can with a nozzle or spray.

Feeling the spray of water, feeling the force of a stream of water. Playing in water in a pool, swirling with stick, using a strainer.

Dropping objects in water, watching patterns made.

Floating different objects: light ones and heavy ones that sink or float.

Wading, swimming.

Bathing the doll baby or helping in bathing a real baby.

Blowing soap bubbles, indoors and outdoors, in sunshine and in wind.

Mixing substances with water: paint powder, powdered clay, flour, dry bread crumbs, salt, sugar, oil.

Dissolving substances like Jell-O and watching them set.

Watching a kettle boil and steam condense.

Observing dew on grass, on cobwebs, on branches.

Observing frost patterns on windows.

Experiences with rain: watching it fall, feeling it on the face, seeing it flow down slopes and in gutters, stepping in puddles.

Experiences with snow and hail: playing in snow, watching snow or hail melt, tasting snow, compressing it into balls, piling it, observing drifts and icicles hanging or melting.

Making ice cubes in refrigerator and using them.

Making ice cream.

Caring for animals that live in water: fish, pollywogs, frogs, turtles, crayfish.

Playing in water with sand and mud, digging channels for the water, putting all kinds of objects in the water, observing properties of water.

Out of these experiences, and many more, the child discovers some of the properties of water (implicit knowledge). She can begin to predict what will happen when she does certain things. She knows that water doesn't run uphill, for example. She can dig channels to lead the water where she wants it to go. She can begin to estimate what will float and what will sink. She has acquired a "bank" of knowledge about water.

How the Teacher Uses Experiences for Explicit Teaching

In addition to providing these experiences, the teacher may call attention to how water behaves. She may ask the child questions. She may make suggestions to extend the child's experimentation. She may describe what is happening and encourage her to describe it. She may give explanations in answer to questions and help the child explore.

The teacher may call a child's attention to the way water paint evaporates in the sun in contrast to what happens in the shade. She may point out the way water acts on the dry sand in contrast to the wet sand. She may point out the steam on the windows in the kitchen.

The teacher may ask questions as the child plays with water in a tub. "I wonder what would happen if you put that big piece of wood in the water?" When the child tries it, the teacher may ask, "What happened?" In other situations the teacher may ask, "What happened when you added water to the clay powder?" or, "Where do you think the steam comes from?" or, "What makes the frost on our window?" or, "I wonder what would happen if we put the ice in the sun?"

Through these experiences the child acquires implicit knowledge about buoyancy, resistance, gravity, wave motion, and other principles. The

Learning takes place when children have real experiences with real objects that are relevant to their lives. Child Development Laboratory, California State University, Chico

teacher guides children in these steps towards "organizing facts already internalized about the real world" (Brearley & Hitchfield, 1966) so that these will be useful to them in the concepts the children are building.

Clearing Up Misconceptions

The child begins early to reason, but her conclusions often reveal the limitations on which her reasoning is based. Four-year-old Melissa, for example, was full of excitement about the birth of a baby to an older sister. When she arrived at school, she told her teacher all about it. The teacher smiled as she remarked, "Now your mother is a grandmother." Melissa stopped, her eyes wide with surprise. Then she shook her head positively. "Oh, no," she said, "my mother still lives with us." One gets an insight into Melissa's concept of grandmother as well as the different viewpoints of child and adult. The incident also illustrates the difficulty a child has in thinking about relationships among people.

In helping the child gradually clear up misconceptions, we may ask "Why do you think that?" or, "How can you tell?" In doing this we help her examine her premises. There are probably few subjects about which the child has more curiosity and more misconception than the subject of where she came from, how she was conceived, how she was born, and how she grew. We can answer her questions by asking, "What do you think?"

following the suggestions given by Selma Fraiberg (1959) in her excellent discussion, "Education for Love," in *The Magic Years*. We can use books such as Sara Bonnet Stein's (1974) *Making Babies*. We can present information in simple words, giving only as much as the child can understand or wants to know at the moment. We should give only accurate, true information. The subject will need repeated clarification, but, bit by bit, concepts will come closer to facts.

In spite of explanations, children's misconceptions will persist until they are ready to understand. Jose said to his mother, "You're going to have to blow up your tummy, so we can have a baby." Jose was eager for a baby to arrive. The child keeps assimilating information in personal ways, weaving it into the fabric of experience. We do not always know what the meaning of it is to a child. Three-year-old Matt was playing in the front yard while his mother was raking leaves. Their very pregnant neighbor came over for a visit. When she left, Matt's mother said, "Mrs. Graham is going to have a baby very soon." Matt didn't say anything. His mother continued, "You know, she has a baby growing in her tummy." Matt looked up at his mother with a wide-eyed expression, almost a look of horror, and said, "Did she swallow it?" The child's world is filled with questions as information is presented. The complex issues of birth will take more time and experience before understanding occurs.

Distinguishing between the Real World and the World of Fantasy

The thinking of children at this stage is largely personal. Kevin, described in an earlier chapter, could exclaim, "It doesn't wait for me," when he saw the water flowing away from him. This perception of the world is revealed in the drawings of young children where the head or face is usually very large. It has long been thought that this is because it is the part of the body that is most important for the child. However, one teacher asked a child to draw the back of the face and was astonished that the face was drawn quite small. She asked the child about this difference, and to her surprise the child replied, "I need more room in the front for the eyes, nose and mouth." We do not always understand what the meaning is for the child. Who would have believed that young children have the foresight to plan ahead in their drawings!!

Fantasy and reality are often confused in young children's thinking. What they think seems true to them whether or not it corresponds to reality. Children need help and time as they struggle to get the real world and the world of magic into their proper places. Children are fortunate when they have help from a parent or a teacher. Imaginative tales can be valued for what they are, delightful figments of the imagination and a method of escape that we can all use at times. Children enjoy making up stories but—should gradually become clear about the differences between the pretend and the factual.

Jamie, a 4-year-old, tended to turn away from difficulties and deny unpleasant realities. He often tried to make his world be what he wanted it to be. He teased and successfully manipulated the succession of baby-sitters who cared for him when he was not in the center while his mother worked. His teacher watched for opportunities to help him enjoy reality without distorting it. It was not difficult, for he was a friendly child, eager to please and to find a place for himself in the group.

Jamie is playing with dough at the table, patting, squeezing and folding it. He suddenly looks down and exclaims, "Hey! Hey, I made a turtle. I made a turtle!" He smiles a big smile and is obviously pleased with this discovery. With his hands he carefully forms the legs and head so they are more prominent. The other children start making turtles, too. Jamie exclaims to an approaching teacher, "Hey, look at my turtle!" He jumps off his chair and joining in excitedly, "Turtle, turtle, see my turtle!" The teacher admires the turtles.

Jamie says, "I didn't know I could make a turtle, but I did. I made a turtle." He then puts his hand behind the turtle and gives it a shove. The turtle sticks to the table and changes form slightly. Jamie frowns and carefully unsticks it and shoves it again. This time it slides on the table but changes shape. He looks up at the teacher with a distraught expression and says, "My turtle can't walk."

The teacher asks thoughtfully, "Do you know why your turtle can't walk?" Jamie frowns, then replies slowly, "No—oh yeah, because he is playdough instead of real." With a smile the teacher confirms his discovery. "Yes, you know why."

Here we see Jamie pleased with himself for making a turtle and then finding that the turtle does not fit in with his dream of a turtle. The teacher helps him return to a satisfying reality.

The Teacher Encourages Imagination

Imagination is valuable. We know that "hunches" and "brain storming" often produce worthwhile ideas in adults. Children are naturally good at using their imaginations, or "taking them out for a run," as someone has called it. As they become clearer about reality and fantasy, they have fun making up stories as well as describing real experiences. They play games of pretending. "Wouldn't it be funny if . . ." or "This looks like a. . . ."

Thinking of alternatives or possibilities is an exercise for the intellect and the imagination. The teacher may ask, "How many ways are there to go to the store?" "What do you think we will see when we get to the top of the hill?" "What would you do if you found you were lost on the street?" "What do you think we could make out of this?" Guessing and risking a guess are often valuable aids in problem solving if one can check on the results. Imaginative solutions are worth cultivating.

How Young Children Are Motivated to Learn

As we observe children, we see that they are most absorbed when they are most interested. They concentrate and persist when they are really intrigued, just as we ourselves do. If we are to teach effectively, we must understand the interests children are likely to have and the particular interests of the individual child. Only as we make available materials and experiences in which the children are truly interested can we facilitate their learning.

Purposeful activity grows out of interests, and it is this kind of activity that generates the energy learning demands. Brearley (1970) puts it this way: "Teaching is a cultural task and our business is to gear these natural curiosities and interests to the traditional skills which the culture has built up and valued . . . ," adding that in teaching we need "the energy of his [the child's] willingness on our side."

Young children are interested in all kinds of physical movement, large and small muscle activities, indoor and outdoor play, which gives opportunities to explore the possibilities of what can be done with movement. Children find great satisfaction in climbing the jungle gym, digging in the dirt, and rolling in the snow.

Many opportunities exist for cognitive learning in most of these activities. There are problems to be dealt with, things to be observed and compared.

Curiosity is a motivating force in children in the sensorimotor and preoperational stages of development. We need to provide a rich variety of firsthand experiences to be explored and acted upon. The curious child can use his experiences in "structured thinking" as he is ready. The teacher can supply words, ask questions, call attention to aspects of the experience and extend it. The teacher can deepen the child's curiosity and interest into explicit knowledge.

The desire for love and appreciation is also a strong motivating force. It is a need that can easily be exploited unless we keep clearly in mind the child's purposes and his level of development. Too often we may be more concerned with our own purposes. If we give the child approval for being "good" by our standards or for doing what we think is best, we may be limiting his development as an individual. We need to make sure that we acknowledge with approval the effort that went into constructing an airplane that satisfied him, or the control he exercised in not acting on the impulse to hit an offending companion, or the spontaneous sharing done among friends, or the imaginative observation, rather than giving approval only for achievements that satisfy us.

The supportive role of the adult is an important one. He or she gives support to the child by showing an interest in what the child does, by treating the child's questions with respect, by giving more attention to the positive than the negative aspects of the child's performance, by generous giving of approval for real accomplishments.

The Urge Toward Mastery

Motivation depends on many factors. One of the strongest is the urge toward mastery of a problem and the satisfaction that all of us feel from performing with skill. We see this in a young child as he persists in working

The learning process is enhanced when a project can be experienced from beginning to end.
Next step: applesauce! *Child Development Laboratory, California State University, Chico*

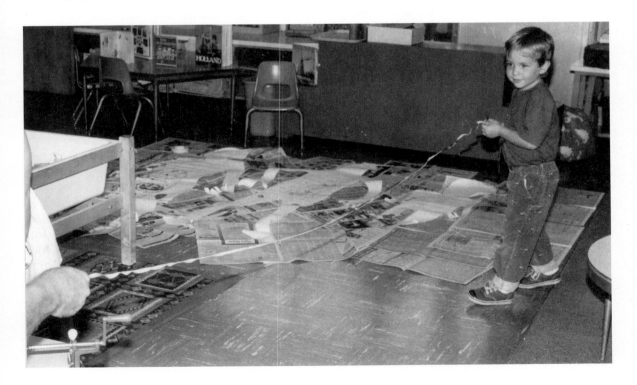

on a fastening until he succeeds in opening it and then turns to fresh fields of endeavor.

This urge toward competence, as psychologist Robert W. White (1968) has called it, is a strong motivating force as long as we believe there is a hope of success. The strength of the urge diminishes if our efforts are continually blocked. The child who has lost hope of any success is not motivated to try. He has lost this powerful urge. When a child has lived in an environment that is largely unfavorable for learning, the teacher must work to reawaken his curiosity and zest for exploring and discovering. Above all she must help the child rediscover faith in his own competence. He must know that he can succeed, if he tries. The child must see himself as someone who is able to achieve. If the teacher is to help, she must herself believe that the child can learn.

Under favorable conditions, the child's natural curiosity and urge toward competence motivate him. He wants to learn and to gain skills. The teacher does not need to depend on extrinsic forms of motivation. The child wants to grow to be like the important adults around him. When these adults present themselves as "models" who work and achieve, they give direction to the child's efforts. He can work and become competent.

Bruner (1966) comments: "The will to learn is an intrinsic motive, one that finds its source and its reward in its own exercise." He points out that the most lasting satisfactions lie in learning itself, not in extrinsic rewards. These do not give reliable nourishment "over the long course of learning." The urge toward competence is strong in a healthy child, who needs little else except encouragement to sustain learning.

The teacher has a responsibility to guard this precious "will to learn" that motivates the child, or to reawaken it in children who may have lost it. She needs to help these children find "the confidence to try and to make mistakes, and the confidence to know that it is worth doing for its own sake. And the daring to like yourself and trust your product." (Vinnette Carroll, as quoted in Christian Science Monitor, November 29, 1969)

Readiness for Learning

Nurturing readiness for formal learning does not imply early teaching of school subjects. Most educators of young children have always opposed such pressures. As long ago as 1962, members of a colloquy held in Washington, D.C., called Basic Human Values for Childhood Education, declared themselves "unreservedly opposed to pressures on children for early formal learning." They felt that "formal learning tasks may displace the informal play-type learning which involves imagination, fantasy, creative activities and the other higher mental processes, and in that way deprive the child of the very activities so necessary for his development." (Association for Childhood Education International, 1962. Report of colloquy on Basic Human Values for Childhood Education. Washington, DC: Author)

More recently, NAEYC pointed out that teachers help children achieve sound intellectual learning through a curriculum that "encourages children to be actively involved in the learning process, to experience a variety of developmentally appropriate activities and materials, and to pursue their own interests in the context of life in the community and the world." (NAEYC, 1991a. *Accreditation criteria . . .* , p. 20)

Children learn easily those things that they are developmentally ready to learn. They construct their own knowledge from experiences and mistakes. But their readiness needs to be nurtured.

> **The vital role** of teachers and other adults is to support children's development both in terms of their actual development and their potential. Vygotsky uses the term "zone of proximal development" to describe the level of development where the child can function with the assistance of adults or more capable peers, the level beyond where the child is able to function independently. The principle of learning is that children can do things first in a supportive context and then later independently and in a variety of contexts. The support of adults and more competent peers provides the necessary assistance or "scaffold" that enables the child to move to the next level of independent functioning. The teacher's role is one of supporting, guiding, and facilitating development and learning, as opposed to the traditional view of teaching as transmission of knowledge. (NAEYC, 1991. *Guidelines for appropriate curriculum content . . .* , p. 26)

A good teacher continually nurtures a child's readiness to move into more advanced activities. For example, when a child has mastered pounding large tacks into a board to her satisfaction, she is ready for other woodworking experiences. The teacher provides nails and then a saw so that the child can proceed to constructing an object, depending on her interests, with all the learning involved in the construction. She also is gaining confidence in her own ability to learn. The teacher will give children choices, too, whenever possible to help them develop their capacities in making decisions. Children can assume increasing responsibility as they are ready.

Each child grows and learns in her own manner and rate, nurtured by opportunities, but without pressures. She becomes a more confident person in the process of learning.

A Special Kind of Learning

Many experiences at the preschool level prepare a child for learning to read. One of the most important of these is a "reading atmosphere" fostered by people who are themselves interested in and enjoy books and who enjoy reading to the child from suitable books. Books become an important part of the child's world. As he sits with the adult, he observes her eye movements and becomes aware of the way she follows the line of print. The adult may use a finger to indicate where the words she is reading appear on the page and when she is ready for the page to be turned.

There are many opportunities to call the child's attention to words and their meaning—a "stop" sign on the street or on the playground to indicate where the wagons and tricycles must stop; a sign "store" or the sentence, "This is a store" on a block construction, which makes the child more aware of the written word. The child's name can be printed over his locker or cubby, on his paintings, or at the table where he sits for lunch. Later he may copy the teacher's lettering and print his own name. There may be discussion of the letters and comparisons with other people's names with the recognition of letters that are the same or different. Lotto games give the child practice in discriminating lines and forms, a skill needed in reading.

Handling tools, using scissors, drawing, and painting are some activities that promote the neuromuscular development which is required for reading and writing. Equally necessary is a wide variety of experiences with objects and people and situations that enable the child to understand what he will be reading later. All of this is part of nurturing readiness to develop appropriate skills necessary for formal reading.

Adult Anxiety about a Child's Learning to Read

Adult anxiety often centers around children's reading. We see this in educational television programs and workbook activities. Learning to recognize and write the letters of the alphabet is not an appropriate activity for most 3-year-olds, but it is often included in programs for young preschoolers. Far more important as a basis for reading are the experiences we have mentioned.

When children have not had this background, we give them help by providing what they have lacked rather than by working with them to master skills for which they have not had the preparation. Skipping a stage does not promote optimum development. Beginning without enough background may mean that the child struggles for months to achieve a level of skill reachable with very little effort later. Some parents and teachers of young children grow anxious and attempt to push the child toward reading, not trusting him to learn and thus not building trust in himself. There is little point in learning to read before one has the background for understanding what is on the page. Partial comprehension may become a habit. One only reads words. There will be individual differences in the age at which children are ready to begin reading, of course, and these differences can be respected.

One mother, when asked about her 4-year-old's talent in reading and writing, said she couldn't explain it. She did nothing to teach her child to read or write, yet the child was writing and reading. Upon further investigation, the mother revealed that books were a very important part of the family's life. Word games were played in the car; rhyming words and being silly with language were part of the fun; drawing letters and numbers on one's arm or back and then guessing what was drawn were favorite activities. The child was having an experience with words, letters, and sounds that contributed to her early writing. The mother was surprised when told that these games contributed to the child's early abilities.

Randy, 3 1/2, was able to read quite well. His parents loved books and were pleased with his precocious development. The child was ready to demonstrate his skill on every occasion, but the other children were not interested. He lacked skill in riding a tricycle. He did not know how to use blocks or climb in the jungle gym. He did not know how to play. It was some weeks before he could make contact on his own with the children. He was full of fears and had wild fantasies. He was a child who needed a group experience.

When Randy left the group more than a year later, he was much more relaxed and was eating and sleeping better at home. While his motor skills were still below average for his age, he had made a great deal of progress in developing them as well as in developing his social skills. He was taking part in active group play in a more childlike way. His parents had revised their goals for him. They were pleased with his development for they could see that he was a happier child. He will do well in school, and he also has a good chance of becoming a well-developed human being. He is sure to be less handicapped socially, emotionally, and even intellectually.

The Characteristics of a Good Thinker

An important characteristic of a good thinker is a child's feeling of self-confidence. Experiences in being successful encourage the child to persist and to believe in her own success. The teacher's belief in the child and her expectations also give confidence. This confidence enables the child to face frustrations and failures and to use them, as the scientist does, for learning what does not work.

The ability to pay attention or concentrate is a characteristic of a good thinker. Providing what is of real interest to the child and allowing her time to complete an activity is one part of the teacher's contribution. She will note which materials call forth the longest attention spans and supply more of them. She avoids interrupting purposeful activities when possible, keeping the schedule flexible to allow for concentration. A teacher reported that one 4-year-old in her group worked for a full hour at the workbench making an airplane, using the tools and materials on hand there.

A good thinker makes a practice of estimating and planning. A child may say, "I need three pieces of wood to finish this." Afterward the teacher may say, if this is the case, "You thought you needed three pieces. Now you know you only needed two." Learning to estimate approximately what will be needed, how far it is around the playground, or how long it will take, and then finding out if the estimations were correct are characteristics of a thinker. The teacher can encourage these traits. She can also help the child check on results and reflect. As he sees similarities and differences, she can ask, "Why?" or, "How do you know?"

Good thinkers use imagination. They are creative. Children often pretend in their play. A child might pretend to be the mother, or the father, or

Good thinkers draw conclusions about honey by tasting and watching its slow drip. Migrant Head Start, Chico, California

the baby, and proceed to imagine and act the role. Or they say, "Pretend I'm a lion and I'm going to eat you." Children exercise their imaginations more actively than most adults do and, in fantasy, deal with all kinds of real situations. Using imagination about personal relationships increases children's awareness of aspects of relationships. Here, too, the teacher can give direction. "What would you have done if you had been this child?" she can say as they read a story together. Or she can ask, "What would you do if you found you were lost and didn't know your way home?" Thinking can take place in these discussions, and a pattern for solving difficulties can evolve as thinking begins to find its place along with action. Dramatic play of all kinds stimulates cognitive growth. Symbolic thinking depends on being able to imagine.

The good thinker needs to be able to communicate her thoughts. Language plays an important role in the development of the intellect. It is a means of clarifying thought as well as a means of communication. It nourishes the growth of the capacity to reason. We will discuss this further in the section on language in Chapter 18.

Overcoming Emotional Blocks in Learning

A child may be blocked in learning because of fears that she may bring to the learning situation. Fear of making a mistake is one of the common fears. These fears may prevent her from daring to take necessary risks.

Emotional blocks in learning may result from the child's attitude toward authority and authority figures. If the child is continually resisting authority, she is blocked in learning because inevitably a measure of authority and discipline is necessary in a learning situation. She must in the end be able to discipline herself. The child needs to come to terms with her feelings about authority before she is free to learn as she might otherwise do. Discriminations of many kinds may inhibit learning.

Cognitive learning is best carried on under relatively conflict-free conditions. There can be an element of surprise or uncertainty or some disequilibrium, as an unanswered question, but not an element of conflict. As part of her teaching role the teacher will try to help the child with any blocks that may hinder learning.

Chapter Overview

In this chapter we have introduced the concepts of implicit and explicit learning. We have emphasized the need for children to have opportunities to discover the properties of objects. This enhances their implicit knowledge base. The conditions that favor intellectual growth are those in which children feel secure and relatively free from conflicts and have confidence in themselves and in their ability to cope with the problems presented. They do not learn readily when they are discouraged and see little hope of success when they feel alienated.

The next five chapters are about areas of learning in a curriculum for young children. We will suggest some activities and their values in each of these areas. Every teacher will want to explore and discover other opportunities to provide children with learning experiences in the areas, depending on the interests of the children in the group.

Projects

1. Select an area in a center and list possible ways in which children may be able to have learning experiences here. Indicate also what some of the explicit learnings might be. In what way might these be valuable for later learning? For example, what are possible experiences with colors, or with sounds?

2. Interview parents about early reading experiences with their child/children. Ask about the books read to the child, the games played with words, the child's interest in "reading" items such as the cereal box, signs and television messages.

For Your Further Reading

Ault, R. L. (1983). *Children's cognitive learning*. (2nd ed.). New York: Oxford University Press. A readable comparison of children's cognitive development from the Piagetian approach and the process (non-Piagetian) approach. Makes research results understandable and interesting.

Brearley, M. (Ed.). (1970). *The teaching of young children: Some applications of*

Piaget's learning theory. New York: Schocken Books. Describes implicit and explicit learning, as well as a simple and sound approach to classroom use of Piaget's theories.

Chess, S., Thomas, A., & Birch, H. G. (1978). *Your child is a person.* New York: Penguin. Written for parents and valuable for teachers in understanding children's temperamental characteristics. Based on a 20-year study that identified children's inborn differences as "easy," "slow-to-warm," and "difficult," which can be influenced by environment and responses of those around them. Helps adults understand children's differences in the learning process.

DeVries, R., & Kohlberg, L. (1990.) *Constructivist early education: Overview and comparison with other programs.* Washington, DC: National Association for the Education of Young Children. Not easy reading, but fascinating discussion of Piagetian constructivist theory and applications to classroom practices. Compares Piaget with Montessori theory and practice and Bank Street theory and practice.

Donaldson, M. (1978). *Children's minds.* New York: W. W. Norton. An interesting book challenging some of Piaget's findings; offers fresh understanding into how children think.

Hendrick, J. (1990). *Total learning: Developmental curriculum for the young child* (3rd ed.). Columbus, OH: Merrill Publishing. Two chapters are particularly valuable about children's learning processes: "Helping children learn to think for themselves: Increasing cognitive competence," pp. 329–345, and "Building for future academic competence: Developing specific mental abilities," pp. 346–369. Helps adults translate Piaget's theories into daily curriculum.

Kantrowitz, B., & Wingert, P. (1989). How kids learn. *Young Children 44*(6), 3–10. Reprinted from *Newsweek*, April 17, 1989. The authors ask, "Why is it that we know so much about how young children learn, and yet we do so little of it in our schools?" An excellent article on how children learn through moving, touching, exploring, yet how difficult the job is to convince parents and some schools. Chart shows learning focus at different ages from infancy to age 8.

Katz, L. G., & Chard, S. C. (1989). *Engaging children's minds: The project approach.* Norwood, NJ: Ablex. Includes theoretical concerns about reward and reinforcement as well as lively examples of how to teach through the project approach: how to get started, materials needed, classroom settings, assessment checklist.

National Association for the Education of Young Children (1991). Guidelines for appropriate curriculum content and assessment in programs serving children ages 3 through 8. Position statement of the NAEYC and the National Association of Early Childhood Specialists in State Departments of Education. *Young Children,* 46(3), 21–38. The first part of the position paper presents long-awaited guidelines for curriculum, starting with definitions and theoretical framework, how children learn, and what children should learn. Eighteen statements describe curriculum content guidelines.

Piaget, J. (1983). Piaget's theory. In P. H. Mussen (Ed.). *Handbook of child psychology* (4th ed.). W. Kessen (Ed.). Vol. I: *History, theory, and methods.* New York: John Wiley & Sons. Jean Piaget writes about his work, of interest to many people who have read books about Piaget rather than by him.

Areas of Learning in the Program: Motor and Sensory Development

Baseball players (*boy, 3 years*)

In this first chapter about *Areas of Learning in the Program* you will learn one of the first things we notice in young children: their enjoyment of sensory activities and their constant use of their muscles in movement. You will explore:

▶ Learning through senses: Kinesthetic, seeing, hearing, touching, tasting, smelling
▶ Organizing sensory impressions: Forming concepts.

DEVELOPMENTALLY APPROPRIATE PRACTICE: When provided with a wealth of experiences to choose from during the day, [young children] seek desired activities or objects . . . and begin to understand, in a practical sensorimotor way, such concepts as cause and effect; the use of tools; and familiarity with distance, spatial relationships, and perspectives. They begin to group and compare. They imitate. They develop patterns of relation to others, including adults . . . They need to be encouraged to explore and learn from a rich array of activities, objects, and people. (Bredekamp, 1987. *Developmentally appropriate practice . . .*, p. 19)

In all the areas of learning in programs for young children, teaching begins at the point where the individual child is in competencies and understanding. We must remember that the child has already had many experiences and has learned a great deal before entering a center. This child implicitly "knows" a great deal. Our teaching must be based on this knowledge.

Our task is to find out where the child is in his abilities and experiences. We need to observe the child, consult with the parents who have guided his earlier learning, and build a relationship of trust with the child.

It is important not to skip any of the stages in intellectual or emotional development. When children have missed important experiences earlier, they need to have these experiences before they can go on to the next stage. Four-year-old Maria, for example, who had had little opportunity for play, at first explored the housekeeping corner more like a 2-year-old child before she went on to make use of the corner as 4-year-olds usually do.

We will discuss curriculum areas in turn, beginning with sensorimotor aspects of learning.

Learning Through the Senses

Skills in Sensory Perception: Foundation for Concepts

Children learn about the world around them through the five senses—seeing, hearing, feeling, tasting, smelling—and through the kinesthetic sense, the sense of muscular movement. The greater the input of sensory impressions, the more material they have from which to build concepts of what the world is like. They improve their tools for understanding the world as they improve the keenness of their sensory perception. Teachers provide for a wide variety of sensory experiences and encourage their use. Their role is an important one here.

A child with a sensory defect, such as a partially sighted child or a hearing-impaired child, is handicapped because he takes in less complete or less accurate impressions. He must make more effort to learn because of the sensory limitation.

Kinesthetic Sense and Motor Skills

The infant begins to perceive the world as he moves his hands, then arms and legs, roots for the breast, and sucks. Much later he crawls, stands, begins to walk, and broadens his horizons as he gains more control over his muscles. The child's kinesthetic impressions increase as he uses his body.

Acquiring skill in using body muscles is important for the young child. He gains confidence when able to control his muscles and can feel "in tune" with his body, able to use it freely, following his own rhythms. His posture and the way he uses his body reveal attitudes he holds about him-

Learning through the kinesthetic sense as the boys mix concrete for the sign post and shovel it into the bucket. Child Development Laboratory, California State University, Chico

self. He has more confidence as he plays with other children and copes with situations.

A healthy child enjoys practicing until a skill is mastered. The toddler goes up and down stairs or climbs over objects until he can do it easily. The preschool age child will try many methods of riding a tricycle after mastering the art of riding. He goes fast on it, cuts corners, and rides close to objects.

He begins to know what it feels like to lift a weight, to roll down a slope, to throw. As he jumps from a box, he experiences distance and depth. Reaching out, falling, climbing, swinging, pushing a wagon, riding a tricycle—all play a part in refining kinesthetic perceptions. He enjoys his competence. It gives him confidence.

Skills in using large muscles develop through vigorous, active play. This kind of play usually takes place outdoors. Activities that develop large muscle skills include:

Lifting and piling large hollow blocks, boxes, or short boards.
Pulling a loaded wagon or using a wheelbarrow for carrying objects.
Digging with shovel or spade.
Climbing on a jungle gym, rope ladder, or in a tree or over a box.
Swinging in a swing or on the rungs of a bar or a horizontal ladder.
Riding wheel toys.
Pounding nails, sawing, and using other carpentry tools.
Balancing by walking on low boards or on bouncing boards or on the trampoline.
Running, sometimes barefoot, on sand or grass.
Throwing balls through a hoop or throwing beanbags at a target, or just throwing.
Rhythmic activities to music.

Activities that develop coordination in the use of small muscles include:

Activities in connection with dressing, buttoning, lacing shoes, pulling on boots, hanging up a coat or towel.
Activities in connection with eating, such as using a spoon and fork, pouring juice or milk from a small pitcher into a cup or glass.
Play with all kinds of manipulative toys like trucks, cars, interlocking blocks, puzzles.
Using a paint brush or large crayons or felt pen, or cutting with scissors.
Finger plays.

Good posture is important, too. It is encouraged by active play. It is also encouraged by making sure that chairs are of the proper height so that children's feet are on the floor when they are seated and by making sure that children sit only for short periods. Good posture may also be developed by dancing and games.

Motor activities form an important part of the curriculum for young children. As teachers observe the play, they may extend the range of experience by introducing a game of throwing beanbags at a target or of balancing on a walking board. They may rearrange the boards and boxes in new patterns to encourage more climbing. Part of their teaching will consist in making sure that children have a range of activities to develop coordination of large and small muscles.

With opportunity children can develop surprising skill.

Carlos, a 4-year-old, had extraordinary skill with tools. He could hammer a nail accurately, saw through boards, and use a screwdriver. His father had a workshop in their basement, and he had provided a small one for his son with proper tools. They often worked there together. This boy took the lead in constructing a playhouse at the center. The project lasted several weeks, and he continued his interest in the project throughout the time, helping sustain the interest of other children in it.

There are many implicit cognitive learnings in motor activities. The child who has balanced on a walking board, built a tower of blocks, bounced on a springing surface, swung on a set of rings or the horizontal ladder, rolled down an incline, or ridden a tricycle fast around corners knows implicitly some of the principles of physics that will later be the basis for explicit learning. The child's understanding of the abstract principles will be based on his own body experience with them in play.

Seeing

Visual impressions are one of the most constant and valuable sources of learning for young children. An infant responds in an excited way to the sight of the breast or bottle being brought near him. He has learned a sequence of sights and sounds that allows him to anticipate the breast or bottle and predict this event. The older infant experiences an object as completely as possible by touching it, rolling it, pulling and twisting it, chewing on it, looking at it from all angles, and finally dropping it when he "understands" it. Donald Winnicott (1957) in his chapter, "Further Thoughts on Babies as Persons," gives a delightful description of how a 10-month-old baby comes to "know" a spoon by playing with it. Preschool children continue to learn by looking at, feeling, and doing something with the objects around them.

In favorable environments young children have many opportunities to see and come to know objects. In unfavorable environments they may have fewer of these experiences. The effect of fewer experiences is that there are fewer impressions, which discourages children's curiosity and their urge to explore.

The teacher should be alert to the possibility of visual impairment in individual children. It is easy to misjudge the cause of behavior. The child with poor vision may be easily distracted or clumsy and may hold objects very close to his face. It is important to correct visual defects at an early age because defective vision impedes learning, especially in the very young child whose learning takes place largely through sensorimotor experiences. The teacher can make a simple vision test and consult with the parents if a problem seems likely.

Beauty in line, form, and color are important for children. They are helped to become more aware of beauty by having lovely things to look at in the center, such as hanging plants, a beautiful picture in the entrance hall, and some of their own paintings attractively mounted and hung at a child's eye level.

Shapes and forms interest children. The teacher can help make these differences more explicit. Blocks can be arranged on shelves according to shapes and sizes. Big and small, long and short, wide and narrow are terms to learn in relation to objects seen as well as felt. There are different textures and patterns to be looked at as well as felt: the bark on trees, the tracks in sand or mud, ripples made by waves. Experimenting with shadows, children can change shapes and sizes. Every teacher will build on what is available to give children more material for developing concepts through looking and examining what they see.

Hearing

Interest in sounds and the capacity to hear and to discriminate sounds contributes to the development of speech. Children discover many sounds on their own as they explore materials. The teacher can extend these experiences by her comments: "You made a different sound when you hit the spoon against the can" or, "Is it higher or lower this time?" Children often play with words and make up nonsense lines. They like the sounds of some phrases. The teacher can select stories and poems in which the words make music, or she can call attention to sounds.

Children today may live in such a confusion of noises that they fail to learn to identify individual sounds or to listen. The teacher helps children listen to sounds—bird songs, the sound of an airplane, the eggbeater in the kitchen, the clock, a whisper, the rumble of a truck, the swish of feet in the leaves. She helps them make different sounds, hitting two things together, ringing a bell, making musical sounds by using a variety of instruments. A keen ear is a help to children as they go on learning and enjoying experiences.

A child may seem inattentive because of a hearing loss. The teacher can make a simple test such as speaking to the child in a normal tone when his back is turned, or moving a ticking clock toward him and noting when he pays attention. If the teacher suspects any hearing loss, she can consult with the parents. The child may need tests by a professional. Many children have been disadvantaged in school because of an undetected hearing loss.

Touching

Children are responsive to the feel of things. They learn from touching and need a wide variety of experiences with touching in order to develop adequate concepts about the world around them. They need help in making discriminations and in using the correct descriptive words. A teacher can

Infants enjoy different textures, like grass, as they learn to creep and walk. Migrant Head Start, Chico, California

exercise ingenuity in providing children with touch experiences and encouraging their personal descriptions of the feel of things.

Objects feel hard or soft, rough or smooth, firm or spongy. A "feel box" with items hidden in it gives a child the chance to identify objects by their feel. Sorting games based on the feel of materials of different textures, or on shapes or sizes or forms, may interest children. Children enjoy collecting things that have special "feels," like stones and shells made smooth by the water, smooth nuts, or other objects that are smooth and hard. They enjoy the sensory delight of feeling things.

The teacher can provide a variety of materials of different textures in the "dress-up" area, such as squares of filmy gauze or chiffon, velvet, silk or soft wool or cotton, along with synthetic fibers. In each case the teacher uses the correct designation as she talks about the different materials.

The same object feels different at different temperatures, like the handlebars of a tricycle in the sun or the shade. Water feels different when it has turned to ice. The feel of a leaf when it is green and when it is dry is different, as is the feel of bark on different trees or the feel of different animals—a worm, a baby chick, a kitten. There is the feel of food as well as its taste to identify it. Some foods are soft and some are crunchy. The feel of clay when it is dry is different from its feel when wet and "gooshy." The child experiences these things, but the teacher reinforces and extends the experience by her comments or descriptive words.

Up to her elbows in shaving cream, the child learns through sensory exploration. Santa Monica College, Child Development Center, Santa Monica, California

She may share the experience by describing it without asking any response. Children learn by touching and feeling.

Tasting

Children often comment on taste, saying, "It tastes bad," or "good." There are more accurate terms, however, to describe the discrimination of tastes, and the teacher can introduce children to the terms sweet, sour, bitter, and salty with samples. Things that look the same do not always taste the same, such as pineapple and grapefruit juice, or a pinch of sugar and a pinch of salt. The most likely place for children to be interested in taste discrimination is at the table when they are eating.

Most of us know the taste of paste, playdough, and a variety of other things used in school. Many young children also will bring objects and materials to their mouths to explore their taste and feel. Experiencing and describing tastes not only increase the child's awareness but also challenge the ability to express his perceptions. Enjoying tastes and flavors increases enjoyment in eating.

Smelling

There are many kinds of smells in the child's environment: the smell of food or flowers; the smell of clay, paint, or soap; the smell of freshly washed towels; the smell of wool when it is wet; the smell of new shoes. Some smells are pleasant; some are unpleasant. The smell of food is good when one is hungry. Some flowers have a strong fragrance; some have a delicate fragrance. Almost everything has an odor that helps us identify places, things, people, and animals.

Describing smells increases children's ability to express their perceptions and to describe their experiences. The teacher will comment on different odors or respond with appreciation when a child comments. The teacher may help the child develop more awareness of odors by asking, "What does it smell like?" or, "Can you find where the odor comes from?" The teacher supplies a variety of experiences and can reinforce the child's learning by showing interest and attention.

Organizing Sensory Impressions: Forming Concepts

As children use their senses, they store up a multitude of impressions. In doing this they begin to classify these impressions and to make distinctions. All furry animals are not kittens. An animal can be a kitty or a dog. Other children have mothers and fathers. Some children are bigger than others. When does tomorrow really come? It is often a confusing matter, and there is an endless amount to learn. We can help children to organize, classify, and discriminate.

Identifying, associating, organizing, classifying, and perceiving relationships are important aspects of learning in the early years. Children do much of this in their play, but some happens through games and experiences devised to focus on developing these skills. They are learning to perceive basic relationships involving objects, space and time relationships, and cause and effect relationships.

To organize impressions, a child must be able to identify and label objects. All objects have names. The teacher will use the names of things in speaking to a child by calling the child's attention to names, such as her own name on her locker or on her painting; pointing out signs when they are walking, like the name of a street or a "stop" sign; and giving the child the name of any new object she meets.

Objects also have characteristics by which they can be identified. They may differ in color. They may be heavy or light or large or small. As they talk with children, the teachers will use descriptive words. The cup one is using is green. The box is large, but it is also light. Another box may be large and heavy. The teachers make sure the child has a chance to have experiences with many objects with different characteristics. They might introduce games that depend on identifying characteristics, such as, "What can you find that is heavy?" or, "What can you find that is light?" or, "What can you find that is blue?"

It is important for the child to know the uses and functions of objects as a way of learning about them. For example, she paints with a brush, and she cuts with scissors. The teacher may ask, "What do you need when you want to cut the paper?" Some things have more than one use. We use water for several purposes. The teacher may ask, "What do we use water

Motor learning takes place through experimentation: Kicking the ball doesn't work, nor does throwing it. He rolls it—success! Migrant Head Start, Chico, California

for?" In conversations the teacher and the children can talk about what things are used for, or what they might be used for.

Objects are related in different ways. They may be the same, or they may be different. They may be similar, like plates and saucers. They may belong together in sets, like cups and saucers. There are size relationships. Some objects are large and some small. There may be an order in size, from smallest to biggest. There are relationships in quantity, too, from a few to a lot. Some objects may be the same because they are soft or hard, or they may be different in these ways. They may be rough or smooth.

Making explicit the way in which things are alike or different is important. Things may be alike because of their function or their color or their size. They may both be used for drinking but be different in color. Through many experiences with objects the teacher tries to help the child sharpen the ability to perceive, to make distinctions, and to classify. Matching and sorting games are useful here.

There are labels that refer to position in space, too, such as under, over, inside, outside, beside, on top of, below. Teachers can use these words as they give directions: "Put the block on top of the box beside the truck." They can encourage the children to use specific words in describing where a thing belongs. They may introduce games in which children follow directions about placing or hiding objects.

Teachers can also help the child become more aware of time and the place of events in time. There is a time for lunch and a time for rest. One event comes before another, or after it. There are days for being at the center and days for being at home. There is a long time and a short time, and even a beginning and an end to an experience.

Things change, and some of the changes relate to time. A child is 3, and then she is 4. After the daytime comes the nighttime. Other changes are not related to time. Water freezes when it is put into the freezer or when it is very cold outdoors. A child is cold, and she gets warm when she runs. The teacher calls attention to these things, making them more explicit for the child, helping her to build concepts and to clear up misconceptions as she organizes her impressions.

Recalling and remembering involve making associations. Children enjoy recalling what they did once or what they saw when they were on a walk or trip. "Remember the fire engine . . ." or, "Remember the baby colt and how he looked. . . ." It is good to be able to think about what one has experienced. It helps one learn and it solves problems. "Remember when you . . ." may help the child solve the problem of how to make an airplane. Deciding what she needs to finish an airplane or boat may necessitate recalling what materials were used before and where they were found. She begins to plan this way.

Recalling will depend on giving attention in the first place. The teacher may introduce games that depend on paying attention and remembering, such as a game where the child first looks carefully at objects placed in front of her, then closes her eyes while one of these is removed and, when she looks again, tries to remember the name of the missing object.

Many times children will surprise us by the new patterns they see or the associations they make. Children often have a fresh approach that can be nurtured by our appreciation.

Chapter Overview

As we have seen in this chapter, through motor and sensory development children begin to learn about their world. Skills in using large and small muscles come about by providing a curriculum that includes many opportunities to play. Planning experiences that use the senses—seeing, hearing, tasting, touching, smelling—provide a developmentally appropriate framework for enhancing motor and sensory skill development. Finally, this chapter has demonstrated how helping children organize their perceptions by recalling and remembering contributes to sharpening young children's ability to make connections in their experiences.

Projects

1. Observe and record five questions asked by a child. Indicate the circumstances briefly. How was each question answered? How would you evaluate each as a learning experience for the child?
2. Observe and record incidents in which a child added to his store of sensory impressions (touch, sight, sound, smell, taste).
3. Observe and record incidents that give evidence of a child's learning:
   A. Perceiving characteristics of an object.
   B. Perceiving functions of an object.
   C. Perceiving relationships.
   D. Ability to recall or associate perceptions.

For Your Further Reading

Baker, K. R. (1966). *Let's play outdoors.* Washington, DC: National Association for the Education of Young Children. Still in print, this little book gives practical tips on educationally sound play areas and equipment. Suggests how teachers can make outdoor play worthwhile.

Carr, R. (1973). *Be a frog, a bird, or a tree: Creative yoga exercises for children.* New York: Harper & Row. A simple, delightful book suggesting movement activities. Each page contains a poem, a drawing (of the grasshopper, the swimmer, the bridge), and a photograph of a child acting out the movement. Encourages creativity rather than imitation.

Hill, D. M. (1977). *Mud, sand and water.* Washington, DC: National Association for the Education of Young Children. This perennially popular book presents how children's learning is advanced through natural, messy materials, and the importance of providing such materials in the program for young children.

Kamii, C., & DeVries, R. (1980). *Group

games in early education: Implications of Piaget's theory. Washington, DC: National Association for the Education of Young Children. Explains the role of competitive games in children's development; includes game directions.

Miller, K. (1989). *The outside play and learning book: Activities for young children.* Mt. Rainier, MD: Gryphon House. An activities book full of ways to help teachers create enriched outdoor experiences, with emphasis on learning as well as enjoyment in natural settings. The planning chapter suggests interest centers, safety and health reminders, turn-taking skills, and supervision. In addition to chapters on outdoor activities usually provided, like sand, mud, and water, the book includes ideas for infants and toddlers, fantasy play, art, and age-appropriate games.

Poest, C. A., Williams, J. R., Witt, D. D., & Atwood, M. E. (1990). Challenge me to move: Large muscle development in young children. *Young Children 45*(5), 4–10. Makes a case for providing planned motor activity centers and guided movement experiences, rather than just providing children with well-equipped motor equipment and expecting them to develop motor skills through maturation.

Skeen, P., Garner, A. P., & Cartwright, S. (1984). *Woodworking for young children.* Washington, DC: National Association for the Education of Young Children. Another excellent how-to book from NAEYC. Helps even adult beginners to teach children the use of tools and woodworking.

Sullivan, M. (1982). *Feeling strong, feeling free: Movement exploration for young children.* Washington, DC: National Association for the Education of Young Children. Detailed teaching ideas for a movement program, including the teacher's role. Sections for 3- and 4-year-olds, 5- to 8-year-olds, and even a child and an adult working together.

Areas of Learning in the Program: Language and Literature

"Once upon a time" story (*girl, 4 years, 8 months*)

This chapter explores a most delightful aspect of young children, their language, and a related interest, literature for young children:

▶ Language.
▶ Special problems with speech.
▶ Language as self-expression.
▶ Emergent literacy.
▶ Literature.

CRITERION: Staff speak with children in a friendly, positive, courteous manner. Staff converse frequently with children, asking open-ended questions and speaking individually to children (as opposed to the whole group) most of the time. Staff include child in conversations; describe actions, experiences, and events; listen and respond to children's comments and suggestions. Children's communication skills develop from verbal interaction with adults. Open-ended questions prompt the child to talk because they cannot be answered by *yes* or *no* or one word. Other questioning techniques which contribute to language development should also be used. (NAEYC, 1991a. *Accreditation Criteria . . . ,* p. 16)

Language

Increasing the child's language competence is an important part of any program for young children. Social relations of all kinds are extended and improved as speech develops. Language is necessary for higher forms of thought processes.

Early Stages in Learning Language

Learning to talk is a complex process, and parents rightfully feel that the baby's first words mark a milestone. A great deal of cognitive growth has taken place to make it possible. Yet it is worth noting that the ordinary, healthy child learns to talk with no formal teaching if she is in an environment where she hears plenty of speech.

The infant communicates by crying and by body movements, including mouth movements. She wriggles all over with delight when she is pleased. She stretches out her arms for what she wants and later she will point. She vocalizes and blows bubbles. Her mouth movements and her other body movements tend to resemble those of her mother as she talks with her. She pays attention to sounds and uses visual cues in understanding meanings. She begins to understand that a word stands for an object long before she herself uses the word. Her mother has used the word "bottle" as she brings it to her, and she understands.

As she moves into the stage where she becomes aware of the permanence of objects, the awareness that something exists even when she can not see it, she recalls the bottle when she hears the word. The word calls up the image, an important function of language. Without the experience the word is of no use to her. When she comes to the stage of using words, she can communicate the idea of "bottle" by using the word herself or some reasonable attempt at the word, another significant achievement. For a long time the gesture is still the preferred method of communication if the object is in sight.

In the early stages a word often stands for a whole object or an experience. "Hot," for example, may mean the stove as well as the heat it gives off and the warning given to control action. With more experience the child will discover that the word refers to only one attribute of a stove and can be applied to other objects.

In this sensorimotor stage of development nothing takes the place of a wide variety of appropriate firsthand experiences. The child needs to see, to touch, to taste, and to do something with the object if she is to understand its nature and the meaning of the label attached to it. If she can roll a ball, sit on it, bounce it, watch it float in the water or sink, and bite it, and if she can use several different types of balls, she stores up impressions that create a more complete concept of "ball." She knows about balls. As adults we still learn in this firsthand way although we have added other ways of knowing.

Individual Differences in Use of Speech

In any group of children we observe great individual differences in their competence with language and their verbal "styles." Some children are always talking as they play. They sing or talk to themselves. When they are with other children, they chatter with them, describing what they are doing, giving directions, agreeing and disagreeing. Other children use few words in the same situations, going quietly about the business of play although they show that they understand and are listening to what is being said. They practice less with speech. They may have other interests at the moment.

We can appreciate how much children are influenced by the speech they hear when we listen to the telephone conversations carried on during play in the housekeeping corner. Some children conduct long conversations about going to work, caring for babies, arranging parties. Other children, probably from homes where language use is restricted, tend to be monosyllabic in their telephone conversations. They are the children who may need help if they are to develop competence with language.

We know that the child needs (1) variety and richness in experience, adapted to her level of understanding and (2) many experiences with speech, hearing it and trying out its many forms, if she is to develop com-

Dramatic play provides opportunities for talking, especially with props like a telephone.
Hill 'n Dale Family Learning Center, Santa Monica, California

petence in the use of speech. Parents and teachers encourage children's speech by talking with them, by paying attention when children speak, and by responding appropriately, so that the communication is mutually rewarding.

The Young Child Develops Competence Without Being Corrected

One study on language found that at home mothers do very little correcting of a young child's speech. They may correct errors of fact, but they tend to ignore errors in speech. Cazden (1981), who has done extensive research on how children learn to speak, considers it a myth that children learn a language by imitation and by having errors corrected. Learning by imitation and by correction is true only in a general sense, according to Cazden. Children appear to imitate some people and not others, depending on the affectional ties. They pick their own speech models. The adult who accepts and respects the child is more likely to be imitated.

The Logic of Children's Speech

In learning to talk all children go through stages that are strikingly similar from child to child and quite different from the adult speech that they hear. Children themselves are actively discovering language and trying to make sense of its structure. In this effort they apply their own logic. At one stage, for example, almost all children will say "foots" or "mouses." These are not words they are likely to have heard, but it shows that they have observed that an "s" is used to form plurals. They try applying this rule, a logical operation, only later to discover that there are exceptions. The same thing happens when they reach the conclusion that past tense is indicated by *-ed* and they begin saying "comed," "goed," "teached."

Here is an example of how some children correct their own mistakes.

Tawanda, 4 years, 9 months, seeing the mice, called excitedly to the others, "Look, mices," Jason ran over to see and called to his companions, "Come and see the mouses." Later, Tawanda, sitting with her elbows on the table while she watched the mice closely, suddenly asked, "When will the mice grow up?"

In phrasing her question Tawanda shows that she had become aware of the correct singular and plural forms and had corrected her own usage. She had taken this step on her own, adding to her confidence in herself as an independent learner. Jason remained at the "mouses" stage, not yet ready for this discovery in language structure.

The child sometimes shows us the logic of experience as she views it.

Susie, 2 years old, shared in the excitement of welcoming her grandmother and her aunt who always came to visit together. Susie cried, "Grandmother, grandmother!" The family discovered that Susie thought the word grandmother applied to both.

When the family insisted that the aunt's name was Aunt Helen, Susie would whisper in Aunt Helen's ear, "Grandmother."

The attempt to construct a logical grammar is evidence of an advance in thinking, although the errors introduced may seem more like a regression. The errors diminish as the child adds to her observations. This goes on, not in any conscious way, but as a formulation out of implicit knowledge from experiences. The process continues throughout life in the attempt to make sense of conflicting evidence.

Coming to a conclusion by one's own efforts sets a constructive pattern for learning in the future. Children are more likely to remember what they themselves have discovered. Correcting children and calling attention to their errors tends to put them on the defensive unless they are very confident. It may take away from the excitement of learning. The healthy child is an eager learner unless corrected too often and discouraged in making the effort.

Cognitive Skills Developed by the Need to Master Language

Recent studies in early language development suggest that "certain cognitive skills are exercised and thereby developed solely because of the need to master language." While it is enough for the child to use her senses to discover the meaning of many words, she begins to meet words that she cannot understand by this method. She must deal with words like "how"

A child learns new vocabulary and concepts in hands-on activities.
Child Development Laboratory, California State University, Chico

and "why" by some other means. She uses the word in order to get enough responses to build a concept of its meaning. As Blank (1974) has put it, the child must "engage in a concentrated course of hypothesis testing." To do this she keeps asking "why" and "how" types of questions. From the answers she gets, she begins to attach meaning to abstract terms about relationships or purposes.

The Importance of Questions

Mastering the question form is an evidence of intellectual growth. The question itself gives clues to the child's level of thinking, which makes answering questions an important matter that deserves thought and attention. Tawanda's interesting question in the situation with the mice, "When will they grow up?" reveals that she is working on the aspect of time. The teacher's answer was, "In about two weeks. Mice grow very fast." The answer was correct but probably inadequate for Tawanda's concerns. How long is two weeks? Evidently it is connected with "fast." She will go on searching. Tawanda will be going to kindergarten soon. The teacher might have asked, "Are you thinking about growing up and going to a new school?" This might have led to a discussion on a subject important to Tawanda. Young children are often confused about time intervals, days of the week, years and phrases like "a little while ago." Until children have asked questions, tested out the answers, and corrected and refined their understanding, they can not appreciate the meaning of these concepts.

When the Language at Home Is Different

A special situation exists in any group where some of the children speak a first language other than English or speak a dialect other than standard English. Gone are the days, we hope, when children were not allowed to use their "mother tongue" in school. All children should be encouraged to use all the speech they have. When children do not speak English, it is important that they have someone in the center who speaks what is spoken at home. If the minority group happens to be Spanish or Hmong, for example, there should be a teacher or aide who knows their language to talk with them, help with explanations, and encourage them to learn to use English. If no teacher is available who can do so, maybe a volunteer, a parent, or another child can help and can spend some time in the group.

The center will help English-speaking children learn about language differences. Songs, games, and stories other than English open the door for more learning. American children whose experience with other languages may be limited need such opportunities. Children learn readily at this age if all languages are introduced and valued. A center with a mixture of nationalities has a chance to broaden the experience of all its children.

When a whole group consists of children with a first language other than English, they adjust more readily if the language of the classroom is their own at first and English is introduced as secondary. The teacher or some other person must be bilingual. There is considerable information about teaching English as a second language (ESL) that may help the teacher in this situation. (Kagen & Garcia, 1991)

Other questions arise when children in the group speak a dialect other than standard English. Here again, it is important to respect the child's home dialect. Our attitudes are changing because of recent studies about language. These studies indicate that all dialects are "systematic, highly structured language codes," different from but not inferior to one another. "The language variety one learns simply reflects where and with whom one lives, not the intelligence with which one is endowed." (Cazden et al, 1981) Black dialect arose out of the culture of black people when this culture came in contact with white, Western culture. Dialects have developed in some Native American groups in the same way.

Since it is important for children to speak standard English if they are to succeed in an English-speaking country, the center should help them toward that competence while they remain comfortable with their home language or dialect.

Ways in Which the Teacher Promotes Language Competence

The teacher stimulates language learning in several ways. She serves as a model for the children in speech. They identify with her, and her warmth and responsiveness encourage their verbal expressions. In serving as a model she avoids using any direct way of changing children's language. She does not correct errors, although she may repeat correctly a word that has been mispronounced in the case of a very young child. She accepts the fact that children use the speech they are accustomed to hearing.

There will be nonverbal communication at times. A child brings his painting, and the teacher smiles and nods approval. There may be unspoken meanings behind some questions or statements a child makes. The teacher needs to be alert to the possibility of the doubt that may be hidden in a question. She can put the feeling into words that may help the child express his feelings more directly the next time.

An Environment that Stimulates Language Learning

We feel sure of some points: (1) Children learn the words they put to use, so we encourage speech and give children a great deal to talk about. For example, the teacher extends the child's vocabulary. The child exclaimed, "It went to the bottom," when he dropped a pebble into a pail of water. The teacher responded, "Yes, the pebble sank." At lunch the teacher may encourage children to recall their experiences, saying, "Do you remember when . . . ," and encourage each one to recount his version. (2) Talking with other children in play tends to stimulate more extensive and sustained speech than talk with adults, in most cases. Opportunity for play, especially for sociodramatic play, should be provided. (3) One-to-one conversation between a child and an adult on a subject of interest to the child advances development in more complex forms of speech; so the teacher takes time for conversation with individual children.

The teacher stimulates children's growth in language competence in the following ways:

1. The teacher models grammatically correct speech. She uses complete sentences and explicit words, as in, "Please bring me the red truck on the top shelf," rather than, "Please bring that truck." The child has a pattern of exact speech in the first sentence but not in the second.

2. The teacher uses variety in her speech to help increase the child's vocabulary. She makes comments introducing new words as in the example, "The pebble sank."

3. The teacher asks open-ended questions rather than questions that can be answered by "yes" or "no." "What do you think will happen?" "What would you do if . . . ?" "What is the problem?" in the case of a dispute. "I wonder if . . ." "Where did the water go?"

4. The teacher listens carefully to what the child says and responds relevantly. She wants the child to feel that she values his words. Meeting with indifference when one speaks is discouraging to anyone.

5. The teacher encourages talking. Children gain speech competence by having many opportunities to use speech and by having a chance to talk about matters of interest to them to an interested listener. They gain language competence, too, as they talk among themselves as they play.

6. The teacher monitors her conversations with children to make sure she is not doing too much talking and to make sure she is encouraging speech in all the children.

7. The teacher allows plenty of time for conversations with individual children. They may carry on a conversation as they wash the paint brushes together or prepare the snack. Conversations at the table may be between two children or between teacher and a child. On the way back to the center after a trip, conversations recalling the experience often take place.

8. Above all, the teacher plans activities that promote language. These will include such things as providing plenty of time, space, and props for dramatic play. Sociodramatic play is an excellent stimulus for speech production, as are small-group projects like cooking or a construction project. The teacher uses games to promote language such as describing objects, finishing a story, or guessing games where each child in turn guesses what a picture will be about when he has a peek at one small bit of the page. This guessing game appeals to 4-year-

olds. Puppet play encourages language just as simple role playing does for older children. Excursions to places of interest stimulate conversation, as do reading stories and poems and telling stories to children. The teacher can ask questions, "What do you suppose this book is about?" Interruptions while reading the story are welcomed for their language value. The teacher will need to develop skill in knowing the point at which she should continue the reading.

Special Problems with Speech

Some children may withdraw from trying to communicate because they are afraid, resentful, or disturbed in different ways. The teacher's task here is to build a relationship of trust with the child before doing anything direct about his speech.

Young children often stutter, repeating words or syllables. They are in the process of learning to talk. They are eager to communicate, but they have not developed enough control to get the words out rapidly. Frequent and prolonged stuttering may be a sign the child feels more pressure than he can manage comfortably. The teacher can try to reduce any pressures on the child. She will also help the child by giving her undivided attention when he speaks to her. She will not say, "Speak more slowly." Calling the child's attention to the stuttering by asking him to speak more slowly may make him self-conscious. He becomes afraid of stuttering and is more likely to continue stuttering. It is interesting to note that types of speech defects vary in different cultures. Among certain Eskimos and Native Americans, for example, no case of stuttering has ever been recorded. In our culture, it is more common among boys than girls; but there are cultures where the reverse is true.

Other children may have defects of articulation in speech. They may have difficulty in saying the sounds of "r," "l", or "th." The adult helps a child by pronouncing the sound very clearly herself, repeating the word the child has said rather than asking him to repeat it. She wants him to hear the correct pronunciation and, in time, to imitate it without interfering with spontaneity in verbal communication.

The whole curriculum plays a part in increasing the child's competence with language by offering experiences to talk about and people to talk with. Speech is an important tool.

Language as Self-Expression

Andrea is a delightfully verbal 4-year-old whose spontaneity is enjoyed by two accepting parents. Andrea welcomes approaches by others as gestures of friendliness. She disarms the most aggressive children by her own friendliness. She expresses her feelings freely and it is fun to listen to her language.

"Wouldn't it be funny if I were an egg, or if I were a tomato and someone picked me in the garden?" She laughs as the group is returning from a trip to the farm.

She feels a part of whatever she sees and identifies closely with the world around her. "I'd like to have a comb like that," she says as she looks at the rooster. Patting the setting hen, she exclaims, "I'd like to be a chicken and have someone pat me like this!"

Her imagination seizes on many things and weaves them into fascinating patterns. In the spring the center had two ducks and a white rabbit. Andrea gave this version of the legend of the Easter bunny when she came in one morning: "When this bunny and the ducks grow up, we can teach them to paint eggs, can't we? The ducks will have the eggs, and the bunny will paint them, and when we come to nursery school there will be painted eggs all over, won't there?"

Andrea's feelings tumble out in words, and she finds these feelings easy to handle as she creates pictures of her world through language.

Language Is More than an Avenue of Communication

Not all children use language as freely as Andrea, but for most children language is an important avenue of self-expression, not just an avenue of communication. They use it to express the delight they feel as well as the anger and resentment. They use it without regard to any listener. A young child will chatter to herself as she plays, or she will accompany her more rhythmic activities with singing.

 Cece, 3 years, 3 months, is swinging and she talks to herself. "I'm going to ride a horsey, a horsey, a horsey. It's going to be a real big one. I'll be big, too, 'cause I ate my breakfast this morning."

When children in a group are happy and satisfied, they talk and sing as they play, even though they are not communicating with each other. Sometimes their singing is in the form of a chant, repeating sounds or words in a rhythmic pattern. Sometimes their chanting is an expression of their delight in companionship as well as in sounds. Often these chants have an element of humor, as when Terry sang to the group, "Would you like to eat a hammer?" and the three other children replied together, "No." He continued the song with, "Would you like to eat a tongue?" and they chorused, "No," and so on through a long list of nonsensical questions with the group replying, "No" in great delight. This is not only language expression but it is also a form of group game that begins to make its appearance with 4-year-olds, as we have noted earlier. Teachers or parents should jot down these language expressions for the light they throw on the feelings or ideas and concepts of the child, as well as for their literary interest.

Children are helped by putting experiences into words when the experiences have an element of fear or discomfort. Lynn, aged 4 years, 9 months, reminisces pleasantly as she is swinging about an experience that was not entirely pleasant.

Last night my Daddy got a needle,
A needle, needle, needle, needle,
He took the sliver out of my hand,
And it didn't hurt one bit,
And it didn't hurt one bit,
And I didn't cry at all.
It didn't hurt at all.
Last night my Daddy got a needle,
And he stuck it in my hand,
Took the sliver out,
And it didn't hurt one bit.
And I didn't cry one bit,
No, I didn't, 'cause it didn't hurt,
Because he did it with a needle.
Needle, needle, needle, needle.

 Linda, 3 1/2, climbs high on the jungle gym and says, "I can climb right up here. Now look what I can do. I'm higher than Mommy now. She can't catch me. Now she can, now she can't." She expresses her delight in being up high, out of her mother's reach but not really out of touch. She reveals the ambivalence of her feelings.

Children enjoy hearing favorite songs and poems repeated over and over until they know them by heart. They may sing them as they play. A parent may report that a child is singing songs at home that were learned at the center, sometimes to the teacher's surprise.

We can also encourage the use of language as a means of self-expression. This might be one way we keep open for the child an important avenue through which she can drain feelings, or share them with others, or find creative delight for herself. We also have for ourselves a valuable means of gaining insight into what experiences mean to the child as we listen to what is expressed through her words.

Emergent Literacy

The concept of emergent literacy is a recent innovation to our understanding of how reading and writing take place for the young child. Becoming literate is regarded as not only a cognitive skill to be mastered, but it is also a complex activity influenced by social, linguistic, and psychological aspects. (Strickland, & Morrow, 1989) Children in technological societies are surrounded with written words and very early begin attempting to show how these words look on paper. Written words appear everywhere—television, magazines, newspapers, signs, cereal boxes, books. It is interesting to note that often a young child's scribbles bear a resemblance of how writing looks on paper. Often the left to right sequence is apparent in their scribbles (in cultures where this form is used). Children learn very early the usefulness of writing as they watch their parents and other adults engage in reading and writing activities. Emergent literacy suggests that reading and writing develop at the same time and are interrelated. Teachers should look at the classroom with an eye to making the reading and writing environment reflect the concept of emergent literacy. One teacher with the help of the children set up a table for taking orders for car repairs in the dramatic play corner. The children had visited a local auto repair shop and had come back excited about playing out repairing cars. An order form was developed with the help of the teacher, and the children engaged in many writing activities centered around this part of their dramatic play.

Another teacher set up a "writers' center" with paper, pencils, and drawing materials. She capitalized on the children's interest in talking and writing about their family and home experiences. She based the writers' center on the child's agenda. The following is an observation from one teacher's records about the emotions one child felt concerning rage and how the writers' corner helped this child deal with these emotions. In this account we are reminded of the influence of the social, linguistic, and psychological aspects of expressing emotions in writing.

The Erupting Volcano: Opening the Creative Vent

Leroy, a 3-year-old, certainly had a lot of experience with rage and frustration. He had learned not to hit or bite or kick, but he had not found an outlet for his emotions.

There he stood, eye to eye with Reni, our self-appointed Regulatory Commissioner. "You can't have those beans. You'll break them," she insisted as she snatched the beans from Leroy's hand. Here it comes again, that fury, that rage.

Leroy's face burned red as he harnessed the impulse to strike. From across the room I held my breath. Quickly Leroy's eyes darted to the writers' center where I was working. Within seconds his body followed, furiously running to my side.

"Where's the angry one?" he shouted, pointing to the stacks of papers, each labeled with an emotion. This was Leroy's second experience in the writers' center. This time, he discovered that rage can be expressed and perhaps even dissipated through written words. With his cheeks still burning bright red and his chest heaving with each breath, Leroy dictated his words. "Sometimes I feel angry because Reni took those things away from me!"

"That's all," he announced. Then he scurried off, past Reni, to the blocks.
A.S.

Literature

Experiences with books are part of the daily program in a good center. A variety of well-chosen books should always be available under conditions that will encourage their proper use. It goes without saying that the books should be in good repair.

Bookshelves or a rack for books with plenty of soft cushions or comfortable chairs nearby makes it possible for a child to look at books while

Time spent reading a book with a teacher in a rocking chair provides opportunities for language and relaxation.
Valley College, Campus Child Development Center, Los Angeles

being relaxed. A heap of picture books piled on a small table can only lead to misuse of the books. Children can not be expected to handle books carefully if the space is crowded; nor can they be expected to be interested in reading for long if they are not comfortable.

A few colorful books laid out on a table near the bookshelf may attract the children's attention. Adding a new book or changing the selection stimulates interest. Reading groups should be small, for the child likes to be close to the teacher and the book. He is easily distracted in a large group where he does not have this closeness. Reading need not be confined to one story period. Some children will want many opportunities to listen to stories, while others may not. Small informal groups formed when there is an interest meet these needs. In pleasant weather, reading can be done outdoors in a shady spot, and the new location creates new interest.

Books Should Fit the Interests of the Children

Variety in the books selected for the center library is important, for children differ in their interests, just as adults do.

Lee, age 3 1/2, showed no interest in books. He had evidently had few experiences with books at home, or perhaps his experiences had been with books that were not suited to his level of development. But he did like cars, and one day he found a small book about cars. He looked at it carefully for a long time and then asked the teacher to read it to him while he listened attentively. For days he carried his book around. Sometimes he would stop and find someone to read it to him again. Then he began enjoying other books and joining the group when they listened to stories. Through the one book that was related to his interest, he had begun to discover the world of books.

This case illustrates the importance of having books that are related to the children's individual interests. Each group will enjoy a somewhat different selection of books, depending on their environment and the experiences they have had. Books about trains will be popular in one place and books about dinosaurs in another. Everywhere children will enjoy books about boys and girls and animals, for they are all familiar with these subjects.

Books Should Present the Familiar World

In selecting books we must remember that the function of books for the young child is not to present new information, but to re-create for him the world he knows. By re-creation we strengthen his understanding of it. New knowledge should come from firsthand experiences and not from the printed page. We will find many city children thinking of milk as coming from a bottle no matter how many stories they have heard about the cow and her contribution to the bottle. Stories about cows have more meaning after a trip to a farm. Books such as Harriet Huntington's classic *Let's Go Outdoors* (1939) present information that can be used in connection with experiences in the garden. It is fun for the children to find the pictures of earthworms and read about them after having discovered worms in their digging, or to find the picture of tadpoles when there are tadpoles swimming in the bowl at the center. Whatever the children's experiences, they can be broadened and enriched through books related to those experiences.

In the past many books presented an unrealistic or biased picture of the world. All the children in the stories were white, all mothers were homemakers, and all the strong characters were boys or men. Today many excellent books for children represent the world the child is experiencing: men and boys in caregiving roles, mothers in careers including nontraditional jobs, competent female heroines as well as male heroes, single-parent families, people with disabilities, and people of many racial and cultural groups. The center's own collection of books and those borrowed from a library should reflect this diversity. A few new books added each year can greatly enrich the center's collection in representing many kinds of children, adults, and families.

Poetry Has an Important Place

Children can appreciate the beauty and imagery of good poetry. They need to be introduced to it early and hear it read with expression. They love the rhythmic quality of words, the alliteration and repetition that are all part of poetry, beginning with Mother Goose rhymes and going on to the delightful verse of A. A. Milne or John Ciardi. Holdaway (1979) states, "Chant, song, dance, and linguistic rituals are among the most powerful forms of human learnings, primitively satisfying, deeply memorable, and globally meaningful. Much of poetry's power comes from the sense of security, generated by repetitions, familiarity, and universality." Children who are familiar with good poetry often go on to create beauty with words themselves. Poetry may become a lifelong source of enjoyment for them.

Books Should Be Attractive and Interestingly Presented

Books that are desirable for a center are not only about familiar, everyday subjects, but also are short and written in simple, correct English with many clear illustrations in color. Pictures should be on the same page as the material they illustrate. Many books reputedly for young children fail to hold children's interest because they are not attractive in appearance and their vocabulary is above the child's level. The child who has these books will be less likely to develop an interest in books in general, which is unfortunate because much of what we learn later in life is through books.

When we present stories to children, we must read slowly so that children have no difficulty in understanding. Anyone who has tried to follow a conversation in an unfamiliar language understands how difficult even the ordinary rate of speech may be for the child who is listening. As we read, we need to remember that children are still in the process of learning the language. We must read slowly with inflections that will clarify the meaning as well as add interest and variety. Teachers should be thoroughly familiar with the story and should be interested themselves.

In telling stories one has the advantage of being able to stay close to the audience. Bringing in something related to the story such as caps, shells, or even a carrot adds to the interest. Telling as well as reading stories is an ability that every teacher should develop.

Effect of the Story on the Child

We have mentioned realistic stories as suitable for young children. The suitability of "fairy tales" and imaginative tales in general may well be raised here. At one time folk and fairy tales constituted almost the entire literary fare available to children, along with the moralistic tale. If one has a chance to look at samples of early literature for children, one realizes how much change there has been in books for children in the last hundred years. John Newbery, the "father of children's literature," first took advantage of the market in children's books and published the pocket books of the eighteenth century. He was obliged to throw in sonnets from Shakespeare along with Mother Goose to make it acceptable to the buying public.

In selecting books today we are helped by knowing more about children's development. We know that arousing fear may be damaging, that there is a readiness factor in learning, and that children need help in understanding the world around them before they meet a terrifying unreal world. It is better to omit terrifying elements from stories until the child has had time to develop secure feelings and has confidence in his ability to meet the real world. This doesn't mean that stories for the child should lack action and suspense but that frightening elements should be left out. *Hansel and Gretel* is an example of a story not suitable for younger children. Some children, depending on their level of emotional development, will be ready at an earlier age than others for folk tales. Three- and 4-year-olds are struggling with fears about body assaults and also struggling to sort out the real from the unreal. Disturbed sleep and a child more timid than necessary in facing the new and unknown may be the price of introducing terrifying stories too early.

Imagination is fun when it is a play between the real and the unreal. Listen to the children's "jokes" to gain some concept of what is real and unreal to them. "How would you like to eat a horse?" draws a big laugh because they can perceive how impossible such a thing could be. They laugh at things like this because they know they are not true, but what do they know about monsters and what they might or might not do? There are many stories of animals dressing and talking like people that may not be among the best in books for children. They may distort reality for children. As one child remarked, "I wonder why they make them talk like that."

Imagination is fun, too, when children use it with word sounds.

 Connie talks as she uses the crayons. Holding up a red crayon she says to Estrelida, "Red, red, wet your bed." They both repeat this several times, giggling together. Then Connie adds, "Rain, rain, what's your name?" They repeat this several times with obvious pleasure. Estrelida leaves, and Connie continues, "Know what this is? A baby bat on his back!" She goes on, "Know what this is? Camel with a hammer in his hand. I saw a camel at the zoo. Camel, pamel."

Like many 4-year-olds, Connie likes words and the way they sound.

Selecting Books

A variety of sources is helpful in becoming acquainted with new books being published for children and with children's literature in general. The children's librarian in the local public library can be an important source of help in selecting books. Some centers depend on the library for many of their books. The books can be selected with the interests of individual children in mind, and they can be changed frequently.

The teacher will find sources for help in the Horn Book magazine; resource books such as those by Norton (1983), Meek (1978), Glazer and Williams (1979), Jalongo (1988), and the local library. Teachers should

Looking at books to-gether can be a social experience as the girls enjoy books, conversation, and searching for Waldo.
Valley College, Campus Child Development Center, Los Angeles

read a book before selecting it; so book exhibits at conferences and book fairs are valuable sources. Useful criteria for selecting children's books can be found in *Literature: Basic in the Language Arts Curriculum.* (Stewig, 1983) A growing number of books are available for children on death, the new baby, divorce, stepfamilies, hospitalization, handicaps, and other stressful situations. The book *Growing pains: Helping children deal with everyday problems through reading* (Cuddigan & Hanson, 1988) organizes children's books according to topic and will be particularly useful to teachers who are helping children cope with problems and conflicts. There are a number of excellent sources for multiethnic books. NAEYC has published a resource called *Cultural awareness: A resource bibliography.* (Schmidt & McNeill, 1978) We recommend that all centers purchase a few story, poetry, and informational or resource books each year. It helps a child's learning if the teacher can locate and use an informational or resource book with him when his interest in a particular subject is at a peak.

Chapter Overview

This chapter reviews the early stages in language learning and how young children begin using the grammatical rules of the language they are acquiring. The importance of the child's questions are noted as evidence of intellectual growth. The complicated issues of English as a second language are addressed. It is evident that an environment should be created that stimulates language learning. Special problems with speech are considered along with the idea that children use language for self-expression. Emerging literacy is described as an important trend. Finally, the chapter looks at developmentally appropriate literature for children, setting up the library corner, reading stories, telling stories, and selecting appropriate books for the children.

Projects

1. Select a child and record her speech as completely as possible for three ten-minute periods during one hour. Summarize your record and characterize her speech, covering such points as: Is her speech used for self-expression or communication? Are there defects of articulation or defects in rhythm? How would you characterize her voice quality? For what purposes does she usually use speech? How many questions did she ask? What ideas and attitudes did she express in speech? Is her speech adequate for her purposes? How does her speech aid her in learning?

2. Select five books for this child on the basis of her interests and her development, giving the name of the book, the author, and the reason for your selection.

3. Observe and record a situation in which the teacher made effective use of an experience to increase the child's language competence.

For Your Further Reading

Bos, B. (1983). *Before the basics: Creating conversations with children*. Roseville, CA: Turn the Page Press. This child-centered approach to language includes the use of books, stories, songs, games, sharing, and movement. "Conversations" refers to genuine interchange between child and adult in all of these language-learning activities, the learning that comes from within the child. Delightful, readable, and full of useful ideas.

Cazden, C. B. (Ed.). (1981). *Language in early childhood education* (rev. ed). Washington, DC: National Association for the Education of Young Children. A classic collection of articles, often cited, including English as a second language for preschoolers, attitudes of black parents toward their children's language education, commercial language programs, dialect, and how language relates to reading.

Council on Interracial Books for Children. (1980). *Guidelines for selecting bias-free textbooks and storybooks*. New York: Author. One of the best resources for teachers seeking anti-bias books for young children. Contains the widely quoted "ten quick ways to analyze children's books for sexism and racism" checklist, as well as a helpful "stereotypes worksheet" to help adults identify their own biases.

Cuddigan, M., & Hanson (1988). *Growing pains: Helping children deal with everyday problems through reading*. Chicago, IL: American Library Association. Groups titles of books into thirteen helpful areas of problems encountered by children, including contemporary issues as well as traditional problems. Books are for children from 2 to 8.

Fields, M. V. (1989). *Literacy begins at birth: A revolutionary approach in whole language learning*. Tucson, AZ: Fisher Books. Written for parents; useful for teachers as well. Explains the whole language approach: how oral and written language relate; how children learn to read and write from experiencing an environment rich in print, from play, and from real experiences.

Garvey, C. (1984). *Children's talk.* The developing child series. Cambridge, MA: Harvard University Press. Discusses the importance of talking in children's social development; how children learn intangible rules of conversation.

Genishi, C. (1988). Research in review. Children's language: Learning words from experience. *Young Children, 44*(1), 16–23. Since children's learning of language goes from experience to concept to words, teachers plan rich experiences in and out of the classroom so that children learn in context.

Gottwald, S. R., Goldback, P., & Isack, A. H. (1985). Stuttering: Prevention and detection. *Young Children, 41*(1), 9–14. Identifies danger signs of stuttering; offers ways for teachers to enhance fluency; offers help for stuttering referral.

Harris, V. J. (1991). Research in review: Multicultural curriculum: African-American children's literature. *Young Children, 46*(2), 37–44. Research on literature about African-American culture has been sparse. This article defines and reviews African-American literature and discusses instructional implications for teachers. Not a "how-to" article.

Hendrick, J. B. (1990). *Total learning: Developmental curriculum for the young child* (3rd ed.). Columbus, OH: Merrill Publishing Co. The chapter called "putting it all together for a good group time" offers a unique approach in discussing eight components that group times should include. How to structure the group for success; charts by age groups and examples of poetry, finger plays, and songs.

McAfee, O. D. (1985). Research report: Circle time: Getting past "Two little pumpkins." *Young Children, 40*(6), 24–29. A study of what takes place during circle or large group times; includes practical suggestions to improve group times.

Mills, H., & Clyde, J. A. (1991). Children's success as readers and writers: It's the teacher's beliefs that make the difference. *Young Children, 46*(2), 54–59. In describing the whole language approach in kindergarten, this article offers help to preschool teachers in creating environments for meaningful language learnings. Children learn about literacy long before they start kindergarten.

Schickedanz, J. (1986). *More than the ABCs: The early stages of reading and writing.* Washington, DC: National Association for the Education of Young Children. Sound ways to introduce literacy learning: using books with infants and preschoolers, with suggested titles; how children begin to write; organizing the environment to support literacy learning.

Schickedanz, J. A., Chay, S., Gopin, P., Sheng, L. L., Song, S., & Wild, N. (1990). Preschoolers and academics: Some thoughts. *Young Children 46*(1), 4–13. Discusses early literacy experiences in home and school; proposes that academic learning can be appropriate in preschool, but with home-like teaching methods rather than customary classroom methods.

Schon, I. (1988). Hispanic books: Libros Hispanicos. *Young Children 43*(4), 81–85. Excellent resource for building Hispanic literature collections, good children's books in Spanish, U.S. dealers in Spanish books, and further reading list.

Soto, L. D. (1991). Research in review: Understanding bilingual/bicultural young children. *Young Children, 46* (2), 30–36. Discusses misconceptions educators have about young children learning second languages, and offers helpful instructional suggestions for teachers.

Areas of Learning in the Program: The Arts

The dancing turkey (*boy, 4 years*)

In this chapter you will think about some of the most common activities in a center—the arts—from the view of their value in children's self-expression and communication. Perhaps you will see avenues of self-expression for yourself, as you help children in:

▶ Drawing and painting
▶ Modeling
▶ Cutting and pasting
▶ Other art experiences: Printmaking, weaving, woodworking, mud, sand, and water
▶ Music and movement.

CRITERION: Staff provide a variety of developmentally appropriate activities and materials that are selected to emphasize concrete experiential learning and to achieve the following goals . . . encourage creative expression and appreciation for the arts . . . (NAEYC, 1991a. *Accreditation Criteria* . . . , p. 23)

DEVELOPMENTALLY APPROPRIATE PRACTICE: Workbooks, worksheets, coloring books, and adult-made models of art products for children to copy are not appropriate for young children, especially those younger than 6 . . . Basic learning materials and activities for an appropriate curriculum include sand, water, clay and accessories to use with them; . . . a changing selection of appropriate and aesthetically pleasing books and recordings; supplies of paper, water-based paint, markers, and other materials for creative expression . . . (Bredekamp, 1987. *Developmentally appropriate practice* . . . , p 4)

Art media offer both child and adult an avenue for the discovery of self and the expression of feeling. Creative expression through the arts, whether in language, music or dance, or the graphic or plastic arts, has an important place in the curriculum.

We are interested in creative expression through art because of the satisfactions this kind of expression brings. There is fulfillment and increased awareness in expression of feeling. We are happier when we are creative. All of us have within us warm, loving feelings, a responsiveness to beauty, to laughter, and to the richness of life itself. These are feelings that are good to express. With expression, we grow as people. Art is an important avenue for this kind of growth. When expression through art is blocked, personality growth is limited.

We are also interested in opportunities for creative expression because such expressive experiences can serve as a safety valve, draining destructive feelings that might otherwise pile up to disturb us in unrecognized ways. As tensions mount, it becomes important to have avenues for releasing these feelings.

We appreciate the art products of the child, too, not because of the talent shown, but because we can truly appreciate the effort that lies behind any achievement in controlling and expressing feeling in an art form.

Because of these values, it is essential that children have opportunities for creative expression through art and that we recognize and protect the spontaneity of their expressions. By keeping many avenues of expression open in language, movement, and in the arts, we leave children more free to grow. We protect them against the effects of blocking and inhibitions that result when few avenues of expression are open. We help them find the satisfactions that come from expressing themselves freely, without fear and with confidence.

As we watch children in the center, we may become more aware of the avenues of expression through art that are open to us as adults. In the center we see children expressing a feeling through an art medium, but the need for expression and the values of expression may be as great for us as adults.

Here we will suggest only some of the ways in which children express themselves in language, music or dance, and in the graphic and plastic arts.

Avenues for Expression and Communication

Drawing and painting are important avenues through which young children may express their ideas and feelings. They also use drawing and painting as a means to communicate when they have little language.

Children may be telling something in the drawing or painting. They assume that we can receive the message.

Individual Differences

In art as in other areas there are wide individual differences in pace and rate of working. One child may paint a single picture carefully and slowly. One picture is enough for him. His pace is slow and methodical. Another child may paint a series of pictures in rapid succession. One child moves early to representation, while another scribbles for a long time seeming to enjoy changing the paper. Still others become absorbed in using color or texture and may explore these variables thoroughly. No one way is necessarily best; each child has his own pace of working.

No one art activity is equally satisfying to all children. One child may prefer to use a pencil to draw intricate lines, seeming to plan each stroke. He may prefer a small piece of paper. Another child may prefer paint and a wide brush. He may use a large piece of paper, cover it quickly, and allow the colors to drip. Still another child may find that clay allows him to express his ideas and feelings best. He may enjoy the feel of clay or its potential for creating.

The Adult Role

Our role is to make sure the child is supplied with the materials needed for drawing and painting, plenty of pencils or suitable pens, plenty of paper, paints of several different colors and space for undisturbed working. We may approve what he does when he shows us a product, but we do not give the child directions or set any kind of pattern. The product is the child's, his own creation, an expression in an art form of his feeling. We will encourage his effort. The time will come when the child will ask for something more from us as he matures. It is important that the child is free to express himself without interference from adults.

The Process Rather than the Product Is Important

Experiences in the graphic and plastic arts offer an important avenue through which individuals release their feelings and find satisfaction and an avenue for communication. Too many of us have had this avenue blocked by the teaching we received at home or at school. We are convinced that we can't draw a straight line, and we probably are right. Nothing that we are likely to do will ever rate as a "work of art." But we probably could draw much better than we think. More important, we could have found pleasure and emotional release in the process if we had had sound teaching, or at least had been left alone. The anxious attention on the product rather than the process, the many coloring books, and other "patterns" that were imposed on us have all served to prevent us from expressing ourselves through art. Yet art is an important means of expression and of releasing feelings as well as a source of satisfaction.

As we work with children, we must try to safeguard their use of art media as a means of self-expression by eliminating the use of coloring books or workbooks. For every child, art can serve as an outlet for feeling if the process rather than the product is emphasized. It does not matter that there are differences in artistic ability, just as there are in music. Given an easel, paper and paint, and no directions, every child will paint. For some children painting will remain an important avenue through which they can express feeling throughout their lives.

Drawing

Very young children seem to prefer drawing with a pencil on any kind of paper, often placing the paper on the floor. Pencils lend themselves to simple as well as intricate drawings. Felt markers, flow pens, color ink pens, and even chalk may be used. Children will try these and may discover a preference for one or the other.

For reasons of convenience, many preschool children are limited to crayons in their art experiences at home. Crayons are a much "tighter" medium than paints and are used with more cramped movements. They are more suited to the level of representation that comes later. The child who continues to use crayons in preference to pencils or a brush may be a tense, tight child.

Sok, age 3, had a difficult time adjusting to nursery school, and during this period he used crayons frequently. After he had relaxed and become more comfortable, he turned to the easel where he painted freely, seldom touching crayons again.

We will not waste many words on coloring books or workbooks. They are examples of pattern-setting of the worst kind, preventing children from expressing their own thoughts and feelings. Children who have often used coloring books and workbooks are unlikely to discover or to appreciate what art offers in the way of creative experiences. Heilman (1954) writes, "Children can become dependent upon these workbooks and the youngsters' own creative work can be seriously and negatively influenced."

A Research Study of the Art Products of Young Children

Lark-Horovitz (1976) has made one of the few intensive studies of the art of very young children from earliest childhood. With cooperation of a group of parents she collected all the art products the children had done in their homes or in centers. The parents were instructed to make paper and pencils or pens available without commenting on the artwork produced by their children. The children were selected because the mothers were willing to cooperate, they were under a year old, and lived within traveling distance from Lark-Horovitz. They were not selected because of any indication of possible talent beyond the mother's willingness to participate.

Lark-Horovitz continued to collect samples of the art done by many of these young children after they entered school. She found individual differences in very young children in the amount of artwork produced at home, the creativity displayed, and in the length of time that art was a major interest. Some young children ceased showing interest in drawing after entering school. Only one or two went on to later careers in some form of the arts.

Her study showed some evidence of a relationship between art expression at an early age and language expression. The children in whose homes art had been abundant and creative were later rated by their schools as superior in language development. It was as if the children's spontaneous expression in art had contributed to later expression in language.

Most of the drawings used in this book at the beginning of each chapter have been selected from Lark-Horovitz's collection with the child's age, sex, and the title the child gave to his or her picture.

Painting

Providing opportunities for painting is important. A supply of large sheets of paper, several large brushes, and rich-colored paints should always be available. Two or more easels are needed. Sometimes children prefer to

Talking to a friend about her easel painting.
First Step Nursery School, Santa Monica, California

paint on a large sheet of paper on the floor or outdoors. Children are social. They may enjoy painting and talking together.

Painting needs a location relatively free from distraction. Aprons and a floor covering may be desirable. The primary colors should be supplied. Sometimes the teacher adds black or white if the children are interested in exploring other effects. Children will mix paints and discover other colors.

The opportunity to paint and the availability of appropriate supplies are all the child needs, but we can show our interest and our appreciation when the child wants these. We refrain from asking questions, and we do not give directions. Even the drip from a full brush can make fascinating patterns on paper. Some methodical children will wipe their brushes carefully because they want to make their pictures with no drips. Others may slop on the paint, expressing their own overflowing and as yet less well-controlled feeling, while others may drip the paint deliberately on the paper as they explore the possibilities of the medium. They do not all use paint in the same way.

 Greg, age 3 1/2, picks up the brush from the jar with red paint and draws a circle. He puts red lines and dots inside the circle and then smears red paint in a few places outside it. "All done with this one," he says. On a fresh piece of paper he begins with paint from the orange jar and dabs the bright color on the paper in one spot, then uses broad, brisk strokes to paint with orange across the paper. He picks up the red brush and makes a few more strokes across the paper, covering very little of his previous work. He dabs a small amount of yellow in one spot near the corner of the paper and says again, "All done with this one."

 Kay, age 3, is a child for whom painting became a favorite medium for expression. When she first entered the group, she explored all the possible experiences with paint. The teacher watched her as she approached the easel with evident satisfaction on that first day. She painted on the paper with full brush strokes, using all the colors. Then she touched the tip of the brush to her tongue and stood relishing its taste. Next, she brushed it under her nose, getting its smell. Afterward she carefully painted the palm of her hand. She found out what paint felt like. She had enjoyed all the sensory experiences that paint offered, and she used it often during the time she attended.

 Ginny, age 2 1/2, is a child who delighted in the feel of paint on her skin. She usually ended a session at the easel by carefully painting her hands, arms, and face and then, just as carefully, washing off the paint, enjoying the sight of herself in the mirror all the while.

The youngest children usually do not intend to represent anything when they use paints. They are using art as a means of expressing themselves and paint as a medium whose possibilities they are beginning to explore. By the time they are 3 or 4, they may name and describe what they are doing as they work; but the teacher should be careful to avoid pushing them into naming their pictures by asking questions.

It is Kay who gave us a clue when she put her painting away.

Kay, laughed and said, "What is it? What is it?"
The teacher asked her, "Is that what you think your mother will say when she sees your painting?"
"Yes," replied Kay with a smile.

Left alone, children put down many of their experiences on paper, even though they may not add titles for our benefit. A large barn burned near one center in a spectacular night fire witnessed by some of the children and described vividly to the others. Following that, there were many paintings of "barns burning." Most were splotches of dark paint covered by red color. These pictures appeared again and again, and many of the children were probably helped to drain the fear the fire had roused by expressing it in an art form, thus turning it into a more pleasant and manageable experience.

Zeke, 4 years old, was painting with a hard, circular movement. He talked as he painted. "I'm making a jungle. Look at my jungle. There's a lion. That's a trail and a river that the lion can't cross."

With this painting Zeke may have been expressing feelings about dangerous things that need to be controlled. They can be represented by lions in jungles with a river that sets a boundary. Through his painting he reduces his anxieties to more manageable proportions.

When we leave children free to use art as avenues of self-expression, we gain insight into what they are feeling as we observe what they paint and how they paint.

Finger Painting Is Valuable

Finger painting allows a great deal of spontaneous expression. The pressure to keep clean may be less damaging to a child if this acceptable outlet for sensory experience and for messiness is available. Being messy with finger paints should reduce the need the child feels to be messy in other places and times and lessen the damage she may suffer from having to limit herself at these places and times.

We learn something about the kinds of control that a child has built up as we watch her approach the new experience of using finger paints. Is the response wholehearted and immediate? Does she hesitate and withhold herself, finding participation difficult? In what way does she enjoy the experience—by patting or squeezing or just poking the paint? Does she use a small bit of paint or a whole lot? Does she touch it with only one finger as though afraid of the sensation, or does she use the whole hand or even her arm? Changes in the child's behavior at the finger painting table will offer clues to changes taking place in behavior in other areas, too. Finger painting may

The sensory delight of fingerpaint shows in this girl's face. Santa Monica College, Child Development Center, Santa Monica, California

help free children for more creative activities in other areas. It offers a valuable avenue of release to children who have had too little chance for play with mud or for messy play at other times.

Modeling

Clay Is Another Desirable Medium

Clay may have many of the same values for children as finger painting. It offers a direct, sensory experience.

Children who have felt conflict over toilet training are especially likely to use it for release of feeling. The squeezing, patting, and pounding they do with clay serves to drain some of their resentment at interferences that they may have been unable to express in other ways. We often see a child make something out of clay and then destroy it by flattening it on the table. It is all right to smash clay, and one can get rid of hostile feelings in this way. It is a way of "acting out" that does no harm and may have much value.

Every center should have a crock or a tightly covered pail for storing clay. Because the sensory experiences offered by clay are important, it is wise to encourage handling it with the fingers rather than to introduce tools of any kind. We are less interested in products than in the process, and fingers are the best tools to achieve what we want. By making the clay wetter and thus messier, we may increase its value for some children. Some inhibited children, on the other hand, may be unable to touch clay at first if it is too wet and sticky. These children need to have clay that is only soft and moist until the barriers they have built up against messiness in any form are relaxed. The older preschool child who produces something that he values may find satisfaction in letting it dry and later painting it. It may even be possible to fire the product to give it added value for the older child.

There is no art medium that seems more likely than clay to tempt the inexperienced adult into model making. The idea that one can play with clay, rolling it, patting it and feeling it without making anything seems hard for even a well-intentioned adult to remember. Past experiences in which it was necessary to "make" something operate against one's being content to play with the medium. We all need to be on our guard, or we will find ourselves making models that the children are only too prone to follow. Then we may have deprived them of the creative values in using clay.

Playdough is often used in centers and it provides a different experience than clay. It is easily and inexpensively made, less messy to use, and offers children the opportunity to see raw materials change. Playdough and clay both belong in centers and enhance modeling opportunities.

Cutting and Pasting

Before children can use scissors as a tool, they can tear paper for their use. As children are learning to cut, this activity is important in and of itself and need not serve any other purpose. The child makes snips to change the appearance of the paper. Changing the paper into small or large pieces is the activity. Most children will learn to cut if the teacher sits with them and snips paper herself at their level of cutting. Over time, as children become skilled in using scissors, they can use them as a tool to make shapes for collage, assemblage, or other activities.

Well-constructed blunt scissors with sharp blades should be provided for preschool children. Scissors should cut paper easily, but they must also be safe for children to use. Excellent plastic scissors that cut only paper are now available. Left-handed scissors should be available.

Pasting, like cutting, starts out as an activity that young children enjoy for its own sake. Children often place one piece of material over another with paste sandwiched in between; in this way they learn about the quality of paste. By using paste over time to attach paper and fabric to a variety of background surfaces, children learn how to accomplish their particular purpose. Children can start pasting with paper or cardboard as a background surface and attach materials of various colors, textures, and shapes prepared by the teacher. Library paste is easy to handle and provides a beginning step. As other materials and adhesives are used, children can become more selective in choosing materials and adhesives. Our goal is for the child to feel free and confident in his own expressions through collage.

There are many kinds of adhesives, such as library paste, white glue, liquid starch, vinyl plastic, and rubber cement. Each has its own unique

Pasting is valuable for its own sake. This girl's collage is already layers of glue and shapes, and she is not through yet! Valley College, Campus Child Development Center, Los Angeles

qualities, and each is designed to accomplish a particular purpose. For example, a tissue paper collage can be made with liquid starch or library paste. Liquid starch will dry transparently and give a stained glass window effect to the tissue paper. As children use adhesives with various materials they learn which ones produce the effect they desire.

Many kinds of materials can be used for collage, such as candy wrappers, wire screen, cotton balls, confetti, and velvet. Teachers will search for all sorts of interesting materials with a wide variety of textures, shapes, and colors for children to use and become sensitive to the quality of the materials.

Other Art Experiences

Many other activities are related to art. Simple printmaking and weaving have value, and woodworking should be included in the art activities planned for young children.

The object of these activities is not the product. It is the experience of exploring and experimenting with color and texture, spaces, shapes, relations. Craft work, which may be appropriate for older children and adults, has no place in the young child's art experiences.

Children Need 'Messy' Play Experiences

"Messy" play with clay and finger paints helps lessen the burden imposed on children by the effort to be clean. Because they are sensory experiences,

Wood glue "sculptures" made one day and painted the next provide experimentation with two kinds of creative self-expression. Child Development Laboratory, California State University, Chico

they are deeply satisfying to children. As teachers we must look at our own attitude toward the sensory satisfaction of "messy" play. We may have suffered from training experiences in childhood, so that it is hard for us to see children delighting in using sticky clay or gobs of squishy finger paint. Unless we can accept our own feelings, we may find ourselves avoiding the use of clay or finger paint. We may find ourselves depriving the child of a satisfying experience or, on the other hand, being unable to set limits when limitation is necessary because we are afraid of being too restrictive. We may need to handle our own feelings if we are to offer help to the children here.

It is important to mention that mud, sand, and water offer many of the same values to the child as clay. We might even consider clay and finger paints as sophisticated substitutes for the mud hole or mud puddles that have brought joy to the hearts—and fingers—of many healthy children. Children who have been denied access to mud and water have more need of experiences with clay and finger paints if they are to satisfy the desire for sensory experience that is strong in all young children. But children who use clay and finger paints will have a richer experience if they also know the feel of sand, both dry and wet, through their fingers and have dabbled in mud and explored the possibilities of water play. A good center will supply these "down-to-earth" experiences, for they, too, are avenues of self-expression and among the most direct and satisfying to a child.

Music and Movement

Music offers children an avenue of expression that is closely related to that of language. It is an avenue used by children everywhere. There is significance in the act of a mother as she rocks and sings to her child. The sound of a mother's voice, the feeling tones expressed in it, and the rhythm of rocking are important to a child very early in his life.

The Tone of the Human Voice Tells Us a Great Deal

The child in a center will respond to the tone of the teacher's speaking voice as much as to the words used and will be reassured if the teacher's tone is confident and friendly, regardless of what she says. The "music" of the voice is an important medium for communicating feeling. As teachers and parents we need to be aware of the effect that the tones of our voices have on children.

Just as the child senses meanings through the tone quality of adult voices, so we can be alert to what is being communicated through the tones of the child's voice. The high-pitched, tight, rapid speech of one child, the low, only half-articulated speech of another, and the strong, full tones

*Children enjoy famil-
iar songs and finger
plays at group time.
Migrant Head Start,
Chico, California*

of a third all tell us a great deal about each of these children and what they are feeling. We can learn to identify more accurately what the voices of children reveal as we listen and observe.

Satisfying Activities Stimulate Singing and Dancing

When children are happy and content, when they are engaged in satisfying activities, especially rhythmic activities, they will sing. We can encourage musical expression when we help them find satisfactions and see that they have plenty of opportunity for rhythmic activities such as swinging, bouncing, pounding, running, or pedaling a tricycle. Two swings side by side make companionship possible under simple circumstances, so that the joy of having a friend may find expression along with the joy of movement through space. Swinging and singing go together. One school used a large truck inner tube for many rhythmic activities. Two or three children would sit on it and bounce, or the group would use it for a drum, pounding on it with their hands as they listened to music, or set their own rhythmic patterns. When a long board is placed between two low sawhorses, bouncing may take a rhythmic pattern, too. There are endless ways in which rhythm can be introduced into the experience of children, bringing singing with it.

The teacher who can sing "on the spot" and move freely to music will encourage spontaneous responses. Parents may be glad to bring to the center musical instruments they can play, so the children will have a chance to see and hear wind, string, and percussion instruments. The addition of musical instruments can enrich singing activities, too. Activity and music go together. Singing around the piano may be fun, but it does not take the place of singing in connection with activities. There should be plenty of singing by the children and the teachers on the playground and through all the areas of play activity. There should be the opportunity for dancing given appropriate space and music.

The Ability to Keep Time Improves with Maturity rather than Practice

There is evidence that ability to keep time is not improved by practice but that it depends on maturity and innate ability. At 4, a child keeps more accurate time than she did at 3—whether or not she has had training. One 4-year-old will keep better time than another, regardless of experience, because of innate differences in ability. But if a child has been pressured to "keep time with the music," she may find less enjoyment in music and may feel less adequate in this area. There are individual differences in the rate at which a child develops a sense of time, but all children enjoy rhythmic experiences—if this enjoyment has not been interfered with. The more opportunity they have to move freely, either with music or without it, the more pleasure and the more release for their feelings they will find in this form of expression.

The Ability to Sing Improves with Practice

Ability to "carry a tune" responds to training, according to what we know at present. Singing with the teacher gives a child practice, but the teacher must value singing as a means of self-expression rather than as a skill, especially with the young child. He or she can help the child enjoy this avenue of self-expression by bringing songs within the measure of the child's ability to sing them rather than setting difficult patterns. Children's singing voices as a rule are not high-pitched. Children usually pitch their own songs below middle A, for example. Many of their own songs are sung in a minor key, quite different from the songs we often give them to sing. Simple children's songs, used in connection with activities, build skill and enjoyment of singing.

The teacher with a musical background can encourage creative expression in singing by jotting down the songs that the children sing in their play and then playing and singing these songs back to them later, in the same way that she encourages their stories and poems. Her interest will heighten their awareness of the creative possibilities of music.

In one center the violinist who brought her violin began playing the instrument as she walked down the hall. Many of the children heard the music and were eager to listen when she came into the room. She had introduced herself and her violin.

Listening Is Important

Another important experience the program can offer is that of listening to good music through tapes, records, or music played on the piano, the violin, the flute, or any other instrument. If the teacher is not a musician, she often can find someone who likes children and who will enjoy sharing music with them. This adds to the variety of the children's experience with music and increases their interest. Not all children may wish to listen each time such a music experience is offered. There should be no compulsion about listening, for this does not build desirable attitudes toward music. The child who does not wish to listen can respect the needs of the listening group for quiet by playing at the other end of the room or playing outside. Many times curiosity about a new instrument will bring even a nonlistener into the group for a time.

When a record player or audio cassette recorder is used, it should be of good quality, and it should be played where a child can listen undisturbed. Some children will want to listen far more often than others will. They should be free to listen without interfering with the play of other children or being interfered with themselves as they listen. A listening center with headphones may be helpful to children's listening without interruption. With the proper physical setup, listening to music may form a large part of the music curriculum for some children at some periods.

Teachers can encourage a variety of experiences in listening, such as listening to bird songs, the peeping of baby chicks (if the center has raised some), and the many sounds to be heard on a city street. Watching and listening to a band practicing is an absorbing experience for children. They often re-enact it later in their dramatic play.

Sometimes we find a child who spends a great deal of time listening to music or stories. She may be doing this as a form of escape from facing difficulties, such as attempting to adjust to other children in play situations. The teacher needs to recognize this situation and take steps to encourage the child to extend her interests. She can give the child more support in her group relations and build her confidence. It is important that the total pattern of the child's adjustment be understood. Music meets many emotional needs and should not serve only as an escape.

Children Enjoy Using Different Instruments

Every center needs a variety of musical instruments for the children to use freely, sometimes on their own and sometimes in a group under the teacher's direction. Drums and bells of all kinds are fun and can be easily available. But there are many other instruments: triangles, tambourines, cymbals, maracas, and xylophones as well as simple shakers or sand blocks. An autoharp is a useful addition, easily used outdoors as well as indoors. Most children love to play the piano, and many will go to the piano to play and sing, turning the pages of a favorite songbook, perhaps with a friend beside them. With little supervision children can use and enjoy the piano by themselves.

Body Movement Is a Natural Outlet for the Expression of Feeling

Dancing as well as singing will occur in many areas when children are free to act spontaneously. Running in the wind through falling leaves, crunching dry leaves underfoot in a marching rhythm, rolling down a grassy slope on the first warm spring day when space and sunshine seem to make everything burst into song and movement—all may be experiences in body movement for children.

One of the most natural and spontaneous forms of expression for a young child comes through body movements. The teacher may be able to encourage the child to use her body, saying, "How can you make your body into a round ball?" or, "Can you make your body small or big?" When body movements become rhythmic and are used for the expression of feeling, they form a creative outlet.

When there is plenty of space, all children take delight in large, free body movements. A gymnasium or a large room equipped with full-length mirrors for modern dance practice, for example, inspires joyful and graceful experimentation with movements, especially if it is accompanied by

The guitar enriches the singing experience with the teacher. Children enjoy instruments.
First Step Nursery School, Santa Monica, California

music. It seems likely that opportunities to dance and play in front of full-length mirrors may add a dimension to the child's concept of herself as a person, especially for a child who has had little or no opportunity to see herself in a mirror.

Marching to music with a strong beat brings a response from children as well as adults. The strong beat sets the pattern, and the teacher enjoys the experience with the children. Drums and bells will extend the experience for the group. With opportunity and encouragement and increasing skill in using their bodies, they can translate many feelings into body movements.

The value of gymnastics for very young children is open to question. The regimentation required in training, the competitive aspects, the many failures: all these may interfere with healthy personality development. Young children at this stage are struggling to gain confidence in themselves and in their ability to use their initiative and make decisions. The regimentation in the training required in gymnastics may distort this personal growth.

Body Movement Is a Natural Outlet for the Expression of Feeling

Music and movement have their greatest value for young children as avenues of self-expression. Children will use them in this way unless adults block them by offering patterns. The values we seek are those that come with creativity.

To be in tune with one's body helps free a child from doubt about herself. It gives her confidence. For young children, simple actions like rolling over and over, getting up very slowly or very quickly, or pretending to lift something heavy help them learn to control their movements and to have fun in doing so. Teachers, too, can discover the pleasure in free movement as they dance with the children in unpatterned ways.

Elaborate settings are not necessary for rhythm and music. In one of the World War II child-care centers a group of 2-year-olds was playing in the limited area available to them. They had little in the way of play materials and less in the way of stable, continued contacts with reassuring adults. Their long day at school was followed by a home experience that offered little security to most of them. In the tiny court where they played, the wind was blowing one day. It picked up some stray pieces of toilet tissue (used to wipe drippy noses) and swirled them round and round in the corner of the cement courtyard. Observing this, one of the 2-year-olds suddenly began turning and whirling with the bits of paper. Several children joined her, and in that bleak corner they did a graceful dance with the bits of tissue in the wind for a few brief minutes, and then ran off, laughing.

Children who are in groups in which there is plenty of expression through music have less need to drain off feeling in undesirable ways. They are likely to have fewer difficulties in working out relationships as they play together. When teachers are aware of the values that music and rhythm offer and the dangers of patterning these expressions, they can offer children many experiences in these areas, limited only by their own talent and resourcefulness and the limits imposed by the physical environment. The children will welcome these opportunities and profit from them. They will use them in creative ways.

Setting patterns for musical expression will serve to block the use of music or movement as a means of self-expression. If the teacher tries to teach the child how to keep time, to fit her response into the pattern of the music being played, the child may be blocked in the expression of her own feeling in response to the time. The skillful teacher will, instead, adapt the music to the child's own rhythm. She will give the children many opportunities to respond to music, but she will not attempt to dictate what their responses will be.

Chapter Overview

This chapter presents ideas concerning creative expression. Drawing and painting are viewed as avenues of expression and communication. The process rather than a finished product is emphasized. Children use creative materials in a variety of ways. Messy experiences are a part of the creative process. Finger paints, clay, and playdough all have usefulness as a child begins expression in the arts. Music and movement provide satisfying experiences for children. Keeping time to the beat of the music, singing, listening, using instruments, and expressing feelings are all important parts of this creative outlet.

Projects

1. Look at a series of paintings done by one child over a period of weeks. What seems to remain the same? What changes in his paintings over the period? How would you characterize this child from looking at his paintings? What meaning does painting seem to have for him?
2. Over a period of observation note (a) the kinds and amounts of experience the children have with rhythm and music, (b) the sounds that they appear to notice, and (c) their participation in musical or rhythmic group experiences. What differences do you observe in individual interest here and in ability?
3. Draw a floor plan of the room where you are observing and note how materials are arranged for art and music. Is there evidence of self-initiated activities? Where is the water supply? What colors are available for painting? Is the clay in a covered crock? Are the musical instruments available at the child's level? What musical instruments are there? Is there a record or tape player? An autoharp? A piano? Assess the areas from the standpoint of developmentally appropriate activities for children under 5.

For Your Further Reading

Bos, B. (1978). *Don't move the muffin tins: A hands-off guide to art for the young child.* Carmichael, CA: The Burton Gallery. An exuberant book of ideas for art activities. Includes the facilitating environment, role of adults, and presentation of materials in creative and developmentally appropriate ways.

Clemens, S. G. (1991). Art in the classroom: Making every day special. *Young Children*, 46(2), 4–11. Art that is developmentally appropriate, including basic philosophy of values of creativity to children, some recipes, and mention of unsafe art supplies.

Goodnow, J. (1977). *Children drawing*. The developing child series. Cambridge, MA: Harvard University Press. Discusses how children's drawing often indicates their development, thinking, and problem solving. Takes the reader through the stages of children's drawing with illustrations.

Jalongo, M. R. (1990). The child's right to the expressive arts: Nurturing the imagination as well as the intellect. A position paper of the Association for Childhood Education International. *Childhood Education 66*(4), 195–201. Looks at what imagination adds to learning, counters myths that de-emphasize the creative arts in classrooms, and recommends ways to reaffirm the expressive arts in children's programs. Excellent references for further reading.

Lasky, L., & Mukerji, R. (1980). *Art: Basic for young children.* Washington, DC: National Association for the Education of Young Children. How art is important in children's learning, with many ideas for activities for 2- to 10-year-olds. Why worksheets and patterns are never art.

McDonald, D. T. (1979). *Music in our lives: The early years.* Washington, DC: National Association for the Education of Young Children. Assists teachers who may believe they lack musical skills to develop a program with instruments, singing, and listening to good music. Simple and practical.

Smith, N. R. (1983). *Experience and art: Teaching children to paint.* New York: Teachers College Press. Not a "how to" book, but one that discusses the teacher's role and cognitive processes behind the painting of children from 1 1/2 to 11 years.

Taylor, B. J. (1991). *A child goes forth: A curriculum guide for preschool children* (7th ed.). New York: Macmillan Publishing Company. A well-tested activities guide, with each section discussing main principles, developmental characteristics, and application of principles as well as specific activities. Excellent music and art chapters.

Areas of Learning in the Program: The Sciences

Car, policemen, stop light (*boy, 4 years, 4 months*)

This chapter explores several areas we may call "science": mathematics, natural and physical science, as well as "social science," which includes cultural understanding and acceptance, and the child's community. You will learn about:

▶ The sciences
  Mathematics
  Physical science
  Natural science
▶ Social studies
  Understanding cultural differences
  Community, as young children know it.

CRITERION: Staff provide a variety of developmentally appropriate activities and materials that are selected to emphasize concrete experiential learning . . . [to] encourage children to think, reason, question, and experiment. (p. 23)

Staff equally treat children of all races, religions, family backgrounds, and cultures with equal respect and consideration. . . . Cultural diversity is the American norm. Recognition of and respect for a child's unique cultural heritage is essential. Culture provides a source of identity, a framework for interpreting the world, the basis for a feeling of belonging, and the basis for esthetic values. (p. 16)

Developmentally appropriate ... materials and equipment that project heterogeneous racial, sexual, and age attributes are selected and used. We live in a heterogeneous society. Materials and equipment should reflect the diversity that exists in society and avoid stereotyping of any group. (p. 22) (NAEYC, 1991a. *Accreditation Criteria* . . .)

The Sciences: Mathematics, Physical Science, and Natural Science

Young children are explorers. They are curious and they investigate. Our role as adults is not to teach but to foster and protect children's urge to discover. We can provide an environment that invites exploring and discovering, and we can avoid depriving children of the excitement of discovery and learning. It has been said that one truly knows only what one has discovered oneself. Healthy young children begin early discovery of the world around them.

Drew, a 4-year-old, says, "My boat went to the bottom. It didn't do that yesterday." Drew is learning the properties of water. When his metal boat fills with water it sinks. Yesterday it didn't do this because he had put it in the water in such a way that it didn't take on water. Drew's teacher says, "I wonder how you can get your boat to stay on top of the water." Drew discovers a way to get the boat to float. "I did it, I did it!" Indeed, Drew "did it," and he played with other objects, figuring out properties of water, properties of objects, and learning a great deal. Drew has confidence that he can figure things out. He is encouraged to think, reason, question, and experiment.

Children in favorable environments come in contact with many scientific experiences. The young child runs downhill and falls. He tries to pull a loaded wagon up the hill. He watches snow melt in the sun. He discovers a worm as he digs. He feeds a leaf of lettuce to the turtle. He watches a bulb sprout and finally blossom. He becomes aware of quantity, too. He has three candles on his birthday cake when he is 3 years old. He needs two blocks to finish his building.

From these experiences the child develops ideas about the nature of the world. The teacher helps him extend these ideas by providing the opportunities for added experiences. By comments and questions a teacher gives more meaning to what the child is experiencing.

Mathematics

As children play, they handle objects and become aware of quantity. "I need more blocks to close up my wall," says Mark, as he figures out what he needs for his structure. Children store up impressions of amounts and relationships that are essential for later stages in understanding mathematical concepts. "These are too big. I need smaller blocks," Mark tells Sue, who is putting the play animals inside the enclosure. Learning that some objects are big, some small, and some in between provides an important piece of information for the child in laying a foundation for understanding mathematical principles. The teacher may make the learning more explicit, saying, "You found just enough blocks to close your wall" or, "It took just two blocks to close your wall." The teacher uses language that will help the child make sense out of the experience. Words such as different, the same as, high, low, balance, top shelf, bottom shelf, heavy, and light enable the child to begin not only to understand what is happening but also to describe what is happening.

Kamii and DeVries (1976) state, "Young children seem to have an interest in numbers when [their] use is at the appropriate level for them." Mika says, "There are four cookies left." Her teacher responds, "Do we have enough for everybody to have one?" Piaget makes it clear through his observations that learning to count does not mean the child understands the numbers. The child gains this from his experiences. He "knows" two from having had many experiences with two. He has two hands and two feet. At the table there is a chair for him and one for his friend. The teacher says, "Here are two chairs for two boys, just enough." Later the teacher may say, "Do we have enough chairs for everyone at this table?" or "Do we have too many cups? Bring just enough cups for everybody at your table." Here the child is having direct experience with the very basis of number concept, one to one correspondence. "In beginning to construct number concepts it is best to avoid telling children to count. . . . The ability to count is one thing, and quantification is quite something else." (Kamii & DeVries, 1976)

The child playing in the doll corner selects the biggest doll. Then he sorts the doll clothes and finds the ones that fit this doll, discarding the smaller sizes. Children playing at the clay table want a lot of clay. They try to divide it, and one says, "You have more" or, "Yours is biggest." They are having experiences that are part of understanding in mathematics.

In the sand area a child arranges containers in a row on the ledge. As she fills the containers, she sees that they need different amounts. It takes much more sand to fill the big container than it does to fill the little one. The teacher may comment on these differences and on the relation of size and amount. The child may line the containers up in order from biggest to smallest.

In the housekeeping corner a child may line up the doll dishes and survey them with satisfaction. There are a lot! In contrast there are only a few cooking dishes. Things sometimes come in sets. The teacher may comment, "Are there enough lids for the pans?"

"How long do you think this rug is? Let's find out." Mathematical concepts are constructed through concrete experiences. Child Development Laboratory, California State University, Chico

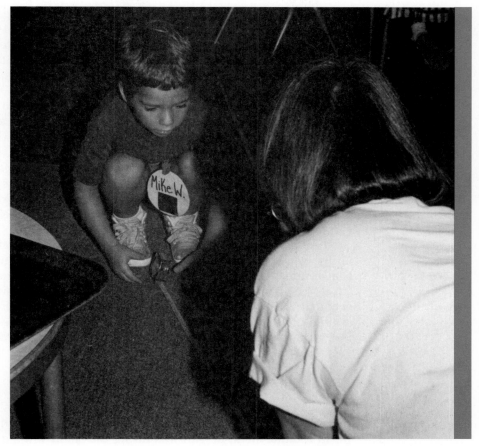

With a balance scale available, the child has a chance to weigh things and to compare weights. The teacher helps him put discoveries into words by asking, "I wonder what would happen if you put this rock on the scale."

The teacher provides measuring cups, one-cup, two-cup, or four-cup sizes, and measuring spoons. There are measurements to be made in cooking. It takes a cup of water to soften "this much" Jell-O. A teaspoonful of salt is needed here, and two tablespoonfuls of sugar. The child at the workbench uses a ruler to measure the length of the piece he needs to complete his airplane. He measures it and saws the piece to fit.

There are many situations in which the child makes estimates of quantity, the number of pens the box will hold as he puts away the pens, the number of blocks needed to go from the wall to the door, the amount of juice to pour into the cup, the size of the serving on the plate. With the guidance of an alert teacher the center offers many experiences that give children a basis for understanding mathematical concepts.

Teachers may help children grasp sequencing of events by using language to expand what has happened. "We made playdough," says Jaimie. The teacher asks, "What did you do first . . . next . . . last?" helping Jaimie put into words the sequence of events.

The concept of time is difficult for young children to grasp. As a child is bathed, dressed, played with, fed, and put to bed at somewhat regular times from birth, he has opportunities for experiences that begin to form the basis for time perception.

By the time a child is 2, he has learned to anticipate an immediate event, and he refers to time in the present "now." Later he will learn to place events in the past, present, and future. He lacks precision about ideas. "A long time ago" may mean yesterday or last week, and "soon" may mean in the immediate future or in the next week.

Leo asked his teacher, "What time is it?" He was really asking, "When is my father coming?" A 3-year-old understands time in terms of events that relate to him—"time to get dressed," "time to go outside and play," "time for a snack." A teacher who responds with a simple sequence of events is most helpful in teaching the child about time. For example, when a child says, "Help me, teacher!" it is more useful to say, "I'm helping Maria; I'll help you next" than to say, "In a minute" or, "Soon."

Physical Science

Every child is interested in how things happen and where things come from. There are many opportunities in the simple, daily experiences of children to build up a fund of knowledge about the nature of the physical world around them. Megan was filling the small wading pool. She walked slowly and awkwardly with the heavy pail, carefully pouring it into the pool. She proceeded to run back to the faucet with her empty pail for more. She begins to know intuitively what heavy and light mean by experiencing these terms with her own body. Arsenio tries to pull a heavy load in his wagon, and the teacher says, "It is too heavy. How can you make it lighter?" The language experience together with the real experience help the child gain understanding.

Rebecca gets off the tricycle and climbs into the wagon Michael is pulling. She spies the pedal car and jumps off the wagon and climbs into the car. She rides the wheel toys and discovers differences in the ease of riding wheel toys of different sizes. She pulls and pushes toys on wheels. She steers with the wheel. Later, she turns the wagon upside down and tries the wheel, watching it rotate freely. She slows it down. She uses a pulley, pulling objects up and lowering them. She is laying a foundation for understanding concepts in physics.

She wonders about many aspects of nature—the snow falling, hail bouncing on the roof or sidewalk, the rain evaporating in the sun and stay-

Riding tricycles on different levels develops physical knowledge of up, down, faster, higher, lower. John Adams Children's Center, Santa Monica, California

ing on the damp grass under the shade of the tree, the force of the wind that blew off the top of her shelter. She may blow soap bubbles outdoors and watch their colors and the direction they take as they float and burst. The teacher will give her simple explanations and suggest ways to find out more about the things that interest her. She will raise other questions. Rebecca's interests seem to be in physical science. All healthy young children are interested in the sciences as part of the world around them.

Natural Science

Children are interested in all living things. They enjoy watching growth and the changes it brings. A garden offers rich opportunities for learning and extending concepts about plant life. Children enjoy digging and planting seeds. There are many kinds of seeds, from the tiny carrot seed to the big, wrinkled nasturtium seed. They find seeds in pods as they gather nuts, peas, or beans. Picking fruit from a low tree and gathering the products of a garden are satisfying experiences for children. Beans can be sprouted in a jar, and children can watch the unfolding of seeds kept moist in a dish. Bulbs will grow and flower in a window. The teacher and the children can talk about what they have planted and what will happen. Some children will participate eagerly, with a sustained interest. Others will show only a casual interest, but all will gain something.

There are seasonal changes to be noted in the garden. The leaves fall and can be gathered or heaped into piles for play. The children discover roots as they dig in the ground. They pick flowers or sprays of berries in the fall.

Watching pets and caring for them give children a chance to learn more about animals, how they eat, sleep, eliminate, and reproduce. The child can observe and discuss these things with other children and with the teacher. Fish need to be fed only occasionally, while the rabbit and the chickens are hungry many times a day. The bird splashes in the bath, but the baby ducks go right into the water. The turtle moves very slowly, and the bird has to be kept in a cage because it flies away so fast and so far. Tadpoles slowly change into frogs. The baby chick is fluffy at first, but it finally grows feathers like the hen. There are many similarities and many differences among the animals children observe. These experiences make up a background for understanding.

In one center it was usually possible each spring to have a lamb for a few weeks. The children loved to give the lamb her bottle of milk in the morning. She would play with them. Often to the delight of the children, she managed to slip in an unguarded door and make straight for the kitchen, the direction from which her bottle appeared. A young kid in another center proved as adept as the children on the walking boards and in jumping over boxes. The children enjoyed learning about a baby goat.

Examining a bone with a magnifying lens may also raise questions about death.
Child Development Laboratory, California State University, Chico

When there are pets in a center, it is important to have adequate provisions for caring for them, a proper shelter and pens that can be cleaned easily and thoroughly. This, too, is part of what children need to learn about animals.

Trips to a farm are sometimes possible to see a cow with a calf, or sheep and pigs. It is enlightening to visit a hatchery at a time when chicks are hatching in the incubators. Children in the city may extend their experiences with animals through visits to the zoo. Many zoos have a petting area, planned for children, in which there are barnyard animals and other animals that can be fed and played with. City gardens may be limited to window boxes, but the feel and the smell of earth and the growing plants can still be there; only the space is restricted.

The young child constructs her knowledge from her own experience. She learns through direct involvement with the objects and through changes in the objects. Telling her answers that we ourselves have discovered will not help her in this process. The child has to structure her knowledge for herself. A teacher can be helpful in providing the opportunities for a child to learn ways of thinking, to learn ways to ask and answer questions, but can not shortcut the process for the child.

Experiences with Animals Bring Contact with Death

If the children have many experiences with animals, they are sure to come into contact with death. The baby rats sometimes die, or a dog may get in and kill a chicken. The children may see a dead lamb when they visit the barn during lambing season, or they may discover a dead bird in the yard.

In their response to these experiences the children will reflect the attitudes of the adults with them. It is important not to hide death from children or try to escape from facing it with them. It is a mystery, like life, and sometimes far less of a tragedy. The children will want to understand why the animal died, and they may be helped in their acceptance of the reality of death by touching and feeling to see how the dead animal differs from the living ones they have known. They will not be greatly disturbed if the adult does not dramatize or distort or try to escape from the death. If the children can have sound, reassuring experiences in this area, they will be helped to face life as well as death with less fear. There is an end to everything: Plants die, animals die, people die.

Questions About Babies

All children are interested in knowing where babies come from and how they grow. They are really interested in how they themselves were born. They are trying to develop concepts about where they came from and how they got here. They need simple, factual information. Occasions for giving this information may arise when the pets in the school reproduce, and the children follow the sequence of events.

Seeing a baby nursing seems to be a new experience for this girl.
Jean Berlfein

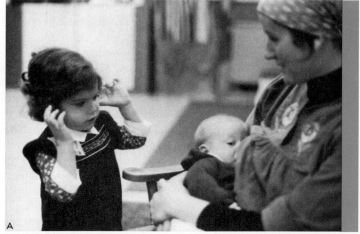

A

The mother explains to the group, and they listen intently.
Jean Berlfein

B

They have accurate information now. All watch the baby nursing.
Jean Berlfein

C

Children need to feel that it is all right to ask questions about birth. Teachers need to answer questions freely and with appreciation for the great significance of the subject for children. They should not burden the children with more information than they want, but the teachers will make sure that they are given information when they want it. The information is needed in small doses, with time to digest it, and with many repetitions. Teachers will listen to conversations among the children and will be ready to clear up misconceptions. They will give simple information: "Babies start growing from an egg inside the mother. The father starts the egg growing."

Discussions about where they came from and how they were born will follow—how each one of them grew from an egg inside their mother, were fertilized (or started growing) by the father, and protected inside the mother until they were big enough to be on their own outside. Later the children will need more information about the father's part.

Before offering information in answer to questions here, the wise teacher will ask the child, "What do you think happens?" The teacher who understands what the child is imagining in interpreting these matters is in a better position to clear up misconceptions and give the information the child seeks. The teacher may comment to clear up points, but she will understand that it takes time to build correct concepts. She will not discourage thinking that may be incorrect at first. We need only remember the richness of myth and legend that has come from attempts in the past to account for the wonder of creation.

As we can see in the photographs, watching a mother nurse a baby is a fascinating experience for children. The children are absorbed in what they see. It seems apparent that the child in the first picture has never seen an infant nursing. She responds with astonishment. The mother explains, and all the children look at her intently. The mother is a trustworthy source of information. This mother seems "in tune" with the children and is enjoying their interest. After the explanation all quietly watch the baby nursing, completely wrapped up in the wonder of the experience. Accepting attitudes are being formed. The children are getting accurate information.

A few children who are interested may enjoy looking at pictures of prenatal growth. There are many books with stories about babies that all children will enjoy. The center can buy several good titles for its collection. Conversations about babies also are important for young children. Negative feelings may be expressed. The teacher should listen without discouraging such expressions, but can suggest other interpretations or aspects.

Gaining some understanding about reproduction is an important part of learning in the early years.

Strategies for Teaching Conservation and Ecology

With books and activities teachers can help children develop positive attitudes about conservation and the ecology of Earth. It is important that children not be burdened with guilt concerning the condition of the world's ecosystem; rather the goal should be to educate children in the ways that they can preserve and protect our precious natural resources. Appropriate books and magazines for young children address conservation issues. Schools should have recycling programs and water conservation plans. We can help children develop a cooperative, responsible spirit and begin to understand that a better world "begins with me."

Social Studies

Children live in a community, and they want to understand it. Watch young children as they play out the roles of people they have met or experiences they have had. Becoming the truck driver, the doctor, the store clerk, the service station attendant, or the garage mechanic in dramatic play enables young children to begin to understand the roles of different people. The teacher helps children by talking over questions of interest such as where people work or what firefighters or police officers do. Real experiences with these people as well as books, stories, and pictures depicting them help children better understand the roles of people in a society.

As children learn social roles, they also learn about the places where people work, both the physical structures and the surrounding environment.

Will and Jaime, both 4 1/2, built an elaborate ramp for parking cars and included a block to represent where the attendant collected the money. Will said, "My brother collects the money here." Will was representing with blocks a situation he knew about.

Children's experiences may be enriched by having visitors come to the school or by going on trips. The person who washes and polishes the floors in one school was invited to come and show the children the electric scrubber. Walking to a local library, to a shoe repair shop, or to a post office enables children to gain an understanding of how the community functions. They can talk about what they see and re-enact these roles in their play later. A parent may bring to the center tools or a product that is part of his or her job, so that children will have clearer ideas of what parents do at work. It may be possible to arrange a trip to places of parents' employment. One center in a large office complex visited the snack bar owned by one of the parents. Children saw the big coffee maker, the rows of sandwiches being prepared, and the trays of fruit and cookies stored on shelves waiting for the noon rush. They came back to their classroom and played snack bar for several days. A group on a college campus was invited to visit a college classroom one day. Their dramatic play afterwards reflected what they had seen in "playing school."

Understanding Ethnic Differences

At a very early age children are aware of people's physical and cultural differences. (Council on Interracial Books for Children, 1983) There are racial differences. They can be seen, and children see them. A healthy racial/cultural identity plus skills in recognizing and combating racism are essential to all children's self-esteem and ability to function productively in a society. Racial identity is based on a concept of "groupness," which young children have trouble understanding. A teacher or parent may help by using the family concept that is easier for the child to grasp. Children's physical and cultural characteristics are acquired from belonging to their family.

A consultant in a school tells the following story:

I was entering a school at closing time, and as I walked up the stairs I heard a young child crying and screaming and the sound of small feet stamping. Around the corner came a little girl about 4 years old, her mother holding her hand. The mother saw me and looked mortified. At this precise moment the child looked at her mother and said loudly, "I told you I want to be black." The child continued to yell, "I want to be black! Can I be black?"

I stopped in front of the girl, looked at her, put my hand out to touch her and said quietly, "You can't be black."

"But I want to be," she said.

"Look at your mother." She did. "You look like your mother and daddy and your grandparents. I look like my mother, daddy, and grandparents. You can't ever be black. Do you have black friends in your class?"

She smiled and said, "Yes."

I continued, "You can have black friends and you can ask your mother to buy you a black doll and some books about black children, but remember, you can't be black."

The important point is that a child learns to accept his own identity. (Council on Interracial Books for Children, 1983) Children whose parents come from differing racial backgrounds may have a further identity problem because they may not look like either parent. Teachers can play an important role here in talking about all families' differences and similarities.

Respect for cultural diversity of staff and children is one of the curriculum goals of accreditation by the National Academy of Early Childhood Programs. Centers that have children of different racial origins within the group are fortunate. Children in these centers know that all people do not have the same color of skin or hair and do not all dress, eat, or even respond in the same way. They also know that all children go to the same center and make friends with people there. If each child feels that his differences are accepted, he can readily accept differences in others. They can all enjoy what these differences may offer.

Creating a Multicultural Classroom

Teachers can create a multicultural classroom that will help all children develop self- and group esteem. They can provide "books, dolls, toys, wall decorations (photos and pictures), and recordings that reflect diverse images children may not likely see elsewhere." (NAEYC, 1991a, p. 16) Pictures should show both sexes and a variety of skin tones, facial features, and hair textures. Children should see pictures of people who look like them and people from their own culture in respected or leadership roles. This is as important in classrooms of homogeneous grouping as in classrooms with cultural diversity. Pictures can be helpful in talking about differences. A teacher and a child were looking at a picture of a Japanese mother and her own child in the grocery store. The teacher asked, "Do you know someone like this?" Their discussion may help the young child talk about cultural diversity and perhaps clear up concerns the child has about racial identity.

The NAEYC *Accreditation Criteria* state: Staff make it a firm rule that a person's identity (age, race, ethnicity, or disability) is never an acceptable reason for teasing or rejecting. Staff initiate activities and discussion to build positive self-identity and teach the value of differences. Staff talk positively about each child's physical characteristics and cultural heritage. (1991a, p. 16)

Using poems, songs, stories, music, and foods from different cultural traditions; hanging signs in a variety of languages; displaying art from other cultures; providing dress-up clothes and kitchen utensils of other cultures in the dramatic play area; and providing toys, dolls, and puzzles that represent all races—all help to make a classroom multicultural. Making or collecting books about people who are different and avoiding any

The center must include familiar household implements from the children's home cultures.
Migrant Head Start, Chico, California

book with stereotypes are other important ways of creating an atmosphere of acknowledging and accepting cultural diversity. *Ten Quick Ways to Analyze Children's Books* is a helpful resource. (Council on Interracial Books for Children, 1980) It is important to give children the opportunity to know from their own experience that people are different. The children themselves are different, but they are all growing up in the same country in one world.

Festivals and Holidays

In helping the children understand the meaning of festivals and holidays, the teacher must first be familiar with the cultural backgrounds represented in the children in her group as well as the area where the center is located. In a neighborhood with a mixture of cultural customs there may be a variety of celebrations.

Children enjoy participating in celebrations, provided the celebrating is suited to the child's pace rather than the adult's and does not intrude on what the child himself is doing. The teacher should let the child choose to enter into the activity, observe from a distance, or not participate.

The celebration of religious holidays is a very personal experience for family members. Living in a pluralistic society where respect for observances is important, teachers must plan carefully if religious observances are to be recognized. Parents should be a part of the planning. Celebrations differ, but many involve the giving of gifts. Children enjoy making gifts for their parents and friends. These should be gifts that the child has planned and made rather than an assembly-line gift suggested by the teacher. Children can be helped with gift-making projects by providing appropriate materials preceded by a planning session where ideas are generated. It is important that such projects be developmentally appropriate for the children and not adult-planned "craft" activities seen all too often in early childhood centers.

There are other celebrations that children are likely to become aware of such as Halloween. Making a face on the pumpkin, carving it with the teacher's help, and putting the candle inside are all part of the tradition of Halloween. Familiarity with Halloween masks, pumpkins, and books at the center may help children avoid being frightened when trick or treating. Costumes and dressing up are a part of the festivities. One teacher collected a variety of costumes, clothing, and accessories to be saved for this special time. She allowed children the opportunity to assemble their own costumes and provided a full-length mirror for them to see how they looked. Some centers emphasize cooking activities with pumpkins and autumn activities to enrich autumn or harvest themes and to play down Halloween's frightening aspects. Ramsey's (1979) article, *Beyond "Ten little Indians" and turkeys: Alternative approaches to Thanksgiving*, suggests creative ways to plan nonstereotyped curriculum around autumn holidays.

In later years holiday celebrations may be remembered as among the most significant events of one's school experience. From breaking the piñata to making valentines, children begin to know their social world. Teachers will need to discuss with the parents what may be appropriate to include in these celebrations.

Birthdays are an important celebration for children. They can be shared with friends in the center and can add to a child's feeling of being an important and valued person. The celebration is best when it is simple. It may include a birthday greeting by the teacher as the child comes in the morning, or the children may make cookies that day with one specially decorated for the birthday child. These may be served at snack time or lunch as children sing "Happy Birthday." It is wise to establish a policy of no presents or favors brought in by parents. The center birthday should not be like the one at home. Birthdays provide opportunities for discussions about growing, about family celebrations, and about people getting older.

Children sometimes are not permitted to enter into celebrations in the classroom due to religious restrictions. It is important to find this out when the child is starting school. The child must understand why he is not permitted to participate, and then arrangements must be made for the child while the celebration is taking place. Respect for the family's belief system is important. The child from a religious affiliation that enforces nonparticipation in celebrations knows about this at an early age. However, a young child may not understand why the other children in the center get to celebrate and he does not. Sometimes the child can be a part of a group activity in another classroom or perhaps help the director in the office. This is a sensitive issue that will demand parent and teacher working at a solution. The child's emotional welfare is at stake.

Trips Outside the School

In Chapter 9, we referred to trips as a way of learning more about the world in which children live. To young children their "community" means their street, their immediate neighborhood, the neighborhood around the center, and perhaps their town or city. In making field trips, the children may use some of the community services. They may go by bus to a park, a museum, or a zoo. Travel time should be short.

Trips may be made to places that provide community services, to meet the people whose business it is to protect or provide the service. There are many such opportunities for children to extend the range of their experiences about the role of workers. The teacher can make use of the experiences her community offers, visiting local shops or businesses that are within the range of the children's comprehension.

Preparation for a trip is important. The children need to know what they are going to see, what to look for, and what to expect. They can be

A trip to a local farm gives surprising information about where milk comes from. Child Development Laboratory, California State University, Chico

prepared for any unusual or unexpected events and are less likely to be startled. They can enjoy and profit more from the experience. In a prior visit to the trip destination, the teacher can also prepare the hosts by making sure they know what to expect from young children.

Any instructions or prohibitions should be clearly stated before the children start. They should know what is expected of them, what they can do, and what is not permitted. They can enjoy being responsible people if they understand what fits this role. Adults accompanying the children should also understand the rules. There should be enough adults to enable each child to feel free to explore at his own pace.

In planning trips the teacher will keep in mind that children learn most when there are familiar elements in the experience and when they can relate the unfamiliar to something they know. A child is likely to enjoy watching a cement mixer and men at work putting in a new driveway more than he will enjoy a trip to a factory with a lot of big machinery that he cannot understand. A hatchery with incubators full of eggs and tiny chicks is of great interest because the child already knows something about eggs and chicks. He gets the most satisfaction out of simple experiences in which he can see clearly and, if possible, touch.

On most trips some children will want to spend more time than others to satisfy their curiosity about some aspect of the experience.

Serena, 4 years, 3 months, was most interested when the group visited the sheep barns one day, arriving just after a ewe had given birth to a lamb by a Caesarean section. Serena had recently been in the hospital for emergency surgery and had many questions. When the group moved on, she stayed behind with an assistant teacher who talked with her about how one feels about operations. It was important for Serena to explore the subject thoroughly. It probably helped reduce some of the anxieties that remained from her hospital experience. The rest of the children did not need this much time there.

Children profit from trips outside the center. If the group is small and there are at least two adults, it is easier for the teacher to be sure of the experience each child is having and to explain what may need interpreting. Emergencies arise, such as having to find a toilet for one child or taking a child back to the school. Many times parents are able and eager to help with trips and with transportation. It is of real value for a parent and a teacher to share such an experience.

Chapter Overview

The sciences play an important role in cognitive development. Children embark on adventures that allows them to think, reason, question, and experiment with physical and natural conditions in the environment. As children play with water, sand, mud, blocks, clay, woodworking, and dramatic play they have opportunities to figure out the "why" of conditions they encounter. The natural sciences allow children opportunities to learn and experience living things. The cycle of life and its mysteries are examined at a level appropriate to development. The area of social studies opens up the larger world for the young child as trips into the community provide knowledge of the roles of different people. An understanding of ethnic differences begins early, and as we have seen in this chapter the center is a good place to set the stage for dealing with racism and cultural differences. Finally, participation in festivals and holidays is examined and some ways are suggested for making these times developmentally appropriate.

Projects

1. Make a list of field trips that are desirable and possible for the children in your group that might expand concepts about work done in the community or about community services.
2. Outline a plan for a field trip for these children, indicating the purposes of the trip, what preparations would be made beforehand by the staff, how the children would be prepared, and possible follow-up activities.
3. Talk with people whose cultural or ethnic background differs from your own. Find out how their culture acknowledges celebrating a religious observance. Ask them to share a recipe for preparing an ethnic food or to tell a folk tale that can be used with young children. Put these in a notebook called "cultural awareness materials." You may want to include pictures of children in their native dress and games children play.

For Your Further Reading

Social Science and Cultural Diversity

Derman-Sparks, L., and the A.B.C. Task Force. (1989). *Anti-bias curriculum: Tools for empowering young children.* Redefines the efforts of teachers and centers to move beyond superficial observances of holidays and the "tourist approach." Full of practical suggestions for integrating racial and ethnic diversity into early childhood programs, and also gender and abilities. How to work with parents in developing a true anti-bias curriculum.

Derman-Sparks, O. (1988). *Anti-bias curriculum.* (30-minute videotape; $35 plus tax and shipping.) Available through Pacific Oaks Extension Services. Accompanies the book, *Anti-bias curriculum.*

Derman-Sparks, L., Gutierrez, M., & Phillips, C. B. (1989). *Teaching young children to resist bias: What parents can do.* Brochure #565; single copies $0.50. Washington, DC: National Association for the Education of Young Children.

Dimidjian, V. J. (1989). Holidays, holy days, and wholly dazed: Approaches to special days. *Young Children, 44*(6), 70–75. Considers questions like whether religious holidays should be celebrated in our pluralistic classrooms, and whether holidays of many cultures and religions should be observed. Useful charts, strengths and weaknesses, guidelines. Makes a distinction between learning about a holiday in contrast to observing the holy day.

Ramsey, P. G. (1979). Beyond "Ten Little Indians" and turkeys: Alternative approaches to Thanksgiving. *Young Children, 34*(6), 28–32, 49–52. Five alternative curriculum themes that avoid stereotypes in observing Thanksgiving with young children.

Saracho, O. N., & Spodek, B. (1983). *Understanding the multicultural experience in early childhood education.* Washington, DC: National Association for the Education of Young Children. Helpful chapters on Mexican-American, black, Native American, and Asian cultures; working with bilingualism; and practices and materials for teachers.

Schmidt, V. E., & McNeill, E. (1978). *Cultural awareness: A resource bibliography.* Washington, DC: National Association for the Education of Young Children. Detailed resources on Asian, black, Native, and Spanish-speaking Americans, with multicultural books, posters, records, films, slides, and even dolls and museums listed.

Warren, J., & McKinnon, E. (1988). *Small world celebrations. Everett WA:* Warren Publishing House, Inc. A resource book offering experiences from fifteen cultures, including African-American, East Indian, Vietnamese, Eskimo-Indian, and Intertribal Native American. A folk tale for each culture as well as ideas for art, language, science, music, and food are developmentally appropriate for young children.

Mathematics, Physical Science, and Natural Science

Althouse, R. (1988). *Investigating science with young children.* New York: Teachers College Press. A "process approach" is explained with its theoretical foundations; presents activity ideas complete with resources.

Althouse, R., & Main, C. (1975). *Science experiences for young children.* New York: Teachers College Press. Ten practical booklets on science topics (air, color, magnets, water, wheels, food, growing, pets, seeds, and senses) presented sequentially in order of age appropriateness and concepts from simpler to more complex.

Baratta-Lorton, M. (1976). *Mathematics their way*. Reading, MA: Addison-Wesley. An exciting approach to hands-on experiential math, with photographs, materials, and math categories. Many teachers have learned about this method through workshops.

Kamii, C., with DeClark, G. (1984). *Young children reinvent arithmetic: Implications of Piaget's theory*. New York: Teachers College Press. According to Piaget's theory, children construct number concepts on their own. Kamii is an eloquent spokesperson for how teachers can provide a constructivist mathematics curriculum through actual games and activities that help children construct a real understanding of number.

Koblinsky, S., Atkinson, J., & Davis, S. (1980). Sex education with young children. *Young Children, 36*(1), 21–31. Also in J. F. Brown (Ed.). (1982). Curriculum: Planning for young children. Guidelines for teaching and bibliography of sex education books for children.

Leeb-Lundberg, K. (1985). *Mathematics is more than counting*. Wheaton, MD: Association for Childhood Education International. A valuable pamphlet emphasizing how children learn through play the basis for later abstract thinking: number, conservation, one-to-one correspondence, counting and sequencing, ordering, classifying, sets, equivalence.

Nickelsburg, J. (1976). *Nature activities for early childhood*. Reading, MA: Addison-Wesley. Forty-four projects with small animals, plants, and activities indoors and in the ground. Science concepts are clear and simple. The author's delight and wonderment are conveyed as well.

Redleaf, R. (1983). *Open the door and let's explore: Neighborhood field trips for young children*. St. Paul, MN: Toys'n Things Press. Easy field trips; includes learning goals, vocabulary, activities before and after the trip, songs, fingerplays, and books.

Williams, R. A., Rockwell, R. D., & Sherwood, E. A. (1987). *Mudpies to magnets: A preschool science curriculum*. Mt. Rainier, MD: Gryphon House. Arranged both by ages and by topic. Emphasizes science as investigation.

Educational Technology
in the Center

A monster, "Frankenstein" (*boy, 4 years, 6 months*)

In this chapter you will look at uses of, and controversy about, educational technology with young children—here to stay, but does it have a place in developmentally appropriate centers? You will explore the use of:

▶ Computers
▶ Television
▶ Technology.

Television, videotape, and other forms of media have the potential to be effective educational tools for children; media can be used constructively to expand children's knowledge and promote the development of positive social values . . . This criterion is intended to support the positive uses of media while also eliminating the potential misuse of the media. (NAEYC, 1991a. *Accreditation Criteria . . .* , p. 23)

> DEVELOPMENTALLY APPROPRIATE PRACTICE: Knowledge is not something that is given to children as though they were empty vessels to be filled. Children acquire knowledge about the physical and social worlds in which they live through playful interaction with objects and people. Children do not need to be forced to learn; they are motivated by their own desire to make sense of their world. (Bredekamp, 1987. *Developmentally Appropriate Practice . . .* p. 52)

The era of technology has arrived, and with it have come many changes in the environment. Computers, interactive video discs, synthesized speech, electronic games, television, video cassettes, audio cassettes, and electronic piano keyboards are part of the rapid movement into technology. Television has brought many social changes, and computers will bring even more. Using this technology so that it enhances rather than diminishes our humanness should be a matter of concern to everyone.

Throughout this book we have emphasized how young children learn through real experiences. They actively seek out learning from observing, exploring, making mistakes, succeeding, repeating over and over, trying something yet another way. Adults help as they make available materials, time, and space for these primary hands-on learning activities. They help by their responding, by their putting language to the child's discoveries, and by their encouragement.

How, then, can educational technology have a place in quality centers for young children? The presence of electronic technology is so ever-present in the lives of young children that we cannot ignore it in their school experiences. Some teachers strongly oppose the use of any technology in the classroom. Some centers misuse television by employing it to "entertain" children and misuse computers with inappropriate software programs. But television, video tapes and films, audio tapes, computers, electronic games and keyboards and the use of video cameras are found in many quality centers and need to be used effectively.

Computers

Materials usually found in early childhood settings include blocks, dress-up clothes, paints, paper, mud, sand, water, and books. They have been selected because they invite active involvement and problem solving at a level developmentally appropriate for children under 5. Do computers belong with these materials? Researchers disagree in their views regarding computer use by children under 5. Some suggest that using computers too early may be asking children to work on a developmental plane that is too high and thus may be creating the kind of "hurried child" that Elkind decries in his book, *The Hurried Child* (1988). Others view the computer as a material with many potential benefits and potential problems. (Davidson, 1989) Computers are still rather recent additions to the field of early childhood education, and much more research is needed before their values for young children can be established.

Let us look into an actual classroom experience with 3- and 4-year-old children in a center in which a computer was placed in an area of the room easily accessible to all. The teacher began by introducing small groups of two or three children to the computer using the program LOGO, which was developed by Seymour Papert at the Massachusetts Institute of Technology. LOGO is a computer language designed to introduce children to the world of computer programming using graphics. Children can create designs using a small triangle, referred to as a turtle, which can be made to move forward, back, right, or left. Simple line designs are created by moving the turtle around the screen. The graphics created provide immediate results. The children see the results of the movements on the monitor. The child is in control of what is happening and literally tells the computer what to do.

What kind of control does the child have at the computer? The young child building with blocks is aware of how she controls the blocks. The child playing with different objects in water is able to observe what happens and see the difference between the objects that float and those that sink. No one has to give her directions. She constructs her own knowledge. When using a computer, a child must follow specific instructions given by the teacher, and the teacher must supervise closely what the child does until she has memorized the steps to take. When problems occur, the teacher must provide the answers. It is difficult to be sure what knowledge the child is gaining at the computer.

What must the child understand before she is able to control the computer without the teacher's directions? LOGO requires not only number and letter recognition on the keyboard but also recognition that some numbers are larger or smaller. Most children of 3 or 4 years have usually acquired understanding of true number concepts only up to the numbers three or four. Rote memorization of numbers occurs with children of this age but not concepts of *larger than* or *smaller than*. Many young children have number recognition and can count up to ten or more but do not have a true concept of what these numbers mean. Number concepts develop gradually from firsthand experiences.

LOGO is a graphic procedure in which children can make squares, circles, and other shapes. To make shapes involves knowing that squares, rectangles, and triangles have specific geometric features. The teacher in one center used games, paper, crayons, paints, stories, and songs to teach the children the concepts they needed to know in order to use LOGO. After much "teaching" the teacher decided that LOGO was inappropriate for children of these ages. Trying to hurry the process may interfere with sound learning.

Computer Assisted Instruction (CAI) is another educational approach in which the computer program takes on the role of the teacher and drills or questions the child. The program, often in a game format, tells the child what to do. The child responds and is rewarded for the correct answer by a "happy face" appearing on the screen or by some other computer recognition. If a wrong answer is given, the child is informed by some sign. Sometimes the acknowledgment of an answer is so abstract that the child does not seem aware that the program is responding to something he has done. CAI at first was largely designed along the lines of workbooks and ditto sheets. The majority of the software is still the drill and practice type, but more open-ended programs are available that promote thinking and problem solving.

One popular game children play at the computer is called "memory" in which thirty-six cards appear on the screen, all lined up in the correct order. The child presses a key to start the game and turns off the power to end it. The computer makes such games very tidy and solves conflicts in social relationships, the problem of keeping track of the parts, of arranging the parts, and figuring out what to do when there is a missing part. The computer games are already designed, and there is no opportunity for children to use their own imagination in creating their play. Young children at play often make up their own games, changing the rules as they go. Games with set rules will appeal to children when they are older.

What is the value of originality and creativity? How much can computer experiences stimulate a child's creative capacity? The answers to these questions depend on what the teacher believes about the learning process. At present, computer instruction appears to offer little to stimulate the child's creative capacities. These qualities are developed by self-initiated activities.

The teaching of shapes, colors, number recognition and the alphabet serves as the basis for most computer games for young children. Some of the programs attempt to teach spatial relationships such as on top of, next to, beside, bottom, top, or visual discrimination of, for example, the same or different shapes. These concepts are probably better learned in routine daily activities, such as when children are handling objects, moving a play car next to another car, or putting a block on top of another one to build a tower. The young child is a doer rather than a watcher. Early childhood educators should avoid educational materials that are not in keeping with developmentally appropriate experiences for children.

Social Experiences and Impulsive Behavior

Children approach the computer with different temperamental styles, different cognitive styles, and different social needs.

Matt, 3 1/2 years old, had trouble settling down to activities and was often disciplined because of his behavior. When he sat at the computer to play a game, he seemed able to control his impulsive behavior, carefully pressing the keys so the computer would do what he wanted. Matt appeared to feel motivated to gain control

Developing independence at the computer: handling the floppy disk, inserting it into the disk drive, pressing the restart key.
Hill 'n Dale Family Learning Center, Santa Monica, California

over his body. When he first sat down at the computer his chubby fingers were dancing with action. After a few unsuccessful attempts to type in the instructions necessary to play the game he finally got his hands under control and very deliberately pressed the keys with success.

Vardin-Barker (1984) has reported that impulsive children are often able to develop the controls needed to program and focus at the computer. Again, we may wonder if this is the best way to develop body control and impulse control.

Children can be actively involved in games played at the computer, talking to each other, taking turns, and watching what is happening on the screen. The computer can contribute to social development and arouse interest, but so can playing together with blocks or in the housekeeping center. There are many other experiences that probably enhance social development more effectively than the computer does.

Emotional Responses of Young Children to the Computer

Some children seem to benefit emotionally from using a computer as a way to make the transition from home to center. One child who was new to the center in September used the computer in this way.

Danny, age 4, entered the classroom and the first thing he did was to go to the computer. The computer was near the entrance and the teacher. Danny recognized numbers and letters, so he found the computer games satisfying. As time went by Danny played less with the computer and more with the other children, and he enjoyed the many activities that were available. By December he was not using the computer at all. He had become comfortable with this experience of being in the center. Children will find different sources of security in their transition from home to center.

Some children at the computer may show signs of stress such as sucking a finger or strained facial expressions suggesting anxiety when they do not know what to do and need help. Usually a frustrated child will leave. Observant teachers can see when this occurs. Favaro (1983) warns against beginning computer use at too young an age, especially if the tasks are too difficult and frustrating.

The attention spans of young children at the computer differ. Few children use the computer as long as Danny did, although some return to it frequently. The novelty of the computer, along with a screen like that in a television and the presence of an adult, may contribute to the popularity of the computer in a center.

Differences Between the Interest of Boys and Girls

Observational records were kept at one center that indicated how often and how long children used the computer. Girls and boys showed equal interest in the computer. There were individual differences in interest and ability, but there was no evidence to suggest boys took to the computer more than girls. Studies provide contradictory answers to this question. In the later grades research has shown that boys tend to use computers much more than girls. (Clements, 1987) Clements further states that "most studies reveal lack of sex differences in the computer use of younger children. Several authorities have suggested, therefore, that the early years are the ideal time to introduce the computer in school."[1] We believe it would be better to set up a nonsexist environment where girls and boys have opportunities to play and work together at many activity centers that interest them.

Concerns about Computer Appropriateness

The question remains whether these experiences at the computer enhance learning. More research is needed. Early childhood teachers support the belief that the child must be actively involved in doing and making as a foundation for later learning. Most agree that concept development does not result from using workbook and ditto sheets. A child does nothing at the computer that can not be done in the classroom. Davidson (1987) sums this up nicely when she says, "Although the computer has much to offer an early childhood classroom, its absence from the classroom will not be disastrous."

More study is needed about the age at which a child will profit most in learning to use computers. At present, teachers may question the use of computers for children under 5. At first, computers may require a great deal of a teacher's time with one or two children. Computers are an expensive addition to an educational program for young children, and few early childhood teachers are trained in their use. Repair and replacement of equipment must be budgeted. A 3-year-old in one center stuffed his little counting bears into the disk drive, closed the door, and said, "Go to sleep, bears." The disk drive had to be replaced.

Selecting good software for the early childhood classroom is a concern for all teachers. Buckleitner (1991) has written a reference book for teachers and parents that provides a comprehensive review of computer programs for children aged 3 to 7, published by High/Scope Educational Research Foundation and updated yearly. Buckleitner suggests that software is now available that gives young children opportunities for open-ended experiences, graphic programs that allow children to draw, estimation games that allow children an opportunity to guess, memory games that enhance social skills and concentration, and a wide range of concept formation games. Adults have the responsibility of being informed and knowledgeable about the software available.

---

[1]J. Parker. (1984). Some disturbing data: Sex differences in computer use. Paper presented at the annual National Educational Computing Conferences, Dayton, OH

Development proceeds by stages, and each stage contributes to sound growth. No stage can be skipped. It takes time for a child to grow. Pushing children's development may create problems later. We can conclude that the computer has some values in a classroom when used in developmentally appropriate ways, but these values can be obtained in less expensive and more effective ways when teaching young children under the age of 5.

Television

Television viewing and computer use by young children have some similarities. However, television sets are found in most homes and many schools while computers, as yet, are not. In homes with children, the television may be on as much as sixty hours a week. (Hesse, 1989) Most children do a lot of television viewing, and no one doubts this is having an effect on their lives. Television viewing limits the child's time for play, which is his natural avenue for learning. Play is an active process in which the child is doing and imagining, while in television he is viewing what is on the screen. Television may reduce the child's capacity for self-initiated activities. Watching television may take the place of reading.

Television serves many purposes in the average home. It serves as a baby-sitter for the tired parent at the end of the day. It serves as a source of information, an entertainer, and for some as a companion. Parents should be cautioned, however, that there are serious problems with young children watching television. Commercials are presented in an inviting way, and young children do not have the maturity or the experience with this type of salesmanship to discern the problems with truth in advertising. The content of programs is often inappropriate for young children where violence, biased reflections of people from other cultures, and sexist attitudes are too often the favorite topics.

Television is a mass medium. It can not be adapted to the individual needs of children and their individual readiness for an experience. The personal element so necessary for the young child is lacking. Misconceptions can not be discovered and cleared up. Amassing facts, partially understood, does not promote sound learning. For older children television can offer material that broadens their horizons, just as reading does, with television adding the vividness of pictures and movement. For young children, the excitement, speed, noise, and constantly changing stimuli are probably bewildering and overwhelming. Children lack the background for interpreting the rapidly changing sequence of events. Children need concrete experiences and the world presented in small doses. This is not what television offers. Young children believe what they see on television. They are still trying to sort out what is real from what is fantasy or fiction, and television does not make this easier for them.

Television Viewing Is Likely to Impoverish and Distort Play

Television is having an effect on the dramatic play of young children. Patterns appear in the child's play that reflect what he has seen on the screen. In some of the portrayals of aggressive behavior on television programs, children seem to find patterns for playing out their own aggressive feelings. While we are not sure what the effect of television may be on young children, it may be helpful for the child to reenact what he sees on television programs. In this way he is doing something about what he sees, trying to understand it better and make it less frightening. At the same time it is important to remember that if these roles are too frightening, disorganizing, or if they cause a child to lose control, playing them out will not enable him to cope and may do the very opposite. Teachers must redirect, limit, or stop this play as well as accept the child's feelings.

Several years ago a television program often watched by children dealt with emergency rescue episodes. In one center children reenacted the themes by racing their tricycles around a corner of the concrete path and falling off onto the lawn. They then called out loudly, "Emergency!" and "rescuers" rushed to help. At first the teachers saw it as simply playing out what the children viewed on television. As the play continued undiminished for months, it became clear that they were playing out situations with elements of fear and anxiety and which they did not understand. Perhaps they were grappling with concerns about death. Clearly they were worried about injury and recovery. Rather than stopping the "emergency" play, as teachers had contemplated, they decided to provide additional legitimate ways for children to cope with these fears. Through setting up dramatic play like hospital, police car, or ambulance, by inviting visitors who were rescue workers, and through books and discussions, teachers helped children to play out and reduce their anxious feelings.

Programs Planned for Children

When television programs are planned by people who are well-informed about children's developmental needs and who have had experience with children, the programs may be of benefit. "Mr. Rogers" and "Sesame Street" are examples of such programs. "Mr. Rogers" is slow-paced, deals with situations familiar to most children, and has a format that promotes kindness to others. "Sesame Street" emphasizes letters and numbers and cultural diversity in a format that children find entertaining. Both programs feature theories of concern to children—death, pregnancy, illness, disability. Both make available related books or magazines.

Many television programs designed for family viewing are also watched by young children. They may show parents as being stupid or unable to solve everyday problems, as well as being the objects of disrespect. These programs often do not portray a healthy family situation; they threaten the trust on which the child depends. Such caricatures of family relationships possibly damage the child's confidence in adults.

Another issue involves the stereotypes and biases seen on some family shows and cartoons. Recognizing that television is a powerful social learning experience, adults must point out to children negative images portrayed. Some family programs and cartoons billed as entertainment actually exploit issues of gender, race, culture, and disabilities. Fortunately, through the efforts of organizations such as Action for Children's Television (ACT), we are seeing more ethnic representation and some sensitive handling of people with emotional or physical disabilities. However, when old programs are rerun, children are exposed to models that may contribute to perpetuating bias and stereotypes. Continued vigilance is necessary.

Some programs for children are planned to satisfy parents who feel it is important to push young children into learning to read, write, and count. A confusion exists for these parents between learning the ABCs or counting to ten and the true education that is the result of understanding what young children gain through concrete experiences in doing and making. A child who has had numerous experiences in playing with blocks, for example, understands the meaning of many or few or one, two, three. He has laid a foundation for later understanding of mathematics. The child who has had many experiences of looking at books, having books read to him, and finding out what books have to offer, is usually a child who learns to read easily. Each child has his own rate in learning. Pushing a child before he has a basis for understanding is likely to disrupt and undermine later learning.

Concern Over Violence in Television Programs

One of the gravest concerns about television viewing for young children is the amount of violence they see. Violence on television may give adults some release and a chance to drain off hostile, aggressive feelings, but children are still in an acting-out stage. They have not developed much inner control. They tend to hit, bite, or kick, and their impulses are strong. They are not sure of the difference between acceptable and unacceptable behavior. Television seldom makes the difference clear. It does not offer young children much help in controlling impulsive behavior or limiting the acting out of feelings. Conflicts are usually resolved violently on television with no apparent consequences. Evidence from studies suggests that adults are wise to protect young children from terrifying, incomprehensible material that too often makes up television viewing.

Another concern about television programming comes from the Center for Psychological Studies in the Nuclear Age. The enemy in cartoons often is stereotyped as a foreigner. The appearance is frightening, and the voice and the accent are threatening. The fear is that these portrayals foster prejudices against different cultures and races. The cartoon format

A listening center with audio tapes and the accompanying books introduces children to another approach to language experience.
Valley College, Campus Child Development Center, Los Angeles

encourages alienation from other cultures and aggression against them. The enemy is seen as a thoroughly evil torturer and aggressor. Children might mistake these characteristics for the people of the races and cultures the enemy represents. Conflicts are resolved through violence. The serious concern is that children may become desensitized to aggressive behavior. The adult should watch television with the child and talk about what they have seen. ACT has been able to get some commercials banned but has been less successful in reducing the violence that has increased in American children's television programs during the 1980s. (Pearl 1987)

Other Technology

In this last decade of the twentieth century, we are overwhelmed by the influx of electronic devices that have entered our offices and homes. Much of the equipment will find its place in our child-care centers in the form of listening centers with audio tapes, interactive video discs, synthesized speech, or electronic keyboards. In each case the teacher must determine that the activity is developmentally appropriate and that the emphasis is on active rather than passive behavior.

In some centers teachers or parents videotape special activities. Later, children can see themselves painting at the easel, building an elaborate block structure, or walking to the neighborhood mailbox. Such video tapes can be enjoyed by parents or shown at a community open house. We recommend that if video equipment is available, it should be brought in for occasional special uses and not become a regular part of the classroom.

Video tapes, video monitors, and video cassette recorders are popular items in many homes. Video tapes of cartoons, stories, and children's programs are readily available for low rental fees. A word of caution concerning young children and the use of video cassettes in centers is suggested. Children thrive on active experiences appropriate to their stage of growth and development. Television is a passive experience and, as stated earlier, does not belong in centers.

Chapter Overview

In this chapter we have noted what needs should be considered as teachers make decisions about appropriate uses of technology in their centers. We have noted the variety of ways young children learn. Children's learning styles may be primarily sensory—auditory, visual, or tactile. We may ask if electronic technology is suitable for an individual child's way of learning.

Another consideration is the developmental appropriateness of the video tape, audio tape, or computer program being selected, both in the content and in the manner in which it is used. Does the child have opportunity for independent experience? Does he have the right to come and go? Teachers should consider how these kinds of educational technology can be tied to real experiences that the children are having. Finally, the use of educational technology will require teacher assistance as children learn to use the equipment.

Projects

1. Visit a local early childhood center that uses computers. Observe how they are used, which programs are used, sex differences, teacher involvement, children's attention span, location of the computer in the classroom, and value of the experience for children.
2. Watch several television cartoons and note what national, racial, or ethnic groups are represented and who is the "enemy." Count how many times violence is used to solve a conflict both by the "good guys" and the "bad guys." Evaluate the quality of the program based upon your knowledge of early childhood principles.

For Your Further Reading

Anselmo, S., & Zinck, R. A. (1987). Computers for young children? Perhaps. *Young Children, 42*(3), 22–27, Indicates computers in early childhood classrooms should be used only after a sound, experiential, appropriate curriculum has been developed. Positive values can be the interactiveness of computers with appropriate software; difference in interest by ages; experimentation and action in computer activities; and keyboard letter-matching as an aid to reading.

Beaty, J. J. (1991). Computer center. In J. J. Beaty, *Preschool appropriate practices.* pp. 65–95. Fort Worth, TX: Harcourt Brace Jovanovich College Publishers. Begins with good discussion of reasons for including a computer center in the early childhood classroom. Specific suggestions for setting up the center and selecting appropriate software. Suggests activities to promote development, and concludes with the teacher's role.

Burns, M. S., Goin, L., & Donlon, J. T. (1990). A computer in my room. *Young Children* 45(2), 62–67. Helpful principles for teachers on what they expect children to learn from computers in the early childhood classroom, how teachers expect learning to develop, and selecting software that encourages problem solving by children. Includes practical classroom suggestions.

Clements, D. H. (1987). Computers and young children: A review of research. *Young Children, 43*(1), 34–44. Looks at investigations of gender equity in use of computers; social-emotional, language, and mathematics/problem solving; a mention of special needs children; and the importance of quality software, amount of time spent with the computer, and the ways in which it is used.

Greenfield, P. M. (1984). *Mind and media: The effects of television, video games, and computers.* The developing child series. Cambridge, MA: Harvard University Press. Urges using research to see how instructional media can promote social development and thinking skills. Is encouraging on positive aspects of the three media discussed in this chapter.

Haugland, S. W., & Shade, D.D. (1988). Developmentally appropriate software for young children. *Young Children, 43*(4), 37–43. Discusses how software can be developmentally appropriate for young children's learning, using ten criteria including child control, progressive complexity, discovery process, trial and error, and clear instructions. Evaluates eight programs according to these criteria.

Honig, A. S. (1983). Television and young children: Research in review. *Young Children, 38*(4), 63–76. Considers a child's functioning in relation to TV: passive versus active learning, achievement, violence and aggression, sex role learning, prosocial programs, and effects on family life. Concludes with how adults can take charge.

Kaden, M. (1990). Issues on computers and early childhood education. In C. Seefeldt, *Continuing issues in early childhood education.* Columbus, OH: Merrill Publishing. pp. 261–275. Examines use of computers in relation to NAEYC's developmentally appropriate practices in social, emotional, and cognitive development, thinking skills, and physical capabilities. Concludes that "the time has come for teachers to decide how, not if, they want to incorporate technology into their curricula."

National Association for the Education of Young Children. (1990). NAEYC Position statement on media violence in children's lives. *Young Children* 45(5), 18–21. Supports efforts to use media constructively to expand children's knowledge and promote the development of positive social values. Takes a strong stand against violent television programming and other forms of media aimed at children. Makes sound recommendations for policymakers, broadcasters, teachers, and parents.

National Association for the Education of Young Children. (1990). *Media violence and children: A guide for parents.* Brochure #585; single copies $0.50. Washington, DC: Author. Brief overview from research on problems associated with repeated viewing of television violence, and guidelines for parents.

Winick, M. P., & Wehrenberg, J. S. (1982). *Children and TV II: Mediating the medium.* Wheaton, MD: Association for Childhood Education International. Relates age traits of children 2 to 3, 4 to 6, 7 to 9, and 10 to 12 to television viewing. Suggests ways to incorporate Piagetian process activities into children's viewing. Offers ideas to guide parents.

PART SIX

Concerns of Parents and Teachers

Teachers and Parents Work Together

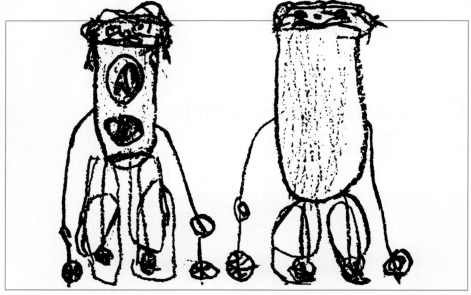

Mummy and Daddy on skis (*boy, 4 years, 7 months*)

In this chapter you will explore some important relationships, in which beginning teachers may find a particular challenge. Let us look at how:

► Parents are important people to children
► Parents present different problems
► Parents learn parenting skills and confidence
► The center supports parents.

GOAL: Parents are well informed about and welcome as observers and contributors to the program.
RATIONALE: Young children are integrally connected to their families. Programs cannot adequately meet the needs of children unless they also recognize the importance of the child's family and develop strategies to work effectively with families. All communication between programs and families should be based on the concept that parents are and should be the principal influence in children's lives. (NAEYC, 1991a, *Accreditation Criteria . . .* , p. 26)

"To bring up children in personal and tolerant ways, based on information and education rather than tradition, is a very new way; it exposes parents to many additional insecurities. . . ." (Erikson, 1959)

The twentieth century has brought so much that is new that we may find it difficult to appreciate how many "additional insecurities" parents face, as Erikson puts it. Through the centuries, in different parts of the world, there have been traditional ways of bringing up children. Only recently has a body of knowledge developed that might be useful for parents in the way that knowledge is useful to an engineer or a doctor. Being a parent is different from being an engineer or a doctor. Being a parent is a deeply personal experience as well as one that calls for information. It demands "personal and tolerant ways" as well as "informed ways" of functioning. We are just beginning to give attention to the possible ways in which parents can be helped, not only to gain the information and education available, but also to use the knowledge in their individual ways, with respect for the individuality of their child.

Parents have a tremendous job, and they do it remarkably well. Some of them face obstacles because of health, housing conditions, single parenting, and the demands of their jobs. We are interested in the problems of parents. We are interested in how centers can help parents do their job.

When a child enters a center, she begins living in two environments, each requiring different adjustments. The child's parents will continue to carry the primary responsibility. They are the ones who know the child more intimately. The teacher brings knowledge of child growth and development and understanding of a number of children. Many teachers are themselves parents. All teachers gain in understanding the children in their group when parents share knowledge of their own child. The insights of both parent and teacher may grow in the sharing. Such sharing will depend on communication and also on the basic respect parents and teachers have for one another. If there is mutual respect, the parents and the teacher can give optimum support to the child as she moves from home to center and back to the home.

Parents are Important People to Children

Of most importance to children are their parents and what they think, feel, and do.

Oscar, 4 years, 9 months, spent most of the morning in school making a table. After he had made it, he painted it, working intently with long strokes of the brush. He asked the teacher if it could be painted different colors. When she agreed that would be a good idea, he used blue, yellow, and orange, and then he painted a part with one color over another to make another color. He announced that he had made the table for his daddy. He asked the teacher almost pleadingly, "Do you think my Daddy will love it?" "Yes, I think he will love it," she answered.

As he intently brushed the table with paint he said, "I am doing a good job. A painter should do a good job. I can paint better than other children." He seemed satisfied as he looked at the table, and he said hopefully, "We'll wrap it up with a string around so it won't come open. It is a surprise. Will he know what it is?"

The teacher answered, "If he doesn't, you can tell him." Oscar excitedly answered, "I can tell him it is a table for him." Here we see a child eager to please a parent, putting his best effort into a product, planning and anticipating, hoping it will be a good thing.

A less confident child can be seen in this example.

Tommy, a 3-year-old who had never attended a center, and his mother arrive on the first morning with anxiety showing plainly on their faces. They had met the teacher and visited the day before, but they still do not seem at all sure what to expect. Tommy's mother sits down on the chair the teacher indicates is for her. When Tommy finally leaves her to explore some trucks and calls for help, she goes to him only after she asks the teacher, "Is it all right for me to help him?"

She watches him closely and only occasionally appears to notice what other children are doing. She quickly turns away when she observes a dispute. Once another child grabs the small truck Tommy is using. He burst into tears and rushes to his mother, who holds him tightly and does not conceal her concern. One feels her uncertainty and her disapproval of many of the situations that occur. She volunteers few comments. When she relates an incident about Tommy to the teacher, she says, "I know what I did was wrong." She seems to pass judgment on herself and others and expects the same from them. Perhaps being in a center makes her feel like this because of her own childhood experiences.

The anxiety Tommy's mother feels makes it more difficult for Tommy to feel secure in the center. The teacher will try to reassure this mother of the staff's interest in Tommy. The teacher will help Tommy find activities he enjoys, and she may manage to interest a friendly, sociable child in including Tommy in the play. Whenever possible, the teacher will join the mother in observing and commenting on what is happening. It may take time before Tommy and his mother really trust the center and its program. The wise teacher needs to understand that parents may have mixed feelings about leaving their child.

Entering a young child in a center means taking a step that will contribute to important changes in the parent-child relationship. The child may quickly become more independent. He will have experiences in which the parent does not share. If the child is developing well, he will find satisfying relationships with other children and with his teachers. Parents may find it hard to share responsibility for the child with the teacher.

Parents who have enjoyed their child's babyhood may find it difficult to accept his liking the center and his readiness to leave them. A parent who may have found the care of a young child unusually trying may also be reluctant to let him go. Parents may be afraid of shirking their responsibility. They may find it hard to accept their realistic need to have some time free for outside work or studies, or time free from the demands that every young child makes. Centers help meet the needs of parents as well as the needs of children.

The mother who is enrolling a child in an early childhood program because she expects to work outside the home will be influenced in her feelings about the center by the way she feels about her job. She may look forward to working and may be satisfied about arrangements at home. She is likely to be glad, in this case, to have the child enter the center even though she has some regrets about the separation. If she wishes she did not have to work, she may find it difficult to help the child enter into the group, and she may need reassurance from the staff. Most parents are able to help the child with separation if they feel confident in the center.

Children who have had brothers or sisters in the center usually adapt more easily than those who have not, less because they are familiar with the program than because their parents feel at home there. If the parent has accepted group experience for the child, the child likely will find it easy to do the same.

Most parents enjoy watching the growth spurt that usually occurs in the child during the first few months in a center. Changes appear in the child's language, his social skills, ideas about himself, and in what he can do. As one mother remarked, she found herself enjoying her child much more after he started attending the center. He seemed more like a person to her.

Teachers Need to Be Aware of the Feelings of Parents

Most parents feel strongly about matters pertaining to health. Frequently teachers are less alert than parents to adjusting a child's clothing to changes in temperature or activities. They may be less concerned about wet feet or wet sleeves. Teachers are not the ones who are up at night with the sick child, nor do they have the same heavy emotional investment in the child as the parent. Inexperienced teachers must train themselves to be very careful in matters involving health. With experience, they will come to appreciate the parents' viewpoint. If they are careful, they relieve the parents of a source of anxiety and make a better relationship possible. Good parent-teacher relations are based on mutual understanding.

Teachers should provide aprons and smocks for "messy" play and have changes of clothing available. Parents often have errands and shopping to do on their way home from their workday. Parents appreciate teachers who are aware of their feelings about the child's appearance. This is another way to build good relationships between the school and the home.

Some parents feel anxious about the behavior of their children. Parents who are older than the average parent of a preschool child, or who have professional experience unrelated to young children may have had little background to help them understand a child's growth impulses. They are likely to see failure for themselves in the childlike behavior of their offspring.

Parents want to be assured that their child's physical needs are cared for in the center.
First Step Nursery School, Santa Monica, California

They need reassurance from a teacher who accepts them and their children as they are.

Parents may differ in their cultural or ethnic traditions and their attitudes about the child's center. They may have difficulty understanding what the center is attempting to do for their child. They are likely to have met discrimination and may find it difficult to trust the teacher and the center. The teacher needs to give special consideration to the needs of these parents. She must learn as much as possible about their expectations and make any suitable adjustment in the program. She should become familiar with the cultural beliefs and practices of the families in the center. The program may be strengthened by incorporating elements from the different cultures with the help of the parents. All parents will have something to contribute. Doing so helps confirm for the children the validity of our culturally diverse society.

Parents Present Different Problems

Parents Want to Know about Their Child in the Center

Parents may see rapid changes taking place in their child, and not all of the changes will seem desirable. Growth seldom proceeds smoothly. They may find a quiet, docile child becoming more aggressive and defiant after she has been in the center for a while. She may not share toys as willingly. Her vocabulary may be increasing rapidly, but it may contain words that the parents find unacceptable. These parents may criticize aspects of the program.

The teacher should consider these criticisms carefully to see whether situations should be handled differently as well as to identify and understand what may lie behind the complaint. It is a step in the growth of understanding when a criticism is expressed by the parent, accepted by the teacher, and a mutual understanding is reached. Questions and criticisms can often be cleared up by frank discussion so that they do not block the growth of more positive relationships.

Some parents may not ask questions because they have little time to observe, or it may be easier for them to leave matters to the teacher, or they may find it difficult to question a teacher. It is important in these cases for the teacher to tell the parent something about what the child did that day, such as painting a colorful picture, or observations of the child's interest in a special activity or skill with puzzles. The teacher may raise a question about the child's behavior. Doing so shows interest in the child and may help the parent ask questions. If the caregiver is not the parent, the teacher needs to help the caregiver in the same way.

A teacher shares informally with a parent the day-to-day progress of a child in the center.
Child Development Center Laboratory, California State University, Chico

Sometimes a parent may be late in coming for the child. A late parent means a longer day for the teacher. It requires patience and understanding from the teacher, but there often are good reasons for a parent's being late. The teacher needs to accept the reason and handle the situation matter-of-factly. If a parent is repeatedly late, the teacher must discuss the situation with the parent. She should state clearly what it means to the staff and discuss with the parent what can be done about the problem. It may be better to hold the discussion in the morning or by appointment rather than at the time the parent arrives late. The teacher must take into account her own feelings as well as those of the parent, but she needs to make a firm statement for the sake of the staff. If the problem lies in the parent's hours of employment, for example, the parent will need to talk the situation over with the employer so that the hours can be adjusted. If this can not be done, the parent may need to find another center.

Parents Are Concerned about Their Child's Safety

Teachers are always alert to protect the physical safety of children, but they define safety more in terms of a well-arranged environment and good supervision. Parents are reassured to see climbing equipment that is sturdy and positioned on resilient surfaces, dangerous appliances and substances not accessible to children, safety rules followed on walks, visible fire extinguishers and fire drills, and other procedures showing care for physical well-being.

Parents have deep concerns about protecting their children from abduction, sexual molestation, and physical abuse, often because of widespread publicity about a few cases. They seek help in knowing how to protect their children from such terrifying experiences. Some divorced or separated parents have to alert the center to the threat of the child's abduction by the noncustodial parent. Parents ask more frequently if it is permissible for them to visit the center unannounced at any time. Teachers must respond with understanding and reassurance to these concerns.

Upset parents need to be listened to even more than they need explanations of the center's policies. However, the center does need clearly defined policies and procedures, and parents need to be informed about them when the child is initially enrolled. Reminders of the center's policies can be made on a parent bulletin board or in a newsletter. It may be uncomfortable to challenge a person who is not authorized to pick up a child, but parents are grateful in the long run to know that teachers exercise such caution. Some centers now include discussions of personal safety as part of the curriculum. Some excellent books for young children have been published, several of which are listed in "For Your Further Reading." These books and curriculum activities are designed to help children feel reassured and competent.

It is wise not to overemphasize to young children the fearful aspects of abduction and sexual abuse. Young children are seldom able to grasp what a "stranger" is, and we know that most molestation occurs by adults known to the children. It is more appropriate to incorporate such discussions into all kinds of safety education, such as monthly fire drills or emergency practices, safety in crossing streets, avoiding poisonous substances, and other age-appropriate concepts. Most of all, we know it is the responsibility of the adults to keep children safe.

If parental concerns about child safety issues such as molestation and abuse are persistent, teachers may wish to plan a group discussion. Workshops have been given in many communities to help parents and teachers gain confidence in dealing with child safety. Teachers can also make available to parents recent books and articles through a newsletter, bulletin board, or lending library. Parents appreciate knowing about community resources, such as how to contact a poison control center or where to get help when abuse or molestation is suspected. Teachers need to have this information for their own use as well as to give to parents. Teachers play an important role in providing information and reassurance to parents in this sensitive area.

Goals in Working with Parents

In working with parents there are two main goals. The first goal is to help parents gain confidence. Parents who feel confident are better able to enjoy their children, to learn about the needs of children, and to use this knowledge effectively.

The second goal is that of helping parents gain the insights and the knowledge that may improve their contribution to a child's development. The teacher who helps parents feel more confident and who is skillful in providing sound information has achieved important goals.

How Do We Help Parents Gain More Confidence in Themselves?

The center and the teacher may help parents feel that they are important in many small but significant ways.

Does the center provide a comfortable place for parents to sit when they are waiting, a bulletin board with attractive, interesting material on it, and some magazines and books for browsing or lending? Do the teachers try to make parents feel welcome? Do they take time to point out something of interest that may be happening in the center? Have they been clear about the acceptable times to bring and call for the child and about decisions that are theirs to make and those that the parents should make?

The parents will gain confidence if the teacher takes the time to listen to what the parent wants to say. The teacher will try to "listen with the third ear" to understand the meaning behind the words. It is important for parents to feel that they are being understood. In their relationships with parents, teachers will show interest, give encouragement, and avoid blame and criticism.

Teachers want to make parents feel welcome when they bring or pick up children.
Louise Dean

As teachers we must respect the deep feelings involved in any parent-child relationship. We must remember that life with young children brings many frustrations and makes many demands, although it also brings much satisfaction and joy. We must respect parents if we are to help them feel confident. Good relationships are built on awareness and sympathy.

What Knowledge Will Be Useful to Parents?

Our second goal in working with parents is to help them gain more understanding about children and their needs. Along with the intuitive understanding most parents have about their own child, they can benefit from added knowledge. Much of what we have learned as teachers of young children will also be useful to parents. We have a responsibility for sharing our knowledge of child development with them and for doing this in a way that does not interfere with the parents' own unique knowledge of their child.

What knowledge may be especially useful to parents? What might be included in a parent education program? We will suggest some information that might be included in a discussion program:

1. The values of play and of activity for the young child, with emphasis on letting the child touch things and explore as much as possible.
2. The kinds of play materials and play opportunities that are appropriate at different ages and stages, with emphasis on simple, raw materials, dramatic and creative materials, and homemade equipment.
3. Ways in which a child is helped to develop competence in speech, including the importance of talking with a child and listening to his speech, the importance of opportunities with books and stories, and the importance of expanding the child's own language.
4. Information about the way in which a child learns, and the value of answering a child's questions, of helping him ask questions, and of helping him to discover for himself.
5. Understanding about the kind of help that promotes development, such as giving directions or making suggestions in a positive rather than negative way; giving a child developmentally appropriate experiences; letting him take his time; preparing the child for new or difficult situations; playing a supporting role rather than a critical one.
6. The value of helping a child learn to distinguish between fantasy and reality while still enjoying and using his imagination.
7. The importance of putting feelings into words as a way of understanding and controlling action and how this verbalization may be done.
8. The value of play with other children and ways in which a child is helped in getting along with others.
9. Information about development and growth needs, especially about the extent of individual differences in children.
10. Understanding of the stages in cognitive growth, concept formation, the value of imagination in the thought process, and the contribution made to intellectual growth by a rich variety of experiences.

With more knowledge, parents' expectations for the child become more reasonable. Parents can take more interest in the child's development, watching growth patterns evolve that are reassuringly similar to those of all children, yet unique in wonderful ways. Parents are better able to treasure the individuality of their child as a result of their increased understanding of growth and development.

How Parents Learn

Parents, or any of us, learn in a variety of ways. We learn by observing a skillful person as he or she performs a job. We learn by discussion, raising questions and expressing feelings and attitudes. We learn by doing, putting into practice what we have seen and discussed. When observation, discussion, and active participation take place under favorable conditions, they result in sound learning. A good parent education program will include opportunities for all three kinds of activities.

Observations

Parents should feel free to observe at any time. Observation in centers is an important opportunity for parents to realize that their child in some respect is like others and in other respects is unique. Through observation parents may find ideas for play materials, activities, and ways of handling situations. Sometimes the child's behavior with other children and adults will need to be interpreted by the teacher, who can explain why a situation was handled in one way and not another or what the teacher believes a bit of behavior may mean. Observations may make clear a significance in behavior that parents may not have noticed before.

Parents should be encouraged to observe and have an opportunity to talk with the teacher about what they see. Such discussions can be arranged after center hours. If the center has adequate observation space, parents will find it easier to observe without distracting their child and other children.

The teacher may wish to observe a child at home to gain insight into her behavior at the center or to help build a relationship with her. To do so, the teacher arranges with the parent and child for a visit. The teacher can gain understanding about the child's interests, skills, abilities, and relationships with others from a home visit.

For a child, and for the parents, too, the visit of the teacher may have a great deal of significance. The visit demonstrates to the child that she is an important person to the teacher. And parents, even though they may feel somewhat anxious and strained, may still appreciate the visit. Parent-teacher relationships can be more comfortable as a result of this opportunity to visit outside the center. Afterward, it may be easier for a parent to ask questions and for the teacher to understand what these questions mean.

Individual Parent-Teacher Conferences

Individual conferences represent one of the most valuable ways in which teachers and parents can share their observations. The teacher and the parent may hold many informal conferences at arrival or dismissal times or by telephone. Planned conferences may be scheduled, as well. As parents and teachers look at what is happening and pool their thoughts, they may gain new appreciation for what the child is like.

The initial contact between teacher and parent is important even if it takes place by telephone. The parents' first impressions will influence their attitude toward the center and will somehow be conveyed to the child. The first conference (described in Chapter 9) will probably occur as the child is about to enter the center. At this time parents are encouraged to talk about their child, and they also have the opportunity to raise questions about the center. The teacher listens and, with the parents, tries to understand what the experience of entering the program may mean to the child. They decide the roles each will play in helping the child adjust. There may be several short conferences for parents and teacher to share information during the adjustment process. The communication between parents and teacher at this time establishes conferences as matter-of-course events. Teachers accept the responsibility for creating an atmosphere in which communication is easy, honest, and direct.

Individual conferences can be held at regular intervals during the year, perhaps near the midpoint and at the end of the year. The NAEYC *Accreditation Criteria* (1991a) specify, "Conferences are held at least once a year and at other times, as needed." At these times, the teacher's observation of the child's progress on a variety of dimensions can be discussed. The teacher's observations of the child can be compared with the parents' observations of the child at home. The teacher knows the child at the center, and the parents know the child at home.

An annual conference between parent and teacher allows for mutual sharing about the child.
Child Development Center Laboratory, California State University, Chico

In conferences with parents, the teacher helps them approach problems, not by giving answers, but by listening to which solutions the parents have tried. She helps the parent select a course of action from those discussed. Only the parents know the child, the situation in the home, and what they can do. The responsibility for solving most problems belongs to the parent, and the teacher should not attempt to take over this responsibility any more than she should attempt to solve a child's problem. She tries only to help the parents solve a problem by listening, asking questions to clarify a point, or suggesting factors that may be related. She may point out the possible meanings of a course of action to a child and help parents think about alternative solutions. The experienced teacher does not offer advice or pass judgment, but she needs to show confidence that a solution can be found.

Every teacher needs education and experience in holding a conference. She also needs the opportunity, especially as a beginning teacher, to plan and later discuss the parent conferences with a professional person, such as her director, a supervisor, or a consultant. A beginning teacher may benefit from participating in some conferences with an experienced teacher. She learns from analyzing her own experience and identifying the meanings in both her responses and those of the parents. In-service education is important for developing skills in holding a parent conference.

Group Discussions and Parent Meetings

Group discussions provide parents with the opportunity to have contacts with other parents. They can share their concerns and talk about common problems. As a group they are all concerned about their children. It is often a relief for them to know that they are not alone in facing some problems.

Some single mothers with young children are likely to feel isolated, as are single fathers or a grandparent. Some employed mothers have few opportunities to talk with other parents of young children. They need contact with other adults who are interested in children. With the support of other parents, a parent may find it easier to let the child be more independent. Many adults live far from their own families and can not turn to their relatives for support. They may feel alone in facing uncertainties that they hesitate to share with friends. They need the extended family experience, which the center offers through group meetings.

There are many kinds of group experiences. Some centers have general group meetings, held in the evening, for mothers and fathers. The more chance for parent participation, the more the individual parent will gain. Techniques can be used to bring about participation even when groups are large. If the parents share responsibility with the staff for making plans, or take on the responsibility themselves, the experiences are likely to come closer to what parents really want and thus be more valuable. A parent committee may plan the programs.

It is only natural that parents wish to discuss the particular problem of their own child, but the discussion leader will need to keep relating the specific example to general principles or group interests. "Is this a problem that occurs frequently?" "Have some of you met this problem in other types of situations?" "Shall we look at reasons why this behavior appears in children just at this point in their growth?" Parents can be encouraged to present typical situations for discussion at a meeting. Problems that are not typical are better discussed by parent and teacher in a conference.

Prior agreement should be reached on the length of a meeting. It is seldom wise to have a discussion of more than an hour and a half, but frequently small groups will stay to talk more informally about points that have been raised. This can be a valuable part of the experience.

When meetings are being planned, teachers must consider the busy lives and diverse work hours of those who will attend. Some centers have arranged to have informal coffee hours during times when children are at the center. A discussion is led by someone on the staff. Other centers have had success with Saturday morning open houses for parents and children, in which the parents can experience some of the children's activities and chat informally with teachers over puzzles and playdough. There also are work meetings in which parents and teachers repair and paint equipment and talk as they work. Whether parents and teachers meet in the evening in a discussion group or in some other manner, it is important to meet the convenience of parents.

A lending library with books and pamphlets is useful to parents as a useful supplement to group meetings. A bulletin board provides a place where teachers and parents can share ideas or questions. A parent newsletter can also raise issues that have arisen at the center and which parents may want to discuss at parent meetings.

Parents as Classroom Participants

Parents also learn from participating in the center, and most centers welcome their input. Volunteers are always needed to go on an excursion or field trip, bring in a musical instrument to play, provide objects of interest, help with a cooking project, tell stories, or dance. In a culturally diverse center it may take special effort by the teacher to encourage parents to share their culture in the classroom. Discussion and evaluation by parents and staff afterward make parents' participation a valuable experience for all.

Head Start programs, campus child-care centers, and cooperative nursery schools use parents as assistant teachers. They need an adequate orientation in the procedures of the program for the particular center in which they will be sharing responsibilities with a trained teacher. They need to attend regular meetings in which there is discussion of current problems, review and planning of learning opportunities for the children, and an opportunity to raise questions, especially those about their own uncertainties or resistances.

In addition to the problems routinely faced by teachers, parents who are assistant teachers in the group where their child is enrolled face the added problem of having two roles. Being both teacher and parent at the same time is often a very difficult task. Parents in cooperative nursery schools know this problem. Patience is required on the part of everyone involved. Some children do better on the days when their parents are not present.

The Center Supports Parents

The center has a responsibility for parent education. Much more needs to be done, as we learn more about ways of helping parents. We can ask ourselves, "What would we like to find in a center to help us with the task of being a parent?"

Many centers have waiting lists with names of parents who hope to enroll their children. These parents are interested, and the center can offer them opportunities for learning through discussion groups, through conferences and consultation services, and, in some cases, through home visits and home teaching. Classes for expectant parents have proved valuable, as have parent-infant and parent-toddler classes. Centers need to be doing much more to help both fathers and mothers find success and satisfaction in carrying on their roles in "informed" ways.

Parents who lacked educational opportunities themselves can learn ways of supporting their children's learning. In some experimental and federally sponsored programs, teachers go into homes and help mothers of infants and very young children find ways to enrich their experiences. In other programs, teachers go into homes to work with the child to augment what the school is doing and to demonstrate to the individual parent how she or he may help the child. This kind of home visiting program appears to be very effective in supplementing a child's school experiences. It results in improved performance in learning, according to research done by Weikart and others. (Weikart et al, 1974)

A nationwide call for school reform has made more parents aware of the role they can play in the process of helping children learn. Children will benefit from this greater awareness by parents if all aspects of learning are emphasized. They also will benefit if parents do not work too hard at trying to be teachers.

Teachers remain in a key position to help parents value what the child is and does. They can help the parent see a relationship between a single bit of behavior and the total growth pattern. In this way they may help the parent gain a perspective and yet keep a sense of closeness to the child. They will not stress techniques. Techniques are not enough, however good they may be. They may even interfere with spontaneous relationships. It is not so much what people do as how they feel about what they do that is important. "What parents need all along is enlightenment about underlying causes, not advice and not instruction as to procedure." (Winnicott, 1957)

Chapter Overview

As teachers work with different parents, they will strive to understand the differences in parents' feelings. In working with parents, teachers will gain much that will further their own understanding of children. They, in turn, may help the parents in their understanding. Working together, teachers and parents will find the satisfactions that come with confidence, skill, and understanding. Parents have a tremendous job to do in today's changing society. The care and well-being of their children is extremely important to them.

As we have noted, the parents are the primary people in the child's life and the teacher is the extension of the child's home life. Teachers need to be aware of the feelings of parents about health issues, safety concerns, clothing matters, and cultural or ethnic traditions. Goals in working with parents are presented along with suggestions for parent education programs. Parents should be encouraged to visit the center and observe their child at play and with other children. Individual conferences as well as group discussions allow parents and teachers opportunities to work together. Finally, the center is seen as a parent support place that provides books about parenting and child development and encourages the parent's active involvement in the school setting.

Projects

1. Observe a group of children at the end of the school day. What plans are evident that the day is coming to an end? Note what individual parents do and say as they call for their children. What is the teacher's role as children leave?

2. What concerns do you think parents have regarding their children in the center? Are the concerns the same for parents from other cultural or racial backgrounds? If not, describe what you think the differences might be.

For Your Further Reading

Abbott, C. F., & Gold, S. (1991). Conferring with parents when you're concerned that their child needs special services. *Young Children* 46(4), 10–14. Help for teachers faced with difficult conferencing with parents whose child may not be progressing normally and who may need a referral. How to plan the conference; how to refer; how to follow up.

Brazelton, T. B. (1985). *Working and caring.* Reading, MA: Addison-Wesley. For working parents about how to hold a job and raise a family. Another fine book by pediatrician Brazelton that will assist adults who teach children of working parents.

Bundy, B. F. (1991). Fostering communication between parents and preschools. *Young Children.* 46(2), 12–17. Contains specific helps for teachers; how to work effectively with parents in communicating general information on children and parenting issues; specific information on individual children.

Cataldo, C. Z. (1987). *Parent education for early childhood: Child-rearing concepts and program content for the student and practicing professional.* New York: Teachers College Press. A comprehensive look at parenting education programs; practical helps for teachers who teach parent education. Covers not only how to conduct such programs, but also looks at the parenting process, including fathers.

Coleman, M. (1991). Planning for the changing nature of family life in schools for young children. *Young Children 46*(4), 15–20. How the staff in centers can respect diverse cultural, lifestyle, and economic differences and create strong parent involvement and school-home links.

Elkind, D. (1987). *Miseducation: Preschoolers at risk.* New York: Knopf. Written for parents and teachers on the risks of pressuring young children to learn developmentally inappropriate skills. Discusses Erikson's first three developmental tasks as a model for looking at miseducation dangers.

Galinsky, E., & David, J. (1988). *The preschool years: Family strategies that work—from experts and parents.* New York: Ballantine Books. Sound help in easy-to-read form, with anecdotes and questions-and-answers on discipline, routines, happy and sad times, work and family life, schools and child care.

Galinsky, E. (1990). Why are some parent–teacher partnerships clouded with difficulties? *Young Children, 45*(5), 2–3, 38–39. Examines the notion that tension between teachers and parents may be a common occurrence. Discusses research into the question, looking at such issues as parent perception of teacher support and teacher attitudes toward employed mothers.

McLoughlin, C. S. (1987). *Parent-teacher conferencing.* Springfield, IL: Thomas. Beginning teachers need the kinds of specific help for meeting with parents that this book offers. Good background for utilizing parents in the classroom and communication with families. Step-by-step chapters on organizing conferences, dealing with problem-centered conferences, and do's and don'ts.

Parke, R. D. (1981). *Fathers.* The developing child series. Cambridge, MA: Harvard University Press. The chapter, "Innovations in Fathering," discusses time for fathering, the dual career family, role-sharing families, and societal support for father.

Powell, D. R. (1989). *Families and early childhood programs.* Research Monograph #3. Washington, DC: National Association for the Education of Young Children. Makes readable the research and theory that teachers need in encouraging parent participation in early childhood programs.

Shiff, E. (Ed.). (1987). *Experts advise parents A guide to raising loving, responsible children.* New York: Bantam Doubleday Dell Publishing. Leading authorities including Louise Ames, Richard Ferber, Sol Gordon, Earl Grollman, Burton White, and Benjamin Spock write essays on topics of their expertise. Helpful for teachers as well as parents.

Spilke, F. S. (1979). *What about the children? A divorced parent's handbook.* New York: Crown Publishers.

Spilke, F. S. (1979). *The family that changed: A child's book about divorce.* New York: Crown Publishers. These books offer warm and helpful ideas for children from 3 to 6 and their parents. The parents' book includes issues not often discussed, like grandparents' roles and a parent living with someone without marriage.

Stone, J. G. (1987). *Teacher-parent relationships.* Washington, DC: National Association for the Education of Young Children. Warm, simple help for teachers who may not know how to begin their work with parents—often a difficult issue for beginning teachers.

Books to Help Adults and Children with Sexual Abuse and Uncomfortable Touching

Adams, C., & Fay, J. (1981). *No more secrets: Protecting your child from sexual assault.* San Luis Obispo, CA: Impact Publishers. For parents of children up to age 12. Written in helpful question-and-answer form.

Freeman, L. (1982). *It's MY body. A book to teach young children how to resist uncomfortable touch.* Seattle, WA: Parenting Press. For very young children; pictures, short text.

Freeman, L. (1987). *Loving touches.* A book to help young children distinguish between acceptable and uncomfortable touching.

Hart-Rossi, J. (1983). *A parent's resource booklet.* Everett, WA: Planned Parenthood of Snohomish County. Accompanies *It's MY body.* Activities, concepts, discussion ideas, ways to read the book with young children.

Johnsen, K. (1986). *The trouble with secrets.* Seattle, WA: Parenting Press. A book to help children deal with abusing adults who tell them to keep secrets.

Kehoe, P. (1987). *Something happened and I'm scared to tell.* Seattle, WA: Parent Press. A book for young victims of abuse.

Becoming a Professional Person

Self-portrait (*girl, 4 years*)

In this chapter you will discover a number of ways you can continue to grow as a professional in the early childhood field as you learn about:

▶ Professional growth in ethical conduct
▶ Professional growth in relations with others
▶ How the professional teacher continues learning
▶ Taking care of oneself as a professional person
▶ Becoming a professional in early childhood education.

GOAL: The program is staffed by adults who understand child development and who recognize and provide for children's needs.
RATIONALE: the quality of the staff is the most important determinant of the quality of an early childhood program. Research has found that staff training in child development and/or early childhood education is related to positive outcomes for children . . . (NAEYC, 1991a. Accreditation Criteria . . . , p. 30)

"I am persuaded that good teachers, first of all, must hold strong commitments and convictions from which their practices flow." (Hymes, 1981)

As we begin to work with young children and their families in the early childhood field, how do we develop a philosophy based on commitments and convictions? How does one become a professional person? The following are examples in which beginning teachers were faced with violations of professional standards.

Selma, a student aide in a licensed day-care center, comes in at the busy noon hour to help with lunch and to get children ready for naps. She notices that there often are too many children for the center's licensed number. She brings the matter up with the director, who replies, "Yes, I have to be overenrolled so I'll have my licensed number every day to make up for absences." Selma goes along with this but with growing concern. The director asks her to come in an extra morning because the licensing inspector is expected. Another day the fire inspector arrives, and the director sends Selma out the back door to take several children for a walk.

When Selma mentions these incidents to her college classroom teacher, Rina, a student aide in another center, exclaims, "That's nothing! One of our toddlers bit another child. The teacher bit her back, spanked her, and put her into 'time out.' I didn't know what to do or say."

Professional standards certainly are being violated in these centers. In the process of becoming professional, Selma and Rina should find answers for some of these kinds of problems. They must explore their commitments and convictions as they develop a philosophy.

Teachers need time to become truly professional persons, just as children need time to develop. With time and experience each individual will discover guidelines and will construct a philosophy that will serve as a basis for decision-making as she teaches. Each teacher will develop ethical standards through experience, through learning from wise colleagues, and through adopting standards of the profession.

Every profession should have agreed-upon guidelines for conduct. The medical and legal professions have been traditional examples. Standards and guidelines in early childhood education at first covered only matters such as health care, safety, number of square feet of space, and number of toilets in a facility. Today they include many more areas. Social changes, too, require improved standards. The need for care for infants, toddlers, preschoolers, and school-age children is urgent as increasing numbers of mothers are employed. There is a pressing need to raise standards for quality group care that is accessible and affordable.

The code of ethics adopted by NAEYC will help teachers like Selma and Rina make ethical choices that are supported by the profession. They no longer need to feel they are alone in making ethical decisions.

Professional Growth in Ethical Conduct

One of the most important areas for teachers' professional growth is that of ethical standards. Many questions raised today are ethical issues such as confidentiality of records or obtaining research data from children as subjects. The need to develop a code of ethics for the early childhood profession has become clear. (Katz, 1977), (Feeney & Kipnis, 1985), (Feeney & Kipnis, 1990)

Selma and Rina faced dilemmas for which ethical guidelines are urgent. Teachers can act with more confidence when they have guidelines for correct or "right" behavior, especially when there are temptations to behave otherwise. With ethical guidelines teachers find it easier to act in the best interests of the child, the parent, and the program, rather than to act expediently. They find it easier to be clear about what they will not do or will not allow to be done under any circumstances. Because of the professional code of ethics teachers may now say with confidence, "Our profession will not let us do this."

The following statements from the Code of Ethical Conduct and Statement of Commitment (Feeney & Kipnis, 1990) will help teachers of young children develop a philosophy of ethical behavior.

As an individual who works with young children, I commit myself to furthering the values of early childhood education as they are reflected in the NAEYC Code of Ethical Conduct. To the best of my ability I will:

Ensure that programs for young children are based on current knowledge of child development and early childhood education.

Respect and support families in their task of nurturing children.

Respect colleagues in early childhood education and support them in maintaining the NAEYC Code of Ethical Conduct.

Serve as an advocate for children, their families, and their teachers in community and society.

Maintain high standards of professional conduct.

Recognize how personal values, opinions, and biases can affect professional judgment.

Be open to new ideas and be willing to learn from the suggestions of others.

Continue to learn, grow, and contribute as a professional.

Honor the ideals and principles of the NAEYC Code of Ethical Conduct.

Confidentiality

Ethical codes of conduct include confidentiality. Teachers must consider as confidential all information about families.

Teachers serve many needs, not only for the child but also for families. Decisions made by teachers about what is in the child's and family's best interests should be in accord with ethical guidelines. Teachers may receive glimpses into intimate family situations. Teachers often need to contact public health clinics, child protective services, legal authorities, and other community agencies. They may need to contact a physician who knows the child. When making these contacts they must be clear about what information can be shared without violating confidentiality.

Confidentiality means sharing information only with those staff members who are directly involved. It means keeping any notes on children and families carefully filed and not left out for others to read. It means making sensitive telephone calls in private. It means never talking to one parent about another parent. It includes asking permission from a family before talking with any outside agencies. Beginning teachers must respect the policies of the center concerning ethical standards. They need to consult with their supervisor when difficult situations arise, as they clarify their own feelings and beliefs.

The NAEYC professional code of ethics covers more than confidentiality. It includes responsibilities to children, families, colleagues, the community, and society. Ethical guidelines become important when teachers are confronted with difficult choices that may carry a risk to themselves,

Research in a center must be handled in a confidential and ethical manner.
Child Development Center Laboratory, California State University, Chico

the child, the parent, or the center. There are no easy answers, but resources and support are available from others in solving ethical problems. Above all, people working with young children shall do nothing to harm them. This takes precedence over all other codes.

Professional Growth in Relations with Others

With Children

In working with children, teachers use all the knowledge they have gained about child growth and development and about children's needs at different stages. Throughout this book we have presented material about understanding children and ways to meet their needs. We have pointed out the dangers of labeling children and the need for objective observations.

Teachers responding professionally look for the meaning of children's behavior. They look at the curriculum and the physical environment to see if better planning could benefit children's learning and prevent difficulties from occurring. They look at age-expected behaviors for the children and above all at what they know about the individual child from careful observation. (Katz, 1984)

With Parents

The relationship between teacher and parent differs from the personal relationship between friends. It is a professional relationship, concerned with an educational experience and the individual child's well-being. Teachers who can offer such a relationship to parents must have a real understanding of themselves. They must be able to respond to parents' needs.

Teachers need to listen carefully when parents discuss problems with them. They are ready to share their knowledge and their experiences when a parent is ready. If teachers feel that a problem needs specialized help, they should be familiar with resources in the community so they can refer a parent appropriately. For example, teachers are frequently the first to observe that a child may have a hearing impairment or a vision problem. Teachers can suggest a referral and may assist in making appointments, but the parent must be the one to make the decision.

Teachers often are faced with difficult dilemmas in their work with parents. Below are some examples. Decisions are not easy to make in these cases:

A father angrily insists that the teacher spank his child when the child "misbehaves" at the center.

A mother demands that her unusual dietary preferences for the child be followed, even though there is no health reason involved.

A child who has been kidnapped in the past by the noncustodial parent sees that parent watching outside the fence of the center.

A child tells the teacher information indicating that the parent may be breaking the law.

A never-married noncustodial father insists to the teacher that his child's last name is to be listed as his name, while the mother fills out all the forms legally with her last name as the child's last name.

Teachers who suspect that a child may be abused physically, emotionally, or sexually must report it immediately to the appropriate authorities. Professional teachers put the welfare of the child above any conflicting concerns. In many states there are penalties for failure to report. Reporting suspected abuse is not a dilemma or choice: it is a necessity.

With Colleagues

Teachers of young children are likely to be part of a teaching team. Close working relationships, frequently in sensitive situations, make it important to maintain professional relationships with colleagues and all staff involved in the center.

Some aspects of the working conditions of teachers in centers leave much to be desired. Staff turnover may be frequent because of low pay and status, unpaid overtime, lack of adequate breaks, unequal division of labor among staff, and inadequate opportunities for decision-making. (Whitebook et al, 1982) Centers in many states find difficulty in recruiting and retaining teachers. Turnover of teachers had tripled to 41 percent in 1988, from 15 percent in 1977, as reported in the National Child Care Staffing Study. Employment benefits like health insurance and retirement plans were found to be offered to fewer than half of the teachers surveyed. (Whitebook et al, 1989)

Other centers may be more fortunate with good staff morale in spite of inadequate pay. While improved pay and working conditions are real issues, there are ways teachers can support each other to make the center a more satisfying workplace.

The center may bring in consultants, preferably on a regular basis, to provide staff development or to focus on problems of individual children. It is helpful when the center's director observes in individual classrooms and gets acquainted with children in order to consult with teachers. Individual conferences between the director and the teachers are important.

Professional growth for teachers includes learning to listen to colleagues' points of view. Flexibility and compromises often are necessary in working with others if these do not damage the standards of the center. Regular discussions about teaching methods and different situations at the center help to prevent conflict.

Teachers should be careful to share the workload as equally as possible and to be fair about breaks, substituting, or carrying an extra load. They need to take their share of chores such as shopping for curriculum materials, cleaning up in the kitchen, mending books or broken equipment, and doing the laundry. Teachers may volunteer to assume responsibilities, such as revising a parent handbook, working with menus and the food service person, or chairing the school's annual Week of the Young Child activities or holiday program. When teachers support one another, they create a center in which morale is good.

The Professional Teacher Continues Learning

Learning to teach seems to occur in developmental levels, just as children go through stages of development. Teachers have their own patterns as they learn to teach, but awareness of stages may be helpful to teachers as they think about their own professional development.

Lilian Katz (1972) has proposed one way of looking at developmental stages that teachers of young children may experience. The first stage may be one of *survival*, during which teachers may be surprised at the gap between their high hopes and the realities of day-to-day work with children. The next stage is *consolidation*, when they pull together what they have learned and look forward to gaining more skill in working with individual children. Then may come *renewal*, when teachers begin looking for ideas about new materials, procedures, and approaches. Teachers reach a stage of greater *maturity* after several years. They feel freer to develop their own ideas and to become more creative in teaching. They become more concerned about the underlying philosophy of early childhood education.

Katherine Read as part of a panel at a professional conference.
Child Development Center Laboratory, California State University, Chico

Teachers in each developmental stage have different kinds of needs for supervision, training, and support.

Teachers continue their learning through educational activities, support, and opportunities appropriate to their professional experience.

Professional Affiliation

1. Joining professional organizations, such as the National Association for the Education of Young Children and an association specific to the affiliation of the center (such as family day care, Head Start, church-related school, or campus child-care associations).
2. Attending professional conferences and workshops, local, regional, and national.
3. Subscribing to professional journals and newsletters.

Continuing Education

4. Working toward the Child Development Associate credential, a certificate of competence and degree from a community college, or a four-year-college or university degree in early childhood.
5. Planning for future study, possibly a further degree.

Job Market

6. Investigating career opportunities in the field including career ladder opportunities.
7. Preparing and maintaining a professional résumé. Preparing well for job interviews.

Activities for Professional Renewal

8. Visiting other early childhood programs.
9. Participating actively in staff meetings and in-service training sessions; assuming responsibility for some staff learning activities.
10. Participating in accreditation like that of the National Academy for Early Childhood Programs (NAECP) for centers or National Association for Family Day Care (NAFDC) for family day-care providers.
11. Keeping up a useful curriculum activities file, with ideas gained from reading, observing other teachers, and attending conferences and workshops.
12. Maintaining a comprehensive file of books, articles, pamphlets, clippings, and ideas for oneself, for colleagues, and for parents.
13. Participating in research projects, which may be the teacher's own systematic collecting of information about "what works."
14. Serving as a mentor to newer teachers as a means of continuing professional growth.
15. Joining in advocacy efforts to improve not only conditions for children but also the status, pay, and professionalism of adults in the early childhood field.

A responsible professional person is an advocate for the early childhood field. Community participation in the Week of the Young Child *offers opportunities.* Child Development Center Laboratory, California State University, Chico

Teachers become more professional by speaking out effectively for children. James Hymes (1981) calls on "all teachers of young children to take on the role of child advocate. . . . The continuing shortage of programs plus the increasing threats to quality create a pressing need for teachers to be good friends to all young children, and to know how to act on their allegiance."

Teachers must also speak out for adults who work with young children. A large-scale education campaign called "The Full Cost of Quality Must be Paid" was launched by NAEYC in 1990. It is clear that early childhood staff subsidize the actual costs of programs through receiving inadequate pay and benefits. The "Full Cost" campaign is aimed at a "full-scale public education effort" to improve rates paid for early childhood services and quality aspects that strongly affect costs of programs. (National Academy of Early Childhood Programs, 1990)

Taking Care of Oneself as a Professional Person

In becoming professional, teachers need to maintain good health, learn to handle stress, and use social support systems and the evaluations of self and others for continued learning.

Self-Care and Maintaining Good Health

Teachers of young children need to be in good health to have the energy and vitality to maintain enthusiasm for their work. It takes stamina to work long hours with a group of lively children. Habits of good nutrition, vigorous exercise, sufficient sleep and relaxation, and regular breaks for recreation are needed to maintain health and energy.

Teachers need to cultivate interests of their own and to participate in leisure activities outside teaching hours. Achieving a healthy balance between work and leisure is essential.

Stress Management

Closely related to self-care is stress management. Stress and "burnout" in the child care profession have been the subject of study. (Whitebook et al, 1982) Staff turnover because of stress results in "talent drain" and is expensive for centers and for the individual.

The nature of the work makes heavy demands on the teachers' energy. Close personal relations with young children who have many needs and require constant attention can drain a teacher's strength by the end of the day. Combine these factors with low pay, lack of benefits, and low status, and it is easy to see that teachers of young children face stress.

In spite of these factors, working with children gives real enjoyment. Supportive staff relationships also bring satisfaction along with personal growth opportunities.

Teachers can join together to work toward higher pay, better job benefits, and improved working conditions such as smaller child-staff ratios and group size, availability of substitutes, and more control over policy and decision making. (Whitebook et al, 1982) Some communities and businesses have hired a child-care coordinator to advocate for such issues. Resource and referral agencies in some areas offer community support and leadership in advocacy.

Social Support Systems

The presence of a network of supportive people helps teachers grow professionally. Regular staff meetings are very important in providing such support. Staff meetings have been found to be directly related to good staff morale if teachers have felt helped by them in dealing with difficult situations. (Maslach & Pines, 1977) In full-day centers it can be difficult to find hours when the staff can be together to conduct business, make decisions, and fulfill a supportive function for one another. In staff discussions everyone should feel free to express ideas and feelings and to bring up problems. Staff meetings may also be used for in-service training. When everyone is encouraged to contribute, staff meetings will be seen as a productive use of time.

Using Staff Evaluations

All centers do some evaluating of the work of staff members in formal or informal ways. The NAEYC includes evaluation in its system for nationally recognized accreditation. "The director (or other appropriate person) evaluates all staff at least annually. . . . The evaluation includes classroom observation. Staff are informed of evaluation criteria in advance . . . Staff have an opportunity to evaluate their own performance." (NAEYC, 1991a)

The director or head teacher is usually the person who formally evaluates teachers. She is most effective when she is encouraging and supportive and able to point out to the teacher what has been done well and where improvement is needed. Evaluation should be a two-way process with both supervisor and teacher contributing. Evaluation should be a positive experience, helping the teacher to become more effective, to discover strengths, and to gain confidence.

Teachers evaluate each other in informal ways, and they need to be sensitive in recognizing and benefiting from these evaluations. One teacher can ask another for feedback.

Parents, too, do some evaluating. Parent-teacher conferences may give teachers an opportunity to discover how parents feel. Some centers formally include parents' evaluation of teachers in yearly reviews.

Children do some "evaluating" as shown in their behavior when they feel free to express their feelings.

Self-evaluation is possibly the most important form of evaluation. Some centers use videotaping to assist teachers here. Self-evaluation enables teachers to consider all the sources of evaluation.

The NAEYC accreditation criteria state, "At least annually, parents, staff, and other professionals are involved in evaluating the program's effectiveness in meeting the needs of children and parents." (NAEYC, 1991a). Such annual evaluation provides areas for professional growth for improvement in the center and for individual teachers. Teachers are fortunate to work in centers where positive, growth-producing evaluations of several kinds are held regularly.

Becoming a Professional in the Field of Early Childhood Education

It takes time and experience to become a professional in early childhood education, and the process continues through one's working life. Much depends on circumstances and opportunities. One person may begin teaching in a favorable situation with plenty of support and inspiration from working with good teachers as models. Another person may find it harder to become confident and competent but should find the effort worthwhile. It may be hard work with discouraging moments, but teaching can become more interesting and satisfying each year.

We do not always see clearly the progress we have made. A successful episode in handling two aggressive boys; the development of an exciting new curriculum unit; a gratifying conference with a troubled parent; an exciting regional workshop with new ideas—all of these experiences add to our growth as professionals.

Chapter Overview

We have seen in this chapter that beginning teachers' work with children and families is an evolving process. Developing a philosophy, working out professional standards, and adopting a code of ethics are part of this environment. Professional growth in relations with children, parents, and colleagues is an ongoing process. Professional affiliation in organizations or associations, conference attendance and participation, keeping current by reading journals and newsletters, and working on advanced degrees are all a part of becoming a professional. Activities for renewal and advocacy have been outlined. Finally, suggestions for self-care and maintaining good health are viewed as important ingredients that contribute to professionalism.

Projects

1. Arrange to attend a staff meeting in a center. Observe how ideas are introduced, the process of decision-making, and how involved the staff members appear to be. Is there a written agenda? How are individuals' ideas listened to?
2. In a center where you participate, note some ways in which teachers get help in staying "alive" professionally. How does the center encourage staff development activities? Interview several teachers about their own professional development plans.
3. Interview someone who has worked in early childhood education for more than ten years to find out why the person chose the profession, what kinds of work he or she has done in the field, what he or she sees as problems and new trends in the field, or something else that interests you.
4. Discuss with others some of the moral dilemmas that have occurred in your center. Using the code of ethics developed by NAEYC, locate principles that can help you solve your questions.

For Your Further Reading

Census Alert: When the census asks, "What do you do?" what do you say? *Young Children, 45*(2), 48. NAEYC worked with the Census Bureau for the 1990 census to redefine the occupational titles that early childhood professionals can use to clarify the field. A handy chart says, "If this is what you do, this is what you should say" to describe your position.

Dresden, J., & Myers, B. K. (1989). Early childhood professionals: Toward self-definition. *Young Children, 44*(2), 62–66. Challenges conventional views of professionals as several myths: the myth of power and hierarchy, the myth of career ladders, the myth of career commitment excluding other commitments such as to family. Concludes with a call to political activity.

Feeney, S., and Kipnis, K. (1990). *Code of ethical conduct and Statement of commitment: Guidelines for responsible behavior in early childhood education.* Washington, DC: National Association for the Education of Young Children. Available as NAEYC leaflet #503 ($0.50). Every early childhood professional should be familiar with these guidelines for our responsibilities to children, families, colleagues, community, and society.

Jorde-Bloom, P. (1988). *A great place to work: Improving conditions for staff in young children's programs.* Washington, DC: National Association for the Education of Young Children. Defines a healthy work climate on dimensions such as collegiality, professional growth, support from supervisors, staff autonomy in decision-making, and physical setting. How to improve the organizational climate to benefit staff, children, and families.

Katz, L. G. (1972). Developmental stages of preschool teachers. *Elementary School Journal, 23*(1), 50–54. A classic description of stages teachers may go through as they progress in their career, along with kinds of support and training they need at each stage for optimum professional growth.

Katz, L. G. (1984). The professional early childhood teacher. *Young Children, 39*(5), 3–10. An important definition of behaviors used by professional, nonprofessional, and unprofessional teachers in relation to what is being taught by adults and learned by children.

National Association for the Education of Young Children. (1991). *Accreditation criteria and procedures: Position statement of the National Academy of Early Childhood Programs.* Washington, DC: Author. Presents well-tested guidelines for quality programs as the basis for accreditation. Every early childhood professional should be acquainted with this publication.

National Association for the Education of Young Children. (1990). *NAEYC Position statement on guidelines for compensation of early childhood professionals.* Washington, DC: Author. Strongly urges that early childhood professionals receive commensurate compensation to that of other professionals with comparable requirements. Adequate benefits and career ladders should be made available and should not be based on the ages of children served.

Seaver, J. W., Cartwright, C. A., Ward, C. B., & Heasley, C. A. (1984). (Rev. ed.) *Careers with young children: Making your decision.* Washington, DC: National Association for the Education of Young Children. A helpful workbook for choosing an early childhood career. Five strands of careers for the teacher-in-training: serving children directly, serving families directly, organizing services for children and families, providing information to professionals, and providing goods and services that affect children and families.

Spodek, B., Saracho, O., & Peters, D. (Eds.). (1988). *Professionalism and the early childhood practitioner.* New York: Teachers College Press. A fine collection of essays on how the early childhood profession should best train and educate its practitioners. Three parts define professionalism and raise questions about whether the early childhood field truly meets the criteria for professional behavior.

Accepting Our Common Responsibilities

A balloon ride (*girl, 4 years, 6 months*)

In this chapter you will look at responsibilities shared by all of us who are committed to advocating for early childhood education and care as you learn about:

▶ Common responsibilities to families
▶ Common responsibilities of educational and state institutions
▶ Beneficial changes taking place.

NAEYC believes that for young children care and education are integrally related; the younger the child, the more impossible it is to make any distinctions between the two. For very young children, all learning is embedded within a caregiving function, whether provided by parent or another individual. Even as children mature and education becomes more distinct from care, caregiving remains important. Good programs for young children serve both care and education functions. (Willer, 1990. p. viii)

There has been a realization that child care responsibilities cannot be placed on families alone, but that both the private and the public sectors have a role in supporting quality early childhood programs. Rather than ask "why" they should be involved, increasingly businesses, governments, and charitable organizations are asking "how" they can help. (Galinsky, 1990a. p. 27)

Common Responsibilities Relating to Families

As we move closer to the twenty-first century, children's and families' needs remain central in this nation's planning. "Children are growing up today in an ethically polluted nation where instant sex without responsibility, instant gratification without effort, instant solutions without sacrifice, getting rather than giving, and hoarding rather than sharing are the too-frequent signals of our mass media, popular culture, business, and political life." (Children's Defense Fund, 1991) This must change if the nation is to survive. Among our common responsibilities are those relating to families and children. There have been many changes in this century. Many of these have benefitted families. Others have created problems.

Research has greatly increased our knowledge in many areas. How much of this research has advanced our knowledge about the development of children? How much more do we know about their needs for healthy growth and the development of their capacities? How much of this knowledge is made easily available to those caring for young children? How much is society doing to implement what we know so that all children may grow up in favorable environments? What standards exist, and how are they enforced? These are some of the questions that need to be raised, and we share this responsibility. Parents, teachers, employees, the business world, the public, and the government need to be concerned.

The Role of Education

In a period of such rapid change, education plays an important role in helping people adapt. Throughout this book we have looked for ways to increase our understanding of children and the ways in which they grow and learn. We have found that observing them will teach us a great deal about human behavior, and also that, if we are to handle children wisely, we must understand something about ourselves. The kind of people we are influences what we do for children.

The longer we study, the more we appreciate the complexities of human behavior and the more we hesitate to propose ready-made formulas for solving problems or setting standards for what a child ought or ought not do.

We have taken a big step when we have learned to observe children, to recognize the uniqueness of each individual, to search for the meaning behind an act, to accept the child and have confidence in his potential growth. We have taken a big step when we have learned to contribute to the child through reducing the difficulty of the problems he must face, through enriching his experiences, through providing him with optimum opportunities for learning, and through helping him find avenues for creative satisfactions; we contribute nothing when we resort to admonition and interference. We can assume responsibility for defining and maintaining limits for the child's behavior with confidence because we understand better his developmental needs.

Research findings have stressed the importance of infancy and toddlerhood in giving direction to development in physical, intellectual, and personality growth. Healthy parental bonds established in this sensitive period influence all aspects of development. Yet very few employers are willing to give women leave, paid or unpaid, to take care of a baby. Many mothers feel that they cannot afford to take such leave, either because of the needed earnings or because their job status would be in jeopardy.

Common Responsibilities of Educational and State Institutions

While interest in early childhood education grows steadily along with the demand for it, there remains a serious shortage of well-trained teachers for young children. Teacher education programs are at risk because of reduced budgets. The problem exists primarily because of the low pay and low status in this field. Licensing standards deteriorate when teacher shortages exist. The gravity of this situation demands state and local help.

The nutritional status of children who live in families below the poverty line has declined through the 1980s as federal food programs have been reduced. (Children's Defense Fund, 1984) Many of these families have unemployed adults, and all members of the families suffer.

Some changes have been beneficial, such as the improved status of women and greater educational opportunities, along with conveniences that can lighten housework. Other changes have not helped, such as crowding in the cities with problems of pollution, lack of decent housing, lack of parks, playgrounds, and public transportation. Through the centuries parents have been concerned about the welfare of their children, but parents today may be less able than those in the past to provide their children a healthy environment. Families need governmental support if they are to fulfill their functions.

Homelessness

Since 1980 homelessness has become a problem afflicting families with children. Nationwide, one in every five homeless persons is a child. Homelessness is a direct result of falling family incomes and a sorely inadequate supply of low-cost housing. Homelessness hurts children in a variety of ways. Poor health, emotional distress, and disrupted schooling are barriers to healthy development and academic achievement that these vulnerable children face daily. (Children's Defense Fund, 1991) Every era has seen the need for quality care of young children to meet some social or wartime crisis. The 1990s are no different.

Beneficial Changes Taking Place

Businesses have begun to provide child care for the young children of their employees or provide an allowance to help defray child-care expenses.

More citizens are actively trying to find solutions to problems such as air pollution or dangers in the disposal of nuclear waste, for example, or the burden the rapidly growing budget deficit poses for this and future generations.

NAEYC has taken an important step in its efforts to raise standards in the field of early childhood education. In 1984 it published a position statement dealing with standards of early childhood programs, from which the goals and criteria at the beginning of most chapters in this book are quoted. (NAEYC, 1991a) In 1991 NAEYC published a set of guidelines for appropriate curriculum content and assessment in programs serving children ages 3 through 8. (NAEYC, 1991e) It is not enough just to provide care for young children; we must aim for quality care in all programs. These publications outline the criteria for quality early childhood education programs, based on the best knowledge we have at present.

Only as we continue to study children and learn from them and as we try to understand ourselves better can we expect to judge what will benefit each individual child. Our concern should include all children. As students, teachers, and parents, we must accept the challenge put to us by Chisholm (1949) more than half a century ago: "Dare any of us say that he or she can do nothing about the desperate need of the world for better human relationships?" The center is a laboratory for human relationships and learning.

Chapter Overview

This chapter demonstrates the concerns for children and families facing this nation. The authors have provided their thoughts about the complexities of human behavior and the reasons ready-made formulas for solving problems are not appropriate. Healthy parental bonds, sound nutrition, and a healthy environment are rights all children should enjoy.

Projects

1. Interview the director of your local resource and referral agency to find out about local and state licensing requirements.
2. Call upon a local business employing large numbers of women and ask about its child-care arrangements for employees.
3. Volunteer your services at a homeless center serving children and families.

For Your Further Reading

Children's Defense Fund. (1991). *SOS American: A children's defense budget.* Washington, DC: Author.
Children's Defense Fund. (1991). *The state of America's children.* Washington, DC: Author. Important annual publications from the foremost children's advocacy organization. Detailed, up-to-date demo-

graphics and useful information on the state of children and families in the U.S. today.

Fennimore, B. S. (1989). *Child advocacy for early childhood educators.* New York: Teachers College Press. A book to inspire early childhood teachers into advocating more effectively for the rights of young children; includes ways to advocate politically and in the classroom, with families, and in the community.

Galinsky, E. (1990). Government and child care. *Young Children 45*(3), 2–3, 76–77. Shares common arguments given against government involvement with child care issues. Every early childhood advocate would do well to think through answers to such negative comments as, "Public child care support isn't necessary because most children are cared for by family members" or, "Mothers shouldn't work" or, "Given limited . . . resources, efforts should be aimed at increasing the supply before endeavoring to improve quality."

Goffin, S. G., & Lombardi, J. (1988). *Speaking out: Early childhood advocacy.* Washington, DC: National Association for the Education of Young Children. Teachers of young children need resources to be more effective advocates on behalf of young children and programs and the adults who care for children. Helps with the "how to" as well as understanding how public policy is made.

Goffin, S. G. (1988). Putting our advocacy efforts into a new context. *Young Children, 43*(3), 52–56. Presents several assumptions: negative assumptions that have hindered a family-oriented approach to social policy; alternative positive assumptions underlying the efforts of child advocates; assumptions that early childhood educators hold about advocating for children and parents.

Jensen, M. A., & Chevalier, Z. W. (Eds.). (1990). *Issues and advocacy in early edu-cation.* Needham Heights, MA: Allyn & Bacon. A wide-ranging collection of chapters on current and sometimes controversial issues. Includes the importance of advocating for the professionals as well as for children; also topics like developmentally appropriate curriculum practices, television, child abuse, mainstreaming high-risk children, and multicultural education.

Lombardi, J. (1986). Training for public policy and public advocacy. *Young Children 41*(4), 65–69. A proposal to include training for public policy and advocacy in teacher education programs in order to increase involvement in the political process by early childhood professionals.

Morin, J. (1989). Viewpoint: We can force a solution to the staffing crisis. *Young Children 44*(6), 18–19. A brief plea for stronger advocacy for the adults who work in early childhood programs. Eloquent statement of how parents are protected from the true costs of child care by employees' subsidizing the cost by accepting low pay.

Spodek, B., & Saracho, O. N. (Eds.). (1991). *Issues in early childhood curriculum.* Yearbook in Early Childhood Education Series, Vol. II. New York: Teachers College Press. New issues in curriculum study that challenge teachers and decision-makers: instructional technology, cultural diversity, developmentally appropriate practices, evaluation of children and program, and vast changes in family life.

Willer, B., et al. (Ed.). (1991). *The demand and supply of child care in 1990: Joint findings from the National Child Care Survey 1990 and A Profile of Child Care Settings.* Washington, DC: National Association for the Education of Young Children. Full of facts and figures on the market for early education and care and trends in early education and care. Invaluable recent information for advocates.

Appendix: Organizations, Resources, and Publishers

Administration for Children, Youth, and Families: see Health and Human Services Department.

Adopted Child, P. O. Box 9362, Moscow, ID 83843. Newsletter providing information on raising adopted children.

Afro-Am Education Materials, 819 S. Wabash Ave., Chicago, IL 60605.

American Academy of Pediatrics, Department of Publications, 141 Northwest Point Blvd., P.O. Box 927, Elk Grove Village, IL 60007. Provides leaflets such as the *AAP First Aid Chart* for parents, teachers, and centers.

American Alliance for Health, Physical Education, Recreation, and Dance, 1900 Association Drive, Reston, VA 22091. Publishes many useful materials about physical activities of all kinds.

American Association for Gifted Children, 15 Gramercy Park, New York, NY 10003.

American Dietetic Association, 216 W. Jackson Blvd., Suite 800, Chicago, IL 60606.

American Education Research Association, Early Childhood SIG Group, c/o Educational Testing Service, Rosedale Road, Princeton, NJ 08541.

American Foundation for the Blind, 15 W. 16th St., New York, NY 10011.

American Home Economics Association, 2010 Massachusetts Ave., NW, Washington, DC 20036.

American Library Association, 50 E. Huron St., Chicago, IL 60611.

American Montessori Society, 150 5th Ave., Suite 203, New York, NY 10011.

Anti-Defamation League of B'nai B'rith, 823 United Nations Plaza, New York, NY 10017. Resource on Jewish issues.

Appalachia Educational Laboratory, 1031 Quarier St., P. O. Box 1348, Charleston, WV 25325.

Association for Childhood Education, International, 11141 Georgia Ave., Suite 200, Wheaton, MD 20902. Publishes *Childhood Education,* for teachers of children from birth through adolescence; emphasis on kindergarten and primary grades. Also *Journal of Research in Childhood Education.*

Association for Retarded Citizens, 2501 Avenue J, Box 6109, Arlington, TX 76011.

Association for the Care of Children in Hospitals, 7910 Woodmont Ave., Suite 300, Bethesda, MD 20814. Publishes directories of training programs for Child Life Specialist. National conferences encompass all health-related specialists who work with children in hospital settings.

Association Montessori International/USA, 170 W. Scholfield Road, Rochester, NY 14617.

Bank Street College of Education, 610 W. 112th St., New York, NY 10025. Offers specializations in early childhood and elementary education, reading, infant and parent development, and museum education. Well-known for its Center for Children and Technology and the Publications Group, which issues materials for children and adults.

Bilingual Publications Co., 1966 Broadway, New York, NY 10023. Deals with books in Spanish and other languages.

Black Child Development Institute, 1463 Rhode Island Ave. NW, Washington, DC 20005. Publishes *The Black Child Advocate,* a quarterly newsletter.

Center for Child and Family Studies, Far West Laboratory, 180 Harbor Drive, Suite 112, Sausalito, CA 94965.

Center for Science in the Public Interest, 1755 "S" Street NW, Washington, DC 20044. Publishes *Nutrition Action,* up-to-date and authoritative nutrition information.

Center for Parent Education, 55 Chapel St., Newton, MA 02160.

Centering Corporation, Box 3367, Omaha, NE 68103. Resources for families in crisis; books for children and for professionals; workshops on grief and death for families.

Child Care Action Campaign, 99 Hudson St., Room 1233, New York, NY 10013.

Child Care Employee Project, Box 5603, Berkeley, CA 94705. Publishes *Child Care Employee News,* publications on salaries, benefits, and working conditions, and article reprints.

Child Care Information Exchange, P.O. Box 2890, Redmond, WA 98073. Publishes *Beginnings,* and *Child Care Information Exchange,* a bimonthly magazine for center administrators. Sponsors the Directors' Network.

Child Care Law Center, 22 Second St., San Francisco, CA 94105.

Children's Book and Music Center, 2500 Santa Monica Blvd., Santa Monica, CA 90406. A firm supplying musical materials of all kinds, including culturally diverse records, tapes, instruments, and books.

Children's Defense Fund, 122 C St. NW, Washington, DC 20001. Publishes annual *Children's Defense Fund Budget* and other advocacy publications. Best source of statistics and demographics for decision-makers and child advocates.

Children's Foundation, 815 15th St. NW, Suite 928, Washington, DC 20005.

Child Health Alert, P.O. Box 338, Newton Highlands, MA 02161. Authoritative, short articles on diverse health topics for teachers, health professionals, and parents.

Children's Lobby, P.O. Box 448, Sacramento, CA 95802. Publishes *On the Capitol Doorstep,* a newsletter about legislation on children and family issues.

Children's Television Workshop/Sesame Street. One Lincoln Plaza, New York, NY 10023. Publishes *Sesame Street* magazine for preschoolers.

Child Welfare League of America, 440 1st St. NW, Suite 310, Washington, DC 20001.

Childswork/Childsplay: Center for Applied Psychology, 441 N. 5th St. Third Floor, Philadelphia, PA 19123. Mail-order company specializing in books, toys, and games "addressing the mental health needs of children and their families through play."

Claudia's Caravan, P. O. Box 1582, Alameda, CA 94501. Mail-order company featuring culturally diverse books, tapes, and learning materials.

Community Playthings and Equipment for the Handicapped, Route 213, Rifton, NY 12471. Esthetically beautiful wooden equipment for handicapped and nonhandicapped children in centers.

Council for Early Childhood Professional Recognition. 1718 Connecticut Ave. NW, Suite 500, Washington, DC 20009. Provides recognition for individuals through the Child Development Associate credential, a competency-based certification; administers the CDA Professional Preparation Program.

Council for Exceptional Children, Division of Early Childhood, Dept. 651, 1920 Association Drive, Reston, VA 22091. Publishes *Exceptional Children.*

Council on Interracial Books for Children, 1841 Broadway, New York, NY 10023. Publishes *Interracial Books for Children Bulletin,* a newsletter, eight issues annually, and other materials on interracial publications.

Ecumenical Child Care Network, National Council of Churches of Christ in the USA, 475 Riverside Drive, Room 572, New York, NY 10115.

Educational Equity Concepts, 114 E. 32d St., 3rd Floor, Room 306, New York, NY 10016. Resources on gender equity, especially in educational materials.

ERIC/ECEE (Educational Resources Information Center on Elementary and Early Childhood Education), University of Illinois, 805 W. Pennsylvania Ave., Urbana, IL 61801. Publishes *ERIC/ECE Newsletter,* resource lists, leaflets on current research topics, and provides literature searches. Valuable resource for researchers and teachers.

Family Communications, Inc., 4802 Fifth Ave., Pittsburgh, PA 15213. Publishes Mister Rogers books, videos, cassettes, and leaflets on emotionally sensitive topics for adults and children.

Far West Laboratory for Educational Research and Development, 1855 Folsom St., San Francisco, CA 94103.

Folkways Records and Service Corporation, 632 Broadway, Ninth Floor, New York, NY 10012. A fine source of music from all over the world, not only for children. (See Smithsonian)

Global Village, 2210 Wilshire Blvd., Box 262, Santa Monica, CA 90403. Mail-order company emphasizing materials of global awareness, multilingual, social responsibility, anti-bias products.

Growing Child, 22 N. Second St., P. O. Box 620, Lafayette, IN 47902. Publishes newsletters for child care providers (*Growing Together*), professionals (*Research Review*), parents and teachers grades K-12 (*Growing Up*), and for parents of children up to age 6 (*Growing Child*).

Head Start: See Health and Human Services Department.

Health and Human Services Department, Head Start Bureau, Administration for Children, Youth, and Families; Office of Human Development Services, P.O. Box 1182, Washington, DC 20013.

Health and Human Services Department, Bureau of Education for the Handicapped, Administration for Children, Youth, and Families; Office of Human Development Services, P.O. Box 1182, Washington, DC 20013.

Health and Human Services, U. S. Office of Education, 7th and D Streets SW, Washington, DC 20036.

High/Scope Educational Research Foundation, 600 N. River St., Ypsilanti, MI 48197. Publishes newsletter and books and offers teacher training. Includes The Center for the Study of Public Policies for Young Children. Valuable resource on computers and movement; best known for longitudinal research on benefits of quality early childhood education for low-income children.

Hispanic Books Distributors, Inc., 1870 W. Prince Road, Suite 8, Tucson, AZ 85705. Deals in books in Spanish.

Human Sciences Press, Inc., 72 Fifth Ave., New York, NY 10011. Publishes *Day Care and Early Education,* for young children's educators and child-care professionals. Also more than forty children's books on sensitive topics not found elsewhere.

Iaconi Book Imports, 3030 Pennsylvania Ave., San Francisco, CA 94107. Distributes books in several languages, including Spanish.

International Nanny Association, P. O. Box 26522, Austin, TX 78755. Resources on being a professional nanny.

Mental Health Materials Center, Inc. 419 Park Avenue, New York, NY 10016. Publishes pamphlets and materials useful to professionals; e.g., "Feelings and your child," a series of ten pamphlets about family life with young children, prepared by the Canadian Mental Health Association.

Mexican American Cultural Center, 3019 W. French Place, San Antonio, TX 78228.

National Association for Family Day Care, 815 15th St. NW, Suite 928, Washington, DC 20005. Provides the first accreditation program for family day-care providers and homes.

National Association for Gifted Children, 8080 Springnally Drive, Cincinnati, OH 45236.

National Association for Mental Health, 10 Columbus Circle, Suite 1300, New York, NY 10019.

National Association for the Education of Young Children, 1834 Connecticut Ave. NW, Washington, DC 20009-5786. Publishes *Young Children,* a bimonthly journal, covering early childhood education from practical curriculum ideas to theory and research; also *Early Childhood Research Quarterly.* Includes divisions National Academy of Early Childhood Programs, Child Care Information Service, Week of the Young Child sponsorship, National Institute for Early Childhood Professional Development, and other services.

National Academy of Early Childhood Programs, 1834 Connecticut Ave. NW, Washington, DC 20009. A division of National Association for the Education of Young Children. Provides accreditation for early childhood programs.

National Association of Early Childhood Teacher Educators, Family and Child Ecology, Michigan State University, East Lansing, MI 48824.

National Association of Child Care Resource and Referral Agencies, 2116 Campus Dr. SE, Rochester, MN 55904. Regularly updated resource file of agencies; education about availability, affordability, and quality of child-care services; promotes development of resource and referral services nationwide.

National Association of Hospital Affiliated Programs, Shawnee Mission Medical Center CCC, 9100 W. 74th St., Shawnee Mission, KS 66201.

National Center for Children in Poverty, Columbia University, 154 Haven Ave., New York, NY 10032.

National Center for Clinical Infant Programs, 2000 14th St. N, Suite 380, Arlington, VA 22201. Publishes *Zero to Three* journal.

National Coalition for Campus Child Care, Inc., Southern Illinois University at Edwardsville, Early Childhood Center, Box 1076, Edwardsville, IL 62026.

National Commission on Children, 1111 18th St. NW, Washington, DC 20036.

National Committee for the Prevention of Child Abuse, 332 S. Michigan Ave., Suite 950, Chicago, IL 60604.

National Congress of Parents and Teachers (PTA), 700 N. Rush St., Chicago, IL 60611.

National Dairy Council, 111 N. Canal St., Chicago, IL 60606. Resources on dairy foods, useful for foods curriculum.

National Safety Council, 444 N. Michigan Ave., Chicago, IL 60611. Numerous resources on safety of all kinds for children and adults.

National Wildlife Federation, 1412 16th St. NW, Washington, DC 20036. Publishes

Ranger Rick Magazine and other materials for children on wildlife subjects. Several publications for children of different ages.

Navaho Curriculum Center, Rough Rock Demonstration School, Chinle, AZ 86503.

New Society Publishers, 4527 Springfield Ave., Philadelphia, PA 19143. Books on peace and nonviolence, cooperative games, and the environment.

OMEP (Organisation Mondiale pour L'Éducation Prescolaire), World Organization for Early Childhood Education, 24000 Lahser Road, Southfield, MI 48034.

Opportunities for Learning, Inc. 20417 Nordhoff St., Dept. NB, Chatsworth, CA 91311. Source of children's puppets, videos, cassettes.

Pacific Oaks College, 5 Westmoreland Place, Pasadena, CA 91103. Undergraduate and graduate degrees in professional preparation for teaching. Publishes on topics of teacher development and anti-bias curriculum, among many topics.

Parent Action, 380 W. Maple, Suite 301, Vienna, VA 22180.

Parent Cooperative Preschools International, P.O. Box 90410, Indianapolis, IN 46290.

Purple Crayon, 4110 Opal St., Oakland, CA 94609. Mail-order company featuring culturally diverse books, tapes, and learning materials.

Redleaf Press (formerly Toys 'n Things Press), 450 N. Syndicate, Suite 5, St. Paul, MN 55104. Publishes *Family Day Caring* magazine bimonthly, as well as many other books for centers as well as family daycare providers.

Resources for Child Care Management, 261 Springfield Ave., Suite 201, Berkley Heights, NJ 07922.

Roots and Wings, P. O. Box 350, Jamestown, CO 80455. Mail-order firm carries materials on Native American, bilingual, sign language, ecological, and gifted/talented topics.

Scholastic, Inc., P. O. Box 2075, Mahopac, NY 10541. Publishes *Pre-K Today: The Magazine for Teachers of Infants to Fives,* eight issues yearly. Firefly Book Club, low-cost books for children.

School-Age Child Care Project, Center for Research on Women, Wellesley College, Wellesley, MA 02181.

School Age NOTES, P.O. Box 120674, Nashville, TN 37212. Bimonthly newsletter for professionals in school-age programs.

Scienceland magazine. 501 Fifth Ave., Suite 2101, New York, NY 10017. Beautiful book-like magazine with teachers' guide, on science topics.

Smithsonian/Folkways Recordings, Office of Folklife Programs, 955 L'Enfant Plaza, #2600, Washington, DC 20560.

Society for Research in Child Development, University of Chicago Press, 5801 Ellis Ave., Chicago, IL 60637. Publishes *Monographs, Child Development*, and *Child Development Abstracts and Bibliography*.

South Carolina-ETV/Early Childhood, 2712 Millwood Ave., Drawer L, Columbia, SC 29250. Produces educational videos on early childhood topics, including many for NAEYC.

Southern Association on Children Under Six, Box 5403, Brady Station, Little Rock, AR 72215. Publishes *Dimensions,* a journal for professionals who work with young children.

Stop War Toys Campaign, Box 188, Hampton, CT 06247. Publishes resources and promotes media presentations opposing war toys for children.

Superintendent of Documents: See U. S. Government Printing Office.

Texas Department of Human Services, Corporate Child Development Fund, 510 S. Congress, Suite 122, Austin, TX 78704. Publishes *Texas Child Care Quarterly*.

United Cerebral Palsy Association, 66 E. 34th St., New York, NY 10016.

United States Committee for UNICEF, 331 E. 38th St., New York, NY 10016. Publishes materials depicting children of the world, including books, games, calendars, greetings cards.

U. S. Department of Education, 555 New Jersey Ave. NW, Washington, DC 20208.

U. S. Government Printing Office, Superintendent of Documents, Office of Human Development Services, Washington, DC 20402. Prints informational publications on an astonishing array of topics, many in Spanish; ask for publication lists of Children's Bureau, children and youth topics, Head Start, day care, mainstreaming, child abuse, and more. Publishes *Children Today* six times yearly.

Waldorf Kindergarten Association, 9500 Brunett Ave., Silver Spring, MD 20901.

Wheelock College, 200 The Riverway, Boston, MA 02215. Undergraduate and graduate degrees in professional preparation for nursery school, kindergarten, and primary grades teaching.

Women's Action Alliance, 370 Lexington Ave., New York, NY 10017. Publishes *Equal Play* semi-annually, and other materials on gender bias.

Work/Family Directions, 9 Galen St., Suite 230, Watertown, MA 02712. Excellent resource on corporate-related child care issues.

Bibliography

Abbott-Shim, M., & Sibley, A. (1987). *Assessment profile for early childhood programs*. Atlanta, GA: Quality Assist, P. O. Box 15035.

Adams, C., & Fay, J. (1981). *No more secrets: Protecting your child from sexual assault*. San Luis Obispo, CA: Impact Publishers.

Adcock, D., & Segal, M. (1983). *Play together, grow together: A cooperative curriculum for teachers of young children*. White Plains, NY: Mailman Family Press.

Ade, W. (1982). Professionalization and its implications for the field of early childhood education. *Young Children, 37*(3), 25–32.

Alexander, N. (1986). School-age child care: Concerns and challenges. *Young Children, 42*(1), 3–10.

Alger, H. A. (1984). Transitions: Alternatives to manipulative management techniques. *Young Children, 39*(6), 16–25. Also in J. F. Brown (Ed.). (1984). *Administering programs for young children*. Washington, DC: National Association for the Education of Young Children.

Allen, K. E. (1980). Research in review: Mainstreaming: What have we learned? *Young Children, 35*(5), 54–63.

Almy, M. (1975). *The early childhood educator at work*. New York: Teachers College Press.

Almy, M., & Genishi, C. (1979). *Ways of studying children: An observational manual for early childhood teachers* (rev. ed.). New York: Teachers College Press.

Althouse, R. (1988). *Investigating science with young children*. New York: Teachers College Press.

Althouse, R. (1981). *The young child: Learning with understanding*. New York: Teachers College Press.

Althouse, R., & Main, C. (1975). *Science experiences for young children*. New York: Teachers College Press.

Ames, L., & Haber, C., & the Gesell Institute of Human Development. (1982). *He hit me first: When brothers and sisters fight*. New York: Warner Books.

Anselmo, S., & Zinck, R. A. (1987). Computers for young children? Perhaps. *Young Children 42*(3), 22–27.

Asher, S. R., & Gottman, J. M. (Eds.). (1981). *The development of children's friendships*. New York: Cambridge University Press.

Association for Childhood Education International. (1962). *Report of colloquy on basic human values for childhood education*. Washington, DC: Author.

Association for Childhood Education International. (1979). *The most enabling environment: Education is for all children*. Wheaton, MD: Author.

Association of Teacher Educators, & National Association for the Education of Young Children. (1991). Early childhood teacher certification: A position statement. *Young Children, 47*(1), 16–21.

Ault, R. L. (1983). *Children's cognitive learning*. (2nd ed.). New York: Oxford University Press.

Ayers, W. (1989). *The good preschool teacher: Six teachers reflect on their lives*. New York: Teachers College Press.

Baden, R. K., Genser, A., Levine, J. A., & Seligson, M. (1983). *School-age child care: An action manual*. Boston: Auburn House.

Baghban, M. J. (1984). *Our daughter learns to read and write. A case study from birth to three*. Newark, DE: International Reading Association.

Bahan, B., & Dannis, J. (1990). *Signs for me: Basic sign language for children.* Berkeley, CA: Dawn Sign Press.

Baker, G. C. (1983). *Planning and organizing for multicultural instruction.* Reading, MA: Addison-Wesley.

Baker, K. R. (1966). *Let's play outdoors.* Washington, DC: National Association for the Education of Young Children.

Baker, K. R. (Ed.). (1972). *Ideas that work with young children.* Washington, DC: National Association for the Education of Young Children.

Balaban, N. (1985). *Starting school: From separation to independence.* New York: Teachers College Press.

Balaban, N. (1987). *Learning to say goodbye: Starting school and other early childhood separations.* New York: New American Library.

Baratta-Lorton, M. (1976). *Mathematics their way.* Menlo Park, CA: Addison-Wesley.

Baumrind, D. (1972). Socialization and instrumental competence in young children. In W. W. Hartup (Ed.). *The young child: Reviews of research* (Vol. 2, pp. 202–224.) Washington, DC: National Association for the Education of Young Children.

Beardsley, L. (1990). *Good day/Bad day: The child's experience of child care.* New York: Teachers College Press.

Beaty, J. J. (1986). *Observing development of the young child.* Columbus, OH: Merrill Publishing.

Beaty, J. J. (1991). Computer center. In J. J. Beaty, *Preschool appropriate practices.* pp. 65–95. Fort Worth, TX: Harcourt Brace Jovanovich College Publishers.

Beaty, J. J. (1991). *Preschool appropriate practices.* Fort Worth, TX: Harcourt Brace Jovanovich College Publishers.

Beaty, J. J., & Tucker, W. H. (1987). *The computer as a paintbrush: Creative uses for the personal computer in the preschool classroom.* Columbus, OH: Merrill Publishing.

Beginning Equal Project. (1983). *Beginning equal: A manual about nonsexist child-rearing for infants and toddlers.* New York: Women's Action Alliance and Pre-School Association.

Belsky, J. (1986). Infant day care: A cause for concern? *Zero to Three, 7*(1), 1–7.

Belsky, J. (1988). The "effects" of infant day care reconsidered. *Early Childhood Research Quarterly 3,* 235–272.

Bentzen, W. R. (1985) *Seeing young children: A guide to observing and recording behavior.* Albany, NY: Delmar.

Bergen, D. (Ed.). (1988). *Play as a medium for learning and development: A handbook of theory and practice.* Portsmouth, NH: Heinemann.

Bergstrom, J. M. (1984). *School's out—Now what? Resources for your child's time.* Berkeley, CA: Ten Speed Press.

Berrueta-Clement, J. T., Schweinhart, L. J., Barnett, W. S., & Weikart, D. P. (1984). *Changed lives: The effect of the Perry Preschool Program on youths through age 19.* Ypsilanti, MI: High/Scope Educational Research Foundation.

Bettelheim, B. (1987). *A good enough parent: A book on child-rearing.* New York: Vintage Books.

Biber, B. (1967). *Young deprived children and their educational needs.* Washington, DC: Association for Childhood Education International.

Biber, B. (1977). A developmental-interaction approach: Bank Street College of Education. In M. C. Day & R. K. Parker (Eds.), *The preschool in action* (2nd ed., pp. 423–460). Boston: Allyn & Bacon.

Biber, B. (1985). *Early education and psychological development.* New Haven: Yale University Press.

Bissex, G. (1980). *Gnys at work: A child learns to write and read.* Cambridge, MA: Harvard University Press.

Bjorklund, G., & Burger, C. (1987). Making conferences work for parents, teachers, and children. *Young Children, 42*(2), 26–31.

Blank, M. (1974). Cognitive functions of language in the preschool years. *Developmental Psychology, 10*(2).

Boegehold, B. D., Cuffaro, H. K., Hooks, W. H., & Klopf, G. J. (Eds.) (1977). *Education before five.* New York: Teachers College Press.

Boehm, A. E. & Weinberg, R. A. (1987). *The classroom observer: Developing observation skills in early childhood settings.* (2nd ed.). New York: Teachers College Press.

Bos, B. (1978). *Don't move the muffin tins: A hands-off guide to art for the young child.* Roseville, CA: Turn the Page Press.

Bos, B. (1983). *Before the basics: Creating conversations with children,* Roseville, CA: Turn the Page Press.

Bos, B. (1990). *Together we're better.* Roseville, CA: Turn the Page Press.

Bowlby, J. (1982). Attachment and loss: Retrospects and prospect. *American Journal of Orthopsychiatry, 52*(4), 664–678.

Bowlby, J. (1975). *Separation anxiety: A critical review of the literature.* New York: Child Welfare League of America.

Brady, E. J., & Hill, S. (1984). Research in review: Young children and microcomputers: Research issues and directions. *Young Children, 39*(3), 49–61.

Braun, S. J., & Edwards, E. P. (1972). *History and theory of early childhood education.* Worthington, OH: Charles A. Jones.

Brazelton, T. B. (1984). *To listen to a child: Understanding the normal problems of growing up.* Reading, MA: Addison-Wesley.

Brazelton, T. B. (1974). *Toddlers and parents: A declaration of independence.* New York: Delacorte.

Brazelton, T. B. (1981). *On becoming a family.* New York: Delacorte.

Brazelton, T. B. (1983). *Infants and mothers: Differences in development.* New York: Delacorte.

Brazelton, T. B. (1985). *Working and caring.* Reading, MA: Addison-Wesley.

Brazelton, T. B. (1989). *Families: Crisis and caring.* New York: Ballantine Books.

Brearley, M. (Ed.). (1970). *The teaching of young children: Some applications of Piaget's learning theory.* New York: Schocken Books.

Brearley, M., & Hitchfield, E. (1966). *A guide to reading Piaget.* New York: Schocken Books.

Bredekamp, S. (1989). *Regulating child care quality: Evidence from NAEYC's accreditation system.* Washington, DC: National Association for the Education of Young Children.

Bredekamp, S. (1990). Achieving model early childhood programs through accreditation. In Seefeldt, C. (1990). *Continuing issues in early childhood education.* (pp. 301–309). Columbus, OH: Merrill Publishing.

Bredekamp, S. (1990). Extra-year programs: A response to Brewer and Uphoff. *Young Children 45*(6), 20–21. (See Brewer (1990), and Uphoff (1990).)

Bredekamp, S. (Ed.). (1987). *Developmentally appropriate practice in early childhood programs serving children from birth through age 8.* (Exp. ed.). Washington, DC: National Association for the Education of Young Children.

Bredekamp, S., & Apple, P. (1986). How early childhood programs get accredited: An analysis of accreditation decisions. *Young Children, 42*(1), 34–38.

Bredekamp, S., & Berby, J. (1987). Maintaining quality: Accredited programs one year later. *Young Children, 43*(1), 13–15.

Bredekamp, S., & Shepard, L. (1989). How best to protect children from inappropriate school expectations, practices, and policies. *Young Children, 44*(3), 14–24.

Bredekamp, S., & Willer, B. (1992). Of ladders and lattices, cores and cones: Conceptualizing an early childhood professional development system. *Young Children, 47*(3), 47–50.

Brewer, J. A. (1990). Transitional programs: Boon or bane? *Young Children 45*(6), 15–18.

Briggs, D. (1970). *Your child's self-esteem: The key to his life.* Garden City, NY: Doubleday.

Brown, B. (1985). Head Start: How research changed public policy. *Young Children 40*(5), 9–13.

Brown, J. F. (Ed.). (1982). *Curriculum planning for young children.* Washington, DC: National Association for the Education of Young Children.

Brown, J. F. (Ed.). (1984). *Administering programs for young children.* Washington, DC: National Association for the Education of Young Children.

Brown, N. S., Curry, N. E., & Tittnich, E. (1971). How groups of children handle common stress through play. In G. Engstrom (Ed.). *Play: The child strives toward self-realization.* (pp. 26–38.) Washington, DC: National Association for the Education of Young Children.

Bruner, J. S. (1966). *Toward a theory of instruction.* Cambridge, MA: Harvard University Press.

Bruner, J., & Cole, M. (1990). *Infancy: The developing child.* Cambridge, MA: Harvard University Press.

Buckleitner, W. (1991). *Survey of early childhood software.* Ypsilanti, MI: High/Scope Press.

Bundy, B. F. (1991). Fostering communication between parents and preschools. *Young Children, 46*(2), 12–17.

Burg, K. (1984). The microcomputer in the kindergarten. *Young Children, 39*(3), 28–33.

Burke, E. M. (1990). *Literature for the young child* (2nd ed.). Needham Heights, MA: Allyn & Bacon.

Burns, M. S., Goin, L., & Donlon, J. T. (1990). A computer in my room. *Young Children 45*(2), 62–67.

Caldwell, B. (1977). Aggression and hostility in young children. *Young Children, 32*(2), 4–13.

Caldwell, B. (1987, March). Advocacy is everybody's business. *Child Care Information Exchange,* pp. 29–32.

Caldwell, B. M., & Hilliard, A. G. III. (1985). *What is quality child care?* Washington, DC: National Association for the Education of Young Children.

Campbell, P. F., & Fein, G. G. (1986). *Young children and microcomputers,* Englewood Cliffs, NJ: Prentice-Hall.

Carlevale, J. M. (1985). *Observing, recording, interpreting child behavior: A workbook.* (2nd ed., rev.). West Greenwich, RI: Consortium Publishing. (To accompany Cohen, Stern, and Balaban, *Observing and recording the behavior of young children,* 3rd ed.)

Carlsson-Paige, N., & Levin, D. E. (1985). *Helping young children understand peace, war, and the nuclear threat.* Washington, DC: National Association for the Education of Young Children.

Carlsson-Paige, N., & Levin, D. (1986). The Butter Battle Book: Uses and abuses with young children. *Young Children, 41*(3), 37–42.

Carlsson-Paige, N., & Levin, D. (1987). *The war play dilemma: Balancing needs and values in the early childhood classroom.* New York: Teachers College Press.

Carlsson-Paige, N., & Levin, D. (1990). *Who's calling the shots? How to respond effectively to children's fascination with war play and war toys.* Philadelphia: New Society Publishers.

Carr, R. (1973). *Be a frog, a bird, or a tree: Creative yoga exercises for children.* New York: Harper & Row.

Caruso, J. J., & Fawcett, M. T. (1986). *Supervision in early childhood education.* New York: Teachers College Press.

Cataldo, C. Z. (1987). *Parent education for early childhood: Child-rearing concepts and program content for the student and practicing professional.* New York: Teachers College Press.

Caughey, C. (1991). Becoming the child's ally—Observations in a classroom for children who have been abused. *Young Children, 46*(4), 22–28.

Cazden, C. (Ed.). (1981) *Language in early childhood education* (rev. ed.). Washington, DC: National Association for the Education of Young Children.

Cazden, C., Baratz, J., Labov, W., & Palmer, F. (1981). Language development in day care programs. In C. Cazden (Ed.). (1981). *Language in early childhood education* (rev. ed.). Washington, DC: National Association for the Education of Young Children.

Charlesworth, R. (1985, Spring). Readiness: Should we make them ready or let them bloom? *Day Care and Early Education,* pp. 25–27.

Chattin-McNichols, J. P. (1981). The effects of Montessori school experience. *Young Children, 36*(5), 49–66.

Cherry, C. (1981). *Think of something quiet.* Belmont, CA: David S. Lake Publishers.

Cherry, C. (1986). *Creative play for the developing child: Early lifehood education through play.* Belmont, CA: Fearon Pitman Publishers.

Cherry, C., Harkness, B., & Kuzma, K. (1978). *Nursery school and day care center management guide.* (rev. 2nd ed.). Belmong, CA: Fearon Pitman Publishers.

Chess, S., & Thomas, A. (1987). *Know your child: An authoritative guide for today's parents.* New York: Basic Books.

Chess, S., Thomas, A., & Birch, H. G. (1978). *Your child is a person.* New York: Penguin Books.

Children's Defense Fund. (1984). *A children's defense budget: An analysis of the president's FY 1985 budget and children.* Washington, DC: Author.

Children's Defense Fund. (1990a). *Children 1990: A report card, briefing book, and action primer.* Washington, DC: Author.

Children's Defense Fund. (1990b). *S.O.S. America!: A children's defense fund budget.* Washington, DC: Author.

Children's Defense Fund. (1991). *State of America's Children: 1991.* Washington, DC: Author.

Chisholm, B. (1949). Social responsibility. *Science, 109,* 27–30, 43.

Clarke-Stewart, S. (1982). *Daycare.* (The developing child series.) Cambridge, MA: Harvard University Press.

Clay, J. W. (1990). Working with lesbian and gay parents and their children. *Young Children, 45*(3), 31–35.

Clemens, S. G. (1991). Art in the classroom: Making every day special. *Young Children, 46*(2), 4–11.

Clements, D. H. (1987). Computers and young children: A review of research. *Young Children, 43*(1), 34–44.

Cleverley, J., & Phillips, D. C. (1986). *Visions of childhood: Influential models from Locke to Spock.* New York: Teachers College Press.

Clewett, A. S. (1988). Guidance and discipline: Teaching young children appropriate behavior. *Young Children, 43*(4), 26–31.

Click, P. M., & Click, D. W. (1990). *Administration of schools for young children.* (3rd ed.). Albany, NY: Delmar.

Cohen, D., Stern, V. & Balaban, N. (1983) *Observing and recording the behavior of young children.* (3d ed.) New York: Teachers College Press. (See Carlevale for accompanying workbook).

Cole, J., & Calmenson, S. (1989). *Safe from the start: Your child's safety from birth to age five—at home, at play, in the car.* New York: Facts on File.

Coleman, M. (1991). Planning for the changing nature of family life in schools for young children. *Young Children, 46*(4), 15–20.

Cook, J. T. (1985). *Child daycare.* Davis, CA: International Dialogue Press.

Cooper, T. T., & Ratner, M. (1974). *Many hands cooking: An international cookbook for girls and boys.* New York: Thomas Y. Crowell in cooperation with UNICEF.

Cornell, J. (1979). *Sharing nature with children.* Nevada City, CA: Dawn Publications.

Cornell, J. (1989). *Sharing the joy of nature: Nature activities for all ages.* Nevada City, CA: Dawn Publications.

Corsaro, W. A. (1985). *Friendship and peer culture in the early years.* Norwood, NJ: Ablex.

Council for Early Childhood Professional Recognition. (1989). *National directory of early childhood training programs.* Washington, DC: Author.

Council on Interracial Books for Children. (1980). *Guidelines for selecting bias-free textbooks and storybooks.* New York: Author.

Council on Interracial Books for Children. (1983). Counteracting bias in early childhood education. *Interracial Books for Children Bulletin, 14*(7 & 8).

Croft, D. J. (1990). *An activities handbook for teachers of young children.* (5th ed.). Boston, MA: Houghton Mifflin.

Cryan, J. R. (1987). *The banning of corporal punishment in child care, school and other educative settings in the United States.* A position paper. Wheaton, MD: Association for Childhood Education International.

Cuddigan, M., & Hanson, M. B. (1988). *Growing pains: Helping children deal with everyday problems through reading.* Chicago, IL: American Library Association.

Curry, N., & Johnson, C. (1990). *Beyond self-esteem: Developing a genuine sense of human value.* (Research Monograph, Vol. 4.) Washington, DC: National Association for the Education of Young Children.

Curtis, S. (1982). *The joy of movement in early childhood.* New York: Teachers College Press.

Davidson, J. (1980). Wasted time: The ignored dilemma. *Young Children, 35*(4), 13–21. Also in J. F. Brown (Ed.). (1982). *Curriculum planning for young children.* (pp. 196–204.) Washington, DC: National Association for the Education of Young Children.

Davidson, J. I. (1989). *Children and computers together in the early childhood classroom.* Albany, NY: Delmar.

Day, M. C., & Parker, R. K. (Eds.). (1977). *The preschool in action* (2nd ed.). Boston: Allyn & Bacon.

Decker, C. A., & Decker, J. R. (1988). *Planning and administering early childhood programs* (4th ed.). Columbus, OH: Merrill Publishing.

Deiner, P. L. (1983). *Resources for teaching young children with special needs.* New York: Harcourt Brace Jovanovich.

Deitch, S. R. (Ed.). (1982). *Health in day care: A manual for health professionals.* Committee on Early Childhood Adoption and Dependent Care. Elk Grove Village, IL: American Academy of Pediatrics.

Derman-Sparks, L., & the A.B.C. Task Force. (1989). *Anti-bias curriculum: Tools for empowering young children.* Washington, DC: National Association for the Education of Young Children.

Derman-Sparks, L., Gutierrez, M., & Phillips, C. B. (1989). *Teaching young children to resist bias: What parents can do.* (Brochure #565; single copies $0.50.) Washington, DC: National Association for the Education of Young Children.

Derman-Sparks, L., Higa, C. T., & Sparks, B. (1980). Children, race and racism: How race awareness develops. *Interracial Books for Children Bulletin, 11*(3 & 4), 315.

DeVries, R., & Kohlberg, L. (1990.) *Constructivist early education: Overview and comparison with other programs.* Washington, DC: National Association for the Education of Young Children.

Dimidjian, V. J. (1989). Holidays, holy days, and wholly dazed: Approaches to special days. *Young Children, 44*(6), 70–75.

Dinkmeyer, D., McKay, G. D., & Dinkmeyer, J. S. (1989.). *Parenting young children.* Circle Pines, MN: American Guidance Service.

Dittman, L. L. (1985). *Finding the best care for your infant or toddler.* (Brochure #518; single copies $0.50.) Washington, DC: National Association for the Education of Young Children.

Dittmann, L. L. (Ed.). (1977) *Curriculum is what happens: Planning is the key.* (rev. ed.). Washington, DC: National Association for the Education of Young Children.

Dittmann, L. L. (Ed.). (1984). *The infants we care for.* Washington, DC: National Association for the Education of Young Children.

Donaldson, M. (1978). *Children's minds.* New York: W. W. Norton.

Dunn, J. (1977). *Distress and comfort.* (The developing child series.) Cambridge MA: Harvard University Press.

Education News Service. (n.d.). *Only the best: The discriminating software guide for children preschool—12.* Carmichael, CA, P. O. Box 1789, 95609: Author.

Edwards, C. P. (1986). *Promoting social and moral development in young children: Creative approaches for the classroom.* New York: Teachers College Press.

Edwards, C. P., with Ramsey, P. G. (1986). *Promoting social and moral development in young children.* New York: Teachers College Press.

Eliason, C. F., & Jenkins, L. T. (1990). *A practical guide to early childhood curriculum.* (4th ed.). Columbus, OH: Merrill Publishing.

Elkind, D. (1967). Piaget and Montessori. *Harvard Education Review, 37*(4), 535–545.

Elkind, D. (1986). Formal education and early childhood education: An essential difference. *Phi Delta Kappan,* pp. 631–636.

Elkind, D. (1987a). *Miseducation: Preschoolers at risk.* New York: Knopf.

Elkind, D. (1987b). Multiage grouping. *Young Children, 43*(1), 2.

Elkind, D. (1988a). *The hurried child: Growing up too fast too soon.* (rev. ed.). Reading, MA: Addison-Wesley.

Elkind, D. (1988b). Parent involvement. *Young Children, 43*(2), 2.

Endres, J. B., & Rockwell, R. E. (1985). *Food, nutrition, and the young child.* (2nd ed.). Columbus, OH: Merrill Publishing.

Engstrom, G. (Ed.). (1971a). *Play: The child strives toward self-realization.* Washington, DC: National Association for the Education of Young Children.

Engstrom, G., (Ed.). (1971b). *The significance of the young child's motor development.* Washington, DC: National Association for the Education of Young Children.

Erikson, E. (1959). *Identity and the life cycle* (Vol. 1, No. 1). New York: International Press.

Erikson, E. (1963). *Childhood and society.* New York: W. W. Norton.

Esbensen, S. G. (1987). *The early childhood playground: An outdoor classroom.* Ypsilanti, MI: High/Scope Press.

Essa, E. (1990). *A practical guide to solving preschool behavior problems.* (2nd ed.). Albany, NY: Delmar.

Faber, A., & Mazlish, E. (1980). *How to talk so kids will listen and listen so kids will talk.* New York: Avon.

Fassler, J. (1978). *Helping children cope: Mastering stress through books and stories,* New York: The Free Press.

Fassler, J., & Janis, M. G. (1983). Books, children, and peace. *Young Children* *38*(6), 21–30.

Favaro, P. (1983). My five year old knows BASIC. *Creative Computing* *9*(4), 158–166.

Feeney, S., & Kipnis, K. (1985). Professional ethics in early childhood education. *Young Children, 40*(3) 54–57.

Feeney, S., & Kipnis, K. (1990). *Code of ethical conduct and statement of commitment.* (Brochure #503; single copies $0.50.) Washington, DC: National Association for the Education of Young Children.

Feeney, S., & Maravcik, E. (1987). A thing of beauty: Aesthetic development in young children. *Young Children, 42*(6), 6–15.

Feeney, S., & Sysko, L. (1986). Professional ethics in early childhood education: Survey results. *Young Children, 42*(1), 15–20.

Fein, G. & Rivkin, M. (Eds.). (1986). *The young child at play: Reviews of research* (Vol. 4). Washington, DC: National Association for the Education of Young Children.

Fennimore, B. S. (1989). *Child advocacy for early childhood educators.* New York: Teachers College Press.

Ferber, R. (1985). *Solve your child's sleep problems.* New York: Simon and Schuster.

Ferreiro, E., & Teberosky, A. (1982). *Literacy before schooling.* Portsmouth, NH: Heinemann.

Fields, M. V. (1989). *Literacy begins at birth: A revolutionary approach in whole language learning.* Tucson, AZ: Fisher Books.

Fleming, B. M., & Hamilton, D. S. (1990). *Resources for creative teaching in early childhood education.* (2d ed.). New York: Harcourt Brace Jovanovich.

Forman, G., & Hill, F. (1984) *Constructive play: Applying Piaget in the preschool.* (rev. ed.). Reading, MA: Addison-Wesley.

Forman, G., & Kuschner, D. S. (1977). *The child's construction of knowledge: Piaget for teaching children.* Monterey, CA: Brooks/Cole.

Fraiberg, S. (1959). *The magic years: Understanding and handling the problems of early childhood.* New York: Scribner's.

Freedman, P. (1982). A comparison of multiage and homogeneous age grouping in early childhood centers. In L. G. Katz (Ed.). *Current topics in early childhood education* (Vol. 4). Norwood, NJ: Ablex. Pp. 193–209.

Freeman, L. (1982). *It's my body: A book to teach young children how to resist uncomfortable touch.* Seattle, WA: Parenting Press, Inc.

Freeman, L. (1986). *Loving touches.* Seattle, WA: Parenting Press, Inc.

Friedrich-Cofer, L., & Huston, A. C. (1986) Television violence and aggression: The debate continues. *Psychological Bulletin* 100, 364–371.

Froschl, M., Colon, L., Rubin, E., & Sprung, B. (1984). *Including all of us: An early childhood curriculum about disability.* New York: Educational Equity Concepts, 440 Park Ave. S, New York 10016.

Frost, J. L., & Klein, B. L. (1979). *Children's play and playgrounds.* Boston, MA: Allyn and Bacon.

Frost, J. L., & Sunderlin, S. (Eds.). (1985). *When children play: Proceedings of the international conference on play and play environments.* Wheaton, MD: Association for Childhood Education International.

Frost, J. L., & Wortham, S. C. (1988). The evolution of American playgrounds. *Young Children, 43*(5), 19–28.

Furman, E. (1978). Helping children cope with death. *Young Children, 33*(4), 25–32.

Galinsky, E. (1988). Parents and teacher-caregivers: Sources of tension, sources of support. *Young Children, 43*(3), 4–12.

Galinsky, E. (1989). Update on employer-supported child care. *Young Children 44*(6), 2, 75–77.

Galinsky, E. (1990a). The costs of *not* providing quality early childhood programs. In B. Willer, (Ed.). (1990) *Reaching the full cost of quality in early childhood programs.* Washington, DC: National Association for the Education of Young Children.

Galinsky, E. (1990b). Government and child care. *Young Children 45*(3), 2–3, 76–77.

Galinsky, E. (1990c). Raising children in the 1990s: The challenges for parents, educators, and business. *Young Children, 45*(2), 2–3, 67–69.

Galinsky, E. (1990d). Why are some parent/teacher partnerships clouded with difficulties? *Young Children, 45*(5), 2–3, 38–39.

Galinsky, E., & David, J. (1988). *The preschool years: Family strategies that work—from experts and parents.* New York: Ballantine Books.

Gallagher, J. M., & Coche, J. (1987). Hot-housing: The clinical and educational concerns over pressuring young children. *Early Childhood Research Quarterly, 2,* 203–210.

Garvey, C. (1977). *Play.* (The developing child series.) Cambridge, MA: Harvard University Press.

Garvey, C. (1984). *Children's talk.* (The developing child series.) Cambridge, MA: Harvard University Press.

Genishi, C. (1988). Research in review. Children's language: Learning words from experience. *Young Children, 44*(1), 16–23.

George, F. (1975). Checklist for a non-sexist classroom. *Young Children 45*(2), 10–11. From B. Sprung. (1975). *Non-sexist education for young children: A practical guide.* New York: Women's Action Alliance.

Gibson, L. (1989). *Literacy learning in the early years: Through children's eyes.* New York: Teachers College Press.

Glazer, J. (1991). *Literature for young children* (3rd ed.). New York: Merrill Publishing.

Godwin, A., & Schrag, L. (Eds.). (1988). *Setting up for infant care: Guidelines for centers and family day care homes.* Washington, DC: National Association for the Education of Young Children.

Goffin, S. G. (1988). Putting our advocacy efforts into a new context. *Young Children, 43*(3), 52–56.

Goffin, S. G., & Lombardi, J. (1988). *Speaking out: Early childhood advocacy.* Washington, DC: National Association for the Education of Young Children.

Golant, S. K. (1991). *The joys and challenges of raising a gifted child.* New York: Prentice Hall.

Gonzalez-Mena, J. (1992). Taking a culturally sensitive approach in infant-toddler programs. *Young Children, 47*(2), 4–9.

Gonzalez-Mena, J., & Eyer, D. W. (1989). *Infants, toddlers, and caregivers.* (2nd ed.). Mountain View, CA: Mayfield Publishing Co.

Goodnow, J. (1977). *Children's drawing.* (The developing child series.) Cambridge, MA: Harvard University Press.

Gordon, S., & Gordon, J. (1989). *Raising a child conservatively in a sexually permissive world.* (rev.). New York: Simon & Schuster.

Gordon, T. (1970) *P.E.T.: Parent Effectiveness Training.* Available in Spanish: *Padres Eficaz y Tecnicamente Preparados.* New York: Peter Wyden.

Gordon, T. (1976) *P.E.T. in action.* New York: Peter Wyden.

Gordon, T. (1989). *Teaching children self-discipline: At home and at school.* New York: Times Books.

Gottschall, S. (1989). Understanding and accepting separation feelings. *Young Children 44*(6), 11–16.

Green, M. I. (1977). *A sigh of relief: The first aid handbook for childhood emergencies.* New York: Bantam Books.

Greenberg, P. (1989a). *Encouraging self-esteem and self-discipline: Character development in young children.* Washington, DC: National Association for the Education of Young Children.

Greenberg, P. (1989b). Parents as partners in young children's development and education: A new American fad? Why does it matter? *Young Children 44*(4), 61–75.

Greenberg, P. (1990a). Head Start—Part of a multi-pronged anti-poverty effort for children and their families. . . . Before the beginning: A participant's view. *Young Children 45*(6) 40–52.

Greenberg, P. (1990b). Ideas that work with young children: Why not academic preschool? *Young Children 42*(2), 70–80.

Greenberg, P. (1991). *Character development: Encouraging self-esteem and self-discipline in infants, toddlers, and two-year-olds.* Washington, DC: National Association for the Education of Young Children.

Greenberg, P., (Ed.) (1991). *Beginner's bibliography—1991.* Washington, DC: National Association for the Education of Young Children.

Greenberg, P. (1992). Why not academic preschool? (Part 2). Autocracy or democracy in the classroom? *Young Children 47*(3), 54–64.

Greenman, J. (1988). *Caring spaces, learning spaces: Children's environments that work.* Redmond, WA: Exchange Press, Inc.

Griffin, E. F. (1982). *Island of childhood: Education in the special world of nursery school.* New York: Teachers College Press.

Hale-Benson, J. (1986) *Black children: Their roots, culture, and learning style* (rev. ed.). Baltimore, MD: Johns Hopkins University Press.

Harms, T., & Clifford, R. M. (1980). *Early childhood environment rating scale.* New York: Teachers College Press.

Harms, T., & Clifford, R. M. (1989). *Family day care rating scale.* New York: Teachers College Press.

Harms, T., Cryer, D., & Clifford, R. M. (1990). *Infant/toddler environment rating scale.* New York: Teachers College Press.

Harris, V. J. (1991). Research in review: Multicultural curriculum: African American children's literature. *Young Children, 46*(2), 37–44.

Hartley, R. E., Frank, L. K., & Goldenson, R. M. (1952). *Understanding children's play.* New York: Columbia University Press.

Haswell, K. L., Jock, E., & Wenar, C. (1982). Techniques for dealing with oppositional behavior in preschool children. *Young Children, 37*(3), 12–18. Also in J. F. Brown (Ed.). (1982). *Curriculum planning for young children.* (pp. 221–227.)

Haugland, S. W., & Shade, D. D. (1988). Developmentally appropriate software for young children. *Young Children, 43*(4), 37–43.

Haugland, S. W. & Shade, D. D. (1990). *Developmental evaluations of software for young children.* Albany, NY: Delmar Publishers.

Healy, J. M. (1987). *Your child's growing mind.* Garden City, NY: Doubleday.

Hegland, S. (1984). Teacher supervision: A model for advancing professional growth. *Young Children, 39*(4), 3–10.

Hendrick, J. B. (1987). *Why teach?* Washington, DC: National Association for the Education of Young Children.

Hendrick, J. B. (1988). *The whole child: Developmental education for the early years* (4th ed.). Columbus, OH: Merrill Publishing.

Hendrick, J. B. (1990). *Total learning: Developmental curriculum for the young child* (3rd ed.). Columbus, OH: Merrill Publishing.

Hendrick, J. B. (1992). Where does it all begin? Teaching the principles of democracy in the early years. *Young Children 47*(3), 51–53.

Hesse, P., & Center for Psychological Studies in the Nuclear Age. (1989). *The world is a dangerous place: Images of the enemy on children's television.* (video tape). Cambridge, MA: Harvard University Press.

Hewes, D., & Hartman, B. (1988). *Early childhood education: A workbook for administrators* (rev. ed.). Saratoga, CA: R & E Publishers.

Hill, D. M. (1977). *Mud, sand and water.* Washington, DC: National Association for the Education of Young Children.

Hirsch, E. S., (Ed.). (1984). *The block book* (rev. ed.). Washington, DC: National Association for the Education of Young Children.

Hitz, R., & Driscoll, A. (1988). Praise or encouragement? New insights into praise: Implications for early childhood teachers. *Young Children 43*(5), 6–13.

Hodge, B., & Tripp, D. (1987) *Children and television.* Cambridge, MA: Polity Press.

Hogan, P. (1988). *The playground safety checker: A checklist approach to risk management* (rev. ed.). Phoenixville, PA: Playground Press.

Hohmann, M. (1983). *Study guide to "Young children in action."* Ypsilanti, MI: High/Scope Press.

Hohmann, M., Banet, B. & Weikart, D. P. (1979). *Young children in action: A manual for preschool educators.* Ypsilanti, MI: High/Scope Press.

Holdaway, D. (1979). *The foundations of literacy.* New York: Ashton Scholastic.

Holt, B. (1989). *Science with young children* (rev. ed.). Washington, DC: National Association for the Education of Young Children.

Honey, E., Piatkowska, A., & Brown, D. (1988). *Festivals: Ideas from around the world.* Melbourne, Australia: Thomas Nelson.

Honig, A. S. (1979). *Parent involvement in early childhood education* (rev. ed.). Washington, DC: National Association for the Education of Young Children.

Honig, A. S. (1983). TV violence and child aggression: Research review. *Day Care and Early Education, 10*(4), 41–45.

Honig, A. S. (1985) Research in review: Compliance, control and discipline (Parts 1 & 2). *Young Children, 40*(2), 50–58; 40(3), 47–52.

Honig, A. S. (1986). Research in review: Stress and coping in children. In J. B. McCracken (Ed.), *Reducing stress in young children's lives* (pp. 142–167). Washington, DC: National Association for the Education of Young Children.

Honig, A. S. (1987). *Love and learn: Discipline for young children.* (Brochure #528; single copies $0.50.) Washington, DC: National Association for the Education of Young Children.

Horner, C. T. (1988). *The single-parent family in children's books: An annotated bibliography.* (2nd ed.). Metuchen, NJ: Scarecrow.

Hostetler, L. (1991). Scuds, sorties, and yellow ribbons: The costs of war for children. *Young Children, 46*(3), 2.

Howes, C. (1989). Infant child care. *Young Children, 44*(6), 24–28.

Howes, C., & Farver, S. A. (1987). Social pretend play in two-year-olds: Effects of age of partner. *Early Childhood Research Quarterly, 2,* 305–314.

Hrncir, E. J., & Eisenhart, C. E. (1991). Use with caution: The "at-risk" label. *Young Children, 46*(2), 23–27.

Huntington, D. E. (1939). *Let's go outdoors.* New York: Doubleday.

Hymes, J. L. Jr. (1981). *Teaching the child under six* (3rd ed.). Columbus, OH: Merrill Publishing.

Hymes, J. L., Jr. (1991). *Early childhood education: Twenty years in review: A look at 1971–1990.* Washington, DC: National Association for the Education of Young Children.

Hymes, J. L., Jr., with Ginsberg, S., Stolz, L. M., & Goldsmith, C. (1978). *Early childhood education: Living history interviews. Book 2: Care of the children of working mothers.* Carmel, CA: Hacienda Press.

Hymes, J. L., Jr., with Henig, C., Osborn, D. K., & Horwich, F. R. (1979). *Early childhood education: Living history interviews. Book 3: Reaching large numbers of children.* Carmel, CA: Hacienda Press.

Isenberg, J., & Quisenberry, N. L. (1988). *Play: A necessity for all children.* Wheaton, MD: Association for Childhood Education International.

Jalongo, M. R. (1988). *Young children and picture books: Literature from infancy to six.* Washington, DC: National Association for the Education of Young Children.

Jalongo, M. R. (1987). Do security blankets belong in preschool? *Young Children 42*(3), 3–8.

Jalongo, M. R. (1990). The child's right to the expressive arts: Nurturing the imagination as well as the intellect. A position paper of the Association for Childhood Education International. *Childhood Education 66*(4), 195–201.

Jensen, M. A., & Chevalier, Z. W. (Eds.). (1990). *Issues and advocacy in early education.* Needham Heights, MA: Allyn & Bacon.

Jervis, K. (Ed.). (1985). *A guide to separation: Strategies for helping two to four-year-olds.* Los Angeles, CA: Edna Reiss Memorial Trust.

Jewett, C. L. (1982). *Helping children cope with separation and loss.* Harvard, MA: Harvard Common Press.

Johnsen, K. (1986). *The trouble with secrets.* Seattle, WA: Parenting Press, Inc.

Johnson, B., & Plemons, B. (1978). *Cup cooking: Individual child portion picture recipes.* Lake Alfred, FL: Early Educator's Press; distributed by Gryphon House., Mt. Rainier, MD. Accompanied by Johnson, B. (1978). *Cup cooking starter set: Single step charts for child portion picture recipes.* Lake Alfred, FL: Early Educator's Press.

Johnson, H. M. (1972. Originally published 1928). *Children in "The Nursery School."* New York: Agathon.

Johnson, J. E., Christie, J. F., & Yawkey, T. D. (1987). *Play and early childhood de-*

velopment. Glenview, IL: Scott, Foresman and Co.

Jones, E. (1977). *Dimensions of teaching-learning environments: Handbook for teachers*. Pasadena, CA: Pacific Oaks College.

Jones, E. (1986). *Teaching adults: An active learning approach*. Washington, DC: National Association for the Education of Young Children.

Jones, E. (Ed.). (1978). *Joys and risks in teaching young children*. Pasadena, CA: Pacific Oaks College.

Jones, E., & Derman-Sparks, L. (1992). Meeting the challenge of diversity. *Young Children 47*(2), 12–18.

Jordan, J., Gallagher, J., Hutinger, P., & Karnes, M. (Eds.). (1988). *Early childhood special education: Birth to three*. Reston, VA: Council for Exceptional Children.

Jorde, P. (1982). *Avoiding burnout: Strategies for managing time, space, and people in early childhood education*. Washington, DC: Acropolis Books.

Jorde-Bloom, P. (1986). Teacher job satisfaction: A framework for analysis. *Early Childhood Research Quarterly, 1*, 167–183.

Jorde-Bloom, P. (1988). *A great place to work: Improving conditions for staff in young children's programs*. Washington, DC: National Association for the Education of Young Children.

Jorde-Bloom, P., Sheerer, M., & Britz, J. (1991). *Blueprint for action: Achieving center-based change through staff development*. Lake Forest, IL: New Horizons.

Kaden, M. (1990). Issues on computers and early childhood education. In C. Seefeldt, (1990). *Continuing issues in early childhood education*. (pp. 261–275). Columbus, OH: Merrill Publishing.

Kagan, J. (1984). *The nature of the child*. New York: Basic Books.

Kagan, S. L., & Garcia, E. E. (Eds.). (1991). (Special issue.) Educating linguistically and culturally diverse preschoolers. *Early Childhood Research Quarterly, 6*(3), 303–443.

Kagan, S. L., & Zigler, E. F. (Eds.). (1987). *Early schooling: The national debate*. New Haven, CT: Yale University Press.

Kamii, C. (1982a). Leading primary education toward excellence: Beyond worksheets and drill. *Young Chilren, 40*(6), 3–9.

Kamii, C. (1982b). *Number in preschool and kindergarten: Educational implications of Piaget's theory*. Washington, DC: National Association for the Education of Young Children.

Kamii, C. (Ed.). (1990). *Achievement testing in the early grades: The games grown-ups play*. Washington, DC: National Association for the Education of Young Children.

Kamii, C., & DeVries, R. (1980). *Group games in early education: Implications of Piaget's theory*. Washington, DC: National Association for the Education of Young Children.

Kamii, C., with DeClark, G. (1984). *Young children reinvent arithmetic: Implications of Piaget's theory*. New York: Teachers College Press.

Kantrowitz, B., & Wingert, P. (1989). How kids learn. *Young Children 44*(6), 3–10. Reprinted from *Newsweek*, April 17, 1989.

Kaplan, R. (1987). *The parents' emergency medical guide*. New York: McGraw-Hill.

Katz, L. G. (1972). Developmental stages of preschool teachers. *Elementary School Journal, 23*(1), 50–54.

Katz, L. G. (1977a). *Ethical issues in working with children*. Urbana, IL: ERIC

Clearinghouse on Elementary and Early Childhood Education (ED 144 681).

Katz, L. G. (1977b). *Talks with teachers: Reflections on early childhood education.* Washington, DC: National Association for the Education of Young Children.

Katz, L. G. (1980). Mothering and teaching: Some significant distinctions. In L. G. Katz (Ed.), *Current topics in early childhood education* (V. 3, pp. 47–63). Norwood, NJ: Ablex.

Katz, L. G. (1984). The professional early childhood teacher. *Young Children, 39*(5), 3–10.

Katz, L. G. (1991). Guidelines for the assessment of young children. In *ERIC/EECE Newsletter 3*(2), 2.

Katz, L. G., & Chard, S. C. (1989). *Engaging children's minds: The project approach.* Norwood, NJ: Ablex.

Katz, L. G., & Ward, E. H. (1978). *Ethical behavior in early childhood education* (expanded ed.). Washington, DC: National Association for the Education of Young Children.

Katz, L. G., Evangelou, D., & Hartman, J. A. (1990). *The case for mixed-age grouping in early childhood education.* Washington, DC: National Association for the Education of Young Children.

Katz, P. A. (1982). Development of children's racial awareness and intergroup attitudes. In L. G. Katz (Ed.). *Current topics in early childhood education.* (pp. 17–54). Norwood, NJ: Ablex.

Kehoe, P. (1987). *Something happened and I'm scared to tell: A book for young victims of abuse.* Seattle, WA: Parenting Press, Inc.

Kellogg, R. (1979). *Children's drawings/children's minds.* New York: Avon.

Kemmer, E. (1984). *Violence in the family: An annotated bibliography.* New York: Garland.

Kendall, F. E. (1983). *Diversity in the classroom: A multicultural approach to the education of young children.* New York: Teachers College Press.

Kendrick, A. S., Kaufmann, R., & Messenger, K. P. (1990). *Keeping healthy: Parents, teachers, and children.* (Brochure #577; single copies $0.50.) (Companion poster #777.) Washington, DC: National Association for the Education of Young Children.

Kendrick, A. S., Kaufmann, R., & Messenger, K. P. (Eds.). (1991). *Healthy young children: A manual for programs.* Washington, DC: National Association for the Education of Young Children.

Keyes, C. R., & Schwartz, S. L. (Eds.). (1991). (Special issue). Campus Children's Centers: Coming of age. *Early Childhood Research Quarterly, 6*(1), 1–100.

Kleckner, K. A., & Engel, R. E. (1988). A child begins school: Relieving anxiety with books. *Young Children, 43*(5), 14–18.

Klugman, E., & Smilansky, S. (Eds.). (1990). *Children's play and learning: Perspectives and policy implications.* New York: Teachers College Press.

Kontos, S., & Stevens, R. (1985). High quality child care: Does your center measure up? *Young Children 40*(2), 5–9.

Kritchevsky, S., & Prescott, E., with Walling, L. (1977). *Planning environments for young children: Physical space.* (2nd ed.) Washington, DC: National Association for the Education of Young Children.

Kubie L. S. (1948). The child's fifth freedom. *Child Study, 25,* 67–80, 88.

LaBarre, W. (1949). The age period of cultural fixation. *Mental Hygiene, 33,* 200, 221.

Lark-Horovitz, B. (1976). *The art of the very young—an indicator of individuality.*

Columbus, OH: Charles E. Merrill Publishing.

Lasky, L., & Mukerji, R. (1980). *Art: Basic for young children.* Washington, DC: National Association for the Education of Young Children.

Lay-Dopyera, M., & Dopyera, J. E. (1987). Strategies for teaching, In C. Seefeldt (1987). (Ed.). *The early childhood curriculum: A review of current research* (pp. 13–34). New York: Teachers College Press.

Lazar, I., & Darlington, R. (1982). Lasting effects of early education: A report from the Consortium for Longitudinal Studies. *Monographs of the Society for Research in Child Development, 47* (2–3, Serial No. 195.).

Leavitt, R. L., & Eheart, B. K. (1991). Assessment in early childhood programs. *Young Children, 46*(5), 4–9.

Leeb-Lundberg, K. (1985). *Mathematics is more than counting.* Wheaton, MD: Association for Childhood Education International.

Leighton, D., & Kluckhorn, C. (1947). *Children of the people: The Navaho individual and his development.* Cambridge, MA: Harvard University Press.

Lewis, H. (1966). *Child art.* Berkeley, CA: Diablo Press, P.O. Box 7084, Berkeley, CA 94717.

Lickona, T. (1983). *Raising good children: Helping your child through the stages of moral development.* New York: Bantam.

Liebert, R., & Sprafkin, J. (1988). *The early window: Effects of television on children and youth.* New York: Pergamon Press.

Lipson, E. R. (1991). *The New York Times parent's guide to the best books for children* (rev.). New York: Times Books.

Lombardi, J. (1986). Training for public policy and public advocacy. *Young Children 41*(4), 65–69.

Lombardi, J. (1990). Head Start: The nation's pride, A nation's challenge: Recommendations for Head Start in the 1990s. *Young Children 45*(6), 22–29.

Machado, J. M. (1990). *Early childhood experiences in language arts: Emerging literacy* (4th ed.). Albany, NY: Delmar.

Mallory, N. J., & Goldsmith, N. A. (1990). Head Start works! Two Head Start veterans share their views. *Young Children 45*(6), 36–39.

Manning, M., Manning, G., & Kamii, C. (1988). Early phonics instruction: Its effect on literacy development. *Young Children 44*(1), 4–8.

Marion, M. (1987). *Guidance of young children.* (2nd ed.) St. Louis, MO: C. V. Mosby.

Martyna, W. (1983). Beyond the he/man approach: The case for non-sexist language. In B. Thorne, C. Kramarae, & N. Henley (Eds.). (1983). *Language, gender and society* (pp. 25–37). Rowley, MA: Newbury House.

Maslach, C., & Pines, A. (1977). The burnout syndrome in the day care setting. *Child Care Quarterly, 6*(2), 100–113.

McAfee, O. D. (1985). Research report: Circle time: Getting past "Two little pumpkins." *Young Children, 40*(6), 24–29.

McCarthy, J. (1988). *Early childhood teacher certification requirements.* Washington, DC: National Association for the Education of Young Children.

McCracken, J. B. (1987). *Play is FUNdamental.* (Brochure #576; single copies $0.50.) Washington, DC: National Association for the Education of Young Children. (Also available in Spanish, *El Juego es FUNdamental,* #576.)

McCracken, J. B. (1990). *So many goodbyes: Ways to ease the transition between home and groups for young children.* (Brochure

#573; single copies $0.50.) Washington, DC: National Association for the Education of Young Children.

McCracken, J. B. (Ed.). (1986). *Reducing stress in young children's lives.* Washington, DC: National Association for the Education of Young Children.

McCracken, J. B. (Ed.). (1990). *Helping children love themselves and others: A resource guide to equity materials for young children.* Washington, DC: The Children's Foundation and the Women's Educational Equity Act Program.

McDonald, D. T. (1979). *Music in our lives: The early years.* Washington, DC: National Association for the Education of Young Chidlren.

McGinnis, K., & Oehlberg, B. (1988). *Starting out right: Nurturing young children as peacemakers.* Oak Park, IL: Meyer-Stone Books.

McKee, J. S. (Ed.). (1986). *Play: Working partner of growth.* Wheaton, MD: Association for Childhood Education International.

McKee, J. S., & Paciorek, K. M. (1991) *Annual Editions: Early childhood education.* Sluice Dock, Guilford, CT: Dushkin Publishing Group, Inc.

McLoughlin, C. S. (1987). *Parent-teacher conferencing.* Springfield, IL: Thomas.

McNamee, A. S. (Ed.). (1982). *Children & stress: Helping children cope.* Wheaton, MD: Association for Childhood Education International.

Meek, M., et al. (1978). *The cool web: The pattern of children's reading.* New York: Atheneum.

Meisels, S. J. (1986). Testing four- and five-year-olds: Response to Salzer and to Shepard and Smith. *Educational Leadership, 44*(3), 90–92.

Meisels, S. J. (1987). Uses and abuses of developmental screening and school readiness testing. *Young Children, 42*(3), 4–7.

Meisels, S. J. (1989) *Developmental screening in early childhood: A guide.* (3rd ed.). Washington, DC: National Association for the Education of Young Children.

Meisels, S. J., & Shonkoff, J. P. (Eds.). (1990). *Handbook of early childhood intervention.* New York: Cambridge University Press.

Miller, D. F. (1990). *Positive child guidance.* Albany NY: Delmar.

Miller, K. (1989). *The outside play and learning book: Activities for young children.* Mt. Rainier, MD: Gryphon House.

Mills, H., & Clyde, J. A. (1991). Children's success as readers and writers: It's the teacher's beliefs that make the difference. *Young Children, 46*(2), 54–59.

Modigliani, K., Reiff, M., & Jones, S. (1987). *Opening your door to children: How to start a family day care program.* Washington, DC: National Association for the Education of Young Children.

Monighan-Nourot, P., Scales, B., Van Hoorn, J. V., & Almy, M. (1987). *Looking at children's play: A bridge between theory and practice.* New York: Teachers College Press.

Montessori, M. (1964). *The Montessori method.* Cambridge, MA: Robert Bentley.

Montessori, M. (1967). *The absorbent mind.* New York: Dell Publishing Co.

Moore, R. C., Goltsman, S., & Iacafano, D. S. (Eds.) (1987). *Play for all guidelines: Planning, design, and management of outdoor play settings for all children.* Berkeley, CA: MIG Comunications.

Moore, S. G., & Cooper, C. R. (1982). *The young child: Reviews of research* (Vol. 3). Washington, DC: National Association for the Education of Young Children.

Morgan, E. L. (1989). Talking with parents when concerns come up. *Young Children, 44*(2), 52–56.

Morin, J. (1989). Viewpoint: We can force a solution to the staffing crisis. *Young Children 44*(6), 18–19.

Morrison, G. S. (1988). *Early childhood education today.* (4th ed.). Columbus, OH: Merrill Publishing.

Morrow, R. D. (1989). What's in a name? In particular, a Southeast Asian name? *Young Children, 44*(6), 20–23. See also Johnson & Saechao, (1990). More about Southeast Asian names. (letter to editor). *Young Children 45*(2), 3.

Moukaddem, V. (1990). Preventing infectious diseases in your child care setting. *Young Children 45*(2), 28–29.

Moyer, J. (Ed.). (1986). *Selecting educational equipment and materials: For school and home.* (3rd rev.) Wheaton, MD: Association for Childhood Education International.

Mulrooney, M. (1990). Reaccreditation: A snapshot of growth and change in high-quality early childhood programs. *Young Children, 45*(2), 58–61.

National Academy of Early Childhood Programs (1990). Full cost of quality must be paid. *Academy Update, 4*(2), 5–6. Washington, DC: National Association for the Education of Young Children.

National Association for the Education of Young Children. (1982). *Early childhood teacher education guidelines: Basic and advanced.* Washington, DC: Author.

National Association for the Education of Young Children (1984). *NAEYC Position statement on nomenclature, salaries, benefits, and the status of the early childhood profession.* Washington, DC: Author. (Out of print.).

National Association for the Education of Young Children. (1985a). *Guidelines for early childhood education programs in associate degree granting institutions.* Washington, DC: Author.

National Association for the Education of Young Children (1985b). *Toys: Tools for learning.* (Brochure #571; single copies $0.50.) Washington, DC: Author.

National Association for the Education of Young Children (1986a). *Good teaching practices for 4- and 5-year olds.* (Brochure #522; single copies $0.50.) Washington, DC: Author.

National Association for the Education of Young Children (1986b). *Helping children learn self-control: A guide to discipline.* (Brochure #572; single copies $0.50.) Washington, DC: Author.

National Association for the Education of Young Children (1986c). *What are the benefits of quality child care for preschool children?* (Brochure #540; single copies $0.50.) Washington, DC: Author.

National Association for the Education of Young Children. (1987a). *Careers in early childhood education.* (Brochure #505; single copies $0.50.) Washington, DC: Author.

National Association for the Education of Young Children (1987b). Ideas that work with young children: Child choice—Another way to individualize—Another form of preventive discipline. *Young Children, 43*(1), 48–54.

National Association for the Education of Young Children. (1987c). *More than 1,2,3: The real basics of mathematics.* (Brochure #575; single copies $0.50.) Washington, DC: Author.

National Association for the Education of Young Children (1987d) *NAEYC position statement on licensing and regulation of early childhood programs in centers and family day care.* (Brochure #535; single copies $0.50 each.) Washington, DC: Author.

National Association for the Education of Young Children. (1987e). NAEYC position statement on quality, compensation, and affordability in early childhood programs. *Young Children, 43*(1), 31.

National Association for the Education of Young Children. (1988a). *Appropriate education in the primary grades.* (Brochure #578; single copies $0.50.) Washington, DC: Author.

National Association for the Education of Young Children. (1988b). Children's books: Promote science in your program: Use outstanding science books. *Young Children 44*(1), 72–73.

National Association for the Education of Young Children. (1988c). *Early childhood program accreditation: A commitment to excellence.* (Brochure #538; single copies $0.50.) Washington, DC: Author.

National Association for the Education of Young Children. (1988d). Ideas that work with young children: The difficult child. *Young Children 43*(5), 60–68.

National Association for the Education of Young Children. (1988e). NAEYC position statement on standardized testing of young children 3 through 8 years of age. *Young Children, 43*(3), 42–47.

National Association for the Education of Young Children (1988f). *Testing of young children: Concerns and cautions.* (Brochure #582; single copies $0.50.) Washington, DC: Author.

National Association for the Education of Young Children. (1989a). *Developmentally appropriate practice in early childhood programs serving infants.* (Brochure #547; single copies $0.50.) Washington, DC: Author.

National Association for the Education of Young Children. (1989b). *Developmentally appropriate practice in early childhood programs serving toddlers.* (Brochure #508; single copies $0.50.) Washington, DC: Author.

National Association for the Education of Young Children. (1989c). *Facility design for early childhood programs: A resource guide.* Washington, DC: Author.

National Association for the Education of Young Children. (1989d). *How to plan and start a good early childhood program.* (Brochure #515; single copies $0.50.) Washington, DC: Author.

National Association for the Education of Young Children (1989e). *The crisis is real: Demographics on the problems of recruiting and retaining early childhood staff.* (Brochure #550; single copies $0.50.) Washington, DC: Author.

National Association for the Education of Young Children. (1990a). Census Alert: When the census asks, "What do you do?", what do you say? *Young Children, 45*(3), 48.

National Association for the Education of Young Children. (1990b). *How to choose a good early childhood program.* (Brochure #525. Available in Spanish, *Como escoger un buen programa de educación pre-escolar.* Brochure #510. Single copies $0.50.) Washington, DC: Author.

National Association for the Education of Young Children (1990c). *Media violence and children: A guide for parents.* (Brochure #585; single copies $0.50.) Washington, DC: Author.

National Association for the Education of Young Children. (1990d). *NAEYC Position statement on guidelines for compensation of early childhood professionals.* Washington, DC: Author.

National Association for the Education of Young Children (1990e). NAEYC Position statement on media violence in children's lives. *Young Children, 45*(5), 18–21.

National Association for the Education of Young Children (1990f). *NAEYC Position statement on school readiness.* Washington, DC: Author.

National Association for the Education of Young Children. (1990g). *Playgrounds:*

Safe and sound. (Brochure #552; single copies $0.50.) Washington DC: Author.

National Association for the Education of Young Children (1990h). *The full cost of quality in early childhood programs: What you should know: What you can do.* (Brochure #537; single copies $0.50.) Washington, DC: Author.

National Association for the Education of Young Children. (1991a). *Accreditation criteria and procedures of the National Academy of Early Childhood Programs.* (rev. ed.) Washington, DC: Author.

National Association for the Education of Young Children. (1991b). *Child care and ill children and healthy child care practices.* Washington, DC: Author.

National Association for the Education of Young Children. (1991c). *Facility design for early childhood programs resource guide.* Washington, DC: Author.

National Association for the Education of Young Children (1991d). *Guide to accreditation by the National Academy of Early Childhood Programs.* (rev.) Washington, DC: Author.

National Association for the Education of Young Children (1991e). Guidelines for appropriate curriculum content and assessment in programs serving children ages 3 through 8. Position statement of the NAEYC and the National Association of Early Childhood Specialists in State Departments of Education. *Young Children, 46*(3), 21–38.

National Association of State Boards of Education. (1988). *Right from the start: The report of the NASBE Task Force on Early Childhood Education.* Alexandria, VA: Author.

National Center for Clinical Infant Programs. (1988). *Who will mind the babies?* (2nd ed.). Washington, DC: Author.

Neill, S., & Neill, G. (1990). *The annual guide to highest-rated educational software: Only the best, preschool–grade 12.* New York: Bowker.

Nelsen, J. (1981). *Positive discipline.* Fair Oaks, CA: Adlerian Counseling Center, 4984 Arboleda Drive.

Neugebauer, B. (Ed.). (1987). *Alike and different: Exploring our humanity with young children.* Redmond, WA: Exchange Press.

Newman, J. (1987). *Girls are people too: A bibliography of non-traditional female roles in children's books.* Metuchen, NJ: Scarecrow Press.

Nickelsburg, J. (1976). *Nature activities for early childhood.* Reading, MA: Addison-Wesley.

Norton, D. (1983). *Through the eyes of a child: An introduction to children's literature.* Columbus, OH: Charles E. Merrill Publishing.

Nunnelley, J. C. (1990). Beyond turkeys, santas, snowmen, and hearts: How to plan innovative curriculum themes. *Young Children 46*(1), 24–29.

O'Brien, S. (1984). *Child abuse and neglect: Everyone's problem.* (2nd ed.). Wheaton, MD: Association for Childhood Education International.

Ontario Science Center. (1987). *Foodworks— Over 100 science activities and fascinating facts that explore the magic of food.* Reading, MA: Addison-Wesley.

Opie, I., & Opie, P. (1969). *Children's games in street and playgrounds.* Oxford, England: Clarendon Press.

Paley, V. (1984). *Boys and girls: Superheroes in the doll corner.* Chicago: University of Chicago Press.

Paley, V. (1986). *Mollie is three: Growing up in school.* Chicago: University of Chicago Press.

Papert, S. (1980). *Mindstorms: Children, computers, and powerful ideas.* New York: Basic Books.

Parke, R. D. (1981). *Fathers.* (The developing child series.) Cambridge, MA: Harvard University Press.

Parten, M. B. (1932). Social participation among preschool children. *Journal of Abnormal and Social Psychology, 27,* 243–262.

Pearl, D. (1987) Familial, peer, and television influences on aggressive and violent behavior. In D. H. Crowell, I. M. Evans, & C. R. O'Donnell (Eds.). (1987). *Childhood aggression and violence: Sources of influence, prevention, and control.* New York: Plenum.

Peck, J., McCaig, G., & Sapp, M. E. (1988). *Kindergarten policies: What is best for children?* Washington, DC: National Association for the Education of Young Children.

Pellegrini, A. D., & Glickman, C. D. (1990). Measuring kindergartener's social competence. *Young Children, 45*(4), 40–44.

Pena, S., French, J., & Holmes, R. (1987). A look at superheroes: Some issues and guidelines. *Day Care and Early Education, 15,* (Fall).

Peterson, R., & Felton-Collins, V. (1986). *The Piaget handbook for teachers and parents: Children in the age of discovery, preschool–3rd grade.* New York: Teachers College Press.

Phillips, C. B. (1988). Nurturing diversity for today's children and tomorrow's teachers. *Young Children, 43*(2), 42–47.

Phillips, C. B. (1990). The Child Development Associate Program: Entering a new era. *Young Children 45*(3), 24–27.

Phillips, D. A. (Ed.). (1987). *Quality in child care: What does research tell us?* Washington, DC: National Association for the Education of Young Children.

Phillips, J. L., Jr. (1981). *Piaget's theory: A primer.* San Francisco, CA: W. H. Freeman.

Phyfe-Perkins, E. (1981). *Effects of teacher behavior on preschool children: A review of research.* Urbana, IL: ERIC Clearinghouse on Elementary and Early Childhood Education. ED211 176.

Piaget, J. (1950). *The psychology of intelligence.* London: Routledge & Kegan Paul.

Piaget, J. (1970). *Science of education and the psychology of the child.* New York: Orion Press.

Piaget, J. (1974). *The origins of intelligence in children.* (Trans. M. Cook). (Original publication 1952.) New York: W. W. Norton.

Piaget, J. (1983). Piaget's theory. In P. H. Mussen (Ed.). (1983). *Handbook of child psychology* (4th ed.). W. Kessen (Ed.). Vol. I: *History, theory, and methods.* New York: John Wiley & Sons.

Piaget, J., & Inhelder, B. (1969). *The psychology of the child.* New York: Basic Books.

Pitcher, E. G., Feinburg, S. G., & Alexander, D. A. (1989). *Helping young children learn.* (5th ed.). Columbus, OH: Merrill Publishing.

Platt, E. B. (1992). *Scenes from daycare: How teachers teach and what children learn.* New York: Teachers College Press.

Poest, C. A., Williams, J. R., Witt, D. D., & Atwood, M. E. (1990). Challenge me to move: Large muscle development in young children. *Young Children 45*(5), 4–10.

Powell, D. R. (1987). Research in review: After-school child care. *Young Children 42*(3), 62–66.

Powell, D. R. (1989). *Families and early childhood programs.* (Research Monograph Vol. 3.) Washington, DC: National Association for the Education of Young Children.

Powell, D. R. (Ed.). (1988). *Parents education as early childhood intervention: Emerging directions in theory, research and practice.* Norwood, NJ: Ablex.

Pratt, C. (1990). *I learn from children.* New York: Harper and Row. First Perennial

Library edition (originally published by Simon & Schuster in 1948).

Provenzo, E. F., Jr., & Brett, A. (1983). *The complete block book.* Syracuse, NY: Syracuse University.

Raines, S. C. & Canady, R. J. (1990). *The whole language kindergarten.* New York: Teachers College Press.

Ramsey, P. G. (1979). Beyond "Ten little Indians" and turkeys: Alternative approaches to Thanksgiving. *Young Children, 34*(6), 28–32, 49–52.

Ramsey, P. G. (1986). *Children's understanding of diversity: Multicultural perspectives in early childhood education.* New York: Teachers College Press.

Ramsey, P. G. (1987). *Teaching and learning in a diverse world.* New York: Teachers College Press.

Ramsey, P. G. (1991). *Making friends in school: Promoting peer relationships in early childhood.* New York: Teachers College Press.

Ramsey, P. G., & Derman-Sparks, L. (1992). Multicultural education reaffirmed. *Young Children (47)*2, 10–11.

Ratner, M., & Chamlin, S. (1985). *Straight talk: Sexuality education for parents and kids 4 to 7.* Planned Parenthood of Westchester, Inc. New York: Penguin.

Raver, C. C., & Zigler, E. F. (1991). Three steps forward, two steps back: Head Start and the measurement of social competence. *Young Children 46*(4), 3–8.

Redleaf, R. (1983). *Open the door, let's explore: Neighborhood field trips for young children.* St. Paul, MN: Toys 'n Things Press.

Rescorla, L., Hyson, M. C., Hirsch-Pasek, K. (Eds.). (1991). *Academic instruction in early childhood: Challenge or pressure?* No. 53. San Francisco, CA: Jossey-Bass.

Reynolds, E. (1990). *Guiding young children: A child-centered approach.* Mountain View, CA: Mayfield Publishing Company.

Riley, S. S. (1984) *How to generate values in young children: Integrity, honesty, individuality, self-confidence, and wisdom.* Washington, DC: National Association for the Education of Young Children.

Rogers, C. S., & Sawyers, J. K. (1988). *Play in the lives of children.* Washington, DC: National Association for the Education of Young Children.

Rogers, F. & Sharapan, H. B. (1991). Helping parents, teachers, and caregivers deal with children's concerns about war. *Young Children, 46*(3), 12–13.

Roopnarine, J. L., & Johnson, J. E. (Eds.). (1987). *Approaches to early childhood education.* Columbus, OH: Merrill Publishing.

Rothlein, L. (1989). Nutrition tips revisited: On a daily basis, do we implement what we know? *Young Children 44*(6), 30–36.

Rousseau, J. J. (1974. Reprinted from 1933). (B. Foxley, Trans.) *Emile.* London: J. M. Dent & Sons. (Also published by New York: Teachers College Press, W. Boyd, Trans. & Ed., 1962).

Rubin, K. H., Fein, G. G., & Vandenberg, B. (1983). Play. In P. H. Mussen (Ed.), (1983). *Handbook of child psychology.* E. M. Hetherington (Ed.), Volume IV: *Socialization, personality, and social development.* New York: John Wiley & Sons.

Rudman, M. K., Pearce, A. M., & editors of Consumer Reports Books. (1988). *For love of reading: A parent's guide to encouraging young readers from infancy through age 5.* Mount Vernon, NY: Consumers Union.

Rust, F. O., & Williams, L. R. (Eds.). (1989). *The care and education of young children: Expanding contexts, sharpening focus.* New York: Teachers College Press.

Sampson, M. R. (Ed.). (1986). *The pursuit of literacy: Early reading and writing.* Dubuque, IA: Kendall/Hunt Publishing Company.

Saracho, O. N., & Spodek, B. (1983). *Understanding the multicultural experience in early childhood education.* Washington, DC: National Association for the Education of Young Children.

Sawyers, J. K., & Rogers, C. S. (1988). *Helping young children develop through play: A practical guide for parents, caregivers, and teachers.* Washington, DC: National Association for the Education of Young Children.

Scales, B., Almy, M., Nicolopoulou, A., & Ervin-Tripp, S. (Eds.). (1991). *Play and the social context of development in early care and education.* New York: Teachers College Press.

Scarr, S. (1984). *Mother care/Other care.* New York: Basic Books.

Scheffler, J. N. (1983). *Resources for early childhood. An annotated bibliography and guide for educators, librarians, health care professionals, and parents.* New York: Garland.

Schickedanz, J. A. (1983). *Helping children learn about reading.* (Brochure #520; single copies $0.50.) Washington, DC: National Association for the Education of Young Children.

Schickedanz, J. A. (1986). *More than the ABCs: The early stages of reading and writing.* Washington, DC: National Association for the Education of Young Children.

Schickedanz, J. A., Chay, S., Gopin, P., Sheng, L. L., Song, S., & Wild, N. (1990). Preschoolers and academics: Some thoughts. *Young Children 46*(1), 4–13.

Schiller, P. B., & Dyke, P. (1990). *Managing quality child care centers: A comprehensive manual for administrators.* New York: Teachers College Press.

Schirrmacher, R. (1988). *Art and creative development for young children.* Albany, NY: Delmar.

Schmidt, V. E., & McNeill, E. (1978). *Cultural awareness: A resouce bibliography.* Washington, DC: National Association for the Education of Young Children.

Schon, I. (1988). Hispanic books: Libros Hispanicos. *Young Children 43*(4), 81–85.

Schon, I. (1991). Recent noteworthy books in Spanish for young children. *Young Children 46*(4), 65.

Schoff, L., & Schoff, D. (1988). *Within our reach: Breaking the cycle of disadvantages.* New York: Doubleday.

Schweinhart, L. J., Weikart, D. P., & Larner, M. B. (1986). Consequences of three preschool curriculum models through age 15. *Early Childhood Research Quarterly,* 1(1), 14–46. For responses see ECRQ (1986), 1(3), 287–311.

Seaver, J., Cartwright, C., Ward, C., & Heasley, C. A. (1984). *Careers with young children: Making your decision* (rev. ed.). Washington, DC: National Association for the Education of Young Children.

Seefeldt, C. (1984). *Social studies for the preschool–primary child,* (2nd ed.) Columbus, OH: Merrill Publishing.

Seefeldt, C. (1990a). Assessing young children. In C. Seefeldt. (1990). *Continuing issues in early childhood education.* (pp. 312–330). Columbus, OH: Merrill Publishing.

Seefeldt, C. (1990b). *Continuing issues in early childhood education.* Columbus, OH: Merrill Publishing.

Seefeldt, C. (Ed.). (1987). *The early childhood curriculum: A review of current research.* New York: Teachers College Press.

Seefeldt, C., & Warman, B. (1990). *Young and old together.* Washington, DC: National Association for the Education of Young Children

Sheldon, A. (1990). "Kings are royaler than queens:" Language and socialization. *Young Children 45*(2), 4–9.

Shepard, L. A., & Smith, M. E. (1989). *Flunking grades: Research and policies on retention.* Lewes, England: Falmer Press.

Sherwood, E., Williams, R., & Rockwell, R. (1990). *More mudpies to magnets: Science for young children.* Mt. Rainier, MD: Gryphon House.

Shiff, E. (Ed.). (1987). *Experts advise parents: A guide to raising loving, responsible children.* New York: Bantam Doubleday Dell Publishing.

Shuttlesworth, D. (1977). *Exploring nature with your child.* New York: Abrams Inc. Publishing.

Signorielli, N. (1991). *A sourcebook on children and television.* New York: Greenwood Press.

Silvern, S. B., & Countermine, T. (Eds.). (1983). *Children in the age of microcomputers.* Annual theme issue of *Childhood Education.* Wheaton, MD: Association for Childhood Education International.

Sims, R. (1985). Children's books about Blacks: A mid-eighties status report. *Children's Literature Review, 8,* 9–13.

Singer, D. & Singer, J. (1990). *The house of make-believe: Play and the developing imagination.* Cambridge, MA: Harvard University Press.

Skeen, P., Garner, A. P., & Cartwright, S. (1984). *Woodworking for young children.* Washington, DC: National Association for the Education of Young Children.

Smith, J. (1991). View, p. E1. Los Angeles Times, August 22, 1991.

Smith, M. L., & Shepard, L. A. (1987). What doesn't work: Explaining policies of retention in the early grades. *Phi Delta Kappan, 69,* 129–134.

Smith, N. R. (1983). *Experience and art: Teaching children to paint.* New York: Teachers College Press.

Soderman, A. K. (1985). Dealing with difficult young children: Strategies for teachers and parents. *Young Children 40(5),* 15–20.

Soto, L. D. (1991). Research in review: Understanding bilingual/bicultural young children. *Young Children, 46(2),* 30–36.

Souweine, J., Crimmins, S., & Mazel, C. (1981). *Mainstreaming: Ideas for teaching young children.* Washington, DC: National Association for the Education of Young Children.

Spock, B., & Rothenberg, M. B. (1992) *Dr. Spock's baby and child care.* (6th ed.). New York: Pocket Books.

Spodek, B. (1985). Early childhood education's past as prologue: Roots of contemporary concerns. *Young Children, 40(5),* 3–7.

Spodek, B. (1986). *Today's kindergarten: Exploring the knowledge base, expanding the curriculum.* New York: Teachers College Press.

Spodek, B., & Saracho, O. N. (Eds.). (1990). *Early childhood teacher preparation.* (Yearbook in early childhood education, Vol. I.) New York: Teachers College Press.

Spodek, B., & Saracho, O. N. (Eds.). (1991). *Issues in early childhood curriculum.* (Yearbook in Early Childhood Education Series, Vol. II.) New York: Teachers College Press.

Spodek, B., Saracho, O., & Peters, D. (Eds.). (1988). *Professionalism and the early childhood practitioner.* New York: Teachers College Press.

Sprung, B. (Ed.). (1978). *Perspectives on non-sexist early childhood education.* New York: Teachers College Press.

Stein, S. B. (1974). *Making babies: An open family book for parents and children together.* New York: Walker.

Stevens, J. H. & Mathews, M. (1978). *Mother/child father/child relationships.* Washington, DC: National Association for the Education of Young Children.

Stewig, J. W. (1983). *Literature: Basic in the language arts curriculum.* Urbana, IL: ERIC Clearinghouse on Reading and Communication Skills (ED 232 188).

Stone, J. G. (1978). *A guide to discipline.* (rev. ed.) Washington, DC: National Association for the Education of Young Children.

Stone, J. G. (1987). *Teacher-parent relationships.* Washington, DC: National Association for the Education of Young Children.

Stone, J. G. (1990). *Teaching preschoolers: It looks like this . . . in pictures.* Washington, DC: National Association for the Education of Young Children.

Strickland, D., & Morrow, L. (Eds.). (1989). *Emerging literacy: Young children learn to read and write.* Newark, DE: International Reading Association.

Strickland, D., & Taylor, D. (1989). Family story book reading: Implications for children, families, and curriculum. In D. Strickland, & L. Morrow (Eds.). *Emerging literacy: Young children learn to read and write* (pp. 27–34.) Newark, DE: International Reading Association.

Strom, R. D. (Ed.). (1981). *Growing through play.* Monterey, CA: Brooks Cole.

Sullivan, M. (1982). *Feeling strong, feeling free: Movement exploration for young children.* Washington, DC: National Association for the Education of Young Children.

Suransky, V. P. (1982). *The erosion of childhood.* Chicago: University of Chicago Press.

Sutherland, Z., & Arbuthnot, M. (1986). *Children and books.* Glenview, IL: Scott, Foresman.

Taylor, B. J. (1991). *A child goes forth: A curriculum guide for preschool children* (7th ed.). New York: Macmillan Publishing Company.

Taylor, J. M., & Taylor, W. S. (1989). *Communicable disease and young children in group settings.* Boston: College-Hill Press; Little, Brown and Company.

Teale, W. H. (1986). *The beginnings of reading and writing: Written language development during the preschool and kindergarten years.* In M.R. Sampson (Ed.). (1986). *The pursuit of literacy: Early reading and writing.* (pp. 1–29.) Dubuque, IA: Kendall/Hunt Publishing Company.

Teale, W. H., & Martinez, M. (1988). Getting on the right road to reading: Bringing books and young children together in the classroom. *Young Children, 44*(1), 10–15.

Teale, W. H., & Sulzby, E. (1986). *Emergent literacy.* Norwood, NJ: Ablex.

Texas Department of Human Resources. (1984). *Culture and children.* Austin, TX: Author: Child Development Division, P. O. Box 2960.

Thomas, A., & Chess, S. (1977). *Temperament and development.* New York: Brunner/Mazel.

Thompson, D. (1981). *Easy woodstuff for kids.* Mt. Rainer, MD: Gryphon House.

Tobin, J. J., Wu, D. Y. H., & Davidson, D. H. (1989). *Preschool in three cultures.* New Haven, CT: Yale University Press.

Trawick-Smith, J. (1988). "Let's say you're the baby, OK?": Play leadership and following behavior of young children. *Young Children, 43*(5), 51–59.

Trelease, J. (1985). *The read-aloud handbook.* New York: Penguin Books.

Tribe, C. (Comp.) (1982). *Profile of three theories: Erikson, Maslow, Piaget.* Dubuque, IA: Kendall/Hunt Publishing Company.

Trostle, S. L., & Cohen, S. (1989). Big, bigger, biggest: Discovering dinosaurs. *Childhood Education, 65*(3), 140–145.

Trostle, S. L., & Yawkey, T. D. (1990). *Integrated learning activities for young children.* Needham Heights, MA: Allyn & Bacon.

Tuscherer, P. (1988). *TV interactive toys: The new high tech threat to children.* Bend, OR: Pinnaroo Publishing.

Uphoff, J. K. (1990). Extra-year programs: An argument for transitional programs during transitional times. *Young Children 45*(6), 19–20.

Vardin-Barker, P. (1984, Summer). *Microcomputers, robots, and electronic toys.* (Proceedings of the Early Childhood Education Conference of Teachers College, Columbia University.) New York: Teachers College Press.

Vergeront, J. (1987). *Places and spaces for preschool and primary (INDOORS).* Washington, DC: National Association for the Education of Young Children.

Vergeront, J. (1988). *Places and spaces for preschool and primary (OUTDOORS).* Washington, DC: National Association for the Education of Young Children.

Vogel, S., & Mannhoff, D. H., in cooperation with the National Safety Council (1984). Emergency medical treatment: Children. (Also available in Spanish). Oshkosh, WI: RPM International.

Vogel, S., & Mannhoff, D. H., in cooperation with the National Safety Council (1989). *Emergency medical treatment: Infants.* (Also available in Spanish). Oshkosh, WI: RPM International.

Vygotsky, L. (1978). *Mind in society: The development of higher psychological processes.* Cambridge, MA: Harvard University Press.

Wanamaker, N., Hearn, K. & Richarz, S. (1979). *More than graham crackers: Nutrition education and food preparation with young children.* Washington, DC: National Association for the Education of Young Children.

Wardle, F. (1987). *Integrating parties, celebrations, and festivals into the Head Start curriculum.* Commerce City, CO: Adams County Head Start.

Warren, J., & McKinnon, E. (1988). *Small world celebrations.* Everett, WA: Warren Publishing House.

Warren, R. M. (1977). *Caring: Supporting children's growth.* Washington, DC: National Association for the Education of Young Children.

Weber, E. (1984). *Ideas influencing early childhood education: A theoretical analysis.* New York: Teachers College Press.

Weikart, D., Schweinhart, L., & Larner, M. (1971). *The cognitively oriented curriculum.* Urbana, IL: Educational Resources Information Center, and Washington, DC: National Association for the Education of Young Children.

Weikart, D., Deloria, D. J., & Sawsor, S. (1974). A report on longitudinal evaluations of preschool programs. In S. Ryan. (Ed.). *Results of a preschool intervention project* (Vol. 1). Washington, DC: U.S. Department of Health, Education, and Welfare (No. OHD 74-24).

Weikart, P. (1987). *Round the circle: Key experiences in movement for children ages 3 to 5.* Ypsilanti, MI: High/Scope Press.

Weissbourd, B., & Musick, J. S. (1981). *Infants: Their social environments.* Washington, DC: National Association for the Education of Young Children.

Werner, E. E. (1984a). *Child care: Kith, kin and hired hands.* Baltimore, MD: University Park Press.

Werner, E. E. (1984b). Research in review: Resilient children. *Young Children 40*(1), 68–72.

Werner, E. E., & Smith, R. S. (1982). *Vulnerable, but invincible: A longitudinal study of resilient children and youth.* New York: McGraw-Hill.

Whaley, K., & Swadener, E. B. (1990). Multicultural education in infant and toddler settings. *Childhood Education 66*(4), 238–240.

White, B. L. (1990). *The first three years of life* (rev. ed.) New York: Prentice Hall Press.

Whitebook, M., Howes, C., & Phillips, D. (1989). *Who cares? Child care teachers and the quality of care in America: Executive summary of the National Child Care Staffing Study.* Oakland, CA: Child Care Employee Project.

Whitebook, M., & Ginsburg, G. (1985). *Comparable worth: Questions and answers for early childhood staff.* Berkeley, CA: Child Care Employee Project.

Whitebook, M., & Granger, R. C. (1989). "Mommy, who's going to be my teacher today?" Assessing teacher turnover. *Young Children 44*(4), 11–14.

Whitebook, M., Howes, C., Darrah, R., & Friedman, J. (1982). Caring for the caregivers: Staff burnout in child care. In L. G. Katz (Ed.), *Current topics in early childhood education* (vol. 4). Norwood, NJ: Ablex.

Wichert, S. (1989). *Keeping the peace: Practicing cooperation and conflict resolution with preschoolers.* Santa Cruz, CA: New Society Publishers.

Willer, B. (1988). *The growing crisis in child care: Quality, compensation, and affordability in early childhood programs.* Washington, DC: National Association for the Education of Young Children.

Willer, B. (Ed.). (1990) *Reaching the full cost of quality in early childhood programs.* Washington, DC: National Association for the Education of Young Children.

Willer, B., & Bredekamp, S. (1990). Public Policy Report: Redefining readiness: An essential requisite for educational reform. *Young Children 45*(5), 22–24.

Willer, B., Hofferth, S. L., Kisker, E. E., Divine-Hawkins, P., Farquhar, E., & Glantz, F. B. (1991). *The demand and supply of child care in 1990: Joint findings from the National Child Care Survey 1990 and A Profile of Child Care Settings.* Washington, DC: National Association for the Education of Young Children.

Willert, M., & Kamii, C. (1985). Children teach themselves to read. *Young Children, 40*(4), 3–9.

Williams, L. R., & DeGaetano, Y. (1985). *ALERTA: A multicultural, bilingual approach to teaching young children.* Reading, MA: Addison-Wesley.

Williams, R. A., Rockwell, R. D., & Sherwood, E. A. (1983). *Hug a tree and other things to do outdoors with young children.* Mt. Rainier, MD: Gryphon House.

Williams, R. A., Rockwell, R. D., & Sherwood, E. A. (1987). *Mudpies to magnets: A preschool science curriculum.* Mt. Rainier, MD: Gryphon House.

Wilms, D., & Cooper, I. (Eds.). (1987). *A guide to non-sexist children's books* (Vol. II: 1976–1985). Chicago, IL: Academy Chicago Publishers.

Wilson, L. C. (1990). *Infants and toddlers: Curriculum and teaching.* (2nd ed.). Albany, NY: Delmar.

Winick, M. P., & Wehrenberg, J. S. (1982). *Children and TV II: Mediating the medium.* Wheaton, MD: Association for Childhood Education International.

Winnicott, D. W. (1957). *The child and the outside world.* New York: Basic Books.

Winnicott, D. W. (1971). *Playing and reality.* New York: Basic Books.

Winnicott, D. W. (1974). *The maturational process and the facilitating environment.* New York: International Universities Press.

Winstein, C., & David, T. (1987). *Spaces for children: The built environment and child development.* New York: Plenum Press.

Wolf, D. P. (Ed.). (1986). *Connecting: Friendship in the lives of young children and their teachers.* Redmond, WA: Exchange Press, Inc.

Yonemura, M. V. (1986). *A teacher at work: Professional development and the early childhood educator.* New York: Teachers College Press.

York, S. (1991). *Roots and wings: Affirming culture in early childhood programs.* St. Paul, MN: Redleaf Press.

Zavitkovsky D., Baker, K. R., Berlfein, J. R., & Almy, M. (1986). *Listen to the children.* Washington, DC: National Association for the Education of Young Children.

Zigler, E. F., & Gordon, E. W. (Eds.). (1982). *Day care: Scientific and social policy issues.* Boston: Auburn House.

Zigler, E. F., & Lang, M. E. (1990). *Child care choices: Balancing the needs of children, families, and society.* New York: The Free Press.

Index